Also by Walter R. Borneman

A CLIMBING GUIDE TO COLORADO'S FOURTEENERS
(with Lyndon J. Lampert)

ALASKA: SAGA OF A BOLD LAND

1812: THE WAR THAT FORGED A NATION

THE FRENCH AND INDIAN WAR: DECIDING THE FATE
OF NORTH AMERICA

POLK

Walter R. Borneman

Random House New York

$\mathcal{P}$OLK

THE MAN WHO TRANSFORMED

THE PRESIDENCY

AND AMERICA

Published in the United States by Random House, an imprint of
The Random House Publishing Group, a division of Random House, Inc.,
New York.

RANDOM HOUSE and colophon are registered trademarks of
Random House, Inc.

LIBRARY OF CONGRESS CATALOGING-IN-PUBLICATION DATA
Borneman, Walter R.
Polk: the man who transformed the presidency and America/
Walter R. Borneman.
p. cm.
Includes bibliographical references and index.
ISBN 978-1-4000-6560-8
1. Polk, James K. (James Knox), 1795–1849.   2. Presidents —
United States — Biography.   3. United States — Politics and
government — 1845–1849.   I. Title.
E417.B67 2008   973.6'1092 — dc22   2007014040
[B]

Printed in the United States of America on acid-free paper

www.atrandom.com

246897531

First Edition

Book design by Carol Malcolm Russo

Maps by David Lambert

*F*OR *M*ARLENE,

FIRST, LAST, AND ALWAYS

CONTENTS

PART II

The Conquest

LIST OF MAPS

INTRODUCTION
DARK HORSE, BRIGHT LAND

*I*N THE FALL OF 1843, James K. Polk appeared to be politically dead. Despite seven terms in Congress, two of them as Speaker of the United States House of Representatives, Polk's attempt to win reelection as governor of Tennessee had failed miserably—not just once but twice. Even the political power of ex-president Andrew Jackson, now an aging sage ensconced at the Hermitage, appeared unlikely to rescue him.

Yet eighteen months later, this man was inaugurated the eleventh president of the United States. How did this happen? Was James K. Polk really a dark horse who came out of nowhere to win the 1844 Democratic nomination, as conventional wisdom has long suggested, or was he one of the most experienced and astute politicians of his time?

And what of the country? What forces—Manifest Destiny some called them—were at work not only to annex Texas but also in the span of four years under Polk's leadership to nearly double the American nation with the acquisitions of Oregon, California, and all of the Southwest?

Unabashedly proclaiming the policy of the United States to be one of continental expansion, Polk welcomed Texas into the union, bluffed the British out of half of Oregon, and went to war with Mexico to grab California and the Southwest. Yet a change of just 5,000 votes in New York would have elected Henry Clay president instead. Clay appeared content to let Texas remain independent and Oregon remain in British hands. How different the map of the United States might look today if that had happened.

Polk announced his intent to serve only one term even before his election. He immediately became a lame duck, but it allowed him to spend his political capital freely and he did so aggressively, expanding the powers of the presidency more than any other president before the Civil War.

Along with James K. Polk, this is the story of aging Andrew Jackson, would-be president Henry Clay, cagey Martin Van Buren, feisty Thomas Hart Benton, and a young Whig from Illinois named Abraham Lincoln, who challenged Polk to name the exact spot where American blood had been spilled as his pretense for war with Mexico. It is also the story of bruising presidential campaigns, spoiler third parties, and less than stunning popular-vote triumphs—all suggesting that recent presidential politics is nothing new.

It has long been popular to paint James K. Polk as a dark horse, but the record does not square with that tradition. If he was indeed one, he chose to ride boldly across a bright land and in doing so opened up the American West to half a century of unbridled expansion.

A PROLOGUE IN TWO PARTS

March 6, 1836

$\mathcal{L}$ONG BEFORE DAWN, the rattle of assembling infantry and the jangle of cavalry cut through the night air on the outskirts of the dusty little village of San Antonio. Inside the adobe walls of a 118-year-old mission, some two hundred men—commanded by William Barret Travis and including the legendary David Crockett and James Bowie—waited uneasily, perhaps even impatiently.

For twelve days, this meager band had stalled the northward advance of Mexican president Antonio López de Santa Anna's army of some three thousand. By all tenets of international law, Santa Anna was well within his rights. The Alamo and all of Texas were officially Mexican territory, but these Americans—and tens of thousands more spread from the Sabine River to the Brazos and beyond—had other ideas.

Now the reckoning was to be complete. Mexican bugles blared the strains of the chilling *degüello*. No quarter would be given. The first charge was repulsed; a second also failed to carry the adobe walls. But the attacking lines reformed and swept forward again. Minutes later, there were no Americans left alive within the Alamo save for Lieutenant Almeron Dickenson's wife, their infant daughter, and one of Travis's servants. As Susanna Dickenson assumed the role of surviving matriarch and led these survivors away from San Antonio, legend has it that Santa Anna saluted her.

This day, however, was not an end but a beginning. Over the next dozen years, from the bloodstained courtyard of one Mexican mission to the sweeping dictates of the 1848 Treaty of Guadalupe Hidalgo, the North American continent changed forever. It was, wrote a journalist named John L. O'Sullivan in describing the American national psyche, "the fulfillment of our manifest destiny to overspread the continent."[1]

August 3, 1843

Tennessee politics in the 1840s was a rough-and-tumble game. True, it had been some time since the state's venerable sage, Andrew Jackson, had killed anybody in a duel, but that did not mean that partisan tongues on the stump or words in party newspapers carried any less sting. Now the populace held its collective breath and waited to see whether Jackson's Democratic heirs or Henry Clay's upstart Whigs would triumph in their attempt to elect a governor.

The first returns from Middle Tennessee were not encouraging for the Democrats. Their nominee, James K. Polk, was "Old Hickory's" boy—Jackson's long-appointed political heir. Once, Polk had been Speaker of the U.S. House of Representatives. Once, he had seemed a contender for the vice presidential nomination. But Tennessee politics had not been kind. Now, despite narrowly winning a two-year term as Tennessee governor in 1839, Polk sought to avenge his reelection loss in 1841.

But Middle Tennessee proved a splintered battleground. Waiting in his hometown of Columbia, Polk was too shrewd a political veteran to be given over to wishful thinking that the eastern and western districts might change the apparent outcome. In the mountains of East Tennessee the Democrats almost held their own. In the plantation country of West Tennessee south to Memphis, they even gained some. But it was not enough to plug the hole in the center.

When the final results were tallied, James K. Polk had lost the governorship of Tennessee for the second time. His political career now stood in shambles. Most said that it was irrevocably finished—and many of those were his supporters. Politically, James K. Polk was dead.

JAMES K. POLK INAUGURAL MEDAL

The U.S. Mint commemorated the inaugurations of Martin Van Buren, John Tyler, James K. Polk, and Zachary Taylor by striking a very limited number of presidential medals. The obverse used the presidential likeness from that administration's Indian Peace Medal and the reverse showed the date of the respective inauguration surrounded by a wreath.

Polk's inaugural medal appears to have been struck after February 12, 1846, when Polk noted in his diary that he sat for John Gadsby Chapman, a New York artist commissioned to produce Polk's peace medal likeness. Indian Peace Medals were struck in three sizes (76 mm, 62 mm, and 51 mm) and were long used as gifts for principal Indian chiefs to solemnize treaties and special visits. The four inaugural medals used the medium size (about two and one-half inches in diameter) and were about a quarter of an inch thick in a "mahogany finished " bronze.

Polk's peace medals were ready in July 1846 and had the traditional "Peace and Friendship" with clasped hands and crossed tomahawk and peace pipe on the reverse. It is assumed that his inaugural medal with the March 4, 1845, date reverse was produced at the same time. They are extremely rare and the exact use for which they were intended is unclear.

FROM THE COLLECTION OF THE JAMES K. POLK MEMORIAL ASSOCIATION, COLUMBIA, TENNESSEE; GIFT OF DR. AND MRS. JOHN OLSON TO THE JAMES K. POLK HOME.

KEY DATES IN THE LIFE OF
JAMES K. POLK

1795   Born in a log cabin near Pineville, North Carolina, November 2

1803   Sarah Childress born near Murfreesboro, Tennessee, September 4

1806   Polk family moves to Duck River Valley, Tennessee

1812   Survives surgery for urinary stones

1816   Enrolls in the University of North Carolina as a sophomore

1818   Graduates from the University of North Carolina

1819   Law clerk for Felix Grundy; elected clerk of Tennessee state senate

1820   Admitted to Tennessee bar

1823   Elected to Tennessee house of representatives

1824   Marries Sarah Childress, January 1

1825   Elected to the U.S. House of Representatives, August 4

1825   Attends first session of Congress, December 5

1827   Reelected to second term in the U.S. House of Representatives

1827   Appointed to House Committee on Foreign Affairs

1828   Campaigns for Andrew Jackson for president

1829   Reelected to third term in the U.S. House of Representatives

1831   Reelected to fourth term in the U.S. House of Representatives

1832   Appointed to House Committee on Ways and Means

1833   Reelected to fifth term in the U.S. House of Representatives

1833   Appointed chairman of House Committee on Ways and Means

1834   Defeated for election as Speaker of the U.S. House of Representatives

1834 Announces support for Martin Van Buren as Jackson's successor in 1836

1835 Reelected to sixth term in the U.S. House of Representatives

1835 Elected Speaker of the U.S. House of Representatives, December 7

1837 Reelected to seventh term in the U.S. House of Representatives

1837 Reelected Speaker of the U.S. House of Representatives, September 4

1838 Announces candidacy for governor of Tennessee, August 30

1839 Elected governor of Tennessee, August 1

1840 Promotes his candidacy for vice president of the United States

1840 William Henry Harrison elected president of the United States

1841 Harrison dies in office and is succeeded by John Tyler, April 4

1841 Defeated for reelection as governor by James C. Jones, August 5

1842 Entertains Martin Van Buren in Columbia, Tennessee, and courts vice presidency

1843 Defeated for governor a second time by James C. Jones, August 3

1844 Explosion on the U.S.S. *Princeton* changes Tyler's Cabinet, February 24

1844 Nominated for the presidency by the Democrats in Baltimore, May 29

1844 Elected president of the United States, November

1845 Arrives in Washington with Sarah, February 13

1845 Inaugurated as eleventh president of the United States, March 4

1845 Mentor Andrew Jackson dies at the Hermitage, June 8

1845 In midst of Oregon crisis, begins keeping presidential diary, August 26

1845 Texas admitted to the union as the twenty-eighth state, December 29

1846 Orders General Taylor to advance to the Rio Grande, January 13

1846 Asks Congress to declare war on Mexico, May 11

1846 Oregon Treaty signed with Great Britain, June 15

1846 Battle of Monterrey, September 24

1846 Iowa admitted to the union as the twenty-ninth state, December 28

1847 Battle of Buena Vista, February 23

1847 Veracruz falls to Winfield Scott, March 29

1847 Sends Nicholas Trist to Mexico to negotiate, April 10

1847 Attends cornerstone ceremony for Smithsonian Institution, May 1

1847 Travels to University of North Carolina, May 28–June 5

1847 Tours New England, the only major trip of his presidency, June 22–July 7

1847 Mexico City falls to Winfield Scott, September 14

1848 Treaty of Guadalupe Hidalgo signed in Mexico, February 2

1848 Wisconsin admitted to the union as the thirtieth state, May 29

1848 Attends cornerstone ceremony for Washington Monument, July 4

1848 Treaty of Guadalupe Hidalgo becomes official, July 4

1848 Signs bill establishing Territory of Oregon, August 14

1848 Zachary Taylor elected president of the United States, November 7

1849 Signs bill establishing Territory of Minnesota, March 3

1849 Signs bill creating the Department of the Interior, March 3

1849 Zachary Taylor inaugurated president, March 5

1849 Takes up residence in retirement home of Polk Place, Nashville, April 24

1849 Dies at Polk Place, Nashville, June 15

1891 Sarah Childress Polk dies at Polk Place, August 14

PART I

THE MAN

Strike boldly; it [is] your habit,
and the means of your elevation.

—U.S. Supreme Court Justice John Catron to James K. Polk,
September 27, 1837

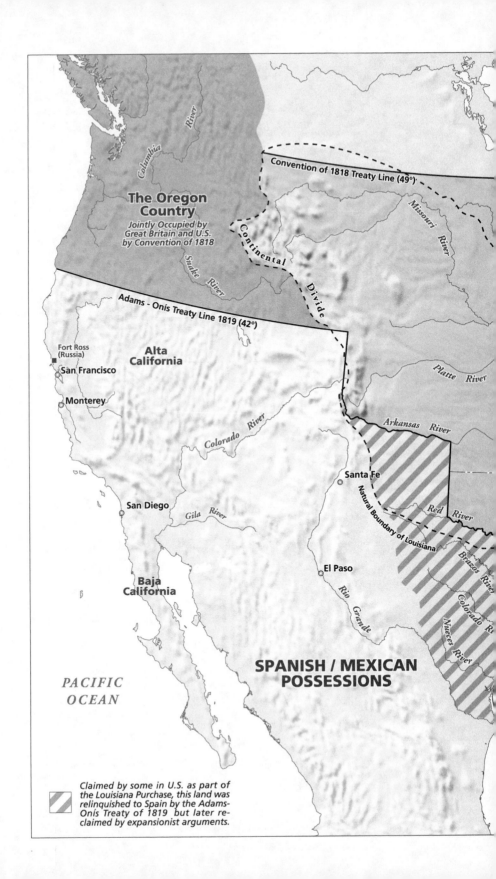

The Oregon Country
Jointly Occupied by Great Britain and U.S. by Convention of 1818

Convention of 1818 Treaty Line (49°)

Columbia *River*

Missouri *River*

Continental Divide

Snake *River*

Adams - Onís Treaty Line 1819 (42°)

Fort Ross (Russia)

San Francisco

Alta California

Monterey

Platte *River*

Colorado *River*

Arkansas *River*

Santa Fe

San Diego

Gila *River*

Natural Boundary of Louisiana

Red *River*

El Paso

Baja California

Rio Grande

Brazos *River*

Colorado *R*

Nueces *River*

PACIFIC OCEAN

SPANISH / MEXICAN POSSESSIONS

Claimed by some in U.S. as part of the Louisiana Purchase, this land was relinquished to Spain by the Adams-Onís Treaty of 1819 but later re-claimed by expansionist arguments.

Polk's America
1819

CANADA

Maine
(Mass.)

Vt.

N.H.

Boston

Mass.

Conn. R.I.

New
York

New
York

N.J.

Michigan
Territory
(1805)

Chicago

Pennsylvania

Ohio

Washington

Del.

Md.

Illinois
(1818)

Indiana
(1816)

Ohio

River

Mississippi River

St. Louis

Virginia

Kentucky

Missouri
Territory
(1812)

Cumberland River

North
Carolina

Nashville

Tennessee

Arkansas
Territory
(1819)

Tennessee River

South
Carolina

Georgia

Louisiana
(1812)

Miss.
(1817)

Alabama
(1819)

River

Florida
Territory
(1822)

New
Orleans

*ATLANTIC
OCEAN*

Gulf of Mexico

CHAPTER 1

Old Hickory's Boy

$\mathscr{J}$AMES K. POLK always had what any politician craves—the un-qualified support of his era's greatest hero. To be sure, some folks vilified the very name of Andrew Jackson. But they were usually in the minority, and from his fabled victory at New Orleans in 1815 until his death in 1845, Jackson cast a huge shadow across the American political landscape. Throughout most of that time, there was never much doubt that James K. Polk was Old Hickory's boy.

It was no small coincidence that the men were born within twenty miles of each other in the frontier hills of the Carolinas. Jackson was the elder by twenty-eight years. Because Jackson's re-cently widowed mother was traveling to join family, there is some doubt which sister's home, and hence which side of the North Carolina–South Carolina border, Elizabeth Jackson was at when her third son was born on March 15, 1767. But young Andrew grew up at his aunt Jane's on the South Carolina side and stayed there until he rode north to Salisbury, North Carolina, to study law seventeen years later.

The law and a lust for adventure soon led Jackson west across the Great Smoky Mountains to Tennessee. In Jonesborough at the age of twenty-one, he fought his first duel, after taking the sarcasm of opposing counsel during a trial a little too personally. Both parties fired into the air, and Jackson left the field satisfied that his reputation was secure. Later in that same year of 1788, he arrived in Nashville.

On the great Cumberland River, Nashville was still very much a fledgling frontier settlement, a town of a few hundred people that nonetheless had already managed to erect both a courthouse and a distillery. Jackson's boisterous personality attracted plenty of attention. In 1796, after helping to draft a state constitution, Andrew Jackson was elected Tennessee's first delegate to the U.S. House of Representatives. He was all of twenty-nine years old.[1]

By then, back in Mecklenburg County, North Carolina, Samuel and Jane Polk had welcomed their firstborn. Jackson's Scots-Irish ancestors had barely reached America when Jackson was born, but the Polks were old-timers, Scots-Irish themselves. Sam's great-great-grandfather had arrived along the eastern shores of Chesapeake Bay in the late 1600s. The Polk clan soon migrated to south-central Pennsylvania and then to the Carolina hill country.

Jane was a Knox, descended from a brother of Scottish Reformation leader John Knox. She was a no-nonsense Presbyterian, and she named the baby she delivered about noon on November 2, 1795, James Knox Polk after her father.

Just about everyone else in Mecklenburg County was also Presbyterian, but there were various shades to their zeal. Sam Polk's father, Ezekiel, was a case in point. After the children he fathered with his second wife all died in infancy, Ezekiel became disillusioned with Presbyterian orthodoxy and began to espouse deism.

When Sam and Jane presented Ezekiel's grandson to be baptized, a young "fire and brimstone" minister named James Wallis chose to interrogate Sam at length about the depths of his own commitment to Presbyterian doctrine. A heated argument ensued and the result was that little James Knox Polk was taken home without receiving the sacrament of baptism. Jane was mortified.

Quite an uproar ensued throughout Mecklenburg County as

Ezekiel voiced his views louder and louder and the Reverend Wallis preached back with equal passion. As if mortification weren't enough, Jane Polk was soon caught squarely in the middle of the debate when her widowed mother married none other than the Reverend Wallis's widower father. But by then, Ezekiel and most of the Polks were looking farther west.[2]

In 1803, Ezekiel Polk led four of his children and their families into the Duck River country of Middle Tennessee in search of new land. At first, Sam and Jane stayed behind in Mecklenburg with their son James and his two younger sisters and a brother. By the time another son was born and the crops of 1806 harvested, Sam and Jane had also left Mecklenburg and made the four-hundred-mile trek over the Smokies to Ezekiel's settlement south of Nashville. Ostensibly a farmer and part-time surveyor, Sam Polk quickly turned to land speculation.

With half the area populated by kin, it wasn't long before the Polk clan was instrumental in establishing the county of Maury and the new town of Columbia as the county seat. Sam Polk was soon a county judge, a respected civic leader, and well on his way to becoming downright wealthy. One of the influential men of Tennessee to grace the Polk house from time to time was Andrew Jackson, by then an ex-judge of the state superior court and a well-established land speculator in his own right.[3]

Sam's son James, however, was not doing well. His schooling to date had been marginal, in large part because of his rather poor health. On a rough-and-tumble frontier where robust men like Andrew Jackson epitomized manhood, James was decidedly frail. In time, his chronic abdominal pains were diagnosed as urinary stones, but in this era before general anesthetic or even proper antiseptic agents, a surgical solution was a major undertaking.

In the fall of 1812, Sam Polk determined to send his almost-seventeen-year-old son to Philadelphia to receive the care of Dr. Philip Syng Physick, later known as "the father of American surgery." Resting uncomfortably on a makeshift bed in a covered wagon, James bounced along as the eight-hundred-mile journey from Columbia began.

But before traveling very far into Kentucky, James "was seized by a paroxysm more painful than any that had preceded it." Doubting that he could survive all the way to Philadelphia, the Polks turned instead to Dr. Ephraim McDowell of Danville, Kentucky, who—relatively speaking—was also a surgeon of some note.

Relying on a liberal dose of brandy as both anesthetic and antisepsis, Dr. McDowell made an incision behind the young man's scrotum and forced a sharp, pointed instrument called a gorget through his prostate and into the bladder. The urinary stone, or stones, were then removed with forceps. Any way one looks at it, the procedure was a ghastly invasion of one's body. James recovered quickly, however, and outwardly appeared no worse for the wear.[4]

Relieved of this health burden, James made the most of his newfound energy. Sam Polk offered to set his son up in the mercantile business, but James was determined to get a proper education. In July 1813, James—despite the fact that his principal biographer chose to call him "Jimmy" and "Jim," there is no evidence that his elders and peers called him anything but James—enrolled at a nearby Presbyterian academy.

After a year, his father agreed to send him to a more distinguished academy in Murfreesboro. James excelled there and by one account was "much the most promising young man in the school." Such promise was to be rewarded, and with Sam Polk by now well able to afford it, James was admitted to the University of North Carolina as a second-semester sophomore in January 1816. He had just turned twenty.

At that time, the University of North Carolina was staffed by a single administrator, one professor, a senior tutor, and two recent graduates who served as additional tutors. The most valuable education may have come from membership in one of the university's two literary societies. James Polk joined the Dialectic Society during his first term at Chapel Hill and was soon engrossed in its weekly debates and essay presentations. It was here that he learned to speak, write, and formulate an argument.

Unfortunately, no detailed minutes remain from the meeting at which the Dialectic Society debated the question "Would an extension of territory be an advantage to the United States?" Which side did young Polk take? A majority voted no. Another topic asked whether an elected representative should "exercise his own judgment or act according to the directions of his constituents." Polk favored the latter, as did a majority of his classmates. A less serious question asked "Is an occasional resort to female company beneficial to students?" The all-male assemblage was unanimous in its verdict.[5]

In due course, Polk was elected to a succession of offices in the Dialectic Society and broke a precedent by winning reelection to the presidency. In presenting a speech on that occasion, Polk told his peers, "your proficiency in extemporaneous debating will furnish you with that fluency of language, that connexion of ideas and boldness of delivery that will be equally serviceable in the council, in the pulpit and at the bar." Considering the large number of his University of North Carolina contemporaries who went on to public service, including his roommate William D. Moseley, who became governor of Florida, Polk's advice was well taken.

Polk graduated with honors in May 1818, but the studious young man had given his all to his academic efforts, and despite Dr. McDowell's successful surgery, his general constitution was still frail. When Sam Polk arrived in Chapel Hill late in July to take his son home, James was in such a weakened condition that Sam returned without him. Not until October was the graduate fit enough to ride the winding mountain roads back to Tennessee. Unbeknownst to Polk, the next time he set foot in Chapel Hill, he would be president of a much larger union than the Dialectic Society.[6]

If James K. Polk came of age intellectually during his two and a half years at Chapel Hill, Tennessee in the interim had also come of age. In fact, the state was booming. Even in Columbia, its population just over three hundred, Sam Polk and his new son-in-law, James Walker, were busy chartering a bank, building a Masonic Hall, and organizing a steamboat company for the Tennessee River.

James Polk might have applied his new education and his meticulous attention to detail to these kinds of business ventures. But the give-and-take of the Dialectic Society had more than whetted his appetite for the public arena, and the most obvious route into it led through admission to the bar. Determined to become a lawyer, James Polk promptly headed fifty miles north to Nashville.

The little frontier settlement that had welcomed Andrew Jackson thirty years before was now a thriving city with three thousand inhabitants and paved streets. It was the commercial hub of Middle Tennessee and was quickly becoming the political center of the entire state.

Jackson had just returned to Nashville from exploits in Spanish-held Florida. His nickname, Old Hickory—as in "tough as hickory"—had been won in the early days of the War of 1812 and his national fame secured by his lopsided defeat of the British at New Orleans at the war's end. Most recently, Jackson had led U.S. army regulars, Tennessee volunteers, and Georgia militia into Florida during the First Seminole War. Largely on his own initiative, he had forced the Spanish to abandon West Florida to the United States.

Now Jackson was building a mansion he called the Hermitage, east of Nashville. Whether Jackson or Sam Polk provided James with an introduction to Felix Grundy is uncertain but probable, and James was soon clerking for one of Nashville's most celebrated lawyers.

Felix Grundy quickly became James Polk's first mentor. Grundy grew up in Kentucky, helped that territory become a state, represented it in the U.S. House of Representatives, and ultimately became the state's chief justice. But Tennessee beckoned, and Grundy climbed a similar legal and political ladder there, representing the state in Congress and achieving some notoriety as one of the war hawks who urged war with Great Britain and then cheered Andy Jackson's every military move.

By the time James Polk came calling in 1819, Grundy was known far and wide across Tennessee for his mastery of juries as well as his wide circle of political connections. Polk readily immersed himself in both Grundy's law library and his school of personal experience.

Polk's fellow clerk was a young man named Francis B. Fogg, who was so studious as to make even the scholarly Polk look like a legal slacker. That year, Grundy was elected to the state legislature, and he suggested that Fogg accompany him to the upcoming legislative session and seek election as clerk of the state senate. Fogg thought a moment and then pronounced himself far too busy with a mountain of legal minutiae to do so. Polk, however, jumped at the chance. After all, to him the law was the vehicle, not the destination.

So, with Grundy's endorsements, Polk accompanied him to Murfreesboro, where the legislature was to meet. On September 20, 1819, the Tennessee senate elected the young man from Columbia as its clerk and proceeded to pay him the then-princely sum of six dollars per day to manage its paperwork. (The legislators themselves were paid only four dollars per diem.) That Polk performed his job effectively and with precision was evidenced by his reelection without opposition when the next legislature convened in 1821. In the process, he learned the full gamut of parliamentary procedure and legislative routine.

Meanwhile, because the legislature rarely met for longer than a month, Polk was able to complete his legal studies with Grundy and gain admission to the state bar when the circuit court convened at Columbia in June 1820. The Polk clan surely celebrated, and Sam Polk even provided his son with his first case by managing to be arrested for public fighting. James secured his father's release with a fine of one dollar plus costs, and Sam was instrumental in paying for the construction of a one-room law office and library for his son's practice.[7]

That young Polk was a stickler for detail became apparent early. When Jackson protégé Sam Houston, who was then practicing law in Nashville and who would later achieve enduring fame in Texas, sent Polk a judgment from a North Carolina court for execution in Tennessee, Polk rejected it. Finding the paperwork "incomplete, and not authenticated in the manner required," Polk advised Houston not "to commence an action on this record" until it was corrected. (In their demeanor, Polk and Houston were polar opposites, and Houston is supposed to have once observed that Polk was "a victim of the use of water as a beverage.")[8]

But Sam Houston wasn't the only one destined for fame who crossed paths with Polk in those early years. Riding to Murfreesboro for the September 1821 session of the legislature, Polk fell in with a newly elected state representative from Lawrence County. His name was David Crockett, and while he, too, was the opposite of Polk in almost every way, Crockett had honed a knack for stump speaking that got him elected by a two-to-one majority.

Some years later, after their political views had diverged, Crockett poked a little fun at Polk and perhaps himself by recounting how in the course of that ride Polk had expressed to Crockett his opinion that the legislature was likely to enact changes in the state's judiciary. "Now so help me God," Crockett later wrote in his autobiography, "I knew no more what a 'radical change' and a 'judiciary' meant than my horse, but looking straight into Mr. Polk's face as though I understood all about it, I replied, 'I presume so.' "[9]

Just when James Polk became close to Andrew Jackson is uncertain. Most likely, it was a relationship begun in passing at Polk's father's house and nurtured by time and Jackson's connections with the extended Polk family. Having no natural children of their own, Old Hickory and his wife, Rachel, were always taking young men of promise under their wings. Similarly, it can't be said with absolute certainty when Polk met the only person to hold more sway over him than Old Hickory. Her name was Sarah Childress.

$\mathscr{S}$arah was born in Rutherford County, Tennessee, within a few miles of Murfreesboro, on September 4, 1803. Her parents, Joel and Elizabeth (Whitsett) Childress, were members of Tennessee's old guard, having also emigrated from North Carolina. They were close friends with Andrew and Rachel Jackson, and anecdotal evidence suggests that Sarah and her siblings addressed the Jacksons as "Uncle Andrew" and "Aunt Rachel." Joel Childress was well established as a merchant, planter, and land speculator, and one well-worn tale avows that Childress personally paid more than five hundred dollars for the full-dress military uniform that Jackson would take with him to New Orleans in 1814.

Certainly, Joel Childress could afford the best that the Tennessee frontier had to offer. His daughters, Sarah and Susan, were schooled at private academies in Murfreesboro and Nashville and then sent east to the Moravian Female Academy in Salem, North Carolina, in 1817, when Sarah was just turning fourteen.

Numerous Polk biographies have attempted—all unconvincingly—to link James and Sarah at an early age, either meeting in passing at an academy in Murfreesboro or while Sarah was in Salem and James nearby in Chapel Hill. It is possible, and indeed Sarah's older brother, Anderson, was enrolled with Polk at the University of North Carolina. But any formal introduction is much more likely to have occurred while James was in Murfreesboro serving as clerk of the state senate and Sarah had just returned home from North Carolina after the death of her father. James was almost twenty-four that fall of 1819, and Sarah had just turned sixteen.

Some nineteenth-century accounts hasten to say that Sarah was everything but beautiful, as if bestowing that compliment would somehow lessen the gravity of her more serious characteristics. She had large brown eyes, long dark hair, and a rich olive complexion. By all accounts, she was vivacious and outgoing, and her formal education was far above the norm for women of her generation.

One way or the other, James K. Polk—as he always signed his letters to her—found those qualities endearing. "See those lovely raven curls clustering around her face, and look in those beautiful brown eyes," Polk mused after Jackson's artist friend, Ralph Earl, painted her portrait some years later. Earl, Polk contended, "has caught exactly the look of mischief that few people outside of myself ever see." Was Sarah Childress beautiful? Look at the portrait and judge for yourself.

The details of their courtship are largely unknown, but one oft-told story of dubious veracity begs telling nonetheless. Supposedly, Polk asked his mentor, Jackson, what he should do to advance his political career. Jackson advised him to find a wife and settle down. Asked if he had anyone in particular in mind, Old Hickory replied, "The one who will never give you trouble. Her wealthy family, education, health, and appearance are all superior. You know her well." It took Polk only a moment to suggest what should have been the obvious. "Do you mean Sarah Childress?" he asked. "I shall go at once and ask her."[10]

No one, however, ever accused James K. Polk of being anything less than insightful, and it is doubtful that he needed Old

Hickory's push to court the daughter of one of Tennessee's most distinguished pioneer families, particularly given Sarah's individual qualities. James later teased Sarah that she would not have consented to marry him had he remained a mere clerk of the state senate.

But in politics, James Polk needed no spur other than his own ambition. At the close of the legislative session in September 1822, he added a postscript to a letter filled with legal business that advised, "I am a candidate for the House of Representatives in the Tennessee Legislature."[11]

In those days, Tennessee elections were held the first week in August in odd years. That gave the young lawyer almost a year to campaign while he practiced law in Columbia, rode the circuit, and continued to court Sarah in Murfreesboro. By election day, just in case persuasive arguments on the stump had not been enough, Polk paid for "twenty-three gallons of cider, brandy, and whiskey in one election district alone."

What his staunch Presbyterian mother and his fiancée thought of the tactic has gone unrecorded, but such refreshments were a requisite of campaigning, and when the results were tallied, James K. Polk was the new state representative from Maury County. The Polk clan alone must have made up half the electorate—or so it sometimes seemed.[12]

Indeed, any election celebration was more than matched by the wedding of James and Sarah on January 1, 1824, in the Childress family home near Murfreesboro. He was twenty-eight; she was twenty. Polk's law partner, Aaron V. Brown, served as best man and would continue to stand by him through the next quarter century of political battles.

Receptions given by Elizabeth Childress in Murfreesboro and by Sam and Jane Polk in Columbia were among the social events of the winter. Clearly, James and Sarah Polk were a young couple on their way up.[13]

$\mathscr{A}$merica was also on its way up. The census of 1820 had counted 9.6 million Americans, double the population of 1790. Almost all of this increase had come from natural growth, not from immigration. Perhaps most significant, only about a hundred thousand Americans had lived west of the Appalachian Mountains in 1790. Thirty years later, owing to migrations such as those that had taken Andrew Jackson and the Polk and Childress clans to Tennessee, there were 2.2 million people west of the mountains.

As a whole, America was still overwhelmingly rural. Less than one American in ten lived in cities of more than twenty-five hundred inhabitants. The agrarian South was experiencing a boom in cotton—thanks mostly to the increased markets of a growing national population. New plantations, run by slave labor, were springing up throughout the rich soil of Alabama and Mississippi on land that Jackson had wrested from the Creek nations during the War of 1812.

The North was also overwhelmingly rural, but life there ran at a little quicker pace. Aside from the urban centers of Philadelphia, New York, Boston, and a fledgling Pittsburgh, the northern states were dotted with small farms. Some areas, however, were beginning to flex their industrial muscles—mills in New England, shipyards on the Great Lakes, and a network of roads and canals were taking shape.

The nascent system of roads and canals encouraged westward migration and tied together the geographic sections of the country. One primary artery was the National Road, initially linking Cumberland, Maryland, and Wheeling, Virginia. But the real revolution in transportation was the steamboat. The days of floating flatboats one-way down the Mississippi were giving way to steam-powered vessels plying the "Big Muddy" and other rivers in both directions.

By 1824, twenty-four stars adorned the American flag, five of them representing the recently admitted states of Indiana, Mississippi, Illinois, Alabama, and Missouri. All were in western lands that had quickly filled up after the War of 1812. Government here, as throughout the nation, was the province of white males over the age of twenty-one. Even then, it was frequently a close-knit fraternity.

But the boom of increased population and new lands fueled a

no-nonsense pragmatism that tended to break down established barriers and to fuel opportunity. For many young men, politics—as James K. Polk had long ago decided—was the way to get ahead.

$\mathscr{J}$ames K. Polk had seen enough of the state legislature during his years as clerk of the senate to know that politics—particularly in Tennessee—was frequently a blood sport. Andrew Jackson carried considerable clout in the state, but that did not mean that all Tennesseeans hung on his every word. In fact, the political factions in the state were complex and their alliances ever-changing. Polk's challenge as a new legislator was to identify with issues he cared about without becoming intractably pigeonholed into any one faction, and this he seemed to do rather well.

At first glance, it might have been assumed that Polk would gravitate to the older conservative faction of landowners and businessmen led by John Overton. This was Felix Grundy's crowd, as well as Sam Polk's. Tennessee's governor, William Carroll, represented a more progressive group. Among other things, this group sought to quash dubious land speculation and to promote the sale of state lands to fund a public school system. Polk not only supported the Carroll position on state lands but also advocated that remaining federal lands in the western part of the state be ceded to the state to endow a higher education system. One of Polk's allies in this endeavor was the "representative from the cane," David Crockett.

These land issues, and other issues such as banking reforms, frequently found Polk opposing the position of his legal mentor, Felix Grundy. When Grundy's normally persuasive oral arguments were stymied by the parliamentary maneuvers and debating skills of his one-time student, he was heard to mutter: "I have been preparing a club here with which my own head is to be broken."

But these political differences were mild compared to the turmoil that ensued when the Overton faction got serious about pushing Andrew Jackson as a candidate for the presidency. The Overton group originally saw Old Hickory's candidacy as a way to build coattails for Overton men throughout the state, and in particular as a way to defeat incumbent U.S. senator John Williams.

Even in Tennessee, no one gave Jackson much chance of actually *winning* the presidency at this point. To be sure, Old Hickory was a military hero—New Orleans and wars against the Creek and Seminole had seen to that. But no military leader—save George Washington—had heretofore been seriously considered for the presidency, let alone elected.

When the Tennessee legislature that was elected in August 1823 met to select a U.S. senator, the pro-Jackson Overton faction found itself divided between businessman Pleasant M. Miller and former congressman John Rhea. Senator Williams, with the support of Governor Carroll, seemed almost assured of reelection. If that happened, Jackson's presidential prospects would suffer.

This likely outcome didn't faze John Overton, who had promoted Jackson's presidential candidacy in the first place merely to aid his own local efforts. But two of Jackson's stalwart friends, Tennessee's other U.S. senator, John H. Eaton, and William B. Lewis, were not so easily called off.

Finding after much bartering that neither Miller nor Rhea had the backing to defeat Senator Williams, Eaton and Lewis had Andrew Jackson's own name placed in nomination. Now James K. Polk faced his first major political decision. Would he continue to vote with Governor Carroll's faction and support Williams, or would he proclaim his allegiance to Andrew Jackson?

While Polk was no doubt lobbied vigorously by both sides, his choice in retrospect seems obvious. Politically, Jackson had begun to voice the sort of "democratic" principles that placed him closer to the Carroll group on some of the issues Polk had been championing, such as land reform and banking. And at a personal level, there was not only the long connection between Jackson and the Polk clan but also Sarah's closeness to "Uncle Andrew" and "Aunt Rachel."

So on October 1, 1823, as David Crockett and most of Governor Carroll's supporters sided with John Williams, Polk voted for Andrew Jackson to become Tennessee's next United States senator. Polk's vote was not the deciding one, but in a relatively close 35–25 race, it was an important one. Senator Andrew Jackson was soon on his way to Washington, and his presidential prospects were suddenly taken seriously in other parts of the country. As for James K. Polk, after his vote for Jackson, there was never any doubt but that he was Old Hickory's boy.[14]

The question that Polk and Tennesseeans now had to ask themselves was this: just how far was Old Hickory bound? Truth be told, Andrew Jackson despised his new role. "I am a senator against my wishes and feelings," the general immediately wrote to his best friend, John Coffee, but "I am compelled to accept." His friends had convinced him that it was his political—nay moral—duty.

And yet, somewhere between Nashville and Washington, Jackson must have realized that the crowds of well-wishers that flocked to see him gave more credibility to his presidential candidacy than any illusion created by his friends in Tennessee. At some point, Old Hickory began to think that he could win it all.[15]

CHAPTER 2

Carrying the Water

$\mathscr{P}$RESIDENT JAMES MONROE had enjoyed little national opposition for the better part of two terms. During his presidency, the
United States embraced the sense of national unity and purpose
that had been forged during the War of 1812 and honed by Jackson's victory at New Orleans. But beneath this national veneer,
what some called the Era of Good Feelings was anything but. Upward of a dozen candidates plotted to succeed Monroe in 1824.

New England's favorite son was John Quincy Adams, Monroe's secretary of state. The South was divided between Georgia's
William H. Crawford, the secretary of the treasury, and South Carolina's young John C. Calhoun, the secretary of war. New York favored its governor, De Witt Clinton, who had promoted the
building of the Erie Canal. Kentucky championed Henry Clay, the
Speaker of the U.S. House of Representatives. Tennessee put forward the name of Andrew Jackson.

With unifying party nominating conventions yet to be developed, these strong regional candidates, each running independently, seemed to promise that no one candidate would receive the

requisite majority of votes in the electoral college. If that happened, the Constitution provided that the U.S. House of Representatives, voting by state delegation with one vote per state, would select the next president from the top three electoral vote-getters.

That is exactly what happened in 1824. John C. Calhoun became almost everyone's choice for vice president and De Witt Clinton fell by the wayside, but the remaining four candidates split the votes among them. When the results were counted, the electoral college vote stood at Jackson, 99; Adams, 84; Crawford, 41; and Clay, 37. Popular vote totals were Jackson, 152,901; Adams, 114,023; Crawford, 46,979; and Clay, 47,217.

It must be quickly added that six states did not select their electors by popular vote—they were chosen instead by the legislatures—and that in some states not all candidates appeared on the ballot. Nonetheless, by either electoral or popular vote standard, Andrew Jackson was the decided choice of the plurality of the people, despite having failed to attain an electoral college majority.[1]

Now the bargaining began. No side was exempt from receiving overtures and no side refrained from making obvious suggestions, no matter how courteous or muted. But the man who scrambled the most was Henry Clay.

Nothing evidences the magnetism of Clay's forceful personality better than the fact that he was elected Speaker of the U.S. House of Representatives as a freshman congressman. From that moment in 1811, Clay set about making the heretofore largely ceremonial speakership a position of true power. He directed debates, interpreted rules, and packed key committees with his partisans, many of whom were western war hawks eager for war with Great Britain.

Throughout the 1824 campaign, Clay had counted on being among the top three finishers and then using his heavy influence over the House of Representatives to elect himself president. He was determined to do so because, more than anything else, Henry Clay wanted to be president of the United States. And now he was not only dead last but also eliminated from the three-way race in the House.

Born in Virginia in 1777, Clay had practiced law in Kentucky. Among his early clients were Aaron Burr, whom Clay represented against the charges that preceded Burr's trial for treason, and Andrew Jackson, whom Clay served as agent in certain trading ventures in Kentucky.

But the Clay-Jackson relationship quickly soured, in part because Jackson got far more adulation for winning the battle of New Orleans *after* the signing of the Treaty of Ghent than Clay received for his role as a peace commissioner in helping to negotiate it. Later, Clay was quick to condemn Jackson's swashbuckling excursion into Spanish Florida.

Certainly, their emerging political philosophies were different. Clay held an elitist top-down view of government; Jackson grounded his beliefs in the grass roots and the sanctity of the common man. Last, these two westerners from neighboring states were vying for the same core constituency. This became particularly apparent when the Kentucky state legislature, having failed to make Clay president, passed resolutions on January 11, 1825, directing its delegates in the House of Representatives to cast the state's vote for Andrew Jackson.

Two and a half weeks later, as the House prepared to resolve the narrow presidential contest, an unsigned letter appeared in a Philadelphia newspaper suggesting that Henry Clay had agreed to swing his support to John Quincy Adams in exchange for an appointment as secretary of state. Clay feigned outrage and published a response "denouncing the anonymous slanderer as a 'baseless and infamous calumniator, a dastard and a liar.' " Clay called upon his accuser "to reveal his identity and give satisfaction" on the dueling grounds.

When the source of the charges was revealed to be an eccentric Pennsylvania congressman who lacked credibility with all concerned, Clay let the matter drop. There was no denying, however, that Clay had indeed spent a long evening of conversation with John Quincy Adams a few weeks before. Undoubtedly, neither man spoke directly to a bargain, but each was far too politically astute to misunderstand the arrangement. In politics, as in love, some things are best left unsaid.[2]

On February 9, 1825, the U.S. House of Representatives met to elect a president. Kentucky's delegation, despite the request of its state legislature to vote for Andrew Jackson, cast the state vote for John Quincy Adams at Clay's urging. "The delegation I believe," Clay blandly observed, "feels perfectly free to vote, as its own judgment shall dictate, notwithstanding the recent request of the Kentucky legislature."

Hearing of this before the vote and surmising that the Kentucky legislature would never again support someone who had so blatantly gone against its directive, Martin Van Buren of New York gasped to a Kentucky colleague, "If you do this, you sign Mr. Clay's political death warrant."[3]

Along with Kentucky, Henry Clay delivered to Adams the votes of the other two states Clay had won, Ohio and Missouri. Jackson received the votes of seven states—Alabama, Indiana, New Jersey, Mississippi, Pennsylvania, South Carolina, and Tennessee. Crawford received the votes of Delaware, Georgia, North Carolina, and Virginia. Ten other states went into the Adams column. Thus, when the dust settled, Adams had won thirteen states—a bare majority of the twenty-four in the union—and was declared the next president of the United States. Five days later, John Quincy Adams offered Henry Clay the post of secretary of state.[4]

Watching all of this from his seat in the Tennessee legislature, James K. Polk could not imagine that twenty years later Henry Clay's actions in the disputed presidential election of 1824 would still play a part in his own campaign for the White House. "So you see," raged Old Hickory after Clay's ambitious maneuver, "the Judas of the West has closed the contract and will receive the thirty pieces of silver—his end will be the same. Was there ever witnessed such a bare faced corruption in any country before?"[5]

In the absence of absolute proof—a smoking gun—history has long debated whether the "corrupt bargain" of Adams and Clay was absolutely prearranged. But it scarcely mattered. Politics, after all, is largely perception.

"We see the predictions verified," an only slightly calmer Jackson wrote a week later, "when we behold two men political enemies, and as different in political sentiments as any men can be, so suddenly unite, there must be some unseen cause to produce this political phenomena." Needless to say, Jackson was one of fifteen "nay" votes out of forty-two total votes cast when the Senate gave its advice and consent to Clay's nomination a few weeks later.[6]

$\mathcal{J}$ackson's loss and Clay's corrupt bargain did not sour Polk's political appetite. The previous August he had thrown his hat into the ring as a candidate for Congress in Tennessee's Sixth District. Now, as Jackson hurried back to Tennessee and started the next presidential campaign even before Adams had time to warm his chair in the White House, Polk pushed his own congressional campaign into high gear.

It proved to be a divisive five-way race. All candidates were expected to "live on their horses for about six months previous to the election," and this Polk did in the extreme. Despite Sarah's worries about his physical health, Polk set a standard that he would follow in subsequent campaigns and relentlessly crisscrossed the district from his home county of Maury south to the Alabama line. When the votes were tallied early in August 1825, his hard work paid off and he placed first in the field of five with a plurality of 3,669 out of 10,440.[7]

There was now no question but that James K. Polk was a man to be watched. Andrew Jackson certainly took notice, as did Governor William Carroll. "Colonel Polk, by whom Colonel Erwin and others were defeated," wrote Carroll to Henry Clay, using a title stemming from Polk's militia service, "is a young man of sprightly talents, and will probably remain several years in Congress; and may hereafter have a share of influence in the political concerns of the state." But for now, Old Hickory's boy was bound for Washington.[8]

During the congressional campaign, some critics had chided Polk that he was too young to be entrusted with such responsibility. He was, after all, only twenty-nine years old, but that was exactly the same age that Old Hickory had been upon his first election to Congress. There was no question that Old Hickory's boy was following in his mentor's footsteps. Meanwhile, as James rode eastward on horseback toward Washington, Sarah remained in Columbia and waited for the children both hoped would come.

———

𝒯he Washington that James K. Polk rode into late in the fall of 1825 was barely more than a quiet little village. The two dominant structures were the White House and the Capitol, each much smaller than future additions would render them. In between, both sides of Pennsylvania Avenue held a variety of boardinghouses, hotels, stables, and shops.

Few members among the 48 senators and 213 congressmen could afford to maintain private dwellings, particularly because sessions of Congress tended to run only from early December to March or April. Most members roomed in boardinghouses and joined together in collegial "messes" to procure their meals. Along with other Tennessee representatives, Polk took a room and joined a mess at Benjamin Burch's house on Capitol Hill.[9]

Polk's next concern was to hasten to the Capitol and stake out his seat. Having suffered extensive damage during the War of 1812, the two initial wings of the Capitol were only then being joined together by the central rotunda. The House of Representatives met in what later became Statuary Hall. It was a cavernous space, warmed by only one fireplace and filled with echoes and dead spots that could vex the most accomplished of orators. Much as he had done as a neophyte clerk of the Tennessee senate, Polk watched the personalities and legislative workings with a keen eye before rising on March 13, 1826, to make his first major speech.

There were many issues facing the country, but the one that Polk first addressed was stoked by partisan outrage left over from the disputed presidential election. At issue was a proposed constitutional amendment either to abolish the electoral college outright and provide for a direct popular vote, or to modify the electoral college and require presidential electors to cast their vote for the candidate receiving a plurality in their district. Polk preferred "the district system," and later assured Jackson that whatever new system was devised, "This important election should in no count devolve upon Congress."[10]

Polk found occasion during the ensuing debate to blast the Adams-Clay contention that Jackson was a dangerous "military chieftain." Edward Everett of Massachusetts noted that if the government was ever destroyed, "it would not be by a President elected

by a minority of the people, but by a President elected by an overwhelming majority of the people; by some 'military chieftain' that
should arise in the land." Polk rose to Old Hickory's defense.

"Yes, sir," replied Polk indignantly, "by some 'military chieftain,'
whose only crime it was to have served his country faithfully at a
period when that country needed and realized the value of his services." If the government was ever to be destroyed, Polk concluded,
it would be by "the alluring and corrupting influence of executive
patronage."[11]

This was a dig at Clay's appointment as secretary of state, but
Polk's remarks were mild compared to those uttered by South Carolina's George McDuffie. Taking exception to Clay's Kentucky allies who now sought to excuse their vote against Jackson despite
the resolution of their legislature, McDuffie referred to Clay as "the
dastardly individual who skulks behind the screen and works the
wires." Tempers flared and McDuffie appeared to invite a challenge. Nevertheless, "the general impression," Polk reported to
Jackson, was that there would "be no fighting."[12]

But that wasn't to be the case in the upper house. In the Senate,
Clay was under assault from Virginia's crusty John Randolph. Clay
and Randolph had never seen eye to eye on even the most trivial of
issues. In fact, when Clay had set about making the speakership a
position of true power upon his first election to that post in 1811, he
had unceremoniously ordered Randolph to remove his dog from the
House floor—something no previous Speaker had dared to do. On
more substantive issues, Randolph vehemently opposed the fixation
of Clay and his war hawks on acquiring Canada.

But now the feud became more personal. Randolph indulged in
a rambling discourse that touched on all phases of Clay's perceived
follies, but most of all upon his "corrupt bargain" with John Quincy
Adams. No longer able to defend himself verbally as a member of
Congress, Clay did the one thing that smacked more of Andrew
Jackson than of his benefactor Adams. He promptly challenged
Randolph to a duel. Randolph was only too happy to oblige.

Never mind that by now most states, including Clay's own Kentucky, had outlawed dueling, or that many in Congress, and Clay
himself, entertained questions about Randolph's sanity. In the end,

Clay determined that "I ought not to be governed by that opinion [of Randolph's insanity] which was opposed by the recent act of my native state electing him to the Senate."

So, on April 8, 1826, despite the entreaties of their seconds to postpone or forgo the matter, the secretary of state of the United States and Senator John Randolph of Virginia faced off at ten paces beneath a cluster of trees just across the Potomac River from Washington.

At the command of "Fire!" both men took aim and discharged their weapons. The ball from Clay's pistol struck the ground near Randolph; the senator's own shot hit a stump behind Clay. "Enough!" cried Senator Thomas Hart Benton, who was witnessing the exchange and who, as first cousin to Clay's wife, had done his best to avert it. But neither combatant was satisfied. Their weapons were reloaded and again came the command, "Fire!" Clay's ball struck almost the same spot. Randolph fired into the air.

"I do not fire at you, Mr. Clay," thundered Randolph, as he quickly advanced toward Clay with outstretched hand. Clay met his opponent halfway and shook hands. Benton and the attendant seconds breathed sighs of relief. Two days later, Clay and Randolph exchanged calling cards, a sign that social relations between the two were formally restored. Such was life in Washington in 1826. As for the electoral college, its structure was never changed, and two centuries later, it remains as enacted in 1804 by the Twelfth Amendment.[13]

𝒜fter Congress recessed, Polk spent the summer of 1826 politicking in Tennessee. When he returned to the capital that autumn, Sarah went with him. She had not taken kindly to her husband's long absence the previous winter and at twenty-three decided to see something of the business of government firsthand. With no sign of children, Sarah occupied her time helping with her husband's correspondence, managing their boarding arrangements at a house on Pennsylvania Avenue, and observing from the House gallery whenever James gave a speech.[14]

The next year, Polk was reelected to Congress in a two-way race despite a strong challenge. After three two-year terms as Tennessee governor, William Carroll was replaced by Jackson protégé Sam Houston. And Jackson, who had used the Tennessee legislature's resolutions endorsing his presidential aspirations as an excuse to resign his detested Senate seat, had his eyes firmly upon the 1828 campaign and a rematch against John Quincy Adams. Throughout it all, Polk and Jackson maintained a steady correspondence.

Jackson told Polk early on that while he took "pleasure to hear from my friends in Congress, still I know their situation too well, to require any apology for not writing to me." But the truly interesting thing is that at a time when both men were extremely busy—Jackson laying the groundwork for another presidential campaign and Polk still learning the ropes in Congress—the length and conversational tone of their letters to each other underscores a deep friendship and mutual respect. Indeed, some of the lengthiest letters in Polk's early correspondence are with Jackson.

Whatever else they had to write about, their common enmity toward Henry Clay gave them a ready topic. So, too, did the coming presidential election. By the spring of 1828, Polk was exhorting Jackson to "expect an excitement during the summer never before witnessed by the country. The administration will make a last desperate struggle to retain their ill-gotten power. We must be prepared to meet it. Your friends are alive to your interest, and will be upon the alert in every part of the Union."[15]

Even though Jackson was his political mentor, Polk did not shrink from offering Old Hickory his own candid advice as the presidential campaign heated up. Jackson's opponents were lambasting him with everything from derogatory attacks upon his beloved wife, Rachel, to pointed accusations about his supposed involvement in Aaron Burr's infamous conspiracy. Don't take the bait, Polk offered. Take the high ground; don't respond to the fusillade.

As unthinkable as that tactic would later become in politics, this was still the era when presidential candidates tried to appear as if they were being *summoned* to the office rather than lusting after it. "First, I deem the result of the election as things now stand entirely certain," Polk counseled Jackson, "and no publication from you can make it more so." Embarking on some campaign swing or publishing direct communications with less than two months left in the campaign would run counter to the image Jackson had cultivated.

Besides, Polk continued, "all that has been said against you has been said by heated partisans and hirelings of 'the powers that be,' and all the base means that have been employed have not detracted from your fair fame, or injured your popularity. . . ." Jackson should "treat every thing that has or may be said, with silent contempt," Polk concluded, because "any notice from you would only give importance to their slanders."

Across the bottom of the last page of Polk's letter, Old Hickory scrawled, "My friend Colonel Polk's letter to be kept as a token of his real friendship."[16]

Less than two months later, Congressman Polk, with Sarah at his side, was hurrying to Washington. Spending a day in Louisville waiting for a steamboat, he reported to a staunch political friend that even Henry Clay's Kentucky seemed to be in the Jackson column. "The Adams men here are dreadfully distressed," Polk confided, "but give up the contest, and admit that General Jackson [is] elected by an overwhelming majority."[17]

𝒯he "military chieftain" was now president, and those who had formed the not-so-loyal opposition to the Adams presidency—including James K. Polk—were in a position to put forward their own agenda. Some issues of that day, such as a national bank, seem decidedly antiquated; yet all—with the possible exception of the bank—tended to intertwine and underscore unsettling sectional differences.

In today's era of automated teller machines and ubiquitous branch banks, it seems strange that one of the major domestic policy debates of the first half of the nineteenth century was over the nation's banking system. In point of fact, was there to be a national banking system? As Washington's secretary of the treasury, Alexander Hamilton had championed a national bank. Chief Justice John Marshall later found it constitutional, but others weren't so sure.

Some favored individual state banks over a national bank, while others were "hard money men" content to carry gold and silver in specie (coined money) and pay the proverbial cash on the barrel-head. James K. Polk professed to be among the latter, but his disdain for the Bank of the United States may also have been influenced by his many constituents, including his brother-in-law James Walker, who were heavily involved in Tennessee state banking.

But the fact remained that a growing national economy required credit. It was difficult to keep local lending practices in line with assets unless the flow of paper notes was occasionally presented for conversion into specie. Under the leadership of Nicholas Biddle, the Bank of the United States routinely did just that and used such credit calls on state and local banks to ensure stability within the entire banking system. Among the shrillest critics of Biddle and the Bank of the United States was Andrew Jackson, who opposed its appearance as a monopoly controlled by eastern elitists, more than he understood and opposed its underlying economic principles.[18]

Then there was the question of tariffs. Put most simply, tariffs were taxes on goods and raw materials imported into the United States. Tariffs raised revenue but also were imposed to "protect" domestic manufacturers and give them a competitive advantage by making foreign products more expensive. In the industrial North and Northwest, tariffs found strong support. In the agricultural South, high tariffs not only meant higher prices on imported goods but also tended to stifle international demand for agricultural exports. New England frequently faced a quandary because its burgeoning manufacturing base favored high tariffs, but its shipping industry preferred the rewards of free trade.

The other burning issues of the day, slavery and westward expansion, were inexorably intertwined. Thanks to New England abolitionists, slavery was an increasingly debated moral issue, but it had been a thorny political issue since the three-fifths compromise of the Constitutional Convention. Both Jackson and Polk were slaveholders. Jackson was of a southern generation that rarely questioned it. Polk seems to have resisted slavery's injection into discussions of public policy far more than he resisted the institution itself.

Many southern gentlemen of Polk's generation sought to ease the moral ramifications by painting distinctions between slaves they had merely inherited and those that had been actively purchased. Other slaveholders couched their trading as noble efforts to keep slave families together by purchasing a husband or a wife. But just as one cannot be a little bit pregnant, one cannot be a little bit of a slaveholder. While Polk went out of his way to keep his slave ownership and active trading discreet, he continued to buy and sell slaves for his plantations, first in West Tennessee and later in Mississippi even after he was elected president.[19]

How much Polk's embrace of slavery as an economic institution influenced his views on westward expansion is an entirely different matter. A man with no qualms about buying and selling other humans probably did not dwell on how expansionist policies might affect indigenous Native Americans or, for that matter, any nationality occupying coveted territory. But to Polk, as indeed to Jackson, the issue of national expansion was imperative to the nation as a whole and distinctly separate from the advancement of a slave-based economic system.

Americans had always looked westward. Even before independence from Great Britain, they sought lands at the forks of the Ohio and across the Great Lakes. The French and Indian War won English-speaking people half a continent; the American Revolution affirmed their independence upon it; and the War of 1812—thanks in no small measure to Jackson's exploits against both Native Americans and the British—filled in the lands east of the Mississippi. By the 1830s, it was the other half of the continent—west of the Mississippi—that some Americans were hungrily eyeing.

Under international law, the boundaries of the American West were relatively well established. As Monroe's secretary of state, John Quincy Adams had had a strong hand in establishing them. In the northwest, the Treaty of 1818 between the United States and Great Britain fixed the boundary between the Louisiana Territory and Canada at the 49th parallel, from the Lake of the Woods west to the crest of the Rocky Mountains. West of the mountains, it provided for "joint occupation" of the Oregon country, which was also subject to overlapping Russian claims reaching south from Alaska, and Spanish claims extending north from California.

In the southeast, under the Adams-Onís Treaty of 1819, Spain ceded Florida to the United States. Andrew Jackson, after all, had already used a mixture of military bluster and claims of self-defense to occupy half of it, and, ironically, Adams had been alone among Monroe's Cabinet in preferring to seize the opportunity rather than demand Jackson's apology.

In exchange for Florida, Spain sought American assurances as to the western limits of the Louisiana Territory. With some justification, Spain claimed the boundary to be the divide between the Mississippi and Sabine watersheds in the middle of the state of Louisiana. Some people in the United States, with far more enthusiasm than legal precedent, wanted to advance the boundary all the way westward to the Rio Grande and include Spain's northern province of Texas, whose capital had been established at San Antonio as early as 1772.

When Adams and Luis de Onís were done dickering, the agreed-upon boundary ran up the Sabine River (the present-day Texas-Louisiana border) and then stair-stepped westward via the Red River (the present-day Texas-Oklahoma border), the 100th meridian, and the Arkansas River to its source deep in the Rockies. From there (near present-day Leadville, Colorado), it ran north to the 42nd parallel and then straight west to the Pacific. Perhaps the most significant part of this arrangement was that Spain recognized American interests in the Pacific Northwest north of 42° even if for the moment those interests were entangled with Great Britain's.

Had Spain retained control of Mexico, it is unlikely that this new border would have become any more inviolate than Florida's had proven. As it was, Mexico declared its independence from Spain in 1821 and was soon recognized by the United States. When this happened, a number of trading ventures were pioneered between the United States and the northern Mexican provinces, principally their capitals of Santa Fe and San Antonio. These brought an increasing number of Americans into what was Mexican territory. By the 1830s, the floodgates were open.

---

*I*n the U.S. House of Representatives, the distinguished congressman from Middle Tennessee continued to win reelection and go about supporting the Jackson administration's position on all of these issues. Debates over the banking system and the tariff remained at the forefront, and Polk carried the water for Old Hickory on relevant legislation.

Jackson's first term was far from smooth. Trusting his faith in the common man and championing a regular rotation of jobs in the government bureaucracy, Jackson instituted a "spoils system" of political patronage. Public participation in government was the goal, but the president was routinely besieged by hordes of office seekers. It was a system that would vex Jackson's successors as well and not be modified until the 1880s.

Perhaps the darkest chapter of Jackson's presidency was the Indian Removal Act of 1830. It authorized the president to purchase tribal lands in the southeastern states and "remove" their occupants to lands west of the Mississippi. Eventually, this policy led to the Cherokees' Trail of Tears and merely postponed any resolution of Anglo–Native American relations.

There was also turmoil in Old Hickory's Cabinet. When Jackson's close friend and secretary of war, John Eaton, married Peggy O'Neill, the daughter of a Washington boardinghouse owner, the Cabinet wives, particularly Floride Calhoun, the vice president's wife, shunned Peggy from formal society. Given Jackson's strong sense of honor, he hastened to Peggy's defense. It was a petty affair—sometimes, in fact, called "the petticoat affair"—but it did nothing to ease relations between Jackson and John C. Calhoun.

Throughout it all, however, Old Hickory retained a huge reservoir of popular goodwill stemming from his military days. This alone kept him in good stead with the rank and file of America— Jackson's common man—as he made plans to win a second term.

By 1832, Henry Clay was again running for president, nominally as the candidate of the National Republican party but more accurately as the leader of all anti-Jackson factions, soon to call themselves Whigs. Clay and his cohorts proposed to use the rechartering of the Bank of the United States against Jackson, surmising that he would veto the measure and lose popularity in the process.

Old Hickory used his veto, but his message lambasting monopolies and championing the common man only boosted his popularity. Jackson easily won reelection over the man he had called "the Judas of the West" eight years before. "Did you ever know such a complete rout?" Polk exclaimed. "The enemy is literally driven from the field."[20]

Sweet victory that November was tempered, however, by the nullification crisis. When a new tariff bill backed by Jackson lowered rates but not nearly as far as some southerners wanted, South Carolina put into practice John C. Calhoun's theory of a state's right to nullify a federal law it found offensive. South Carolina passed the Ordinance of Nullification, prohibiting the collection of *all* tariff duties in the state after February 1, 1833. That alone was enough to incense Old Hickory, but what really enraged him were the additional provisions to raise an army and appropriate money for weapons. This, Jackson avowed, was treason!

Tempers flared on all sides. Calhoun resigned as Jackson's vice president in December 1832, after South Carolina elected him to the Senate. Then, only ten days before the February 1 deadline, Calhoun, whom Jackson had threatened to hang if nullification actually occurred, joined with Henry Clay to push a compromise tariff through Congress. South Carolina used the compromise tariff to save face and repeal its Ordinance of Nullification, but all advocates of states' rights had seen how determined Jackson was to preserve the union.

That summer, in August 1833, James K. Polk was elected to his fifth term in Congress. He became chairman of the powerful House Ways and Means Committee, but the position to which he truly aspired was the speakership itself. Rumors of incumbent Speaker Andrew Stevenson's departure to be ambassador to Great Britain and expressions of support for Polk circulated widely as Congress prepared to convene in December.

But some—including Polk himself—were suddenly very concerned to have Jackson's blessing in the endeavor. It might not look very modest, the argument ran, "to solicit the Speakership for Tennessee, as well as the Presidency." But they need not have worried about Old Hickory's support.

Felix Grundy assured Polk early on that he had discussed the matter and "received an answer from the highest quarter of the most satisfactory and encouraging character." Polk's brother-in-law James Walker also spoke with Old Hickory and reported to Polk that "the President was not only willing but eager to have Polk chosen Speaker of the House."[21]

By December, Andrew Stevenson was still in Congress and was reelected Speaker on the first ballot without serious opposition. When he finally did resign the following June, there was more than one Tennesseean seeking his vacated post. John Bell, a four-term congressman from Nashville, threw his hat into the ring, too.

Bell had once been a strong Jackson supporter, but his close ties to Nashville's business community led to his support of Whig economic policies in general and Biddle's national bank in particular. Ostensibly still a Democrat, Bell orchestrated a coalition of Whigs and Calhounites who supported nullification—and hence were no friends of Jackson or any of his lieutenants. "If Mr. Polk is other than a subservient tool, he is much changed since last session," declared one Bell supporter. "He has been in fact for the two last sessions, the palace slave, or his part has been much misunderstood."

After ten tempestuous ballots, John Bell managed to be elected Speaker and hand James K. Polk his first electoral defeat. Old Hickory, who in anticipation of victory had dispatched his official four-horse carriage down Pennsylvania Avenue to fetch Polk, was devastated when his coachman returned alone with the news. The president ate a solitary meal instead of the prepared refreshments, and Polk was left to plan his revenge on Bell.[22]

In some respects, Bell made it easy. Old Hickory had long ago anointed Vice President Martin Van Buren as his successor. Bell not only worked now to defeat Polk's reelection to Congress in 1835 but also championed Tennessee's Hugh Lawson White as a candidate for president in 1836 against Van Buren. In no other state in the union did national politics foster such bitter intrastate rivalries, rivalries that would intensify and fester in Tennessee for at least a decade.

Hugh Lawson White had taken Jackson's U.S. Senate seat upon his resignation in 1825 and was a longtime supporter of Jackson. But now, persuaded by Bell that White and not some New York dandy should follow in Jackson's footsteps, White became a political enemy.

Bell and White—Jackson would show them! For Van Buren and the presidency, Old Hickory promoted a May 1835 national nominating convention—eighteen long months before the election—to ensure national unity. For Polk and the speakership, Jackson called in political markers around the country. "The New England states will sustain you," Old Hickory assured his protégé in a letter that he instructed Polk to burn after reading.[23]

On December 7, 1835, having easily been reelected to Congress, James K. Polk was elected Speaker of the U.S. House of Representatives over John Bell. It was a clear indication of the power of the Jackson–Van Buren axis, to which was now added the name of Polk. But while this partnership would carry considerable national clout through the presidential election of 1836, John Bell and Hugh Lawson White were far from finished.

Having learned nothing from the four-way-race of 1824, the Whigs put forward Hugh Lawson White, William Henry Harrison, and Daniel Webster as regional candidates. Democrat Van Buren trounced the combined Whig trio in the electoral college. But White—despite all the efforts Jackson and Polk could muster—carried Tennessee and its fifteen electoral votes by 36,168 for White to 26,129 for Van Buren. Four years before, the state had voted for Jackson twenty to one. The rift in Tennessee politics between Old Hickory's supporters and the anti-Jackson camp only got deeper.

David Crockett, who had long ago broken with Jackson and Polk over the issue of federal lands in western Tennessee and had himself suffered a brief attack of the presidential bug, urged that White was "the only man in the nation able to contend against Little Van." If Van Buren was elected, Crockett vowed, he would "go to the wilds of Texas." Even before Van Buren was, Crockett did.[24]

———

𝒜s a national icon, Andrew Jackson was getting out of the White House in the nick of time. The bank wars that he fought so spiritedly on behalf of the common man were drying up credit and about to plunge the country into the Panic of 1837. Leaving that to his handpicked successor, Old Hickory admitted on the last day of his presidency that he had but two regrets: he "had been unable to shoot Henry Clay or to hang John C. Calhoun."[25]

During Jackson's eight years in the presidency, James K. Polk had progressed from Old Hickory's boy to his right-hand lieutenant and Speaker of the House. But now, particularly amidst the growing crescendo of economic unrest, Polk had to make a decision whether to remain in Congress and carry the water as Van Buren's man or return to Tennessee and continue to follow in his mentor's footsteps.

CHAPTER 3

Tennessee and
Old Tippecanoe

THE PANIC OF 1837 emptied the Democrats' ballot boxes as surely as it emptied their pockets. Old Hickory's bank wars had had the unintended consequence of depreciating paper currency, particularly after the federal government began requiring specie (gold or silver coinage) in payment for federal lands. Sales of the public domain during the early 1830s had fueled a speculative land boom that suddenly went bust as easy credit dried up.

As inflation soared, many banks and other creditors also demanded payments in gold or silver. Banks with loans exceeding their gold or silver reserves—and there were hundreds across the country—were forced to close their doors as depositors frantically tried to exchange paper currency for specie. The bubble burst when banks in New York refused to redeem paper money for gold or silver. This tightening of credit quickly permeated all aspects of the American economy, and before the country recovered, one in ten American workers was unemployed and rioters had stormed a New York City warehouse in search of food.

Amidst this turmoil, Polk's Democrats managed to retain a

razor-thin margin in the House of Representatives after the congressional elections. But results in the individual states were devastating. In Polk's own state of Tennessee—once nothing less than Andrew Jackson's personal Democratic fiefdom—the Whigs ran rampant, winning the governor's chair and ten of the state's thirteen congressional seats. That James K. Polk, running unopposed, was one of the few Democratic survivors was not lost on Jackson and other party stalwarts.

Nor was it lost on Polk that with a breakdown of 108 Democrats, 107 Whigs, and 24 assorted others in the newly elected House, his hold on the speakership was tenuous at best. When President Van Buren called a special session of Congress in September 1837 to deal with the economic crisis, Polk urged his Democratic colleagues to be on hand promptly for the initial vote to organize the House, lest the Whigs prevail. Reelected Speaker by just thirteen votes, Polk foresaw that the next election might well result in his demotion to minority leader. What was he to do?

Even if Van Buren had not been in the way, Polk at forty-one was not yet ready to reach for the brass ring. Indeed, he was well aware that even if he retained the speakership in 1839, no Speaker of the House of Representatives had ever been elected president, although Henry Clay had certainly tried his best. (More than a century and a half later, this is still true.) But what if Polk returned to Tennessee and stemmed the Whig tide by recapturing the governorship? Suddenly, he would be a favorite son of a major western state and quite possibly a vice presidential candidate in 1840.[1]

Longtime Polk ally John Catron—his wife, Matilda, and Sarah Polk were first cousins—was among the first to sound out Old Hickory on the idea. Catron had been chief justice of Tennessee, and with Polk's wholehearted support, Jackson appointed Catron to the U.S. Supreme Court on Jackson's last day in office. Now the justice returned the favor by writing to Jackson early in 1838 that Polk was the ideal western candidate to replace Richard Mentor Johnson as Van Buren's running mate in 1840.

"Never have we had such a speaker to the crowd; nor have we a man of so much energy, or character," Catron told Old Hickory, "nor from Kentucky south is there so acceptable a man individually to the Democratic Party. . . . His station as Speaker has quieted asperity—has drawn to him a weight far above any other man. Our state follows men . . . and to a certainty can only be carried by the means of a local candidate."[2]

But Polk was slow to embrace the governorship part of this plan. It was definitely risky. He was, after all, a man of some power in Washington, which he would have to give up, and he had never run a statewide race in Tennessee. Then, too, it was far better to appear the reluctant candidate, urged into the race by one's supporters, than to rush forward with too much ambition. Even Polk's brother-in-law James Walker, who was doing his best to drum up support in Mississippi and Alabama for a future Polk vice presidential bid, thought that it was smarter for him to run again for Congress.[3]

As Polk kept his options open during the spring of 1838, a number of Tennessee Democrats, including James Walker, once again promoted William Carroll for governor. Elected to three additional two-year terms starting in 1829, Carroll was defeated in 1835 by Newton Cannon, whose chief claim was that he was strongly anti-Jackson. Carroll, on the other hand, had remained friendly with Polk from his first days in the state legislature and, despite some policy differences with Jackson, had long been in the Jackson–Van Buren camp.

How much of a stalking horse William Carroll was for Polk is open to question, but it would have been hard to orchestrate a more dramatic event than occurred on August 30, 1838, in Murfreesboro. In a pleasant grove of trees on the outskirts of town, Polk climbed onto the speaker's stand in front of an enthusiastic crowd of some two thousand, including William Carroll himself, and proceeded to denounce Whig policies during a rousing two-hour speech.

After Polk finished speaking, the hungry crowd devoured "forty fat sheep, forty fine shoats [young pigs], six beeves, three hundred pounds of fine ham, and bread and vegetables without limit," all washed down with "the generous juice of the grape, whiskey, and cognac."

Then a toast was raised endorsing Carroll's candidacy for governor. Carroll immediately rose and expressed profound thanks for the honor, but announced that due to poor health "arising from exposure in the late war," he would not be a candidate.

Never mind that "the late war" had been Carroll's stand with Jackson at New Orleans a quarter of a century before. Another toast was quickly offered in support of James K. Polk's candidacy for governor. Polk promptly rose, tried to feign some measure of surprise, and then conceded that "he had been strongly solicited from various quarters" to be ready to step into the breach. Reluctant candidate though he was, he was now ready to declare himself for governor of Tennessee. The crowd erupted in hearty cheers. Polk was running for the governorship but betting on even higher stakes.[4]

After the adjournment of the twenty-fifth Congress in March 1839, James and Sarah Polk left Washington and returned to Columbia. Partisan politics had gotten so bad that opposition members in the House disputed the customary vote of thanks traditionally rendered the Speaker. Nonetheless, Polk graciously accepted the 94–57 vote in his favor and noted that it was "the highest and most valued testimony I have ever received from this House," because, under the circumstances, it was not a mere formality.

"While you were Speaker," Julius W. Blackwell, a congressman from eastern Tennessee, wrote Polk the following December, "your friends praised, and your enemies abused you, but it is now admitted, on all sides, that James K. Polk was the best presiding officer that we have had for many years, and some say the best we ever had."[5]

But there was never a difference of opinion over Sarah Polk's departure from the capital. By all accounts, Sarah left behind nothing but adoring fans who were charmed by her acknowledged wit, vitality, and political acumen. Among her admirers was Joseph D. Story, a longtime associate justice of the U.S. Supreme Court. Upon the Polks' departure, the judge penned a syrupy poem entitled "To Mrs. Polk, On Her Leaving Washington," which began:

Lady, I heard with saddened heart
The melancholy strain:

So soon from these fair scenes to part,
Ne'er to return again.[6]

Perhaps James and Sarah chuckled a bit over that last line, but for the present they both threw themselves into Polk's first statewide contest. Tennessee had three distinct regions, and Polk was definitely a man of Middle Tennessee. He was not as well known in Knoxville and the commercial centers of East Tennessee or in the poorer farming country of the western part of the state. He set out to change that when he opened his formal campaign in April by publishing a lengthy "Address to the People of Tennessee" in the Nashville *Union,* his political mouthpiece.

Significantly, Polk's campaign epistle dealt almost entirely with national affairs. Tariffs, the banking system, and internal improvements were on the minds of most Tennesseeans, but the incumbent Whig governor, Newton Cannon, readily portrayed himself as much more in touch with Tennessee. After the two candidates squared off in Murfreesboro in their first debate, the Whigs' Nashville *Republican Banner* snidely reported that when it came to state issues, Polk knew "very little more than the man in the moon."

But Polk's superior debating skills quickly took a heavy toll on Cannon, and even when the Whigs brought in Polk's old nemesis from the 1834 speakership battle, John Bell, their strategy backfired. Bell unleashed such a vitriolic diatribe that it left even his partisans embarrassed. "The day was clearly ours and our opponents knew it," Polk wrote home to Sarah. "Bell did more for us than I and all our friends could have done."

Governor Cannon spent most of the remainder of the campaign in Nashville professing "important state business," and Polk was given free rein to crisscross the state. During the next two months, Polk rode across the Cumberland Plateau and then north to Knoxville, traveling thirteen hundred miles, visiting "thirty-seven of the state's sixty-six counties, and making forty-three scheduled and numerous impromptu addresses." It was taxing work for even the hardiest of constitutions, and Polk was quick to acknowledge to Sarah via frequent letters that he was greatly fatigued.

Meanwhile, Sarah assumed the role of de facto campaign man-

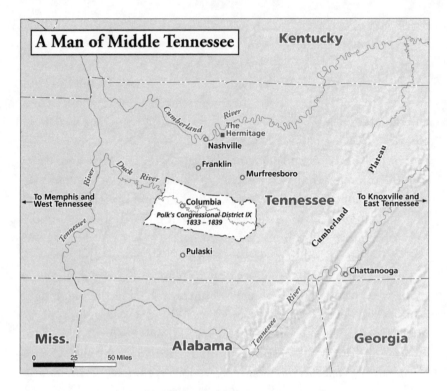

A Man of Middle Tennessee

Kentucky

Cumberland

River

The Hermitage

Nashville

Franklin

Murfreesboro

To Memphis and West Tennessee

Columbia

Polk's Congressional District IX 1833 – 1839

Tennessee

Plateau

To Knoxville and East Tennessee

Cumberland

Tennessee River

Duck River

Pulaski

Chattanooga

Miss.

Alabama

Tennessee River

Georgia

0   25   50 Miles

ager by remaining in Columbia to mail literature, schedule speeches, and generally fuss over the candidate's health. "I am anxious to hear from you," she wrote after Polk spent but one night with her in Columbia and then embarked on a similar swing to West Tennessee, "not political prospects only, but your *health*."[7]

When Cannon ventured into East Tennessee on a last-minute campaign swing, Polk canceled his West Tennessee appearances and rode clear across the state in hot pursuit. He finally overtook the governor in Rogersville, east of Knoxville, just three days before the election.

On August 1, 1839, Tennesseeans showed that whatever else they cared about, they definitely cared about exercising the franchise of voting. An unprecedented 89 percent of the electorate — albeit only white males age twenty-one and over in those days — cast ballots. Democrats regained control of the state legislature and picked up three congressional seats. And, by the narrow margin of 54,102 to 51,396 votes, James K. Polk captured the governor's chair.

Both Whigs and Democrats alike were quick to ascribe the sweeping Democratic victory to Polk's individual efforts and almost herculean campaigning. Andrew Jackson professed it to signal "the return of old democratic Tennessee to the republican fold again," but that was not the case. This was much more the victory of one determined personality and not a wholesale repudiation of Henry Clay's Whig politics.[8]

"I am duly sensible that I have been but the humbler instrument in their hands," the triumphant governor-elect modestly reported of Tennessee voters, but Democrats across the country knew better. Even Senator Franklin Pierce in far-off New Hampshire wrote Polk acknowledging that "this triumphant regeneration of Tennessee is regarded by both parties as of incalculable importance . . . [and] your name is upon the lips of all our friends." That, of course, was exactly what Polk had sought to accomplish.[9]

In state matters, however, Polk found the governor's chair in Nashville to have its limitations. For one thing, the state constitution did not even grant him the power to veto legislative bills. Patronage appointments were limited by the relatively small size of the state government, and many of Polk's pet projects, including banking reforms, fell on deaf ears in the legislature. Nonetheless, the state's Democratic legislators rallied to Polk's greater goals, and no sooner was Polk sworn in as governor in October 1839 than the general assembly passed resolutions promoting Polk as Van Buren's vice presidential running mate in 1840.

Soon afterward, Polk orchestrated the resignations of Tennessee's two Whig senators and watched in satisfaction as the Democratic-controlled legislature elected Alexander Anderson of Knoxville and Polk's first mentor, Felix Grundy, as their Democratic replacements. These gentlemen were dispatched to the United States Senate as if to remind Van Buren that Polk, who had faithfully carried the water for Old Hickory, could be counted on to do the same for him—preferably as vice president.

———

𝒱an Buren's sitting vice president was Richard Mentor Johnson of Kentucky. A former congressman and U.S. senator, Johnson owed his fame to a widely circulated, but largely unsubstantiated, story that he had personally killed the great Shawnee chief Tecumseh at the Battle of the Thames during the War of 1812.

In 1836, "Old Dick" had hardly been anyone's favorite for the number two spot, but Andrew Jackson—swayed more by Johnson's past personal loyalties than future political realities—had insisted. New Yorker Van Buren acquiesced to balance the ticket geographically. Even then, Johnson was not able to poll a majority of the vice presidential vote in the electoral college and per the Constitution was elected by the Senate in a 33–16 vote—the only vice president so chosen.

By the middle of Van Buren's term, the campaign slogan of "rumpsey dumpsey, rumpsey dumpsey, Colonel Johnson killed Tecumseh" had worn decidedly thin. Johnson's rough-hewn western ways paled beside the much more sophisticated Van Buren, and reports of Johnson's having had two mulatto daughters with a black mistress came under heavy scrutiny. Just about everyone in the Democratic party thought that Old Dick should be replaced on the ticket in 1840, and there was no lack of claimants for the honor—James K. Polk among them.

Then, at their nominating convention in Harrisburg, Pennsylvania, in December 1839, the Whigs did the unexpected. Little Van and the Democrats were on the ropes and still smarting from the Panic of 1837. But instead of looking forward, the Whigs were suddenly smitten by "the general bug" and looked backward. They had been quick to lambaste Old Hickory as "a military chieftain," but they had seen his military credentials work at the polls. Now, despite Henry Clay's once more striving to be the heir apparent, the Whigs looked around for their own general.

Major General Winfield Scott, head of the army's eastern command, actively courted the nomination, as did Clay, but when the dust settled, the Whigs selected sixty-six-year-old General William Henry Harrison as their standard bearer. Harrison owed his fame to the Battle of Tippecanoe, a prelude to the War of 1812, where his troops withstood an attack by five hundred Native Americans and then burned their abandoned village.

Still plagued by the stigma of his vaunting ambition of 1824, and having been the Whigs' sacrificial lamb in 1832, Henry Clay simply couldn't believe it. "I am the most unfortunate man in the history of parties," he reportedly bemoaned, "always run by my friends when sure to be defeated, and now betrayed when I, or any one, would be sure of election."[10]

After his nomination, Harrison's managers quickly sought to appease the Clay forces by nominating one of Clay's closest friends, Benjamin Watkins Leigh of Virginia, for vice president. But Leigh declined the nomination, as did at least three others. In desperation, the convention turned to a delegate from Virginia who had reportedly "shed tears" over Clay's defeat and in doing so had "convinced delegates that he was one of those passionate Whigs who idolized Henry Clay." His name was John Tyler, and as a former Democratic governor and senator, he was a strong proponent of states' rights.

Never mind that both Harrison and Tyler were by any measure every bit as patrician as Van Buren. What started as an obscure remark in a Baltimore newspaper—that given a barrel of hard cider, General Harrison would be content to "sit the remainder of his days in a log cabin"—quickly mushroomed into a nineteenth-century media blitz of songs and slogans. The hero of Tippecanoe was made to appear as the very embodiment of the rustic frontier, and as for Tyler, well, the most famous slogan of the campaign said it all. One could get "Tippecanoe and Tyler, too!"[11]

Van Buren's Democrats soon found themselves facing a media-manufactured image of two regular guys sitting in a log cabin sipping hard cider and doing what was right for the common man. It was a page right out of Old Hickory's campaign book, and suddenly rough-cut Richard Mentor Johnson didn't look too bad as vice president.

Because Van Buren's renomination was assured, many Democrats wanted to forgo a formal convention and simply keep their Van Buren–Johnson ticket in place. That didn't sit well with those vice presidential aspirants who coveted Old Dick's spot. But why, the question must be asked, did James K. Polk remain so doggedly among them?

𝒥ust when Polk set his sights on the presidency is unclear. It may have been as early as those days watching Felix Grundy work his magic in a Tennessee courtroom. Most assuredly, by the time he was elected governor in 1839, Polk was determined to win it all — just as his mentor, Old Hickory, had done.

Archibald Yell, a Polk ally running for governor of Arkansas, alluded to Polk's "ultimate wishes" as early as 1839. But Yell advised his friend to have patience — "recollect you are only about 40 years of age, too young for the presidency." Yell maintained that Polk should not unnecessarily antagonize the other vice presidential hopefuls by running prematurely for that office.

But Polk clung tenaciously to the idea of being on the ticket with Van Buren in 1840 and even went so far as to assert that if "nominated for vice president, he would not be a candidate in 1844 for either the first or second office." The pledge hardly squared with his young age or ultimate goal, but it may have been a signal to Thomas Hart Benton of Missouri and John C. Calhoun of South Carolina that he recognized their aspirations for the highest office.

In 1839, another Polk friend, Amos Kirkpatrick, told Polk, "the plan that I had laid off was for you to be our governor six years and then senator six and at the end of Benton's eight years [1848] make you President."[12]

What happened in fact was that Polk's ambition kept him in the vice presidential hunt well past the point of reason. Congressman Cave Johnson, perhaps Polk's best friend, sent the candidate a frank letter concluding that despite "all that can be said or done by your friends, the convention will give it to RMJ [Richard Mentor Johnson]."

Felix Grundy, who had resigned as Van Buren's attorney general to answer Polk's summons to be one of Tennessee's new Democratic senators, was even more emphatic. "To all I have heard upon the subject," Grundy wrote to his former pupil somewhat impatiently, "I have one answer to make — you cannot be nominated by that convention. That I suppose is sufficient."[13]

At their convention in Baltimore in May 1840, the Democrats renominated President Van Buren as expected and then adopted a rather bizarre "no-nomination" strategy for vice president. Both Richard Mentor Johnson and James K. Polk were calculated to be short of the required two-thirds majority if a ballot were to be taken. A host of other candidates circled in the wings. It was essential to avoid a party fracas.

Consequently, the convention deferred the nomination of a vice presidential candidate until *after* the election. Strange as it may seem, the thought was that the electoral college would then select a vice president from the list of state nominees, and should no one achieve a majority, the Senate could well do the honors as it had in 1836.

As it turned out, it didn't matter. Old Tippecanoe won 53 percent of the popular vote and trounced Van Buren. Harrison and his Whigs carried Tennessee by 12,000 votes. Andrew Jackson was horrified and James Polk embarrassed by the outcome. But for Polk, the national results may well have been a blessing in disguise. They may also have proven that Polk was one of the shrewdest political operatives of his day.

Again the question must be asked: why did Polk pursue the vice presidency so aggressively so early in his career and against such odds? The best answer may well be found in the pages of the Nashville *Republican Banner*, the ardently anti-Polk mouthpiece of the Whigs in Tennessee.

Wondering why Polk had received support for his bid from as far away as Massachusetts, Allen A. Hall, the *Banner*'s editor, speculated that Massachusetts Democrats were betting on a perceived future winner. Their support was "probably founded on their abundant faith in General Jackson's power and influence, which they no doubt deem sufficient to make Gov. P. President after Mr. Van Buren."

What Polk had shrewdly tried to do, Hall editorialized, was have the vote of the South concentrated on him for vice president as a means of keeping him before the public and giving him a head start for 1844. It hadn't worked out entirely that way, but Polk had gotten a lot of national exposure and avoided the stigma of being on

Van Buren's losing ticket. Nonetheless, Polk was to have no friends at the Nashville *Republican Banner*. "Henceforth," editor Hall prophesied, "his career will be downwards."[14]

(In 1956, a young Massachusetts senator named John F. Kennedy sought to win the Democratic vice presidential nomination under Adlai Stevenson after Stevenson threw the choice open to the convention. Kennedy narrowly lost the convention fight to Tennessee senator Estes Kefauver but attracted considerable media attention by moving Kefauver's unanimous nomination. The Stevenson-Kefauver ticket went on to suffer a sweeping defeat at the hands of Eisenhower, but Kennedy quickly emerged as a Democratic front-runner in the 1960 presidential race.)

*W*hat James K. Polk had to do next was prove that he could retain the Tennessee governor's chair in the 1841 election and expand his base of Democratic support in the state. In the wake of the national Whig victory, this was far easier said than done.

Taking a cue from the media frenzy of the 1840 presidential campaign, Tennessee Whigs were determined not to be outgunned on the stump again. To oppose Polk, they nominated a thirty-two-year-old state representative from Wilson County just east of Nashville named James Chamberlain Jones. Since he was six-foot-two but weighed only 125 pounds, no one had to ask why his nickname was Lean Jimmy. Scholarly James versus Lean Jimmy. It was going to be quite a race.

Early on, one of Polk's supporters warned him that the Whigs would "attempt to run [Jones] as the log cabin boy taken from the plough," despite the fact that he "never ploughed a day in his life." Jones's very nomination was premised on his mastery of the Whigs' newly hewn techniques of political showmanship that would allow him to make "a perfect 'Tippecanoe run.'"[15]

Certainly, Jones looked the part. His tall, narrow frame was topped by a "solemn, almost grotesque, face that was enough by itself to bring shouts of merriment from his audiences." In fact, he might have been said to look like another young Whig up in Illinois by the name of Abraham Lincoln. And as they did with Lincoln, people seemed to laugh *with* Lean Jimmy Jones, not at him.

Unlike Governor Cannon, who had frequently avoided confronting Polk in person two years before, Lean Jimmy accepted Polk's invitation for joint debates and dogged the governor at almost every campaign appearance. Beginning in Murfreesboro on March 27, 1841, Polk did what he had always done during campaigns and talked about the issues. Jones played to the crowds.

Always deferential to the governor, Lean Jimmy evoked part sympathy and part comic relief. After Polk referred to Jones as "a promising young man" but termed his quest for the governor's chair "all a notion," Jones was quick to refer repeatedly to Polk—not quite forty-six himself—as "my venerable competitor."[16]

That first debate set the tone for the campaign. Throughout, Jones "maintained such an air of courtesy and magnanimity that an opponent could not attack the absurdities in his arguments without arousing sympathy." While Polk expounded on national issues from the tariff to an independent treasury to internal improvements, Jones chipped away at inevitable inconsistencies on those issues over Polk's almost-twenty-year career in politics. "Why, boys, at this rate," Jones told his audience of Polk's long public tenure, "it will never be your turn. You will never get to be constables even!"[17]

The campaign was a grueling schedule of individual town "speakings," but in an age before television, this was the price of election. Routinely, the candidates arrived in the appointed town around noon. In sparsely populated areas, perhaps only three or four hundred might gather in the courthouse, a church, the town square, or a nearby grove. In larger communities, two to three thousand might descend to feast on a barbecue, sample liquid refreshments, and listen to the candidates' stump speeches.

Each candidate would speak for upward of two hours and then be given a thirty-minute rebuttal. It was a full afternoon, and evenings found both candidates exhausted but still pressed to meet with local party leaders and dash off a few letters to supporters. Frequently, they would be off before dawn the next morning, sometimes riding along together to the next appointment. Here was grassroots democracy at its finest![18]

Sarah remained in Nashville and again performed the mundane but essential tasks of a campaign manager while worrying about her husband's health. "When I think of the labor and fatigue you have to undergo," Sarah wrote to James, "I feel *sad* and melancholy, and conclude that *success* is not worth the labor. If Jones does frighten you home by the 15th, you may tell him your wife will be glad to see you."[19]

Polk wasn't frightened by Jones, but he did grow weary of Jones's "aw shucks" manner and portrayal of himself as a common dirt farmer. "Bring on your team fellow-citizens," Polk urged one gathering, telling them that he had been "here cutting the cane a third of a century ago" and had driven "the team afield and followed the plough over the soil of Tennessee many a day."[20]

So, on the campaign went, as the two candidates paced each other from one end of the state to the other. By the sultry days of late July, they were in the bottom lands of West Tennessee and both showing the strain. Jones was "wearied and worn" and "so hoarse that his supporters wondered how much longer he would be able to continue."

Polk was no better off. He became ill at Dyersburg and, fearing his susceptibility to dysentery, was unable to keep the next appointment in Troy. He managed to catch up with Jones two days later at Trenton, but was forced to spend three days in bed before a major engagement at Jackson, after which both candidates followed another week of debates back to Nashville. No wonder Sarah worried herself sick.

Even so, Polk spent only one day at home before hurrying back to East Tennessee to visit counties that he had missed earlier in the spring. Jones gamely followed in pursuit. Campaigning right up until the August 5 election, Polk finally "boarded a stage to race the returns to Nashville."[21]

𝒯he results were so close that the outcome went down to the last votes. Polk had taken a big bite out of the Whigs' 12,000 statewide majority in the presidential race less than a year before, but it had not been enough. Out of 103,900 ballots cast, incumbent governor Polk lost to his hayseed challenger by 3,243 votes. If there was any solace, it was that his statewide efforts had clearly had a coattail effect, and the Democrats gained control of the state senate by one vote and pulled within three votes of the Whigs in the state house of representatives.

If there was an irony to Polk's defeat—save perhaps the whole charade of Jones's campaign—it was that Polk ran weakest in East Tennessee, where he had made a last-minute effort. Here he seems to have incurred the wrath of sympathetic Calhoun-leaning nullifiers who opposed Polk's support of Martin Van Buren. Whether they stayed home or voted for Jones, the result was the same. Polk lost East Tennessee by 3,223 votes.

It was Andrew Jackson who delivered the spin to Van Buren that Polk had succeeded in reducing the Whig majority. "Governor Polk deserves the thanks of the Democracy of the whole union," Old Hickory wrote Van Buren of his protégé. "He fought the battle well and fought it alone."[22]

CHAPTER 4

The Last Defeat

*J*AMES K. POLK'S loss of the Tennessee governorship in August 1841 was a heavy blow, but it did little to blunt his driving ambition or his national image. At worst, the loss was due to voter hangover from the Whigs' smashing 1840 presidential victory, and at best, well, there was still plenty of time to reclaim the governor's chair in 1843 and stand poised on the national scene for the presidential election the following year. Surely, Polk reasoned, by 1843 the voters of Tennessee would have seen Lean Jimmy Jones for the huckster he was and come to their senses.

"We must keep on the armor of our political warfare and continue to do battle in the cause of sound principles," the ex-governor exhorted a gathering of Democratic faithful shortly after Lean Jimmy's inauguration. "The sober second thought of the people is every where producing its effect," Polk declared, and "Tennessee only waits another opportunity to come to the ballot-box."[1]

But there was a more immediate opportunity for Polk. Throughout the gubernatorial campaign, the Whigs had chided the governor that he held little hope of reelection and that his strenuous campaign efforts were merely to elect a Democratic legislature, which in turn would elect him to one of Tennessee's two U.S. Senate seats.

The circumstance of two Senate terms expiring in the same year was unusual. It was occasioned by the normal expiration of Democrat Alexander Anderson's term and the vacancy caused by the death of Felix Grundy. This seat was temporarily filled with the recess appointment of Democrat A.O.P. Nicholson. If Polk had been eager in 1839 to show Van Buren and the national Democrats that he could deliver two Democratic senators to Washington, he was even more determined to do so now in order to maintain his national standing.

No doubt Polk was swayed in his thinking by letters such as he received from Hopkins Turney, a Tennessee congressman from the Cumberland Plateau. Turney wrote Polk from Washington shortly after Polk's gubernatorial defeat, perhaps trying to put a silver lining on it. The governor's loss might prove fortunate, Turney opined, because if Polk could now come to the Senate, "I believe your chance for a nomination for the presidency, would be better than any other man's."

The Democrats had made some gains in the Tennessee legislature, but with a one-vote margin in the state senate against a three-vote Whig majority in the house, the Democrats were still two votes short in the joint session that traditionally elected U.S. senators. But a man of Polk's arm-twisting abilities might just be able to siphon off a couple of Whigs or engineer a compromise whereby he got one seat and a Whig the other.

Behind the scenes, Polk quietly pursued this option. Despite the fact that he had emphatically declared during the campaign that he "wanted nothing that the people of Tennessee cannot bestow" and "would never accept office from any other power," Polk was very tempted by the prospects of a Senate seat.

He secured a couple of Whig converts and then instructed his best friend and faithful lieutenant, Congressman Cave Johnson, to approach a fence-sitting Whig from his district to tip the balance.

Then, before any vote could be taken, a broadside from the Whigs'
Nashville *Republican Banner* seemed to have brought him to his political senses.

"Before the reverberation of the thundertones of the people's
condemnation of his claims to their confidence and support has died
away among the mountains," the *Banner* proclaimed, "we find him
[Polk] obtruding his repudiated pretensions before their representatives and setting up his claim to even a higher station than that
which, but yesterday, they so signally declared he was unfit to occupy."

Should Polk now push his will upon the state legislature, or preserve his image as a man of the people? Perhaps remembering
Henry Clay's vaunting ambition of 1824, Polk chose the latter. "If I
shall ever again rise," he told Tennessee Democrats, "I expect to rise
from the people." He was not and would not be a candidate for the
United States Senate.[2]

But Polk's apparent dismissal of a Senate seat did not end a
stalemate brewing in the Tennessee legislature. Despite numerous
attempts at compromise, the Democrats in the state senate, the Immortal Thirteen as they came to be called, refused to allow the senate's participation in a joint session to elect U.S. senators. While this
maneuver precluded the election of Whig senators, it also precluded
the election of *any* senators and meant that Tennessee was temporarily not represented in the United States Senate.

That this impasse—which some termed a distinct embarrassment—was allowed to continue was perhaps best explained by the
words of Polk biographer Eugene McCormac. "In Tennessee,"
McCormac wryly observed, "politics had precedence over legislation." And in many respects, Tennessee politics mirrored only too
well the increasingly bitter inter- *and* intraparty squabbling on the
national scene.[3]

𝒯he election of 1840 had been a wake-up call to Andrew Jackson's
Democrats. With shouts of "Tippecanoe and Tyler, too," the Whigs
had rallied the common folk to William Henry Harrison and elected
him president, but they couldn't keep him alive. A month after his
inauguration, Old Tippecanoe was dead of pneumonia and assorted

complications at the age of sixty-eight. Suddenly, all eyes were on "Tyler, too."

Log cabin campaign tactics aside, John Tyler was every bit as patrician as William Henry Harrison. In fact, the two were born on nearby family estates in the Virginia tidewater east of Richmond. Tyler's father, another John, succeeded Harrison's father, Benjamin, a signer of the Declaration of Independence, to a Virginia House of Burgesses seat. Now their sons were repeating those roles, and this time a Tyler was succeeding a Harrison to the ultimate office.

John Tyler was born on March 29, 1790, and graduated from William and Mary at seventeen. He studied law with his father and then was elected to Congress in 1817 at twenty-seven. By 1825, he was governor of Virginia, and two years later, a United States senator. Early on, Tyler generally supported Andrew Jackson, but he soon grew disenchanted with Old Hickory's use of presidential power. He disagreed with John Calhoun's theory of nullification but was thoroughly incensed that Jackson should threaten military action against South Carolina. By 1836, despite opposing formation of a national bank, Tyler cast his lot with the Whigs—or so it seemed.

During the 1836 presidential election, Tyler received forty-seven scattered electoral votes for vice president. Although he was not the Whigs' first choice for vice president in 1840, Tyler proved accommodating in accepting the nomination. This time, however, the Harrison-Tyler ticket won, and thirty days after Harrison's inauguration, John Tyler was suddenly president of the United States.[4]

More than a few people were horrified. Given Harrison's age and general health, his chances of surviving four years in the presidency should have been suspect from the start. Only Jackson—age seventy at the end of his second term—had been older in office.

But little thought seemed to have been given by the Whig hierarchy to the possibility, let alone the probability, that Tyler might succeed to the higher office. In part, this may have been because Henry Clay and other prominent Whigs had been determined to exercise a heavy influence over a Whig occupant of the White House no matter who he was.

"The impression which I have," wrote banker Nicholas Biddle to

Daniel Webster even before Harrison was inaugurated, is "that the coming administration will be in fact your administration." Webster became secretary of state but hardly co-president.

But a co-presidency was exactly the role to which Henry Clay seems to have assumed he was entitled. When Clay pushed his choice of Harrison's Cabinet appointments a bit too strenuously, Old Tippecanoe turned to the senator and thundered: "Mr. Clay, you forget that I am the President."[5]

Once Harrison was dead, Clay was even more determined to hold sway over his successor. Amidst the constitutional uncertainties that surrounded this first vice president to ascend to the presidency, Clay "kept referring to Tyler as the 'Vice President' and insisted that 'his administration will be in the nature of a regency.' " And to whom should Tyler turn more in that regency than to the gentleman from Kentucky? After all, hadn't Tyler shed tears when Clay himself was denied the nomination?[6]

"President Tyler is a Whig—a true Whig," the *National Intelligencer* optimistically reported on the day of Harrison's funeral, but John Tyler was to prove an independent cuss and surprise just about everyone.[7]

He quickly set the constitutional standard for later presidential successions by asserting that he was not merely "acting president" but had in fact acquired the full powers of the presidency. And, when Clay forcefully demanded that Tyler wholeheartedly support congressional Whigs in rechartering yet another national bank, Tyler had no qualms about asserting his power in opposition.

With equal the passion of William Henry Harrison, Tyler, too, thundered at Clay: "Go you now, then, Mr. Clay, to your end of the avenue, where stands the Capitol, and there perform your duty to the country as you shall think proper. So help me God, I shall do mine at this end of it as I shall think proper."

That encounter seems to have pushed Henry Clay—who could as the occasion demanded be quite the debonair and persuasive gentleman—into a long-running obnoxious and dictatorial funk. "Clay is unhappy . . . and much more imperious and arrogant with his friends than I ever knew him," New Yorker Silas Wright wrote to Van Buren, "and that you know is saying a great deal."[8]

Indeed, Henry Clay quickly lost sight of any measure of political cooperation. Just as he had ignored the consequences and sought appointment as secretary of state in 1824, Clay was now bound and determined to be not only his party's leader in Congress but also, by virtue of the Whigs' election victory, the country's leader as well. Next, he saw himself as his party's inevitable nominee in 1844 and the duly elected occupant of the White House thereafter.

But throughout the summer of 1841, Clay's demeanor proved far from presidential. At one point, Clay became quite violent and literally screamed at a fellow Whig who had merely noted Tyler's firm stand against a national bank. "Tyler dares not resist," Clay shouted. "I will drive him before me." Even the New York *Herald* reported that Clay "predominates over the Whig Party with despotic sway. Old Hickory himself," the paper noted, "never lorded it over his followers with authority more undisputed, or more supreme."[9]

That supremacy didn't leave much room for John Tyler in the Whig party, and when the president vetoed Clay-sponsored bills for a national bank—not once but twice—Tyler was essentially expelled from his own party. After the second bank veto, Tyler's entire Cabinet resigned in protest save for Secretary of State Daniel Webster, who remained less out of loyalty to Tyler than loyalty to his own presidential ambitions. Tyler, whose own presidential ambitions saw himself being elected in his own right in 1844, looked to the Democrats in the hope of being welcomed as a prodigal son.

But the Democrats had their own problems—and plenty of presidential aspirants of their own—and were hardly willing to embrace a proven maverick. Having alienated his own Whig party, Tyler flirted with becoming a Democrat but then increasingly steered his own course. By the time the wheels began to turn in earnest for the presidential election of 1844, one thing was clear: just about everyone had had too much of Tyler.

In politics, when the going gets tough, it's time for a road trip. With the Democratic party awash with sectional vice presidential candidates—including James K. Polk—and desperately in need of national unity, ex-president Martin Van Buren undertook just that sort of trip in the spring of 1842. After Old Hickory, and perhaps Henry Clay, the man some called "Little Van," "the Little Magician," or "the Red Fox of Kinderhook," was easily the most recognized political figure of the day.

Born in Kinderhook, New York, on December 5, 1782, of Dutch heritage, Van Buren studied law and rose quickly in the political hierarchy of New York State. By 1821, he was a U.S. senator and a key architect of Jackson's emerging Democratic party. As his reward, Van Buren was appointed secretary of state by Jackson in 1828 and was in due course anointed as his presidential successor — much to the chagrin of John C. Calhoun.

Deprived of a second term by the Whig media blitz of 1840, Van Buren nonetheless seemed the logical choice for the Democratic presidential nomination in 1844. So logical, in fact, that John Tyler surreptitiously offered Van Buren a Supreme Court seat to get him out of the way. Silas Wright, one of Van Buren's chief lieutenants, characterized the offer as one to give the whole country "a broader, deeper, heartier laugh than it ever had." The Red Fox politely declined and remained in the catbird seat for the Democratic nomination. Just about everyone was asking "Who else but Van Buren?"[10]

So, Little Van set out on what was billed as a long, leisurely, "nonpolitical" tour that was exactly the opposite. After cajoling the Calhounites in the Carolinas, Van Buren headed west to New Orleans and then arrived in Nashville on April 25, 1842. James K. Polk, ever eager to promote his vice presidential prospects, met the ex-president and accompanied him on the requisite pilgrimage to the Hermitage.

It must have been an intriguing few days for Old Hickory. Here before him were his two favorite political heirs. One desperately wanted to regain the presidency, the other to position himself to attain it four years hence. On their behalf, the old general had freely spent his political capital. Now he was determined to spend what remained of it.

Neither Jackson nor Van Buren left an account of their private conversations. Undoubtedly, Little Van needed no refresher course in Jackson's anti-bank, pro-western-expansion, strong union policies, but he may well have gotten one. Polk seems to have been frustrated by his failure to draw Van Buren into a conversation about his own vice presidential prospects in 1844.

Jackson played the gracious host at a cannon-firing, bell-ringing reception for Van Buren in Nashville on April 28, and Tennessee Democrats generally conceded that Little Van wore better in person than he did in Whig propaganda. James and Sarah Polk fêted Van Buren at a similar reception in Columbia a week later, but despite being a Polk houseguest for two nights, "the Little Magician" coyly avoided any vice presidential discussions. Van Buren was leaving his options open.

What Jackson and Polk thought of Van Buren's next stop can only be imagined. From Tennessee, the would-be president traveled to Lexington, Kentucky, to accept the proffered hospitality of another would-be president. Henry Clay, who had just resigned his Senate seat in contempt for Tyler and in preparation for another White House run, had graciously extended an invitation, and Martin Van Buren, curiously enough, had accepted.

If Clay's correspondence is to be believed, over the course of three days, these two likely opponents in the 1844 presidential race talked little of politics. Not quite the wit that Clay was, Van Buren nonetheless was judged by his host to be "interesting often and some times amusing." Two years later, this seemingly innocent country visit would come back to haunt Clay with incriminations reminiscent of his 1824 "bargain" with John Quincy Adams.[11]

Meanwhile, in Nashville, the Tennessee Whigs were quick to spin Van Buren's recent visit to their advantage. "The bargain is struck, we think," mused the Nashville *Republican Banner*, in apparent reference to the guarantee of a Van Buren–Polk ticket. In part, this report was a Whig ploy to drive a wedge between Polk and Calhoun supporters in East Tennessee who might have been inclined to support a Calhoun-Polk ticket should Calhoun get the top spot.[12]

The truth of the matter was that, despite all appearances and Old Hickory's good graces, there had been no Van Buren–Polk bargain struck. Still, as 1842 progressed, Polk's name was increasingly touted as the perfect vice presidential balance for Van Buren.

*P*olk and his lieutenants did all that they could to fan such talk of the vice presidency, but by the end of 1842, they were faced with a critical strategic decision. In most quarters, Polk was viewed as the logical and strongest candidate to face incumbent Lean Jimmy Jones in the 1843 gubernatorial race. It would be a much-touted re-match.

Without a doubt, the stakes were very high. If Polk won back the governor's chair for the Democrats in Tennessee, the vice presidential nomination was almost assuredly his for the asking. If he lost the governor's race a second time—particularly if the Whigs gained complete control of the Tennessee legislature—Martin Van Buren would look for a running mate more likely to deliver the electoral votes of his home state.

But what if Polk sat out the race? His party standing would still be strong, his record in the House of Representatives intact. He had proven in the past that he could attract statewide votes. Why risk the loss? It is an intriguing question.

Even though Polk remained undeclared into early 1843, there is nothing in his correspondence to suggest that he seriously considered sitting out the contest. He had not avoided an election in almost twenty-five years, and he gave no inclination of doing so now.

A measure of political revenge against Lean Jimmy was part of it, but far more the answer must be that he saw running for governor as his political duty to Tennessee Democrats and as his political ticket to the vice presidency. He was determined to do it. In many respects, this dogged pursuit of what he personally thought to be the correct course, despite the enormous risks involved, is quite indicative of his later presidential actions.

Lean Jimmy, too, knew how high the stakes were. "The contest that is to come off in Tennessee in 1843," wrote the governor eighteen months before the election, "is to be fierce and fearful and who will conquer or be vanquished in the struggle time must determine." Jones professed to wish "an honorable discharge" and to retire from public life, but he, too, was determined to do his political duty for the Whig cause, which now more than ever in Tennessee was the cause of Henry Clay.

Early in February 1843, Jones announced for reelection. Polk immediately declared his own candidacy and reported that he would formally open his campaign in Jackson on April 3. Jones responded that he would not only be with Polk at Jackson but was scheduling six appearances en route. Polk volleyed back with a list of seventy-five additional engagements throughout the entire state that extended until Election Day four months later.

"The labor of canvassing a state like this, of more than six hundred miles in extent, and reaching from the mountains of Virginia and Carolina to the swamps of the Mississippi," wrote Polk to Van Buren in clear hope of imparting to him a little of the sacrifice he was about to make, ". . . is greater than can be estimated by any one who has not performed it." Thus, "the ground was laid for one of the most thorough statewide campaigns ever attempted in the history of American politics."[13]

*P*erhaps the person who felt Polk's sacrifice most keenly was Sarah. Now, eighteen years into their marriage, it seemed certain that they would have no children. Given the tendency for procreation amid the extended Polk clan—James's grandfather, Ezekiel, fathered fourteen children, who in turn "were said to have produced 92 children, who gave him 307 great-grandchildren"—and numerous nephews and nieces on the Childress side, it seems likely that the cause lay with James. The crude surgical procedure in search of his urinary stone as a young man had most likely disrupted far more than was intended.

The result of a childless marriage was that Sarah could and did throw herself into her husband's career far more than the norm of the day. From her early days in Columbia, to her years attending congressional sessions in Washington, to first lady of Tennessee, Sarah was much more than the dutiful political wife. "Present me respectfully to Mrs. P.," wrote a friend to James after one election victory, "and give her my congratulations on her being again a *membress* of Congress-elect."[14]

But now Sarah was quite disturbed by the rigors of the coming campaign. There was a marked departure from her normally upbeat nature that suggests she was among those who wished that her husband would sit out this race.

"I must confess that I feel sad and melancholy at the prospect before me, or I should say before you," Sarah wrote from Columbia after James had barely started down the road for West Tennessee. "The fatigue, exposure and absence for four months cannot present to me a bright prospect. . . . Let me beg and pray that you will take care of yourself and do not become too much excited."[15]

Sarah's pleas were a tall order, given the hectic schedule of five to six hours per day of speech-making, endless rounds of handshaking, and travels by horseback or stage to the next town. At each major stop, James was likely to find a letter from Sarah reporting the latest political intelligence from his hometown friends as well as continuing to express an almost despondent concern for his welfare. "I never wanted to see you more in my life than now," she lamented in early May, shortly before Polk was due home for several days before heading east over the Cumberland Plateau.

Sarah's mood weighed heavily on her husband. "You must cheer up," Polk wrote her on June 9. "It is now but 7 weeks until the election. The worst of the canvass is over." A week later, he tried again to console his wife from Knoxville, clear across the state. "You continue to write despondingly," he noted, "and it distresses me that you are in such low spirits. If I could be with you, you know I would. It is however impossible for the next six weeks, and I hope you will endeavor to recover your former cheerfulness and good spirits."[16]

𝐵y now, the campaign was in full swing. Lean Jimmy Jones was matching Polk speech for speech, handshake for handshake, across the breadth of Tennessee. Polk declared early on that this election "was to be decided by an appeal to reason and not by flags and fiddling," a reference to the log cabin imagery of the Whigs in general and Lean Jimmy's antics in particular.

Indeed, no matter how outlandish the Whig hype became, Polk doggedly spoke about the real issues of the campaign and trusted in the good sense of the voters to separate the wheat from the chaff. The problem was that Lean Jimmy had a proven formula and he was sticking to it.

With jokes and barbs and assorted buffoonery, Jones blasted the Democrats' Immortal Thirteen, who still had not reconciled themselves to the election of U.S. senators, and draped himself in Henry Clay's national Whig banner—figuratively and almost literally.

"There is my banner—and under that flag I will either conquer or die," Lean Jimmy shouted as he pointed to a Whig flag proclaiming CLAY AND A U.S. BANK. Let the chips fall where they may, Jones made no apologies and declared, "I am for Clay first, Clay last, and Clay all the time."[17]

By the time that the circuit reached East Tennessee, Jones was vigorously endorsing Henry Clay for president and John Sergeant of Pennsylvania for vice president. Naturally, Lean Jimmy demanded of Polk that he reveal his preferences, too.

Polk could hardly profess his own vice presidential aspirations, and if he unequivocally announced his support for Van Buren, he ran the risk of further alienating the Calhoun camp—exactly the result desired by Jones. So, Polk's usual reply became that he would support the nominees of the Democratic convention. Then he tried to defuse the question by demanding in return that Jones declare his choices for U.S. senator should the Whigs win the legislature and derail the Immortal Thirteen.

But Jones was not easily distracted and was too astute to open cracks in his own support by speaking only two names from a dozen would-be senatorial candidates. "Sir," he unwaveringly demanded of Polk, "I dare you to name your men, if you do I will hammer them until you won't know them."[18]

And then, as if he needed to be reminded of the stakes, Polk received a letter from Robert Armstrong, who had managed his successful campaign for governor in 1839. "If you succeed as you must and we carry the state," wrote Armstrong, clearly getting ahead of himself, "we must then look to the convention for electing delegates to nominate a candidate for president and vice president. These men must be of the true stripe. There may be a clash between the friends of Van Buren and Calhoun that cannot be settled. Then your prospect as a compromise is best. The friends of Van Buren and Calhoun are Democrats, and could with great propriety agree upon you."[19]

The presidency itself, four years earlier than planned. Now, there was a thought. But first Polk had to dispose of Lean Jimmy, and the entertaining governor was more than countering Polk's well-placed arguments with his down-home appeal and "aw shucks" theatrics. Jones, after all, had little to lose. If he won the state for his party, another two years in the governor's chair were palatable, but if he lost, he had already professed a desire to return to a simpler life.

When the last of their joint appearances concluded at Murfrees-boro, Jones announced that he was striking out for Columbia to de-liver a speech on Polk's home turf on the day before the election. Polk had planned to conclude the campaign in Franklin and then await the results in Nashville. But with Lean Jimmy bearing down on his hometown, Polk cut short his Franklin speech and hurried directly to Columbia, arriving home in time to conclude his twenty-three-hundred-mile campaign with a rebuttal to Lean Jimmy's final act.

*N*ow both men waited. The only thing certain about the outcome was that the tallies would be close. But Polk must have seen the in-evitable coming when early returns from Middle Tennessee showed the Whigs making strong inroads into normally Democratic strong-holds. Bedford and Giles counties, once part of Polk's congressional district, were lost to the Whigs for the first time, and Polk carried his home county of Maury by only 400 votes.

In East Tennessee—thanks in some part to the Calhoun Dem-ocrats—Polk almost broke even, and he even bested Jones in some counties of West Tennessee. But the losses in the central portion of the state were too great to be overcome. By 3,833 votes out of some 110,000 cast, the Whigs' Nashville *Republican Banner* proclaimed the result: "A Whig State, A National Bank State, A Tariff State, A Clay State."

James K. Polk had lost the governor's chair for the second time in two years by almost the same measure of votes. The results showed how closely divided Jackson's common-man Democrats and Clay's big-business Whigs were in Tennessee.

What was more, the Whigs had captured both houses of the Tennessee legislature — doing away with the intransigence of the Immortal Thirteen once and for all. The only bright spot for the Democrats was that they had managed to hold six of the state's eleven congressional seats. (Reapportionment in 1842 had cut the delegation from thirteen to eleven.)[20]

So, what was would-be vice presidential candidate James K. Polk to do now? "It is no time to indulge in a desponding feeling," the defeated candidate wrote bravely to Robert Armstrong. "There must be an immediate and a bold rally of our friends through the [Nashville] *Union*." But for almost two months after the election, Polk's usually bulging correspondence file contained scarcely a letter.[21]

Somehow, Polk found the courage during this hiatus to write Martin Van Buren. With an apparently straight face, he tried to dispel the notion that Tennessee was irrevocably lost to the Whigs in 1844. Despite all the campaign debates about a national bank, tariffs, and presidential candidates, Polk vainly suggested that local, not national issues had occasioned his defeat and that on national issues the Democrats were "now in a clear and decided majority in the state."[22] The implied message was that Polk was still the vice presidential candidate Van Buren needed on his ticket if the Democrats were to capture Tennessee's electoral votes.

Old Hickory also wrote Van Buren urging continued support for Polk, but Van Buren was skeptical. "The politics of Tennessee have been badly managed," the Red Fox confided to Francis P. ("Frank") Blair Sr. of the Washington *Globe* without being so crass as to name names. But that was just the opening some Democrats needed to promote their own vice presidential candidates and take a swipe at Polk. "The Tennessee Dynasty," noted one supporter of Joel R. Poinsett of South Carolina, "were never true to Mr. Van Buren, nor would they be to any man who did not squirt tobacco juice."

Almost five months after the election, Van Buren was still lecturing Polk that "it is as mortifying, as it is incomprehensible" that Tennessee should have been again lost to the Whigs. "You must, and I doubt not will, in good time, seek out the cause and apply the remedy," Van Buren chastised. "It is not to be endured that the Old Chief [Jackson] should go out of the world with his favorite Tennessee in Whig hands."[23]

Meanwhile, in Kentucky, Henry Clay crowed that "the election in Tennessee was by far the most important of the year. . . . Such an event cannot fail to exert a powerful and salutary influence throughout the whole Union."[24] In other words, Henry Clay thought that the brass ring was finally his.

By all accounts, the 1840 prediction of the Nashville *Republican Banner* that "henceforth [Polk's] career will be downwards," had come to pass. After failing to win the vice presidential nomination that year, Polk had suffered not one but two humiliating defeats for governor.

If the best debater and policy guru that the Democrats could muster could not beat a clown prince of Henry Clay and his Whigs in his own home state of Tennessee, who could? For Polk, the answer of "no one" held little solace. After this last defeat, he was finally home with Sarah, but a comeback of any sort appeared all but impossible.

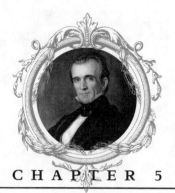

CHAPTER 5

Hands Off Texas

𝒯HE ROCK UPON which the Tyler-Clay relationship broke was the national bank, but John Tyler's lust for Texas made the split inevitable. Independent that he had become—expelled from the Whigs and held at arm's length by the Democrats—President Tyler made no bones about strongly supporting the annexation of Texas. In many respects, it was the latent Jacksonian rising within him. Tyler may have fallen out with Old Hickory over states' rights, but when it came to such core Jacksonian values as national expansion, Tyler looked very much as if he wanted to outdo even the general himself.

By 1844, the Texas question had been simmering for a quarter of a century. As Monroe's secretary of state, John Quincy Adams recognized Spanish sovereignty over Texas as part of the Adams-Onís Treaty of 1819 and agreed to its eastern border at the Sabine River. Spain forbade American settlement in Texas, but no sooner was the treaty ratified than Mexico finally secured its independence from Spain.

The new government in Mexico City reversed policy and ac-

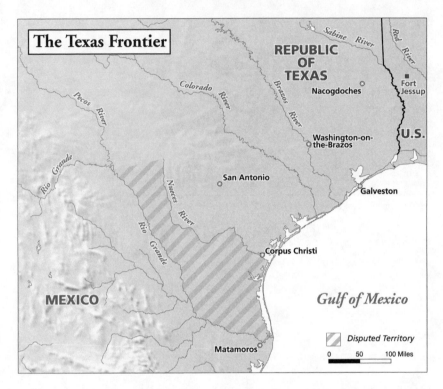

The Texas Frontier

REPUBLIC OF TEXAS

Sabine River

Red River

Colorado River

Brazos River

Pecos River

Nacogdoches

Fort Jessup

Washington-on-the-Brazos

U.S.

Rio Grande

Nueces River

San Antonio

Galveston

Rio Grande

Corpus Christi

MEXICO

Gulf of Mexico

Disputed Territory

0   50   100 Miles

Matamoros

tively encouraged settlement in Texas, not only by Mexicans and Europeans but also by Americans. Mexico's plan was to bolster its northern provinces of Texas and New Mexico with new immigrants and strong commercial ties to the United States. Trade was soon flowing along the Santa Fe Trail and between Louisiana and east Texas settlements, but the numbers of arriving immigrants proved overwhelmingly American. Too late, the Mexican government realized that it had opened the floodgates.

An 1828 fact-finding mission dispatched to Texas by the Mexican government found that far from being gracious and appreciative tenants, the rough-hewn Americans were bent on taking over. "They commence by introducing themselves into the territory which they covet, upon pretence of commercial negotiations, or of the establishment of colonies, with or without the assent of the Government to which it belongs," the commission complained.

The Americans then "proceed, upon the most extraordinary

pretexts, to make themselves masters of the country, as was the case in the Floridas; leaving the question to be decided afterwards as to the legality of the possession, which force alone could take from them." By the time that Mexican president Antonio López de Santa Anna belatedly marched into Texas early in 1836 with an army to exert that "force alone," Americans in Texas exceeded thirty thousand and were determined to stay.[1]

Former Tennessee congressman and onetime Polk ally David Crockett was among some two hundred to fall defending the Alamo in March 1836. "Remember the Alamo" became a rallying cry, but Santa Anna incensed Texans further by ordering the execution of almost twice that number after the surrender of the Texan garrison at Goliad.

Proceeding eastward, Santa Anna thought his mission of chastisement nearly complete, when a ragtag army commanded by another Tennessee expatriate, Sam Houston, routed his napping troops at San Jacinto and made him a prisoner. By the following September, Sam Houston was president of the newly proclaimed Republic of Texas, and most eyes in Texas looked expectantly toward the United States for some sign of welcome into the union.

*C*uriously, while Andrew Jackson long espoused the annexation of Texas, on at least two occasions he uncharacteristically withdrew from the brink of action when more immediate concerns with Spain or the prospect of war with Mexico presented themselves. The first occasion was during the negotiation of the Adams-Onís Treaty. On the verge of coercing Spain out of Florida—in large measure through Jackson's unsanctioned military action—President Monroe requested that John Quincy Adams consult with Jackson before fixing the boundary line between Texas and Louisiana.

Jackson's view before and after their conversations—which included a session with maps at Adams's house—was that Texas was already joined to the United States because it had been part and parcel of the Louisiana Purchase. Where its western boundary lay—be it the Brazos, Colorado, or Nueces River, or even the Rio Grande—might be open to question. But in Jackson's mind, Texas's eastern boundary was not the divide between the Mississippi and Sabine rivers, as the Spanish claimed, or the Sabine River itself, as Adams subsequently negotiated.

If Adams's version in his diary is correct, Jackson nonetheless momentarily agreed with drawing the Sabine River boundary of 1819 to *exclude* Texas. Demanding Texas as well as Florida, Old Hickory reportedly counseled Adams, might jeopardize Spanish willingness to cede Florida, and Old Hickory considered Florida even more essential to the security of the United States than Texas. Later, with Florida secure, with his own animosity toward Adams irrevocable after the election of 1824, and with Texas the next logical step of expansionism, Old Hickory vehemently denied that he had ever uttered such acquiescence.

Jackson's second hesitation regarding grabbing Texas occurred shortly after his inauguration as president in 1829 and continued throughout much of his presidency. Initially determined to undo what he now claimed was Adams's great mistake, Jackson dispatched Anthony Butler to Mexico as his special emissary. Butler was a "free-wheeling, fast-talking land speculator from South Carolina" who "more than matched Jackson's expansionist ardor." Butler also matched Old Hickory's less than tactful style.

After conferring with Jackson and Secretary of State Van Buren, Butler arrived in Mexico City only to be surprised to read in Mexican newspapers that the central purpose of his mission was to purchase Texas for no more than five million dollars. This was true, but with his presidential instructions and monetary limits publicly spelled out, the disclosure left Butler little room to maneuver and angered Mexicans as yet another example of American high-handedness.

Butler, despite no prior diplomatic experience, was soon appointed minister to Mexico. He was not deterred from his original charge, however, and a lengthy charade ensued with Butler making numerous purchase overtures to the Mexican government. He even proposed various schemes to Jackson to bribe certain Mexican officials in order to complete the transaction. Jackson adamantly rebuked Butler for construing that his instructions "authorized you to apply to corruption."

By the time Butler was belatedly recalled, Jackson described him as "a scamp," and Butler's diplomatic bungling fueled continued Mexican resentment toward American intentions in Texas. The Jackson administration's failure to acquire Texas also discouraged Texans who had hoped for a quick annexation and who now faced the prospect of fighting for their independence.[2]

Texans fought, and with Jackson's friend Sam Houston elected president of an independent though tenuous Texas republic soon thereafter, it seemed to many that an annexation mutually satisfactory to the United States and Texas might finally occur. But Jackson continued to drag his feet, not in spite of his long friendship with Houston but because of it.

Save for one career-altering moment, it might well have been Sam Houston that Old Hickory championed for national office rather than James K. Polk. With Jackson's blessing, thirty-five-year-old Houston had been elected governor of Tennessee in 1827 and seemed on his way to reelection in 1829 when he added to his laurels by marrying Eliza Allen, the twenty-year-old daughter of a distinguished pioneer family.

The marriage lasted less than three months. Amid threats and tears, charges and countercharges — one version has Houston falsely accusing his new bride of infidelity with a former suitor — Eliza hurried back to her father's house. In the depths of a deep depression, Houston resigned his governor's chair and slipped away incognito to the west.

Thus, Houston's future was cast with Texas and not Tennessee, but that did not end his friendship with Jackson. In many respects, their bond was strengthened by Houston's being in Texas on the cutting edge of American expansionism, and it was that very bond that Jackson now feared would be made to look like the foundation of a long-prearranged Jackson-Houston plot to wrest Texas from Mexico.

Old Hickory cared little about public opinion when it ran counter to his purposes, but he did care deeply about matters of honor, and he had fought his share of duels to prove it. Maintaining the integrity of the existing treaty between the United States and Mexico and preserving the honor of the United States in the court of international opinion now became Jackson's charge as he directed strict neutrality in relation to the struggle of Texas for independence.

What concerned Old Hickory most was that while Texans had proclaimed their independence and established a government, Mexico still showed every sign of marshaling forces to avenge Santa Anna's defeat and recapture its wayward province. If that happened, then American annexation too quickly, or even diplomatic recognition of the Texas republic by the United States prior to similar recognition by European powers, might well trigger open warfare with Mexico.[3]

Among those urging at least recognition, if not outright annexation, was one of James K. Polk's Tennessee kin who had picked up and "gone to Texas." Thomas J. Hardeman, Polk's uncle by virtue of Hardeman's marrying a daughter of Ezekiel Polk, had been among the emigration from West Tennessee to Texas in 1835. When two of Hardeman's sons were cut off from Texas forces after the fall of the Alamo and suffered hardships, Hardeman sent Polk an account that ended with a plea.

"We are looking to the U.S. to acknowledge our independence and give us all the assistance they can," professed Hardeman before posing a pointed question. "James," his uncle addressed the Speaker of the House, "you have an active tongue, why not use it for Texas as all true Americans should do under existing circumstances?"[4]

But for the moment, Polk deferred to Jackson. Old Hickory's other key concern about Texas was that during the course of his presidency, what should have been an issue of *national* expansion had nonetheless become an issue of *sectional* rivalry entwined with slavery. The question of annexing Texas, Jackson feared, was threatening to divide rather than unify the country. Opponents of annexation claimed that Texas would be divided into four or five pro-slavery states and tip the balance between North and South forever.

No one stood more loudly against Texas annexation and in support of the abolition of slavery than John Quincy Adams. After the Adams-Onís Treaty, Adams had called his negotiations to extend American influence to the Pacific—albeit still jointly occupying

Oregon with Great Britain—"perhaps, the most important day of my life." Seventeen years later on the floor of the House of Representatives, with Polk in the Speaker's chair, Adams sounded much different.

Adams moved to ask the president whether Texas had sought admission to the union and, if so, what response his administration had made. When Adams further asserted, "a very large portion of the people of this country, dearly as they loved the Union, would prefer its total dissolution to the act of the annexation of Texas," it threw the House into such a heated debate that Polk was barely able to restore order. Whatever grand visions John Quincy Adams had once held for continental expansion, they apparently did not apply to Texas.[5]

So, faced with threats of war and disunion, even Andrew Jackson—the very embodiment of what would soon be called Manifest Destiny—failed to annex Texas. He even procrastinated in recognizing it. Only on the afternoon of his last day in office—March 3, 1837—did Old Hickory finally send to the Senate the nomination of Alcée La Branche of Louisiana to be chargé d'affaires to the Republic of Texas. In one of its final acts that session, the Senate concurred in the appointment, and the United States officially recognized Texas as an independent nation.

That evening, as the White House clocks moved toward midnight, William R. Wharton, the Texas minister to the United States and an old friend of Jackson's from Tennessee days, joined Old Hickory in his study and together they raised a toast "to Sam Houston's republic." It would be left to Jackson's successor to bring Texas into the union.[6]

*B*ut Martin Van Buren had other problems. The Red Fox was soon heavily preoccupied with the Panic of 1837. The national banking system—not Texas—was at the forefront of his concerns. Added to this, the American Anti-Slavery Society was flooding Congress with anti-annexation petitions and now warning that Texas would make six or eight states as large as Kentucky.

Consequently, when the Texas minister to Washington delivered a formal request to the U.S. secretary of state on August 4,

1837, that the United States annex Texas, the Van Buren administration responded with a curt no. Annexing Texas before its independence had been acknowledged by Mexico, the State Department professed, would violate the existing treaty between Mexico and the United States.

With no presidential leadership on the issue, southern attempts in Congress to force action also went nowhere. An annexation resolution was tabled in the Senate, and in the House, John Quincy Adams led a three-week filibuster to prevent a vote. Once spurned, Texas withdrew its annexation request.

There the matter of Texas annexation lay until well into John Tyler's presidency. In 1842, Sam Houston, once again president of the Republic of Texas, looked at an empty treasury, mounting debt, and continuing friction with Mexico and resolved that there were but two roads open to his struggling nation: annexation by the United States or closer economic ties with Great Britain. For a while, Houston pursued both options.

Eager for Texas cotton in exchange for its manufacturing exports, and still jockeying for position against the United States in Oregon, Great Britain responded to Houston by extending full diplomatic recognition that same year. Meanwhile, Tyler assured Houston that while he personally favored the annexation of Texas, his hands were tied on the issue as long as Daniel Webster remained his secretary of state.

Webster was the lone remaining Whig from Harrison's original Cabinet. When the balance of Tyler's Cabinet had resigned over the bank vetoes, Webster had stayed at the State Department in order to complete certain diplomatic initiatives—primarily the Webster-Ashburton Treaty fixing the U.S.-Canadian boundary between Lake of the Woods and Lake Superior and between Maine and New Brunswick. By May 1843, however, with the boundary treaty concluded and Tyler's course irrevocably removed from the Whig mainstream, Webster, too, resigned.[7]

For his part, Tyler was only too pleased to replace Webster. Initially, Tyler chose Hugh S. Legaré, his attorney general and an advocate for annexation, to hold both portfolios. But Legaré died suddenly within six weeks of Webster's resignation. Tyler then moved his fellow Virginian and secretary of the navy, Abel P. Upshur, from the Navy Department to the State Department.

Upshur was a gentleman planter from Virginia's Eastern Shore who nonetheless advocated such progressive reforms as the establishment of a naval academy comparable to West Point and the construction of iron steam-driven warships. A Whig in name only, Upshur was ardently pro-slavery and determined to annex Texas.

In September 1843, Upshur informed the Texas ambassador that the Tyler administration would now look favorably on a treaty of annexation. For some reason, most likely because he had been spurned once before and was still receptive to overtures from Great Britain, Sam Houston did not rush to accept the invitation.

But by December, the Texas congress declared its overwhelming support for annexation. It authorized the negotiation of an annexation treaty provided two conditions were met up front: an assurance that the treaty would indeed be ratified by the Senate, and a guarantee that the United States would defend Texas against any attack by Mexico while the negotiations were in progress. Upshur, although he was politically unable to ensure a two-thirds Senate majority and constitutionally unable to commit U.S. armed forces, gave his verbal concurrence to both points.[8]

For his part, Tyler, having been expelled from the Whigs and still wishfully thinking of the Democratic nomination in 1844, was doing everything he could to encourage the annexation of Texas. While he "would deplore any collision with Mexico," Tyler told Congress in December 1843, "[The United States] can not permit that Government to control its policy, whatever it may be, toward Texas, but will treat her . . . as entirely independent of Mexico."[9] To say more would have riled those northern Democrats who were disenchanted with the prospect of another Van Buren nomination and who might have been inclined to support Tyler as an alternative.

So it was that the issue of the annexation of Texas to the United States—with all of its overlying intrigue of sectionalism and abolitionism—was about to come front and center in the presidential election of 1844. Surely, there was no shortage of candidates.

For the Democrats, "Who else but Van Buren?" was still the appropriate question. Proponents of other candidates had somehow convinced Van Buren and his lieutenants to postpone the nominating convention from November 1843 to May 1844, but the Red Fox was not worried. Among the would-be insurgents, John C. Calhoun had momentarily withdrawn from the race, as had Lewis Cass of Michigan and James Buchanan of Pennsylvania.

By January 1844, Van Buren had the endorsements of twelve state conventions, and five others were uncommitted. He made arrangements for historian George Bancroft to write his campaign biography and assured Jackson that the Democratic convention would be "very harmonious."[10]

On the Whig side there was no threat to the heir apparent, Henry Clay. Assured of his nomination and increasingly boastful that "the victory of next year will dim the splendor of that of 1840," Clay embarked from Lexington, Kentucky, on December 14, 1843. He was bound first to New Orleans on what would be a five-month swing across the Deep South and up the Atlantic seaboard—billed as nonpolitical but calculated to put him in Baltimore just in time for the Whigs' national convention early in May.[11]

There was, however, another party in the field. The previous August, the tiny Liberty party, carrying the abolition of slavery as its one and only banner, had nominated James G. Birney, a former slaveholder from Kentucky, as its presidential candidate. The party had done the same thing in 1840, when Birney had managed barely an asterisk by garnering 7,069 votes—three-tenths of 1 percent of the total popular vote.

Few, certainly not Henry Clay, gave Mr. Birney much thought this time around. Meanwhile, John Tyler, who seemed to have decided to win his own term in the White House one way or the other even before Harrison's body was cold, was left to ponder an unlikely last-minute derailment of Van Buren or a third-party bid of his own.

"I think with you," a longtime supporter from East Tennessee wrote to James K. Polk early in January, "that from all indications every where that Mr. Van Buren will be nominated by the Baltimore Convention. But I am far from being sanguine that its nomination will be responded to by the whole Democratic party."

Polk's best friend and congressional confidant, Cave Johnson, was even more dubious. "I fear some secret movements are making here," Johnson reported from Washington, "so as to bring up the Texas question more prominently before the convention meets and to make it operate if practicable against Van in the convention and against Clay in the election." But close as he was to the mark, even Cave Johnson could not have scripted the drama that was about to be played out.[12]

The prologue occurred on February 28, 1844, on the Potomac River just outside of Washington. Secretary of State Upshur was determined to show off the new warship he had championed as secretary of the navy. So, President Tyler, members of his Cabinet, various senators and congressmen, ranking military officers, and a company of their wives and girlfriends all boarded the U.S.S. *Princeton* and were soon cruising down the Potomac toward Mount Vernon.

Designed by the Swedish-born engineer John Ericsson, who would later craft the *Monitor* class of ironclads, the *Princeton* was the prototype of the next generation of superweapons—an iron frigate, powered by steam and driven by a submerged screw propeller instead of a paddle wheel. Its armaments included twenty-four pivoting forty-two-pound carronades and one huge pivoting gun fore and another aft.

Dubbed "the Peacemaker" and "the Oregon," respectively, these guns had fifteen-foot barrels capable of hurling 212-pound projectiles more than three miles. While the Oregon had iron bands around its breech as a precaution against bursting, the Peacemaker—reportedly the largest gun ever forged from wrought iron—did not.

With great celebration, the Peacemaker was fired twice before the dignitaries adjourned belowdecks to a makeshift salon for a sumptuous meal and generous champagne toasts. Afterward, the Peacemaker was readied for another demonstration. President Tyler lingered belowdecks—by one account because he wanted to hear a musical number—but Secretary of State Upshur, Secretary of the Navy Thomas Gilmer, and Senator Thomas Hart Benton were among those who proceeded to the deck for the firing.

This trio gathered on the left side of the giant gun adjacent to its breech, but a navy lieutenant whispered to Benton that he would get a better view if he moved behind the gun and sighted down its long barrel. Benton did so and the gun was fired. With a tremendous explosion, its breech blew apart and wrought iron shrapnel tore away twenty feet of the *Princeton's* hull. Senator Benton was knocked unconscious, but eight others, including the secretaries of state and the navy, lay dead.

President Tyler rushed on deck to survey the carnage. His presence there only moments before might have resulted in another unexpected presidential succession. (Under the Presidential Succession Act of 1792 then in effect, with no vice president in office, the line of succession ran to the president pro tempore of the Senate, Willie P. Mangum.) Three days later, as Washington mourned the victims of the *Princeton* explosion at a White House funeral, the wheels were already in motion to nominate a new secretary of state.[13]

When the name of John C. Calhoun was announced, many questioned his politics but few could question his qualifications: congressman from South Carolina, secretary of war under James Monroe, vice president under John Quincy Adams and during Andrew Jackson's first term, and United States senator from South Carolina. Of course, Calhoun wanted to be president, but that had not stopped him from locking horns with Jackson over states' rights and taking extreme positions on nullification. It also had not stopped him from strenuously advocating the annexation of Texas.

Given the furor that resulted from Calhoun's tenure at the State Department, there has been considerable debate over Tyler's motives in making the appointment. Some historians contend that Tyler confidant Henry Wise, a Virginia congressman, offered the post to Calhoun without Tyler's approval and thus forced the choice upon him.

Others see a Tyler motive to ensconce Calhoun in the Cabinet, make him the pit bull on Texas, and remove him permanently from the presidential campaign. Still others counter that Calhoun's strident *sectional* stand on Texas was hardly what Tyler needed to promote a *national* constituency if he held any hope of winning another term. However the Calhoun nomination came about, one thing is certain. Calhoun accepted and made annexing Texas his top priority.[14]

ℳeanwhile, the negotiations that Upshur had begun before his untimely death had quietly settled the major points of annexation. Texas would enter the union as a territory, not a state—hence no immediate addition of southern senators to rankle the North. Texas would maintain the right to control its own domestic institutions; in other words, to retain slavery. And Texas's public lands would be transferred to the United States in exchange for its assumption of Texas debt at par value. (This point was also calculated to appeal to northern bankers who had been buying Texas bonds for as little as ten cents on the dollar as the republic's financial condition worsened.) Significantly, no territorial boundaries were specified. Once in office, Calhoun made no substantive changes, and on April 12, 1844, the annexation treaty was signed.[15]

On April 22, President Tyler submitted the treaty to the U.S. Senate for ratification. "Should it meet with your approval," Tyler wrote in his transmittal message, "the Government will have succeeded in reclaiming a territory which formerly constituted a portion of its domain." But if Texas were rejected again, Tyler warned, it would undoubtedly "seek the friendship of others." In describing a potential encirclement if Texas were to be added to "Canada, New Brunswick, and Nova Scotia, and islands in the American seas," Tyler left no doubt that by "others" he meant Great Britain.

As for world opinion beyond the British Empire, "Texas voluntarily steps forth," Tyler continued "upon terms of perfect honor and good faith to all nations, to ask to be annexed to the Union." The question, Tyler concluded, "is one purely American." But four days later, when the Senate asked for all diplomatic correspondence related to the treaty, Secretary of State Calhoun revealed a crucial political blunder.[16]

Rather than indisputable fact, British intrigue in Texas had always been more of a bogeyman trotted out for political purposes to urge annexation. However, no less a proponent of Texas annexa-tion—and an ardent Anglophobe—than Andrew Jackson vigor-ously took on this British specter. Old Hickory feared British interests in Oregon were "a peg to declare war against us," said a British alliance with Texas was a prelude to a British army that "marches through Louisiana and Arkansas [and] excites the Ne-groes to insurrection," and claimed a coordinated British invasion from Canada was all but certain.

Even if Great Britain did have modest designs for an expanded empire, Jackson's fears were greatly overstated. Great Britain had in fact abolished slavery throughout its empire in 1833, but the British foreign secretary Lord Aberdeen had also assured the United States as late as December 1843 that "while Britain favored independence for Texas and would be happy to see the Texan gov-ernment abolish slavery," it would not intervene to force abolition or to dominate that government.

Calhoun stumbled onto this dispatch in the State Department after he assumed office and could easily have done no more than file it. Instead, with the Texas treaty about to go to the Senate for ratification, Calhoun wrote the British ambassador, Richard Pak-enham, an impassioned defense of annexation. It was, Calhoun reasoned, the only responsible course for the United States because of British influences—including encouraging the emancipation of slaves—on "the weakest and most vulnerable portion of our fron-tier." Again, Calhoun might have stopped there.

Next, however, Calhoun launched into a lengthy defense of the institution of slavery itself. He essentially argued that freedom was detrimental to the "number, comfort, intelligence, and morals" of slaves and that slavery was "in reality, a political institution, essen-tial to the peace, safety, and prosperity of those States of the Union in which it exists."

Calhoun included a copy of this letter to Pakenham in the treaty documentation requested by the Senate. In violation of the cloak of secrecy that usually attended communications on diplomatic mat-ters, Senator Benjamin Tappan of Ohio "leaked" the Calhoun-Pakenham letter and it appeared in the New York *Evening Post* on April 27, 1844. Suddenly, the annexation of Texas was not only tightly bound to the institution of slavery but was also seen as essential to protecting slavery! Northern abolitionists were outraged.[17]

That Calhoun's startling defense didn't get more immediate attention was due to two other pronouncements that appeared in Washington newspapers the very same day. As front-runners for their parties' presidential nominations, both Martin Van Buren and Henry Clay had been asked with increasing frequency and urgency for their positions on Texas annexation.

By now, Henry Clay was well into his celebratory tour of the South. Never one to doubt that his oratory or written word could sway public opinion, Clay had avoided the question of Texas but had spoken out on a variety of other topics, much to the chagrin of advisers who feared that "his well-known lack of restraint" might produce a misstep. "If St. Paul had been a candidate for the Presidency," one observer counseled to no avail, "I should have advised him to cut the Corinthians and not to let the Hebrews see even his autograph."

But by the time Clay reached Calhoun's South Carolina, the Texas question was staring him head-on. "Are you for or against the annexation of Texas?" demanded the Charleston *Mercury*. "I think I can treat the question in a manner very differently from any treatment which I have yet seen of it," Clay wrote his good friend John Crittenden, with typical ego, and "reconcile all our friends and many others to the views which I entertain."

So, on April 17, 1844, in Raleigh, North Carolina—by one account in the shade of a great white oak on East North Street—Clay sat down and unequivocally put his views on Texas annexation to paper. In what came to be called his "Raleigh letter," Clay contended that "annexation and war with Mexico are identical." The man who had once advocated the conquest of Canada as a young war hawk before the War of 1812 now regarded "all wars as great calamities, to be avoided, if possible."

But even if Mexico should consent to annexation, Clay went on, "I do not think that Texas ought to be received into the Union." Such admission would be "in decided opposition to the wishes of a considerable and respectable portion" of the country and disrupt the balance of power between North and South. Clay was playing to a national audience, and now he was on record as firmly opposed to the annexation of Texas.[18]

And what of Martin Van Buren's position? The Red Fox, too, had been badgered about his position on Texas. Finally, on April 20, 1844, three days after Clay's "Raleigh letter" had been written but not yet published, Van Buren took his stand by answering a letter from Mississippi congressman William H. Hammett. Accusing President Tyler of "acting too secretly and too suddenly," Van Buren said that annexation would be an act of aggression against Mexico that would damage the United States' reputation for reason and justice.

Trying to have it both ways, Van Buren went on to avow that should the majority of the people favor annexation at some point, he would act favorably upon it after he became president. But there could be no mistaking his position, particularly to the ears of southern Democrats. Martin Van Buren was as firmly opposed to the annexation of Texas as was Henry Clay.[19]

Incredibly, Van Buren's position on Texas was published in the Democrats' mouthpiece, the Washington *Globe*, on the very same day—April 27, 1844—that Clay's Raleigh letter appeared in the Whigs' *National Intelligencer*. The apparently coincidental same-day publication even raised speculation that these two political veterans had plotted during Van Buren's 1842 visit with Clay in Kentucky to keep the Texas issue out of the 1844 campaign.

Clay's stand on Texas was predictable, but Van Buren's pronouncement, particularly with its doublespeak designed to appease all parts of the country, set off political tremors. Nowhere did they reverberate more strongly than at Andrew Jackson's Hermitage.

𝒯hroughout the turmoil of the previous year, Old Hickory had kept up a steady correspondence with his old friend Sam Houston. "I have no doubt but that the treaty will be ratified by the Senate," Jackson assured Houston. Now, on May 3, the eastern mail brought to the Hermitage copies of the *National Intelligencer* with Clay's position on Texas. Clay, Old Hickory observed smugly, was "a dead political duck." But then, the other shoe dropped. The next mail brought a copy of the *Globe* with Van Buren's missive.

At first, Jackson refused to believe that the man he had made president could have written such a letter. "I have shed tears of regret," Old Hickory confided to Frank Blair, but he also wrote promptly and directly to Martin Van Buren. Bluntly, Jackson told the Red Fox that given his annexation position, it was now as impossible to elect him president as it would be "to turn the current of the Mississippi." The old general also immediately took charge of one last campaign. In a resolute and determined mood, Old Hickory summoned James K. Polk to the Hermitage.[20]

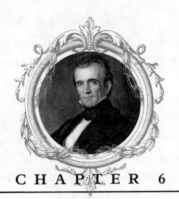

CHAPTER 6

A Summons from Old Hickory

*J*AMES K. POLK, often with Sarah, visited Andrew Jackson at the Hermitage many times over the years. The correspondence between the two men is filled with invitations back and forth and—particularly in later years—Polk's apologies that the press of political business kept him from visiting his mentor more often. But visits to the Hermitage were inevitably political business, and Polk was there on May 3, 1844, when the mood was one of celebration over Clay's anti-annexation stand, and blissful ignorance about Van Buren's recent betrayal.

On Saturday, May 11, back at his home in Columbia, Polk received an urgent summons to return at once to the Hermitage, some fifty miles away. This time, Polk would make no apologies, particularly when the summons came more as a command than an invitation and was delivered in not one but two urgent letters.

One came from Andrew Jackson Donelson, Old Hickory's nephew and trusted political lieutenant. Four years younger than Polk, Donelson had served as Jackson's private secretary while he was president and was well known to Polk. "It is important that you should see us here without delay," Donelson urged. "The division in our ranks threatened by conflicting views about the annexation question must be obviated in time for the convention in Baltimore." As if to underscore the immediacy of the request, Donelson added a postscript in the left margin of the page: "Come directly to General Jackson's."

The other letter to Polk was from Robert Armstrong, a staunch friend of Old Hickory's dating from his campaigns against the Creek during the War of 1812. Armstrong was five years older than Polk, and as the longtime postmaster of Nashville, served Old Hickory as both personal confidant and political informant. "I send you a note from Donelson," Armstrong's letter bearing the salutation "Governor" began. "It is important that you should be here. Start on receipt of this and you may reach the Hermitage *Sunday night*." Armstrong, too, did not want Polk delaying or putting off the trip until after the Sabbath.

Seconding Jackson's view that Van Buren was finished as a viable national candidate, Armstrong sounded a bitter note to Polk: "I cannot see how the South and West who have declared for annexation can support him. [Van Buren] ought to have saved us, as we have here expressed ourselves. He ought to have paid some little respect to the Old Chief's [Jackson's] opinions. He has pierced him badly, and [Jackson] feels it."

But then Armstrong got to the core of the purpose for the summons: "I told you when [you were] here my views. They are not changed. Others think so *now*. Turner is here and believes with me, that [with] you for the Presidency and Woodbury for the Vice, we could redeem ourselves."[1]

The presidency? Nine months earlier, the voters of Tennessee had handed Polk his second defeat for governor. All his enemies and most of his friends had written his political obituary. But Polk didn't stay buried for long. Despite his gubernatorial losses, Polk never gave up his quest for a national nomination, which was what had brought him back to Tennessee in the first place.

Once the stigma of his second gubernatorial defeat wore off just a little, Polk orchestrated a letter-writing campaign—mostly from his close confidants to well-placed Democratic party leaders—promoting his availability for the vice presidential nomination in 1844. His most recent Tennessee loss was either explained away as "local politics" or, more frequently, totally ignored. Polk's fellow Tennessee Democrats obliged him in this effort, and at their state convention in November 1843, the delegates endorsed Polk for the vice presidential nomination.

All this time, it still appeared that Martin Van Buren would be the Democratic presidential nominee. Polk's goal was to appear as strong and as loyal a supporter of Van Buren as possible despite the Red Fox's characterization of Polk's recent gubernatorial loss as "mortifying."

Throughout the early months of 1844, while he remained in Columbia, Polk maintained a lengthy and steady correspondence about this with his most trusted political adviser, Congressman Cave Johnson. Lanky and balding, Johnson was two years older than Polk and had fought with Jackson in the Creek campaign before he was old enough to vote. First elected to Congress in 1829, Johnson had served there continuously except for losing in 1837. Cave Johnson was not only Polk's eyes and ears in the Capitol but also probably Polk's closest personal friend.

Two years before, shortly after Van Buren's celebrated visit to the Hermitage and his failure to broach the vice presidency with Polk, Cave Johnson had written his friend a prescient letter. "I think a serious and powerful effort will be made by some Southern Democrats," Johnson told Polk in May 1842, "to thrust him [Van Buren] aside upon the pretence, that having been beaten, he is not safe for another race . . . and he thrust aside there will be room for another."[2]

Now the "serious and powerful effort" by southern Democrats no longer required a "pretence." They had Texas. Martin Van Buren was openly against annexation. John C. Calhoun, having wrapped his defense of slavery so tightly around the annexation issue, was totally unacceptable to northern Democrats. Thomas Hart Benton was on record in the Washington *Globe* as also opposed to annexation. James Buchanan was supposedly against but was too indecisive to say. Only the recent loser from Tennessee, James K. Polk, still courting a vice presidential slot on a Van Buren ticket, was on record as unequivocally in favor of the annexation of Texas.

Like the queries that had elicited anti-annexation responses from Van Buren and Clay, the query to Polk about Texas had not come from a friendly audience, and the question might have called for circumspection, if not outright obfuscation. Noting all the reasons that "a vast majority" of Ohioans were "irreconcilably opposed" to annexation, a committee headed by Salmon P. Chase of Cincinnati nonetheless asked Polk's opinion. The reply that Polk penned on April 23, 1844—prior to knowing the stand of either Van Buren or Clay, or the uproar that would ensue—must be taken as telling evidence of Polk's strong commitment to principle above politics.

"Having at no time entertained any opinions upon public subjects, which I was unwilling to avow," Polk responded to Chase, "it gives me pleasure to comply with your request. I have no hesitation in declaring that I am in favor of the immediate re-annexation of Texas to the territory and government of the United States." Polk went on to give the Jacksonian defense that Texas "once constituted a part of the territory of the United States" and "should never have been dismembered from it."

Raising the specter of British encirclement, Polk declared it a situation "which no American patriot anxious for the safety and prosperity of his country could permit to occur." Then he went beyond the confines of the question and avowed that not only Texas be annexed, but also the Oregon Territory as well. "Great Britain or any other foreign power," Polk said, must not be allowed "to plant a colony or hold dominion over any portion of the people or territory of either [Texas or Oregon].

"I regret to be compelled to differ so widely from the views expressed by yourselves and the meeting of citizens of Cincinnati whom you represent," Polk told Chase in conclusion. But "differing however with you and with them as I do, it was due to frankness, that I should be thus explicit in the declaration of my opinions."[3]

When Cave Johnson received word of Polk's response to

Chase, the quiet Tennesseean was as ecstatic as his normally calm demeanor would allow. "I have only a moment before the mail leaves to acknowledge the receipt of yours on your return and to express my gratification that you have taken ground for the annexation," Johnson wrote to his friend. "Van's opponents and the friends of Texas are outraged," Johnson continued, "and the chances now seem to be that his nomination will be defeated. Heaven and earth will be moved for that purpose — Calhoun's friends of course in the lead. For this they have been at work, like moles all the winter."[4]

The prospect of a Calhoun presidency concerned Old Hickory almost as much as Van Buren's betrayal regarding Texas. If some southern Democrats made good on their threats to bolt the party and nominate Calhoun as a third-party candidate, Henry Clay might be given a new lease on life. It is unclear whether or not Polk had received Cave Johnson's letter prior to the summons from Old Hickory, but Texas, Calhoun, and his own long-held ambitions were on Polk's mind as he hurried to the Hermitage.

Polk arrived in Nashville on Sunday evening, May 12, and probably met late into the night with Robert Armstrong. Early the next morning, the two of them rode out to the Hermitage. En route, they met Andrew Jackson Donelson coming toward town with a letter from Jackson for publication in the Nashville *Union*, urging the annexation of Texas. Whether or not Polk and Armstrong read Jackson's missive then and there is unclear, but its publication was delayed, and Donelson returned to the Hermitage with Polk and Armstrong to confer with Old Hickory.

By all accounts, Andrew Jackson, ailing and infirm at age seventy-seven, rallied for one last campaign. The old man spoke with all the energy he could muster. His dander was up. "Texas must be ours!" Old Hickory thundered, and he meant it. Oregon, too. Old Hickory was strongly for "extending our laws over Oregon," and Cave Johnson had already reported to Polk "a good deal of feeling in the House upon the Texas and Oregon questions and an effort to unite them."

Van Buren's stand on annexing Texas — without asking, or at the very least even informing his old mentor of it beforehand —

rankled Old Hickory to the core and gave him one last moment on the national stage. Now Jackson was determined not only to fulfill his continental visions but also to resurrect the political career of his most favored lieutenant.

Martin Van Buren might have failed him, but James K. Polk never had. "The scepter shall come back to Tennessee before very long, and your own fair self shall be the queen," Jackson is supposed to have told Sarah Polk at the end of his presidency. Now Old Hickory would do his utmost to see that happen.[5]

The details of what happened at the Hermitage on Monday, May 13, 1844, are best told by three letters Polk sent to Cave Johnson, who was to be a delegate to the Democratic convention in Baltimore. Polk wrote the first on his return to Nashville Monday night. Old Hickory was "not excited but is cool and collected," Polk reported, "and speaks in terms of deep regret at the fatal error which Mr. Van Buren has committed. He says however that it is done and that the convention must select some other as the candidate."

That candidate, Jackson, Armstrong, and others were now determined, had to be Polk, but even to his best friend, Polk was careful about how he announced it. "General Jackson says the candidate for the first office should be an annexation man, and from the Southwest, and he and other friends here urge that my friends should insist upon that point. I tell them and it is true, that I have never aspired so high, and that in all probability the attempt to place me in the first position would be utterly abortive."

Old Hickory was hopeful that Van Buren would come to his senses and withdraw, Polk told Johnson, but "what you can or will do at Baltimore, God only knows." Still being diplomatically coy, Polk reiterated: "I aspire to the second office and should be gratified to receive the nomination—and think it probable that my friends may be able to confer it upon me. I am however in their hands and they can use my name in any way they may think proper."[6]

A day later, still in Nashville, Polk wrote Johnson again. He repeated Jackson's assertion that Van Buren's stand "must be fatal to him"; that "the candidate for the Presidency should be an annexation man and reside in the Southwest"; and that Jackson thought Polk was "the most available man, taking the vice presidential candidate from the North."

Polk told Johnson that he did not expect that to happen. He suggested that the "much greater probability is that a new man for President if one is taken up will hail from the North, and in that event I would stand in a favorable position for the nomination for the second office." But Polk also articulated what had been his strategy to date and what would become his charge to his lieutenants throughout the Democratic convention. It shows how truly shrewd a politician he was.

Polk knew that no matter how things turned out for Van Buren, he needed Van Buren's supporters. If Van Buren somehow still won the presidential nomination, Van Buren's need to balance his ticket geographically and on the issue of Texas would almost assure Polk of the vice presidency. If Van Buren withdrew from the race or was forced aside at the convention by non-Polk delegates, Van Buren's allies could still look favorably on Polk as an ever-loyal follower and thus worthy of their support in the event of a deadlock for the top spot.

Referring to Jackson's soon-to-be-published annexation letter, Polk counseled Johnson: "It will require care on the part of my friends to prevent Mr. Van Buren's friends from becoming excited at the letter and withdrawing from my support in the convention." Apparently still referring to the vice presidential nomination, Polk now told Johnson that he thought he would receive it, "unless Mr. Van Buren's friends should abandon me."

And still again, "should Mr. Van Buren be withdrawn, his friends will probably hold the balance of power and will be able to control the nominations for both offices, and therefore the great importance of conciliating them." Whatever happened, Polk urged, "it will never do to break up in confusion and thus force the party upon Tyler."[7]

𝒫olk left Nashville for Columbia on Wednesday morning, May 15, without mailing his prior night's letter to Johnson. His reason for delaying its mailing was that before starting for Columbia, Polk received a letter from Johnson dated May 8. No doubt Polk was pleased to hear from Johnson that "your letter to Cincinnati [the Chase answer] is in the morning papers and gives great satisfaction to the Texas men." It was another line that seems to have brought him up short.

Johnson reported a conversation he had had with Van Buren's chief strategist and close personal friend, Silas Wright, the same man through whom Tyler had once offered Van Buren a Supreme Court appointment. Some Polk supporters had suggested that Wright might be a more palatable presidential candidate than Van Buren, and Johnson was feeling Wright out on the issue. Wright declined the overture, but then after discounting several other possible candidates, he declared to Johnson that James K. Polk "was the only man he thought the Northern Democrats would support if Van Buren was set aside because [Polk] was known to be firm and true to the cause."[8]

Johnson repeated Wright's comment to Polk without further commentary, but Polk seized upon Wright's sentiment. For Polk to say that he had never desired the presidency or "never for a moment contemplated it," as he'd declared to Johnson the day before, seems highly disingenuous. Such a denial of presidential ambitions runs counter to Polk's long and careful pursuit of the *vice* presidency — rare, after all, have there been those in American politics satisfied with it.

Even if Polk had been elected vice president in 1840 or 1844, he would have been only forty-nine on the latter election and well positioned for 1848, 1852, or even 1856, when he would still have been a few months younger than Old Hickory had been at his election. Polk's assertion that the vice presidency was his ultimate political goal is inconsistent with every political move he made from his first election as clerk of the Tennessee senate.

Arriving in Columbia, Polk scribbled his third letter to Cave Johnson in as many days and then placed it in an envelope marked "Highly Confidential," to be mailed separately from his message of the day before. Noting that the previous day's letter "is strictly true and expresses the opinions which I honestly entertain," Polk admitted that he had "omitted to embrace in it some things which I design for your *own eye alone.*" Quickly, he got to the heart of the matter.

"Mr. Wright's declaration to you," Polk told Johnson, "that I was 'the only man he thought the Northern Democrats would support if Van Buren was set aside . . .' is precisely the opinion which General Jackson expressed to me when I saw him two days ago. The General had previously expressed the same thing to others."

Once more came the perfunctory denial: "You know that I have never aspired to anything beyond the second office, and *that* I have desired." But, Polk continued, if Van Buren were to withdraw—which Polk now suddenly thought probable—"his friends will undoubtedly hold in their hands the controlling power in the selection of *the candidate* and therefore it will be very important to *consolidate* them before the event [Van Buren's withdrawal] occurs."

That might pull Van Buren's supporters into the Polk camp, but what about Van Buren's opponents? "Among the Texas annexation delegates opposed to him," Polk shrewdly observed, "I will undoubtedly have many friends, and if they and the friends of Mr. Van Buren can unite, the whole object will be effected. It will require judgment and delicacy in managing the matter."

If Van Buren did indeed withdraw early in the process, Polk saw "no reason why my friends should not make the effort" to nominate him for the presidency. "If a new man is to be selected, my friends at Nashville think that my position and relations to the party give me more prominence than any other."

There it was. Of course Polk wanted it. And he rushed on to give Johnson the perfect strategy to secure it. "If the feeling of the Northern Democrats continues to be such as Mr. Wright expressed it to be, in the conversation with you—they would probably yield to a compromise—if my friends in the South and Southwest would propose it as a *compromise.* These speculations, arising out of the unexpected events of the last few days, may turn out to be very ridiculous. If so, they are committed to *yourself* alone."

In other words, Johnson was to orchestrate matters so that Polk, the loyal Van Buren lieutenant, would step into the Red Fox's vacant shoes, be acceptable to his followers, and then rally to the banner Polk's natural allies, the Southern Democrats in favor of annexation. Together, they would all save the Democratic party from the likes of Henry Clay and his Whigs.

The day before, Polk confided to his best friend that "someone has to take the lead and no one can do it with more prospect of success than yourself." Now, in his "Highly Confidential" letter of May 15, Polk simply put his faith in Cave Johnson and told him: "You will be on the spot and will be best able to judge."

Referring to the Roman goddess of fortune, Polk concluded, " 'Fortuna is in a frolic,' occasionally and in the midst of the confusion which prevails, there is no telling what may happen."[9]

CHAPTER 7

Baltimore, 1844

*T*HAT THE TWO major political parties should both hold their 1844 nominating conventions in Baltimore was not the coincidence that it might seem. Party nominating conventions were still relatively new creations. The congressional caucus system had been abandoned after 1824, and the nominating convention as a media event had been only recently introduced by the hype and hoopla of the Whigs' 1840 log cabin campaign. With geographic location and favorite-son considerations not yet as important as they would become to future conventions, why not meet in the same city?

Baltimore had numerous advantages. A southern city by demeanor, it was nonetheless centrally located to most of the country and an easy day's travel from Washington. With a population just over one hundred thousand, Baltimore was the queen of the Chesapeake and the second-largest city in the United States, after New York and just before Philadelphia. Commercial competition among these three was fierce, particularly after the opening of the Erie Canal boosted New York's fortunes.

In 1828, after promoters of the Chesapeake and Ohio Canal announced a route along the Potomac River that bypassed Baltimore, city fathers began construction on what was to become America's first railroad, the Baltimore & Ohio. The railroad company built west from Baltimore toward the Ohio River but also began a branch line south toward Washington. Andrew Jackson was the first president to ride the rails, and on August 25, 1835, regular rail service was inaugurated between Baltimore and the nation's capital.

In 1843, Samuel F. B. Morse, a painter by trade, obtained permission from the Baltimore & Ohio to construct an experimental telegraph line along the railroad's right of way between Baltimore and Washington. The first few miles of wire were initially buried alongside the tracks in a lead pipe, but a combination of rocky ground and inadequate insulation quickly led workers to string wire aboveground between wooden poles. By the spring of 1844, Morse had installed one telegraph instrument in the Pratt Street station of the Baltimore & Ohio in Baltimore and another in the Supreme Court chamber in the Capitol in Washington and was about ready to conduct a test.[1]

Henry Clay and the Whigs gathered in Baltimore for their convention on Wednesday, May 1, 1844. This was Clay's third serious bid for the presidency, and the Whigs were certain that this was his time. Clay's role as sacrificial lamb against Old Hickory's 1832 re-election campaign was largely forgotten, but the "corrupt bargain" that made him secretary of state in the aftermath of the four-way race of 1824 was another matter.

At that time, it had been predicted that Clay's actions "will bring home to Clay such a political curse he can't outlive." That seemed to be true. As recently as a speech in Lexington, Kentucky, in June 1842, Clay had been forced to admit, "it would have been wiser and more politic" to decline the proffered Cabinet post.[2]

But it was the faithful, not Clay's critics, who gathered in Baltimore. The city was awash in Clay memorabilia, and the convention quickly took on the aura of a coronation. At 11:00 A.M. the delegates were gaveled to order at the Universalist Church on Calvert Street. Benjamin Watkins Leigh of Virginia, one of Clay's closest friends, immediately took the floor and noted that since the convention was of a single mind, it need not trouble itself with the usual form of nominations. Instead, he proposed that "Henry Clay of Kentucky be nominated unanimously." The hall erupted into great cheers and Leigh's motion was approved by acclamation.

A committee of five was appointed to notify Clay of his nomination and invite him to address the assembly. Expecting the nomination, Clay had planned for this possibility, but his answer was hardly the norm of later conventions. Reverdy Johnson of Maryland, another longtime Clay ally, promptly read a letter from the nominee thanking the delegates for their invitation to speak, but nonetheless declining a personal appearance out of "a sense of delicacy and propriety."

Poor Clay, he should have exhibited such sense when drafting his Raleigh letter. But to the assembled faithful, his determination to absent himself seemed very much in keeping with the proper role of a self-effacing candidate and it endeared him to them all the more.

The vice presidential nomination required only slightly greater effort. Several possible candidates—none household names—immediately declined, and nominations for four other unknowns were eventually made: John Davis of Massachusetts, Millard Fillmore of New York, Theodore Frelinghuysen of New Jersey, and John Sergeant of Pennsylvania.

It took three ballots, but Frelinghuysen, a strong critic of Jackson's Indian-removal policies, was declared the winner, much to the surprise of many, including the presidential nominee. That Clay might have suggested a vice presidential candidate to the convention rather than leave the choice open apparently did not occur to him, or perhaps it smacked too much of just the sort of executive power against which he had long railed.

The only item of business remaining was the adoption of a platform. Only four paragraphs in length, it devoted but one paragraph to the issues. It was vintage Clay except to downplay his prior support for a national bank—even Clay seemed to realize that the majority of the country was against it. The Whig platform favored a tariff to produce revenue, along with what was termed "discriminatory protection" of certain home industries, and it called for the president to serve only one term. Significantly, the Whig platform avoided any mention of Texas.

By the time the convention adjourned, the entire process had taken only a day, and the Whigs were ready to do battle. Even Daniel Webster, who had fallen out with Clay by remaining in Tyler's Cabinet after Tyler's bank vetoes, spoke strongly in Clay's favor at a rally in Baltimore the next day. As for his opponents, "I do not think I ever witnessed such a state of utter disorder, confusion, and decomposition," chortled Henry Clay, "as that which the Democratic party now presents."[3]

*L*ess than a month later, the Democratic party—not quite the empty shell that Henry Clay had characterized it but in disarray nonetheless—descended on Baltimore for its own convention. The presumptive presidential nominee, Martin Van Buren, was not in the city, let alone in the hall, but there was little hope that he would receive a coronation similar to Clay's. Van Buren forces were terribly nervous even though the opposition appeared splintered and unable to agree on little else but the annexation of Texas.

Even the Tennessee delegation was divided—some favoring Van Buren as Polk had directed, others supporting Lewis Cass. Out of thirteen delegates, only five were unquestionably loyal to Polk's directives: Samuel Laughlin of the Nashville *Union*; William G. Childress, a cousin of Sarah's; Andrew Jackson Donelson, the general's eyes and ears; the ever-faithful Cave Johnson; and Gideon J. Pillow, a lawyer and fellow resident of Columbia.

Eleven years Polk's junior, Pillow was an ardent and longtime political ally. Along with Cave Johnson, Pillow was among Polk's few truly close friends. In 1838, Pillow represented Polk's younger brother, William, who had shot and killed a man on the public square in downtown Columbia after a dispute begun several days before in a local tavern. William received a six-week jail sentence and a $750 fine, and Pillow's handling of the matter sealed his bond with Polk.

"You will find Pillow, as soon as he learns how the land lies, a most efficient and energetic man," Polk advised Cave Johnson just prior to Polk's summons from Old Hickory. Afterward, when the stakes suddenly appeared higher than the vice presidency, Polk urged Johnson to work closely with Pillow because "he is one of the shrewdest men you ever knew, and can *execute* whatever is resolved on with as much success as any man who will be at Baltimore."[4]

When the convention opened on Monday, May 27, 1844, many delegates had already been meeting informally in nearby Washington for several days, caucusing among themselves and listening to inevitable arm-twisting. It became apparent early that the first battle of the convention—indeed, the first test of Van Buren's strength—would be over the nominating rules.

The rules question was simply this: would a nomination require only a simple majority, or two-thirds, as had been the case at previous conventions? Van Buren delegates could muster a simple majority, but it was unclear whether Van Buren, or any other candidate, could garner two-thirds. In that event, the convention would be forced either to revise the rules or to dissolve without nominating a candidate.

𝒪ne politician who was content to watch the process from afar was John C. Calhoun, still ostensibly a Democrat. His own chances for the presidency now appeared dim. John Tyler had shrewdly gathered Calhoun into his Cabinet to distract him from the presidential race, but Calhoun had severely damaged his own political prospects with his hideous defense of slavery in the course of the Texas debate.

But that didn't mean that Calhoun's expansionist objectives still might not be achieved. It also didn't mean that Calhoun had given up on the presidency. "I can beat Clay and Van Buren put together on this issue [Texas annexation]," Calhoun reportedly vowed. "They are behind the age. Any man who takes ground against Texas will be set down with those who opposed the last war with Great Britain."[5]

In Calhoun's mind, if the Democratic convention adopted the rule of simple majority, Van Buren would likely be its nominee. If it didn't and no candidate could muster two-thirds of the vote, the result might foster regional candidates. Either way, it would open the door for a pro-annexation third-party bid by Calhoun or by the man temporarily without a party, the incumbent president of the United States.

Significantly, at Calhoun's direction, South Carolina did not send delegates to the Democratic convention. Equally significant, even as Democrats gathered in Baltimore, another convention was under way in the same city to promote John Tyler's candidacy for a term of his own.

The rules debate consumed most of Monday afternoon and spilled over into Tuesday morning, May 28. Monday evening witnessed the ultimate session of horse-trading. Anti–Van Buren forces aggressively promoted the two-thirds rule as the only way to stop the Red Fox. They sought to convince delegation after delegation that if Van Buren could not attain two-thirds, then the nomination should go to each state's favorite.

Michigan was assured that it would be Lewis Cass, not only its own favorite son but also the early champion of the anti–Van Buren pro-Texas faction. New Hampshire was told it would be Levi Woodbury; Kentucky, Richard Mentor Johnson; Pennsylvania, James Buchanan; Tennessee, James K. Polk; and so on.

Following Polk's prior instructions, Cave Johnson and Gideon Pillow were determined to stand by Van Buren and vote against the two-thirds rule, but they could not control the majority of the Tennessee delegation. When Cave Johnson told Van Buren's managers that Tennessee could not be counted on to vote against the two-thirds rule, its passage seemed assured.

Delegates Marcus Morton and George Bancroft of Massachusetts huddled with Johnson to discuss another strategy. Van Buren would likely receive the majority of votes on the first ballot, even if short of two-thirds. Then, with the remaining candidates scattered and unlikely to unite upon one of those already announced, Tennessee would propose the name of Van Buren's chief lieutenant, Silas Wright of New York, as a compromise candidate. Wright would pick Polk as his running mate, just as Van Buren was supposed to have done.

In support of this plan, Johnson and Pillow attempted a compromise within the Tennessee delegation. They and the other Van

Buren–Polk delegates would vote as a unit *for* the two-thirds rule—to Van Buren's detriment—but in return, the anti–Van Buren delegates would vote *for* Van Buren on the first ballot and then support Silas Wright.

Consequently, when the rules vote was finally taken, the two-thirds requirement passed 148 to 116, with Tennessee's thirteen delegates voting unanimously in favor. There was some irony here, but it was even greater in Pennsylvania. Despite the instructions of their state convention to vote for Van Buren, twelve Pennsylvania delegates voted for the two-thirds rule that made Van Buren's nomination all but impossible.[6]

Once the rules conflict was resolved, the delegates reconvened at 3:30 P.M. on Tuesday afternoon after a recess for lunch and proceeded with the presidential balloting. With a total convention of 266 votes, a simple majority required only 134 votes, but under the two-thirds rule just adopted, the nomination required 177 votes. It looked as if it was going to be a long night.

On the first ballot, Pennsylvania—honoring the instructions of its state convention—stuck with Van Buren and gave him its 26 votes. New York remained solidly for Van Buren, as did most of the Northeast. Michigan resolutely stood by Lewis Cass. Richard Mentor Johnson—whether or not he had killed Tecumseh—held his home state of Kentucky, as well as Arkansas and a handful of other votes.

The final tally was Van Buren, 146; Cass, 83; Johnson, 24; and the remaining 13 scattered among James Buchanan, Levi Woodbury, John C. Calhoun, and aging naval hero Charles Stewart.

But how had Tennessee voted? Tennessee, voting as a unit, cast its thirteen votes for Lewis Cass. So much for Polk's strategy of supporting Van Buren until he withdrew. Cave Johnson and Gideon Pillow could not even deliver Tennessee into the Van Buren column on the first ballot.

When Silas Wright heard of the Tennessee vote, he was greatly surprised that the Tennesseeans "would play as bold a hand as they did." He interpreted their vote as a blatant attempt to push Polk's own presidential hopes at the expense of Van Buren, rather than seeing it as the dissension within the Tennessee delegation that it really was. (Apparently, Wright also did not know of the stillborn plan to support him after the first ballot.)

But as a Van Buren man, Wright's real wrath should have been directed against Richard Mentor Johnson. Old Dick belatedly entered the presidential race with visions of personal glory and no reasonable chance of winning. If Van Buren's ex–vice president had loyally supported his former chief and had been able to deliver the 24 votes he received on the first ballot to Van Buren instead, it would have given Van Buren 170 votes—just seven shy of two-thirds.

Whether Tennessee's Cass supporters might then have been convinced to change to Van Buren and assure Polk the vice presidency is debatable, and a what-if of the convention. What is certain in retrospect is that Van Buren never stood closer to the nomination than he did on the first ballot.

Six more ballots were taken on Tuesday evening. Van Buren's support steadily eroded, but neither Cass nor any of the other candidates could break the logjam. Old Dick Johnson proved that at best he was a regional candidate, and peaked with 38 votes on the third ballot. James Buchanan garnered favorite-son support in Pennsylvania after the delegation was released from its preconvention pledge to Van Buren, but he managed no more than 26 votes on the fifth ballot. With only a single delegate voting religiously for John C. Calhoun, it was clear that if the convention was to embrace a southern annexationist, it wouldn't be Calhoun.

By the fifth ballot, Lewis Cass overtook Van Buren 107 to 103, and Van Buren supporters began to realize that the only thing worse than losing was having Cass—who had led the anti–Van Buren charge—winning. By the end of the seventh ballot, the tally stood at Cass, 123; Van Buren, 99; Buchanan, 22; Johnson, 21; and Calhoun, 1. Neither Buchanan nor Johnson alone—or even together—yet had enough votes to play kingmaker, but given the slow desertion in Van Buren ranks, it was only a matter of time.

Van Buren supporters did the only thing they could think of to stop the Cass bandwagon—they frantically called for adjournment. When that failed, they did the next best thing and staged a disruptive fight in the Ohio delegation. The brawl started when one boisterous

Ohio delegate, John K. Miller, stomped to the platform shouting, "I will be heard. I represent ten thousand Democrats. I will be heard."

Miller moved to rescind the two-thirds rule and declare Martin Van Buren the winner based on his first ballot total. This motion was ruled out of order, but any semblance of other order was hopelessly lost on the assembly.

John Hickman of Pennsylvania prevented total anarchy when he bulled his way to the rostrum and wildly announced the nomination of Andrew Jackson, which produced a much-needed round of laughter and applause. Seizing the moment, the chair gaveled the convention adjourned for the evening.[7]

$\mathscr{T}$hroughout these nerve-racking events, Gideon Pillow patiently waited his turn. Now, in the uproar following the seventh inconclusive ballot, as most delegates headed for nearby saloons, Pillow conferred with Massachusetts delegate George Bancroft. Massachusetts and Tennessee—it was not the disconnect that might appear at first glance.

Bancroft was best known as a historian and as author of the multivolume *History of the United States*. He had been corresponding with Polk for some years and was among those New Englanders who had viewed Polk as a staunch Democrat and a ready geographic balance for vice president in 1840. Once the dust settled from the current presidential race, Bancroft again intended to support his southern friend for the vice presidency—with either Van Buren or Silas Wright at the head of the ticket.

But Van Buren was fading, and the Wright-Polk combination suddenly seemed unlikely because of Wright's refusal to become a candidate while his chief was still in the field. Consequently, Bancroft suggested to Pillow that they simply reverse the names. If Polk got the top-line designation, surely Wright would agree to the second.

"I said to them that your name was subject to the will of the convention," Pillow scribbled in his report to Polk late that night. Pillow told of declining to take up Bancroft's offer too quickly and telling Bancroft that "if it was the will of the convention, the name should be brought out by the North." Pillow went on to confide to

Polk: "There is, I think, a strong probability of your name ultimately coming up for President. [But] I do not think it prudent to move in *that* matter now. I want the North to bring you forward as a *compromise* of all interests."[8]

A month later, Bancroft gave Polk his own version of that evening's conversation. "It flashed in my mind," Bancroft recalled, "that it would be alone safe to rally on you." That was exactly the sort of compromise strategy that Polk had already laid out in his preconvention instructions to Cave Johnson. If New England would take the lead, Pillow now quietly assured Bancroft, he was reasonably certain that Tennessee, Alabama, and Mississippi would follow.[9]

But Silas Wright wasn't totally out of the running. Benjamin F. Butler, the chairman of the New York delegation, held Van Buren's letter of withdrawal in favor of Wright. The Red Fox had entrusted it to Butler long before the convention in the event of just such a deadlock.

Somewhere during the long night of May 28, it seems probable that Butler, Bancroft, and Pillow not only crossed paths and compared notes but also surreptitiously joined forces. Whether it would be Wright-Polk or Polk-Wright mattered much less at the moment than did the effort to stop Lewis Cass.

Butler assembled the New York delegation early Wednesday morning before the convention reconvened and attempted to get its unanimous support to override Wright's objections to becoming a candidate. The main problem in that age of delayed communications was that Wright himself was in Washington, some forty miles away. His views on the subject had been entrusted to Judge John Fine of the New York delegation. In the letter Fine held, Wright not only declined to be considered for the presidency but also declared his position on the annexation of Texas to be the same as Van Buren's.

Wright was devoted to Van Buren and had written the letter under much different circumstances, but Judge Fine was adamant that it still contained Wright's current wishes. "If a single vote were cast for Wright," the judge vowed he would read Wright's letter to the convention, including its damning paragraph on Texas.

Butler argued with Fine until five minutes before the convention was called to order, but the judge—true to his client's previously expressed wishes, but not necessarily those the client would have expressed given the exigencies of the moment—refused to allow Wright's name to be placed in nomination. Polk biographer Charles Sellers later suggested that "never before or since has an American politician so clearly thrown away a presidential nomination that was so certainly in his grasp."[10]

Without Wright as a candidate, Butler was left to rally the remaining Van Buren supporters as best he could. To those who showed signs of desertion, "the name of Governor Polk was spoken of as a better one than any person then before the convention." Tennessee's vote on the two-thirds rule aside, Butler thought that Polk "had not been a party to the conspiracies and plots by which we had been destroyed." His nomination "would not only give us a *sound* democrat" but would defeat "with a single blow, the whole posse *by* whom, or *for* whom, the plots [to replace Van Buren] had been set on foot."[11]

$\mathcal{O}$n the eighth ballot, as they had been for the first seven, the states were called in geographic order, beginning in New England. Maine led off and kept eight votes in Van Buren's column and one in that of Cass. But New Hampshire, which had been divided between Van Buren and Buchanan, now cast its six votes for James K. Polk of Tennessee. "You should have heard the cheers," Bancroft boasted to Polk, and they were repeated when Bancroft cast seven of Massachusetts's votes for the Tennesseean.

Two delegates from Pennsylvania and one from Maryland joined the Polk effort, and as the roll call swung south and west to Alabama and Louisiana, those states added their votes to the Polk column. And somehow, intrastate squabbling aside, Gideon Pillow and Cave Johnson were able to twist arms and deliver Tennessee's thirteen votes for Old Hickory's boy. (One of the Tennessee delegates not enamored with Polk was a tailor from East Tennessee named Andrew Johnson, who would later have his own turn at presidential politics.) At the end of the eighth ballot, the vote stood at Cass, 114; Van Buren, 104; Polk, 44; and Buchanan and Calhoun, 2 each.

Chaos reigned. Numerous delegates sought to speak and many did—both recognized and unrecognized. Butler of New York tried to postpone the next ballot to give his delegation time to caucus. When his motion was denied, the New Yorkers left the hall anyway. Meanwhile, Seth Frazer of Pennsylvania took the floor with the Keystone State divided between those still loyal to Van Buren and those pushing Buchanan.

He'd first voted for Van Buren, Frazer explained, because he had been instructed to do so, then for Buchanan as the favorite son of his state. But on the eighth ballot, seeing that neither could be nominated, he had cast his vote for James K. Polk, the man who was "the bosom friend of Old Hickory; the man who fought so bravely and so undauntingly the Whigs of Tennessee."[12]

Then, with New York out of the room and other delegates still clamoring for recognition, the ninth ballot began. Maine switched and gave its eight Van Buren votes to Polk. New Hampshire and Massachusetts—save two Cass holdouts—followed suit. Virginia withdrew to caucus. The roll call attempted to continue, but many delegations passed in order to caucus on the floor.

Long minutes went by until finally it was not the New Yorkers who reappeared but the Virginians. William H. Roane, a grandson of Patrick Henry, announced that all of Virginia's seventeen votes would be cast for James K. Polk. Amid the first burst of truly unified cheering, Roane symbolically extended his hand to Henry Hubbard of New Hampshire, who had cast the first votes for Polk on the eighth ballot.

Meanwhile, the New Yorkers returned to the hall. Unable to agree to vote as a delegation, they had nevertheless agreed that Butler was to withdraw Van Buren's name and that each would then cast his individual vote. Roane of Virginia was still at the platform praising Van Buren despite the Old Dominion's votes for Polk. Butler went to stand beside him and declared that "he always knew that New York and Virginia would ultimately be found fighting side by side."

Butler reluctantly withdrew Van Buren's name and then announced his own vote for Polk, because Polk had met the old Jeffersonian test: capable, honest, and faithful to the Constitution. The rest of the New York delegation, for all of their hesitancy to act as one a few moments before, quickly joined Butler and cast their votes for Polk. That started the stampede.

It was as if the delegates had suddenly seen the way out of the deadlock. One state after another either cast its votes or switched its votes to Polk. Initially, the tally on the ninth ballot was Polk, 233; Cass, 29; but the dissenting votes were quickly "corrected" to make it unanimous. Suddenly, the Democratic nomination for the presidency of the United States belonged to James K. Polk.

Only five days earlier, on May 24, Anne Ellsworth, the daughter of the commissioner of patents, had chosen the phrase "What hath God wrought" for Samuel Morse to use as a test message for his telegraph line between Washington and Baltimore. The test had been a success, and now news of Polk's nomination flashed in an instant across the distance of forty miles to Washington. Many of the Democrats on Capitol Hill knew Polk personally from his service there, and Polk's nomination met with as great a cheer as had filled the hall at Baltimore.[13]

"Your nomination for the presidency unanimously upon the second ballot [of the day] was made today," wrote Cave Johnson to his friend. "Never was there such unanimity and such enthusiasm. . . . Your friends did their duty nobly." And from Gideon Pillow, there came similar sentiments. "Never was there such *enthusiasm* before seen or witnessed in *any body*. I held you up before the convention, as the *'Olive Branch of peace,'* and all parties ran to you as *an ark of safety*." The question for history would be whether James K. Polk was a dark horse who came from nowhere, or one of the most able and determined politicians of his time.[14]

𝒯he excited delegates reassembled after lunch on Wednesday afternoon to take up the vice presidential nomination. Benjamin Butler suggested that in the interest of harmony—as well as a strong Democratic turnout in New York state—the nomination should be offered to Silas Wright. With only eight Georgians voting against it, Wright's nomination was promptly made, and word of it flashed to Wright in Washington by telegraph.

But Wright was still miffed by the convention's rejection of Van

Buren. He had refused the presidential nomination and the probability of a Wright-Polk ticket, and he was definitely not going to accept the vice presidential slot on a Polk-Wright ticket.

Back came Wright's answer by telegraph from Washington that he declined the nomination. Butler was certain that Wright could be convinced otherwise, and a telegraphic exchange ensued. Having said no four times by telegraph, Wright finally dispatched two congressmen in a wagon to drive to Baltimore—the Baltimore & Ohio Railroad did not yet operate at night—and convey his answer in no uncertain terms.

Consequently, the following morning, Thursday, May 30, when the convention reconvened to approve a platform, the vice presidential selection had to be done a second time. For a moment, it appeared that a deadlock similar to the presidential balloting might occur. Southerners and annexationists voted for either Lewis Cass or Levi Woodbury of New Hampshire. The Van Buren faithful tried to rally behind Senator John Fairfield of Maine.

But on the second ballot, Robert J. Walker of Mississippi, a longtime Polk ally, put forward the name of his own uncle by marriage, George M. Dallas of Pennsylvania. Dallas proved acceptable to both factions, and Pennsylvania promised to be a proper geographic balance with Tennessee. By the end of the second ballot, support for the Polk-Dallas ticket was unanimous.[15]

With the delegates heading for the exits, the Democratic platform of 1844 was approved almost as an afterthought. Essentially, it was as true to Jacksonian democracy as the Whigs' platform was to Henry Clay's vision of federal government. The Democrats reiterated their party's historic opposition to: a national bank, an excessive tariff, any federal involvement in internal improvements, federal assumption of state debts, and federal interference with "the domestic institutions of the several states"—not the least of which was slavery.

But there was one startling additional plank that was to go to the core of the coming campaign and redefine the shape of the country during the next four years. The Democrats resolved "that our title to the whole of the Territory of Oregon is clear and unquestionable; that no portion of the same ought to be ceded to England or any other power, and that the reoccupation of Oregon and the re-annexation of Texas, at the earliest practicable period, are great American measures, which this convention recommends to the cordial support of the democracy of the Union."

Interestingly enough, the phrase "at the earliest practicable period" was a far cry from Polk's declaration for "immediate annexation," and if Van Buren had framed his annexation position in those terms, rather than announcing against "immediate annexation," the convention might have turned out much differently.

The other glaring point in that plank was Oregon. Heretofore, joint occupation of that territory with Great Britain had been a concern, but it hardly ranked with the Texas debate. Now, to those who actually read the Democratic platform, the conspicuous position of Oregon seemed to have been included both to take the expansionist furor off Texas and to appease northerners that there was plenty of nonslave territory to be had as well.[16]

Reactions to Polk's nomination ran the gamut from incredulous to ecstatic. "We are more disposed to laugh at it here than to treat it seriously," wrote Whig congressman Joseph H. Peyton of Tennessee. "Are our Democratic friends serious in the nominations which they have made at Baltimore?" asked Henry Clay. "No matter how many candidates or who they bring out, we must beat them with ease if we do one half our duty."

But some Whigs voiced concern. Polk's nomination might be "a ridiculous thing," wrote Senator Alexander Barrow of Louisiana, but Barrow admitted that in his home state "the Whigs will have to fight fiercely to carry Clay even against Jimmy Polk."

Other southerners voiced strong support. John C. Calhoun's political mouthpiece, the Washington *Spectator*, was enthusiastic. "The great mass of the people wanted a man pure in morals, sound in political principles, *and in favor of the immediate annexation of Texas*," the paper boasted, "and such they have in James K. Polk."

On the Democratic side, the Washington *Globe* called Polk "a man of ability, unquestioned probity, untiring industry, and sound judgment." Even Silas Wright quickly jumped on the Polk bandwagon and declared that with "Mr. Van Buren being out of the question, Governor Polk was, by very, very far my choice over all the other candidates."

Then there were those who had known James K. Polk all his career. "I suppose miracles will not cease to exist in the land," mused
old friend Adam Hunstman, who had been in the Tennessee senate
when Polk was elected clerk. "To have supposed it probable that
such a possum looking fellow as you were twenty-five years ago,
would ever have [been] nominated for President of the United
States would then have been deemed quixotism. But so it is, and we
must make the best we can out of you."[17]

In later years, there was no shortage of men who claimed to have
been the leading proponent and chief strategist of Polk's nomination
for the presidency. Cave Johnson, Gideon Pillow, George Bancroft,
Benjamin Butler, and others undoubtedly played important roles,
but the two who had done the most were back in Tennessee, one an
aging icon ensconced at the Hermitage and the other a shrewd lifelong politician waiting expectantly in Columbia.

In the excitement of the moment after Polk's nomination, Andrew Jackson Donelson, who had performed Old Hickory's bidding and summoned Polk to the Hermitage less than three weeks
before, scribbled a hasty letter to his uncle. "The dark sky of yesterday," Donelson exclaimed, "has been succeeded by the brightest
day democracy has witnessed since your election."

Without a doubt, Old Hickory had always done his utmost to
promote his favorite protégé. His recent letters to Jackson partisans around the country promoting Polk for the vice presidency
had been numerous, his arguments determined and persuasive.
Jackson's position and actions after Polk's May 10 summons to the
Hermitage had been no less so.

"I hear it whispered about the streets," wrote a reporter for the
Washington *Madisonian* from Baltimore, "that the nomination of
Mr. Polk was agreed upon at the Hermitage." Agreed upon, no
doubt, but consummated only with every ounce of political clout the
old general could muster.[18]

But what about Polk himself? What about the "dark horse"
label? The usual sense of the definition is a person unexpectedly
chosen, a political unknown, someone who comes from behind or
out of nowhere to win.[19]

If Polk's nomination for the top spot was unexpected by all but Old Hickory's inner circle, there were nonetheless many Democrats who did expect Polk's name to be in contention for the vice presidential slot. After seven terms in Congress—two of them as Speaker of the House—a term as governor of Tennessee, and twenty years of political correspondence with Democrats throughout the country, Polk could hardly be called a political unknown. That Polk did not receive a single vote until the eighth ballot is less evidence of his "out of nowhere" dark horse status than it is evidence of his own strategy to stick with Van Buren (and a likely vice presidential slot) until his lieutenants "on the spot" made his move.

But if some, despite those facts, still call James K. Polk a dark horse, the deeper question might be: how was it that he was even in the race at all? Less than a year before, after his humiliating second defeat for governor, Polk had been judged by many to be politically dead. But he never gave up. With letters, speeches, Jackson's support, and a cadre of loyal friends, Polk went to work almost immediately to extricate himself from political obscurity.

Coy and politically correct though he may have been in denying his ambitions, the evidence is irrefutable that as early as 1839 and most likely much earlier, James K. Polk intended to be president of the United States. He was determined that no obstacle should stand in his way. His nomination in 1844 may have been a little ahead of the plan, but when opportunity presented itself, he and his supporters did not hesitate.

Polk was in fact a known horse, showing his colors, running for the vice presidency and getting ready for his big race four or eight years hence. When the presidential field crowded together and bunched up, he was positioned to run to the outside and win without incurring any great wrath in the process.

In politics, serendipity should never be discounted. But then again, neither should persistence, hard work, and unyielding determination. The stars may have aligned for James K. Polk in 1844, but that he was there at all to take advantage of them was due to his own personal resilience and character.

CHAPTER 8

"Who Is James K. Polk?"

$\mathcal{N}$EWS OF POLK'S nomination for the presidency reached Nashville on Tuesday, June 4, 1844. Only the day before, the eyes and ears of Old Hickory's political machine, postmaster Robert Armstrong, had written to Polk in Columbia that the most recent rumors were from a stage passenger who reported the dissension over the two-thirds rule. "Our friends here are *down* and dispirited," noted Armstrong. "Others in our ranks are *pleased* at the troubles that are upon us."

All of that changed by Tuesday evening. The next morning, Armstrong hastened out to the Hermitage to report to the Old Chief. Jackson was "pleased beyond measure" and expressed no fear of the result. "Daughter," Old Hickory wrote to Sarah Polk shortly thereafter, "I will put you in the White House if it costs me my life!"

As for the "others in our ranks" who had been busy promoting their own agendas, they frantically scrambled to get back in line. No Tennessee Democrat did so more hurriedly than A.O.P. Nicholson. Polk had long nurtured Nicholson's political career, much as Jackson had done his own, even securing for Nicholson an interim appointment as U.S. senator when Felix Grundy died. But Polk was nonetheless always leery of Nicholson's true colors. Nicholson had recently strayed into the anti–Van Buren camp in support of Lewis Cass, and there were whispers that his true ambition was to replace Polk as Tennessee's foremost Democrat.

Now, with Tennessee's foremost Democrat running for the presidency, Nicholson was suddenly among Polk's most visible supporters. When the Nashville *Republican Banner* published the question that was to become the Whigs' campaign mantra and derisively asked, "Who is James K. Polk?" it was Nicholson who responded first. The prodigal son proclaimed to an exuberant Polk rally in Nashville that he would "refer the inquirer to the polls of next November. If he will look *there*," chided Nicholson, "he will *then* learn that James K. Polk is President of the United States."[1]

𝒫olk received confirmation of his nomination in Columbia on Thursday, June 6, via Armstrong's report, a batch of newspapers, and the first flurry of congratulatory letters. Among them was one from his old law partner and best man, Aaron V. Brown. With Cave Johnson and Gideon Pillow, Brown completed the Tennessee triumvirate of Polk's closest friends.

Elected to Congress in his own right in 1839, Brown had won two additional terms and along with Johnson had been Polk's eyes and ears in Washington during Polk's self-imposed Tennessee exile. Brown was a delegate to the Baltimore convention, but the death of his wife less than two weeks before and his own flirtations with the anti–Van Buren movement had kept him out of the majority of Johnson and Pillow's maneuvers.

The day after Polk's nomination, however, Brown jumped right in and gave his friend a rather strident "to do" list. Whether out of familiarity, a touch of arrogance, or both, Brown began by noting, "I write as I have opportunity" and sought to dispel any notion that the convention had adjourned with any hard feelings toward those Tennessee delegates—including himself—who had not stood solidly by Van Buren.

Then, in no uncertain terms, Brown told Polk: "In your acceptance you must some way or other express yourself in favor of the
one-term system. This is important. I might say all important and
you will know exactly *how* it will be highly useful. I need not say
who and how many of our friends expect it."[2]

In later years, a pledge by a candidate that he would seek only
one term as president would become almost unthinkable, but in
1844, there was both political pressure and precedent to make such
a statement. The Whigs had long called for a one-term presidency,
not only because it fit Henry Clay's vision of limited executive government but also because it was a rallying cry against the prospect
of eight years of another Jackson.

William Henry Harrison, the first Whig elected president,
pledged in his inaugural address "that under no circumstances will
I consent to serve a second term." Of course, Harrison lived
scarcely a month thereafter, let alone four more years.

But Polk in the summer of 1844 was not yet forty-nine, and the
Democrats had the two-term tradition of Jackson on their side.
What motivated Brown's adamant advice, and would Polk take it?
"I think you should reflect well before you insert the *one term* suggestion which Brown tells me he put in his letter to you today," delegate Samuel Laughlin counseled Polk. "Perhaps all in all it may be
best, and will be making assurance doubly sure, and put us on an
equality with the Whigs on that question."[3]

Removing the specter of eight years of Old Hickory's protégé in
the White House from Henry Clay's attack arsenal made some
sense. Reading between the lines of Brown's admonition and Laughlin's "assurance doubly sure" comment, however, it seems that they
were far more concerned about the Democrats than the Whigs.

For the moment, Polk suddenly had Democrats of every stripe
rallying to his banner. There were former Van Burenites Levi
Woodbury and Silas Wright in the Northeast; the "intriguer" Lewis
Cass in Michigan, who Van Burenites blamed most for their loss;
James Buchanan in Pennsylvania, finally on record for Texas but
still unsure about Polk's tariff stand; Thomas Hart Benton of Missouri, who despite being against immediate annexation nonetheless
pledged to deliver his state to Polk by a 15,000-vote majority; and

even John C. Calhoun of South Carolina, who seemed, at least temporarily, to be back in the Democratic fold.

All of these men now professed support for Polk, but all—save perhaps Wright—also suffered from various degrees of the presidential bug. Calhoun and Benton were rabidly infected. Cass and Buchanan had inhaled enough that they would both be around again. Eight years was a long time to wait, but if Polk declared his intent to serve only one term, these would-be contenders could enthusiastically unite upon the Polk-Dallas ticket to keep the Whigs at bay and then look ahead to their own individual prospects in 1848.

Polk appears to have had a day or two to ponder Brown and Laughlin's advice before he received the official notification of his nomination via a short letter from a convention committee of which Henry Hubbard of New Hampshire was chairman. The committee trusted that Polk would accept the nomination and not "turn a deaf ear to the call of your country, when in a manner so honorable to yourself, she demands your distinguished service."

Polk gallantly responded on June 12, 1844: "It has been well observed that the office of President of the United States should neither be sought nor declined. I have never sought it, nor shall I feel at liberty to decline it, if conferred upon me by the voluntary suffrages of my fellow citizens." Good words for public consumption, but perhaps more telling was the subsequent characterization that the "distinguished honor" of the nomination was "unexpectedly conferred upon me." In some copies of the acceptance, the word "unexpectedly" was omitted.

Knowing that this letter would get widespread distribution, Polk might have simply stopped then and there, but he chose to remove any and all doubts from Whigs and Democrats alike as to his plans for a second term.

"I deem the present to be a proper occasion to declare," continued Polk, "that if the nomination made by the convention shall be confirmed by the people and result in my election, I shall enter upon the discharge of the high and solemn duties of the office, with the settled purpose of not being a candidate for re-election." At the end of four years, "I am resolved to retire to private life."

Thus, in a single paragraph, Polk neatly neutralized Henry Clay and his Whigs on the issue of a one-term presidency. He also temporarily neutralized his Democratic rivals. In a final sentence, he quickened their pulses when he concluded that a one-term pledge was "the most effective means in my power of enabling the Democratic party to make a free selection of a successor."

And what if Polk's feelings or the situation should change in four years? Was Polk committing the Democratic party to a position not espoused in its platform? Insightful politician that he was, Polk seems to have known exactly what he was doing. Writing to Cave Johnson several weeks later, Polk noted: "I said nothing to commit the party upon the *one-term* principle, but expressed simply my own determination." In other words, having already acknowledged that the presidency "should neither be sought nor declined," who knew what four years might bring?[4]

$\mathcal{P}$olk also moved quickly to neutralize the Whigs on the issue of the protective tariff. Polk's twenty-year public record showed that he had generally supported a revenue tariff, one that imposed the lowest possible duties necessary to fund the operations of the government—there were no income taxes in those days—and one that did not extend protection to individual industries. But now Polk needed northern votes in New England and the mid-Atlantic states, where high duties imposed on imports to protect domestic industries were very popular.

Fortunately for Polk, he had always embraced the fine line of Jacksonian tariff policy, somehow managing to advocate low tariffs without damning any and all degrees of protectionism. That a revenue tariff provided "incidental" protection to certain industries and goods was acceptable even to men such as John C. Calhoun, as long as an ad valorem percentage and not discriminatory rates were applied. So, Polk had left himself some wiggle room that now became critical to his chances of election.

"The Texas question will carry the South," Robert J. Walker of Mississippi counseled the candidate the day the convention adjourned at Baltimore; to win the north, "you must then go as far as your principles will permit for incidental protection. Could you not say that . . . you go first for such a tariff as will supply the wants of the government economically administered; second that within this range you go for such just and fair measure as will embrace all the great interests of the whole union."

This was in keeping with Polk's prior acquiescence with incidental protection, and it was essentially Henry Clay's position, although Clay's federal vision demanded greater "wants" (revenues) than Polk's. "You must recollect," Walker concluded to Polk, "that you now belong not to *one* state, but to the *union*."

So, on June 19, 1844, to checkmate Clay's position on the tariff just as he had done on the one-term issue, Polk issued a public letter to John K. Kane, a fellow Democrat in the critical state of Pennsylvania, and literally quoting from Walker's letter—expressed himself in favor of a tariff for revenue purposes. "In adjusting the details of a revenue tariff," Polk wrote, he had "heretofore sanctioned such moderate discriminating duties as would produce the amount of revenue needed, and at the same time afford reasonable incidental protection to our home industry."

Calhoun wouldn't like the phrase "moderate discriminating duties," but it satisfied Pennsylvania and the rest of the North. "Nothing has surprised me so much," confessed a befuddled Henry Clay, "as the attempt now making in Pennsylvania to represent Mr. Polk as the friend and myself as the foe of protection. If it should succeed I shall distrust the power of the press and of truth."[5]

𝒪ne term, a revenue tariff couched in just enough protectionism to appease the North—that left Texas, and Texas, like it or not, was increasingly entwined with the issue of slavery.

On June 8, 1844, the U.S. Senate voted on the Texas annexation treaty that Secretary of State Upshur—before his untimely death on the *Princeton*—had so confidently assured Sam Houston would pass the Senate by the required two-thirds. Even Old Hickory thought that Clay would "order his majority in the Senate to ratify the Texas treaty to rid him of the question." That, no doubt, would have been the politically astute thing to do, but others doubted that Clay's political judgment could override his ego.

"Clay is exceedingly proud of his opinions, and all his friends are committed," reported one of Polk's longtime friends, Supreme Court Justice John Catron, on the day of the vote. "They too have been treated as boys, and will not be willingly absurd, unless he recants first." Clay did not recant, and twenty-eight of twenty-nine Whig senators were joined by seven Van Buren Democrats to reject the treaty 35–16. Texas remained tenuously independent.

Sam Houston well remembered the Van Buren administration's curt "no" to the formal request by Texas for annexation in 1837. Back in the days of Upshur's assurances, Houston had written Old Hickory that Texas was again "a bride adorned for her espousals. [If] she should be rejected," Houston confessed, "her mortification would be indescribable." Now Texas and Sam Houston had been scorned, not just once but twice.[6]

There was, however, one man in the United States government who wanted the annexation of Texas as much as Andrew Jackson or James Polk. His name was John Tyler, and though deserted on almost every side, he was still president of the United States. And, much to the chagrin of the Polk camp, he was still very much a declared candidate for reelection.

Tyler's rump Baltimore convention of office-holding loyalists had officially put his name in the race, and Tyler electoral slates were being mounted across the country. Incredibly, his designated running mate was "Old Tecumseh" himself, Richard Mentor Johnson, who seemed determined to grab a sliver of national limelight no matter how absurd the circumstances or how devoid of self-esteem.

It wasn't that Tyler held out much chance of winning. But as long as he stayed in the race, Texas remained at the forefront, and the block of stalwart supporters that he did control—by one estimate 150,000—might decide the outcome. Tyler wanted Texas, but he also wanted some measure of assurance that these voters, many of whom had deserted the Democrats to vote for Tippecanoe and Tyler, too, in 1840, would be welcomed back into party ranks and into the favors of Democratic patronage.

Somehow, Tyler had to be convinced to withdraw and throw his support to Polk. But how was this to be accomplished? Polk and his lieutenants quickly came to the conclusion that there was only one man "in the country, who can effect it." That man was dying, but he had already pledged his life to put Sarah Polk in the White House. "I believe General Jackson," Sarah's husband pleaded with Andrew Jackson Donelson, "is the only man in the country whose advice Mr. Tyler would take."[7]

So, trusty Gideon Pillow, who had already engineered one miracle at Baltimore, was dispatched to the Hermitage to see if he could convince Old Hickory to perform not one, not two, but three herculean tasks. What Polk now asked of his mentor, in a hand-delivered letter and in Pillow's private discussions, was threefold:

First, tell Jackson's friend Frank Blair of the Washington *Globe* to "cease his war upon the [Tyler] administration during the pendency of the contest" so that it would not appear that Tyler had been driven from the race.

Second, persuade Tyler that if he wished "to preserve his popularity with the Democratic Party," indeed his place in American history, he should withdraw in favor of the Polk-Dallas ticket.

Third, "write a letter to some friend," which would manage to be published for general circulation, stating that Tyler's supporters, "upon his withdrawal, would be welcomed back with cordiality and joy by the Democratic Party," and be placed on equal footing for patronage appointments.[8]

The first was easy; the second required Old Hickory's consummate skill; and the third, the general firmly and flatly refused to do.

Frank Blair, a long-standing member of Jackson's "kitchen cabinet," was a Washington fixture and had edited the *Globe* since Old Hickory had asked him to move from Kentucky to do so in 1830. Blair had a lukewarm relationship with Polk over the years and had favored Van Buren for the 1844 nomination. His virulent criticism of Tyler seemed in part a result of the antipathy he felt for the Polk-Dallas ticket.

Truth be told, Frank Blair simply wasn't saying much that was nice about anyone. But that changed after Old Hickory pointedly told Blair: "I have but one remark, support the cause of Polk and Dallas, and let Tyler alone. Leave Calhoun to himself, we in the south and west will attend to the Federal Union, it must be preserved." So much for the easy one.

Getting Tyler to withdraw was decidedly harder. Jackson sent letters to two of his own trusted allies who had ready access to Tyler. They could be counted on to disclose "confidentially" to Tyler the contents of what were ostensibly private letters. Knowing Old Hickory's candid views, the theory ran, would nudge Tyler into withdrawing.

The first missive went to William B. Lewis, one of Jackson's oldest friends, who was currently serving Tyler in the Treasury Department. Depending on who was telling the story, Lewis was either sort of an "ambassador at large" to Washington for Tennessee or Jackson's personal Washington mole.

Expressing "his great desire that Mr. Tyler should close his term with credit to himself," Jackson told Lewis that Tyler could not be reelected, might well be charged with handing the election to Clay if he stayed in the race, and would "add great and lasting popularity to himself" by withdrawing. And Texas? "On Mr. Tyler's withdrawal," Old Hickory concluded, "every true American will say, Amen to his patriotism in the case of Texas."

The same message was similarly stated in a letter to John Y. Mason, Tyler's secretary of the navy and, by no small coincidence, a friend of Polk's since their days together at the University of North Carolina. According to Old Hickory, Tyler's withdrawal would afford him "a greater popularity than he ever possessed."[9]

As the Polk campaign awaited Tyler's next move, Old Hickory was lecturing his protégé—who was now not quite, but almost, his political equal—about his third request. In writing to Lewis and Mason, Jackson quite willingly implied—for Tyler's personal benefit—that Tyler's supporters should be "received as brethren" back into the Democratic ranks. Jackson would never, however, consent to the publication of such a pronouncement, nor would he condone Polk's doing so, particularly if it promised those wayward souls political patronage on the same level with loyal Democrats.

"Why my dear friend," Old Hickory lectured Polk the day after Pillow left the Hermitage, "such a letter from me or any other of your conspicuous friends would be seized upon as a bargain and intrigue for the presidency—just as Adams and Clay's bargain." Jackson admonished Polk that "no letter from you or any of your friends must be written or published upon any such subject."

Confessing that he was "scarcely able to wield my pen, or to see what I write," Old Hickory couldn't resist one final imperative. In a postscript, the general added: "Tyler's friends are a mere drop in the bucket, and they nor nothing but such [an] imprudent letter as suggested can prevent your election; therefore all you have to do is be silent."

Here was one last directive from teacher to pupil. The old master was still calling the shots. And the pupil was still deferential. "I concur fully with you in the view which you have taken," Polk wrote his mentor in reply. "I have not written a line to a human being on the subject and will not."[10]

As usual in matters of politics and power, Old Hickory proved correct. It was neither wise nor necessary to appease those whom Frank Blair called Tyler's "handful of prostituted followers" by promising them the retention of their offices. Jackson's letters playing to Tyler's ego and similar laudatory resolutions passed by New York Democrats were enough. Thus convinced that he "held the fate of the Democratic Party in [his] hands" and with pride and ego intact, Tyler wrote to Jackson and then publicly withdrew from the race on August 21.[11]

𝒜eanwhile, the main duel between Polk and Henry Clay promised to be increasingly bruising and bitter. Trying to build on their 1840 success with sloganism, the Whigs seized on the demeaning query of the Nashville *Republican Banner* and incessantly chanted, "Who is James K. Polk?"

In answer, one Clay partisan observed that the Democratic nominee, "having been twice rejected for the office of governor of his own state, [had] no hold upon the confidence or affections of his countrymen at home, and no talent to command respect for us abroad."

But in at least one instance, the Whig attacks backfired. "Who is the opponent of Mr. Clay?" asked a longtime Polk foe, S. S. Prentiss of Mississippi. Why, Polk was nothing more than "a blighted burr that has fallen from the mane of the warhorse of the Hermitage." Blighted burr, was he? In a grandiose speech in New York, the brother of writer Herman Melville expanded on the theme and declared that Polk's seed had indeed fallen from the "old hickory tree," and henceforth Polk would be known as Young Hickory.[12]

On certain issues, the Whigs tried to have it both ways. Some Whig newspapers charged Polk with being a duelist. Others labeled him a coward for failing to respond to an adversary who had plainly sought to provoke him while he was Speaker of the House. Cave Johnson and Aaron Brown came to their friend's defense and acquitted Polk of the duelist charge. As to cowardice, an old letter from no less an expert on dueling than Old Hickory was published in which the general expressed high approval of Speaker Polk for responding to his would-be opponent with mere contempt.

The Democrats were also quick to counter that the proven duelist in the race was Henry Clay. With some evidence against him on each count, Clay was called "a drunkard, a duelist, a gambler, and a perjurer." Certainly, Clay had lifted his share of glasses over the years and was an avid cardplayer. Congressman Thomas J. Henley of Indiana was quoted by John Quincy Adams as saying: "The standard of Henry Clay should consist of his armorial bearings, which ought to be a pistol, a pack of cards, and a brandy-bottle."[13]

Perhaps the most infamous dirty trick of the campaign was what came to be called "the Roorback forgery." On August 21, an article appeared in an abolitionist newspaper in Ithaca, New York, that purported to be an excerpt from a work of fiction titled *Roorback's Tour through the Southern and Western States in the Year 1836*. That book recounted the American travels of a German Baron von Roorback and may have been originally meant as a spoof on Alexis de Tocqueville's famous journey.

The Ithaca *Chronicle* compounded the problem of the book's fiction by inserting a sentence into the book's description of a slave trader in Tennessee taking two hundred slaves to market. The fabricated addition read: "Forty of these unfortunate beings had been purchased, I was informed, of the Hon. James K. Polk, the present Speaker of the House of Representatives; the mark of the branding iron, with the initials of his name on their shoulders distinguishing them from the rest."

Polk was a slaveholder, of course, but the false report of slaves in the South branded with the initials "J.K.P." was meant to inflame northern abolitionists against him. The Democrats cried foul and the *Chronicle* retracted the story. Polk characterized the Roorback falsehood as "the grossest and basest I have ever known," but in the end, it served to remind abolitionists, particularly in New York state, that Henry Clay, too, was a slaveholder. More than a century and a half later, a "roorback" is still used in the lexicon of American politics to describe "any last-minute smear."[14]

$\mathcal{A}$s the 1844 campaign shifted into high gear, the Whigs may well have despised James K. Polk, but at least they knew where he stood—particularly on the issue of Texas. For Clay, it was bad enough that he was repeatedly forced to deny that his same-day announcement with Van Buren against Texas annexation was merely coincidental and not evidence of another corrupt bargain. But when Clay decided to clarify—as only he could—his position on annexation, it looked to some Whigs that, at best, their candidate was flirting with the increasingly popular mantle of expansionism and, at worst, trying to have the issue both ways.

What got Clay into trouble, particularly among abolitionists in the north, came to be called his "Alabama letters." As with his Raleigh letter the previous April, Clay would have been better served if he had never picked up his pen.

It all began when Stephen F. Miller, the editor of the Tuscaloosa, Alabama, newspaper, the *Monitor,* reported to Clay that the Democrats were making inroads in what heretofore had been a Clay state because "you did not leave a door open for annexation at a future time." With typical self-confidence in his skills as a communicator, Clay determined that he and he alone could safely nudge the door open just a crack.

No one who read Clay's subsequent letter could fail to see that his overriding goal was to reclaim as much support in the South as practical by softening his stand against annexation. "Personally," Clay wrote, "I could have no objection to the annexation of Texas, but I certainly would be unwilling to see the existing Union dissolved or seriously jeopardized for the sake of acquiring Texas."

When that ambiguous statement raised more questions than it answered on both sides of the Mason-Dixon Line, Clay again took up his pen. This letter was published in the Tuscumbia, Alabama, *North Alabamian* on August 16, 1844. To his own question of what he would do about Texas if elected president, Clay responded: "Far from having any personal objection to the annexation of Texas, I should be glad to see it, [if it could be accomplished] without national dishonor, without war, with the general consent of the states of the Union, and upon just and fair terms."

Democrats and abolitionists alike seized on the phrase "I should be glad to see it" and turned it to their particular advantage. Democrats accused Clay of flip-flopping and adopting their position on the issue. Abolitionists held Clay a traitor for caving in to southern demands for more slave territory.

One of Clay's most distinguished biographers, Robert Remini, asserted that Clay's statements on Texas were in fact noble attempts to look beyond the current campaign and acquiesce to the inevitable annexation of Texas in due course, just not in "some wild expansionist craze for additional territory that would promote disharmony." But slavery and Texas were by now inexorably entwined in disharmony—Calhoun's letter to Pakenham had seen to that.

Whether Clay's words were patriotic attempts at moderation, compromise, and statesmanship or not, the public perception of his increasingly desperate efforts to explain his views was that he was a waffler, willing to say anything to win votes. One ditty said it all:

> *He wires in and wires out,*
> *And leaves the people still in doubt,*
> *Whether the snake that made the track*
> *Was going South, or coming back.*[15]

*D*espite Henry Clay's early nonchalance about his opponent, and Jackson's early assertion to Polk that "you will get 20 states at least," it was soon apparent to most astute observers that the election of 1844 would be very close. The man who made it a squeaker was third-party candidate James G. Birney, a former slaveholder who had moved north from Kentucky and assumed the editorship of *The Philanthropist*, an antislavery newspaper.

In 1840, Birney received 7,069 votes as the presidential nominee of the Liberty party, a single-issue group bent on abolition in general and the prohibition of slavery in the District of Columbia and the elimination of all interstate slave trade in particular. Capturing only three-tenths of 1 percent of the national vote caused barely a ripple in 1840, but four years later—owing in part to Clay's continued stumbles on Texas—Birney's waves were to crash much louder.

Birney accepted the Liberty party's nomination in August 1843. At the time, the state of New York appeared to be safely in the column of the apparent Democratic nominee, Martin Van Buren. But in the ensuing months, the debate over Texas and slavery became much more heated, and by the summer of 1844, Polk's Democratic strategists in the northern states were carefully calculating how Birney's candidacy might affect the Whig vote.

Arnold S. Harris, a Polk worker touring the north, reported in mid-July that "Ohio is a doubtful state at present and is in great danger of being lost to the cause." Harris feared a coalition between Whigs and abolitionists. "One thing will save the state," Harris predicted, "and the Democrats are doing their utmost to bring it about—induce the Liberty Party to maintain their separate organization. If they do not amalgamate with the Whigs, the state will go Democratic by a handsome vote."

That result didn't occur, but Harris was definitely correct in another prediction: "And now for the main spoke of the wheel—the old empire state with her cartload of votes—the all important state, for as goes New York so I think will the general result be."[16]

Polk's savior in New York was to be Silas Wright. In the aftermath of the Baltimore convention, the two men, who genuinely liked each other, exchanged cordial letters. Wright was quick to tell Polk that he had been "compelled to decide and act instantly" in rejecting the vice presidential slot and that he did so out of loyalty to Van Buren and not out of any dissatisfaction with being named second to him.

Polk responded graciously. While he declined to use any personal influence to persuade Wright to run for governor in New York, concluding "neither I, nor my friends out of the state, can interfere," he was nonetheless delighted when Wright acquiesced to the nomination. Wright put his heart and soul into the New York campaign, and when he polled a larger majority in the state for governor than the national ticket did, he would be called "an outstanding hero."[17]

The presidential election of 1844 was conducted in the twenty-six states over the course of twelve days. Pennsylvania and Ohio went to the polls on November 1, followed by most of the states on November 4 and New York on November 5, but the canvass was not complete until Delaware and Vermont cast ballots on November 12.

In some respects, Texas had been the paramount issue of the campaign. Without the concerted Van Buren–Clay opposition to its annexation, the Democratic convention and the subsequent campaign might have been much different. James K. Polk would have been, at best, only a vice presidential nominee.

Texas was not, however, the overriding issue that decided the election. There was a clear choice in 1844 between the candidates and their views of government, Clay representing the Whig policies of higher tariffs, big business, and increased federal spending, and Polk upholding the Democrats' Jacksonian ideals of westward expansion, limited government, and faith in the common man.

Polk managed to straddle the tariff issue and champion Texas; Clay badly fumbled the Texas issue. But the election of 1844 was also decided by party turnout, the increased abolitionist sentiment in the North that fueled the Liberty party, and the Whigs' last-minute flirtation with nativism.

The sentiment of nativism, decidedly against foreign-born citizens and frequently anti-Catholic, had recently manifested itself in the American Republican party, which won city elections in New York in the spring of 1844. Late in the campaign, Clay was favoring tighter naturalization laws, while the Democrats were welcoming immigrants into their ranks with open arms. The day before the election in New York City alone, Democrats registered 497 new voters at Tammany Hall.[18]

Out of twenty-six states, Polk carried eleven with relative ease for a total of 111 electoral votes: Maine; New Hampshire; Pennsylvania, thanks to the tariff letter; Virginia; South Carolina, where no popular vote was held but electors appointed by the legislature voted

Election of 1844

CANADA

Maine 9

Vermont 6

N.H. 6

Mass. 12

New York 36

R.I. 4

Conn. 6

Michigan 5

Penn. 26

N.J. 7

Illinois 9

Indiana 12

Ohio 23

Delaware 3

Maryland 8

Virginia 17

Missouri 7

Kentucky 12

Tennessee 13

N. Carolina 11

Arkansas 3

S. Carolina 9

Alabama 9

Georgia 10

Republic of Texas

Miss. 6

La. 6

Polk   Clay

Democrat   Whig

Polk: 1,337,243 votes; 170 electoral votes
Clay: 1,299,062 votes; 105 electoral votes
Birney: 62,300 votes; 0 electoral votes

By a plurality of 5,000 votes, James K. Polk won New York State and its 36 electoral votes, and with it the presidency.

Gulf of Mexico

for Polk (no doubt to Calhoun's satisfaction); Georgia; Alabama; Mississippi; Missouri—Benton's railings against annexation aside, the state gave Polk a 10,000-vote plurality; Arkansas; and Illinois.

Clay had little trouble in ten states and picked up 92 electoral votes: Vermont; Massachusetts; Rhode Island; Connecticut, from where a correspondent later informed Polk that *"the lords of the spindles"* (mill owners) had compelled their operators to vote for Clay; New Jersey; Delaware, by a 282-vote margin; Maryland; North

Carolina; Kentucky, Clay's home state; and Ohio, despite the Liberty party's maintaining its separate organization and polling 8,050 votes there.

That left the outcome of the election to hinge on five states: Michigan, Indiana, Louisiana, Tennessee, and New York. In three, Birney and the Liberty party were on the ballot. It is not fair to suggest that *all* of Birney's votes would have gone to Clay if Birney had not been in the race; and even if most had, it probably would not have made any difference in Michigan and Indiana. Their seventeen electoral votes went to Polk by narrow margins.

Louisiana had voted overwhelmingly for Harrison over Van Buren in 1840. Now results showed Polk winning the state by 699 votes. The state's six electoral votes would go to Polk, but closer scrutiny revealed a startling anomaly.

In Plaquemines Parish on the Mississippi River south of New Orleans, the Democrats in 1840 had delivered a 250–40 Democratic advantage. Four years later, the reported vote showed a 1,007–37 Democratic advantage. This Democratic vote was larger "than the entire white male population, of all ages, in the parish in 1840," and ten years would pass "before Plaquemines parish could muster half as many Democratic votes as she gave that year to Polk." One explanation of what some called "the Plaquemines fraud" was that two steamboats took boatloads of Democrats downriver from New Orleans and stopped at three different places in Plaquemines Parish to vote three different times for Polk.

Tennessee's thirteen electoral votes were a matter of great personal pride to Polk, as well as a perceived political necessity. He had to have them. Never before had a winning candidate lost his home state and still managed to win the presidency. Even in the final days of the campaign, Polk continually urged his trusted Tennessee lieutenants to keep up the pressure lest Clay prevail on his home turf.

Ten thousand more Tennessee voters cast ballots than voted in the 1843 gubernatorial race, but the final results were the same. By a 113-vote margin, Henry Clay carried James K. Polk's home state. For the third time in a little over three years, the voters of Tennessee had failed to give James K. Polk a statewide majority. With 138 electoral votes needed to win, and the count standing at Polk with

134 and Clay with 105, the 36 votes of New York would decide the outcome.

On the ballot in the thirteen northern states, James G. Birney and the Liberty party received 62,300 votes, or 2.3 percent of the total cast nationwide. More than a quarter of these votes, 15,812, came in New York. Polk bested Clay in the Empire State 237,588 to 232,482, a plurality of 5,106 votes.

The what-ifs jump off the page: What if Birney had not been in the race at all? What if more than 5,107 of Birney's New York votes—one in three—had gone to Clay instead? What if the Whigs had been as aggressive in new recruits as the Democrats?

In the national popular vote, Polk polled a plurality of 1,337,243 (49.6 percent) to Clay's 1,299,062 (48.1 percent) and Birney's 62,300 (2.3 percent). If 5,107 votes had gone from Birney into Clay's column in New York, Clay would have won New York's 36 electoral votes, and even without a popular-vote plurality nation-wide, Clay would have won the electoral vote 141 to 134 and with it the presidency. Instead, New York's electoral votes went to Polk.

Thus, the electoral college registered a 170 to 105 Polk victory that looked much larger than it really was. One ardent Clay sup-porter in Illinois bemoaned the outcome in New York. "If the Whig abolitionists of New York had voted with us," sighed Abraham Lin-coln, alluding to Birney's showing, "Mr. Clay would now be presi-dent."[19]

One hundred and fifty-six years later, in the razor-thin election of 2000, a third-party candidate would siphon off votes and cost a major party two or three states that would have changed the outcome. In that race, too, the Democratic presidential candidate, Albert Gore, was from Tennessee, and he, too, failed to carry his home state.

While the loss of Tennessee clearly rankled Polk, this third statewide loss was quite different from his two previous defeats. This time, instead of being a defeated gubernatorial candidate, James K. Polk—Tennessee with him or not—was the president-elect of the United States.

As usual, it was Old Hickory who summed it up succinctly: "Who is J. K. Polk, will be no more asked."[20]

PART II

THE CONQUEST

In any event I intend to be <u>myself</u>
President of the United States.

— James K. Polk to political confidant Cave Johnson,
December 21, 1844

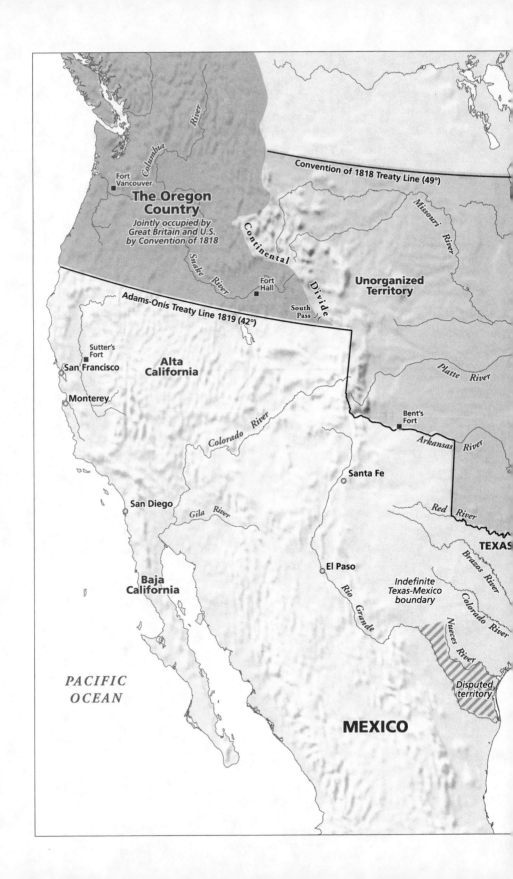

Polk's America
1844

CANADA

Maine
(1820)

Vt.

N.H.

Michigan (1837)

New
York

Mass.   Boston

Conn. R.I.

Chicago

New
York

Pennsylvania

N.J.

Ohio

Illinois

Indiana   Ohio   River

Washington   Md.   Del.

St. Louis

Mississippi River

orth

Missouri
(1821)

Kentucky

Virginia

Cumberland   River

Compromise Line
36°30'N

Nashville

North
Carolina

Tennessee

rkansas
(1836)

Tennessee   River

South
Carolina

Georgia

ATLANTIC
OCEAN

ouisiana   Miss.

Alabama

New
Orleans

Florida
Territory

Gulf of Mexico

CHAPTER 9

Making Good on Texas

𝓡EACTIONS TO THE election of James K. Polk to the presidency ran the full gamut of American political opinion. Only the Texas question, huffed one Whig, had caused the people to elect "a mere *Tom Tit* over the Old Eagle." John Quincy Adams was convinced that Polk's election meant the end of the civilized world and that the followers "of a ruffian"—meaning Andrew Jackson—had sealed "the fate of this nation."

Henry Clay seemed in a state of shock and blamed just about every factor for his defeat except his own handling of the Raleigh and Alabama letters. "If the recent foreigners had not been all united against us," Clay wrote John M. Clayton of Delaware, "or if the foreign Catholics had not been arrayed on the other side; or if the Abolitionists had been true to their avowed principles; or if there had been no frauds, we should have triumphed."

As for the outgoing president, John Tyler smugly predicted that Polk's administration "will be a continuance of my own, since he will be found the advocate of most of my measures." Tyler was only too happy to see Clay, the man who had once presumed to be his "co-president" and who had subsequently dismissed him from the Whig Party, banished into political exile.[1]

International reaction was mostly critical. *The Times* of London—very aware of Great Britain's continuing interest in Texas—called Polk's election "the triumph of every thing that is worst over every thing that is best in the United States of America. It is a victory . . . by the partisans of the annexation of Texas." Perhaps what *The Times* really feared was expressed by *Le journal des débats* of Paris: "Mr. Polk begins the reign of other men for whom the horizon is the [only] limit for America."[2]

Polk partisans cheered. "Allow me to congratulate you, on your election to the highest office in the gift of the people," wrote William C. Bouck from Albany, New York. "The majority in this state is not so large as I supposed it would be," Bouck noted, but he blamed that not on "the popularity of Mr. Clay, but the tariff and Texas question."

Of the Tennessee triumvirate of Cave Johnson, Aaron Brown, and Gideon Pillow, Brown worried about possible assassination attempts after the close election. He advised his friend to "take some thought of *where* you go and eat and drink for a little while . . . in the midst of the desperado spirit which now prevails." But so as not to alarm Sarah, Brown added: "Throw this in the fire that Mrs. P. may not see this note."

Another letter that Polk received was just as personal. It came from one of the Polk family slaves, a man named Harry, who had been hired out for some years as a blacksmith in Carrollton, Mississippi: "I have been betting and losing on you for the last several years but I have made it all up now," Harry wrote. "I must tell you what I have won on your election and I got near all in hand: cash $25 and 11 pair boots, 40 gallons whiskey, 1 barrel flour, and lots of tobacco, but you must not think that I will drink the whiskey myself. . . . I am in hopes that you will come to this state before you go to the White House and let me see you once more before I die."

And what of Old Hickory? "The glorious result of the presidential election has rejoiced every democratic bosom in the United States," Jackson wrote to Andrew Jackson Donelson when the results were known. "And as to myself I can say in the language of Simeon of old 'Let thy servant depart in peace,' as I have seen the solution of the liberty of my country and the perpetuity of our glorious Union."[3]

But the aging warrior was not quite finished. As he had promised Sarah Polk, Jackson had literally given the last ounce of his strength to see her in the White House—the preconvention strategy, numerous arm-twisting letters of support, the deft massaging as only Old Hickory could do of Tyler's ego to facilitate his withdrawal. But after all that, there was still one final matter. There was still Texas.

Whatever John Tyler, John C. Calhoun, James K. Polk, and Andrew Jackson might disagree on, all four were adamant in their commitment to the annexation of Texas. There was perhaps no better evidence of this than the appointment Tyler hastily made in September 1844 as chargé d'affaires to the Republic of Texas.

British and French intrigues in Texas were still high, as was the threat of a Mexican invasion. Sam Houston, his second tenure as president of Texas coming to a close, was greatly annoyed by the Senate's rejection of the promised annexation treaty—by his count, the second American spurning. Anson Jones, Texas secretary of state and Houston's soon-to-be elected successor, was of a like mind and thought that Texas had been "shabbily used."

After the rejection of the treaty, Houston and Jones nonetheless reminded Secretary of State Calhoun of Tyler's earlier promise to defend Texas in the event of an attack by Mexico. When the presidential campaign was in full swing, Tyler and Calhoun were more circumspect on Texas than Clay, and they refrained from any public pronouncements. However, they quietly instructed Tilghman A. Howard, the chargé d'affaires to Texas, to assure Houston and Jones privately that the American government stood behind the promise and would maintain troops along the Sabine River and naval vessels in the Gulf of Mexico.

A week after sending this assurance, Tyler and Calhoun received word that Howard had died of yellow fever. It was essential to appoint a replacement quickly, someone who had the standing to reassure Houston and keep him from leaning further toward Great Britain.

For this difficult assignment, Tyler and Calhoun prevailed upon Andrew Jackson Donelson. He was not only Old Hickory's nephew but also a longtime confidant of both Polk and Houston. Even though he was heavily involved in Polk's campaign, Donelson—with the blessing of Jackson and Polk—quickly wrapped up his Tennessee affairs and hastened to Texas, arriving in Galveston on November 11, 1844.[4]

By November 21, Donelson was settled into a log cabin adjacent to Houston's at the rustic Texas capital of Washington-on-the-Brazos. Donelson found his old Tennessee comrade deeply worried that Tyler's pledges of military protection would not be fulfilled and all too eager to talk on and on about closer ties between Texas and Great Britain. Donelson reported to Calhoun that prompt congressional action on annexation was essential and that "every day's delay is adding strength to the hands of those who are playing the game for the ascendancy of British influence in this Republic."

Significantly, when Houston delivered his farewell address to the Texas congress, he chose to extol the proud future awaiting Texas as an independent republic rather than call for annexation by the United States. When president-elect Jones likewise made no mention of annexation in his inaugural address, it only added to Donelson's worries.

Meanwhile, in Washington, the final session of the twenty-eighth Congress convened on December 2, 1844. The following day, John Tyler submitted his last annual message. There would forever be debate on how much the issue of Texas really changed votes in the election of 1844, but Tyler pulled no punches and put the best possible spin on the outcome.

"A controlling majority of the people and a large majority of the states have declared in favor of immediate annexation," Tyler reported, stretching the mandate just a little. "It is the will of both the people and the states that Texas shall be annexed to the Union promptly and immediately." Then, rather than fight Clay's Whigs in the Senate for the two-thirds vote required to ratify a *treaty* of annexation, Tyler asked Congress to invite Texas into the union by passing a *joint resolution,* which required only a simple majority.[5]

On December 12, the House began debate on a resolution of annexation that contained essentially the same provisions as the treaty that the Senate had rejected the previous June. One major difference was that rather than merely *annexing* Texas as a territory, the resolution provided for its *admission* as a state.

Not only did the resolution spark renewed debate over substantive issues—such as delineation of the Texas boundary, assumption of its debt, and disposition of its public lands—but it also raised the new question of the constitutionality of acquiring territory without the two-thirds advice and consent of the Senate. Heretofore, all territorial expansions beyond the original thirteen colonies had been by treaty, such as the Louisiana Purchase, or by treaty after conquest, as in the case of Jackson's saber-rattling in Florida.

But the pro-Texas camp had little time for such constitutional debates or, for that matter, patience for complicating the basic issue with details. Tyler and Calhoun wanted the debate kept as simple as possible: should Texas be part of the union, yes or no? Resolve that question and there would be plenty of time to argue over the details, even if many arguments might prove acrimonious. From Texas, Andrew Jackson Donelson could only concur in the urgency: "Let us get annexation on any terms we can," he pleaded.[6]

𝒯hroughout the remainder of December and well into January 1845—while James and Sarah Polk wrapped up their affairs in Columbia and made plans to return to the capital they had left six years before—Congress debated resolution after resolution on Texas. In mid-January, Milton Brown, a pro-annexation Whig congressman from Tennessee, offered what was viewed as a compromise plan that went well beyond a simple yes or no vote.

Constitutional arguments aside, Texas, upon its consent, would be admitted into the union as a state. No attempt would be made to interfere with its internal institutions, that was to say slavery. The exact delineation of its boundary would be determined *after* its admission and would be the responsibility of the United States.

If the original state of Texas agreed, four additional states could be created within its borders. Those additional states lying south of the Missouri Compromise line of 36°36' could decide for themselves whether to be slave or free; those north of the line would be free. The United States would not assume the Texas debt, but Texas would retain its public lands and the sale of the same would be available to pay the debt. On January 25, 1845, the House voted 120 to 98 to approve Brown's resolution.

Over in the Senate, another pro-annexation Tennessee Whig, Ephraim Foster, introduced a similar joint resolution. After lengthy debate on the constitutionality of annexation by joint resolution, the Senate Foreign Relations Committee finally voted against it. That left the venerable Thomas Hart Benton of Missouri to step forward with a compromise of his own.

In some respects, Benton was the preeminent Jacksonian expansionist. Benton would be quick to call himself the preeminent *Bentonian* expansionist. A fellow North Carolinian by birth, Benton had come of age in Tennessee, practiced law in Nashville, and served under Jackson early in the War of 1812. Benton and his brother, Jesse, however, soon got into a gunfight over a matter of honor with Jackson in the lobby of Nashville's City Hotel. When the smoke cleared, the Benton boys were bound for Missouri, and Old Hickory had a pistol ball in his chest that he would carry for twenty years.

By the mid-1820s, Benton and Jackson were both U.S. senators from their respective states. They quickly reconciled and joined forces to fight against a national bank and for their shared ideals of low tariffs, limited government, westward expansion, and hard money. Benton's stance on hard currency even earned him the nickname "Old Bullion."

Now Benton's opposition to the immediate annexation of Texas was based not on any lack of territorial appetite but on his fear that annexation meant certain war with Mexico. His opposition was also calculated on the lingering ambition that he might still be president himself some day. In nurturing that goal, Benton hoped to appear presidential and finesse the Texas issue by getting Mexico to recognize Texas's independence.

Nonetheless, on February 5, 1845, Benton seemed to drop this requirement. He simply offered a Senate resolution that "a state, to be formed out of the present republic of Texas" should be admitted as soon as a new treaty was negotiated.[7]

A *treaty*, however, once again meant two-thirds concurrence by the Senate, and at first glance, Benton's resolution may have been a ploy to provoke yet another Texas stalemate. But the political atmosphere changed on February 13, when the president-elect arrived in Washington. Still almost three weeks shy of his inauguration, the man who as a young congressman had urged Old Hickory to arrive in the capital early after his own election in 1828 was himself determined to see firsthand the lay of the political landscape, particularly as it pertained to Texas.

Even if James K. Polk's election mandate on Texas had not been as sweeping as Tyler characterized it, there was nonetheless a strong pro-Texas tide running. Polk was determined to capitalize on it. "Texas will be brought into the Union," bemoaned a fellow Whig to Thurlow Weed of New York. "We must prepare for it. There is no escape. . . . It is idle to think of resisting the current. It will sweep over every obstacle."

Other Whigs concurred. "The arrival of the President-elect has given a powerful impulse to party action on this subject," observed Clay stalwart Senator Willie P. Mangum of North Carolina. Immediately after the Baltimore convention, Mangum had predicted that the Whigs would "literally crush" Polk, but now Mangum was left to confide that Polk "is for Texas, Texas, Texas; and talks of but little else."[8]

But how were the differences between the detailed House resolution and Benton's blank sheet to be resolved? Polk did his own lobbying with many members of Congress, but he also relied heavily on one of the strong supporters of his nomination at Baltimore, Senator Robert J. Walker of Mississippi. Walker coveted a Cabinet post as secretary of the treasury, and Polk was inclined to oblige him.

Walker introduced a Senate amendment to the House version of the joint resolution. It gave the president—presumably the president who was to be inaugurated on March 4 and therefore James K. Polk—the choice between offering Texas annexation on the terms of the House resolution or reopening treaty negotiations under the Benton plan.

Late on the evening of February 27, with the current Congress due to dissolve at midnight on March 3, the Senate approved Walker's amendment by the narrow margin of 27 to 25. Six Democrats who had voted against the treaty the previous June, including Thomas Hart Benton, became the votes needed to push through the Walker amendment affording a presidential choice.

Ever after there would be whispers that they had done so only because Polk had declared, or was said to have declared, or maybe even only hinted, that he would choose the Benton plan and appoint commissioners to renegotiate a treaty. The following day, the original resolution, with the Walker amendment attached, passed the House by a wider margin than the first time, 132 to 75.

So, on March 1, 1845, a joint resolution authorizing the president to choose between immediate annexation or a renewal of negotiations arrived on the desk of John Tyler. No matter how accidental his ascendancy or how stormy his course, John Tyler was still the president of the United States. Texas had always been Tyler's issue and now he was in the position to see it through. Tyler signed the resolution authorizing the presidential choice, and Secretary of State Calhoun immediately suggested that Tyler next choose between annexation and negotiation.

During the debate on Walker's amendment, some congressmen had questioned whether the president doing the choosing might not in fact be John Tyler. No, George McDuffie of Calhoun's own South Carolina reassured the Benton camp, Tyler and Calhoun "would not have the audacity to meddle" with it. The presidential choice, McDuffie maintained, would be Polk's, and—real or imagined—Thomas Hart Benton seemed convinced that Polk would choose the Benton plan to renew negotiations.

George McDuffie must not have known Calhoun as well as he thought, because Calhoun *was* a meddler. He desperately wanted to resolve the issue of Texas once and for all, and he urged Tyler to act immediately for annexation. A Cabinet meeting on Sunday, March 2, found unanimous support for Calhoun's position. But even in the face of this chorus, Tyler appears to have made his own decision—

just as he had done so often. Having made it, Tyler was polite enough to ask Calhoun to call on the president-elect that very afternoon and inform him of it.

The following day, March 3, 1845, Tyler dispatched instructions to Andrew Jackson Donelson, still his chargé d'affaires to Texas. Donelson was to inform Sam Houston, Anson Jones, and all Texans who would listen that the United States stood ready and willing to admit the Lone Star Republic into the union as the twenty-eighth state. John Tyler had decided that he wasn't going to wait for his successor to make good on Texas.[9]

If Polk was surprised or upset by Tyler's last-minute act, the president-elect gave no indication of it. With Sarah and official Washington looking on, James Knox Polk stood in a steady rain on the east steps of the Capitol and took the oath of office as the eleventh president of the United States. In his inaugural address, the new president left no doubt about his view of the status of Texas, even if Texas had not yet assented. Polk counted the number of states at twenty-eight and noted that "two of these"—referring to Florida and Texas—"have taken their position as members within the last week."

If there were those who, because of Texas or anything else, viewed him as a southerner first, Polk also left no doubt that he was irrevocably cut from Old Hickory's cloth. "Every lover of his country must shudder at the thought of the possibility of its dissolution," Young Hickory proclaimed, "and will be ready to adopt the patriotic sentiment, 'Our Federal Union—it must be preserved.' "

With language that must have made Henry Clay cringe, Polk further declared that "all distinctions of birth or of rank have been abolished. All citizens, whether native or adopted, are placed upon terms of precise equality. All are entitled to equal rights and equal protection." Yet, somehow, in espousing this Jacksonian triumph of the common man, Polk failed to count Harry the blacksmith in that number.

Indeed, Polk defended the institution of slavery without mentioning it by name. "It is a source of deep regret," Polk continued, "that in some sections of our country misguided persons have occasionally indulged in schemes and agitations whose object is the destruction of domestic institutions existing in other sections—institutions which existed at the adoption of the Constitution and were recognized and protected by it."

Did Polk remember that the votes of some of those "misguided persons," withheld from Clay by the schemers and agitators of the Liberty party in New York, were the reason he was standing there at all?

Polk's views on other domestic issues were consistent with the planks of the Democratic platform. "We need no national banks," he said, or federal involvement in internal improvements. The national debt resulting from the Panic of 1837—which few Democrats were willing to acknowledge was really a result of Jackson's near-sighted monetary policies—could and should "be speedily paid off." And almost verbatim, Polk repeated the careful wording of his Kane tariff letter during the campaign—"a tariff for revenue" with incidental protection and just enough discrimination to appease the North.

The second half of Polk's speech was devoted to foreign affairs—*expansionist* affairs, one might conclude. Reprising annexation's long-sung theme, Polk insisted that "Texas was once a part of our country—was unwisely ceded away to a foreign power—is now independent, and possesses an undoubted right . . . to merge her sovereignty as a separate and independent state in ours." Congratulating neither Tyler nor Congress, Polk instead chose to "congratulate my country that by an act of the late Congress of the United States the assent of this Government has been given to the reunion."

Polk went on to warn that he regarded "the question of annexation as belonging exclusively to the United States and Texas." In other words, it was not the concern of Great Britain or France and it was certainly no concern of Mexico. "Foreign governments do not seem to appreciate the true character of our Government," he lectured with condescension. With the country's stated purpose of peace, "to enlarge its limits is to extend the dominions of peace over additional territories and increasing millions."

Polk hurried on to assert that he would act just as dutifully to maintain "the right of the United States to that portion of our terri-

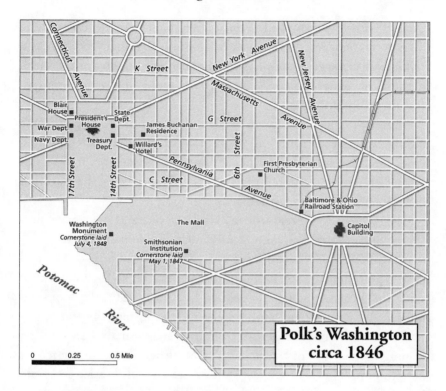

Connecticut Avenue
K Street
New York Avenue
New Jersey Avenue
Massachusetts Avenue
Blair House
State Dept.
President's House
War Dept.
Navy Dept.
Treasury Dept.
James Buchanan Residence
G Street
Willard's Hotel
Pennsylvania
6th Street
First Presbyterian Church
17th Street
14th Street
C Street
Avenue
Baltimore & Ohio Railroad Station
Washington Monument
Cornerstone laid July 4, 1848
The Mall
Smithsonian Institution
Cornerstone laid May 1, 1847
Capitol Building
Potomac River
0   0.25   0.5 Mile

Polk's Washington circa 1846

tory which lies beyond the Rocky Mountains." With British ambassador Richard Pakenham in the crowd, Polk repeated the pledge of the Democratic platform: "Our title to the country of the Oregon is 'clear and unquestionable,' and already are our people preparing to perfect that title by occupying it with their wives and children." This was no military operation but "the peaceful triumphs of the industry of our emigrants." And to us, the president concluded, "belongs the duty of protecting them adequately wherever they may be upon our soil."

Finally, recognizing that "in our country the Chief Magistrate must almost of necessity be chosen by a party and stand pledged to its principles and measures," Polk nonetheless resolved that "in his official action he should not be the President of a part only, but of the whole people of the United States."[10]

With that, cannon thundered and the rain-soaked crowd escorted the Polks down Pennsylvania Avenue to a reception at the White House. James was forty-nine, the youngest person yet to assume the presidency and a full decade younger than the average age of his predecessors. Sarah was forty-one. Together they made a striking and energetic couple who signaled the passing of the torch to the next generation in a way that would not reverberate so sharply again until 1960.

Sarah wore a stylish gown of blue satin and carried a handsome folding fan adorned with ivory. An inauguration gift from her husband, the fan featured portraits of his ten predecessors and one of himself on one side, and an image of the signing of the Declaration of Independence on the other.

But few would ever accuse Sarah of putting style over substance. During the campaign, a lady in Columbia had voiced a preference for Mr. Clay because his wife was a good housekeeper and made fine butter. Sarah replied: "If I should be so fortunate as to reach the White House, I expect to live on twenty-five thousand dollars a year, and I will neither keep house nor make butter."

To quell the rush to dinner from the reception area on her first evening as mistress of the house, Sarah ordered the marine corps band to play "Hail to the Chief" and turn a would-be stampede into a regal procession. By the end of her White House years, that old Scottish anthem—"Hail to the chief who in triumph advances"— would become the traditional announcement to clear the way for the president.

That evening, there were two very different inaugural balls. The highbrow crowd charged ten dollars a ticket and convened at Carusi's Hall. The Democratic Association of the District, backed by the rank and file and the Washington *Globe*, charged five dollars for its gala at the National Theatre. The Polks put in an appearance at Carusi's and then "supped with the true-blue five-dollar Democracy."[11]

𝒮o, where did that leave Texas? Tyler's action on Texas and Polk's inaugural address fanned two firestorms, one foreign and somewhat anticipated, the other domestic and indicative of the way Polk would conduct his administration.

On the international front, the Mexican ambassador to the United States, Juan N. Almonte, had standing instructions to ask for his passport and return to Mexico if an annexation measure passed the American Congress. No less an interested party than British ambassador Richard Pakenham counseled Almonte to wait and assess the situation. But Almonte immediately packed his bags and left for Mexico City, after characterizing annexation as "an act of aggression the most unjust which can be found recorded in the annals of modern history."

Once home, Almonte reported about U.S. military capabilities with just enough inaccuracy that he stoked the determination of Mexico to resist annexation militarily, rather than pursue further diplomatic channels.[12]

On the domestic front, no one was more surprised than Thomas Hart Benton that Polk did not countermand Tyler's orders to Donelson and appoint commissioners to open treaty negotiations. In fact, there was considerable debate in Polk's initial Cabinet meetings about *changing* Donelson's instructions, but not, it appears, about ever *rescinding* them. While Donelson's original instructions from Calhoun permitted Texas to modify the details of the House resolution, by the time the Polk Cabinet was done with its discussion, Donelson was told to urge Texas to accept the terms without modification or delay.

Like Tyler, Polk wanted the basic matter of annexation resolved. The devil could fight over the details later. Polk was so concerned with the instructions to Donelson that he entrusted them to Archibald Yell, one of his oldest supporters. Yell was another Tennessee boy who had moved farther west and made good. He became governor of Arkansas and was now a congressman from that state.

Yell departed for Texas armed with the president's private assurance to Houston and Jones that the United States would not only defend Texas militarily but also "not be satisfied with less than the whole of the territory claimed by Texas—namely to the Rio Grande."[13]

As for Benton, the senator promptly prevailed upon the Senate to request that the president provide that body with a report of his actions toward implementing the joint resolution on Texas. Essentially, the Senate asked Polk what his instructions were to Donelson. Had Polk countermanded Tyler's orders, or not?

Benton and his colleagues soon learned that Young Hickory was just as tough as his namesake was. Claiming executive privilege, Polk refused to provide copies of his instructions to Donelson and Yell "lest such a communication [to the Senate] might delay and ultimately endanger the success of the great measure which Congress so earnestly sought to accomplish."

Whatever his actions in executing that resolution, the actions could not, Polk told the Senate, "at this time and under existing circumstances, be communicated without injury to the public interest." Significantly, Polk deemed it proper, however, to provide the requested copies of Mexican minister Almonte's inflammatory letter severing diplomatic relations.

So, the question must be asked: did Polk, prior to the passage of the House resolution, deceive Benton and his allies into thinking that he was committed to choosing the Benton alternative of negotiating a treaty? When Calhoun called on Polk on March 2 to inform him of Tyler's decision to act on his own and not wait for Polk, the president-elect professed no opinion. Was Polk in fact relieved that Tyler had acted for Texas and gotten him off the hook with Benton?

Once in office, Polk might have countermanded Tyler's orders, but he favored their execution. He strengthened them in print and dispatched not just a courier but the trusted Yell to the scene. Toward the end of his term, when the issue of what he had or had not said or intimated became an issue in the 1848 campaign, Polk adamantly vowed that any deception felt by the Benton group had been merely a misunderstanding. He definitely favored the annexation of Texas, but "if any such pledges were made" as to the method, Polk claimed, "it was in a total misconception of what I had said or meant."

In hindsight, that seems to be a case of selective memory. Polk was a stickler for detail. Witness his early days in Tennessee when he criticized the form of one of Sam Houston's legal documents. It seems very unlikely that Polk would not have carefully compared the two options, as he claimed later, or that he gave such "little importance" to Calhoun's visit telling him of Tyler's decision that he did not think of it again until years later.

Did Polk, in his rush to secure the annexation of Texas that Tyler had so greatly advanced, cross the line between being merely a shrewd politician and being one who at best told all what they wanted to hear and at worst was decidedly duplicitous? Polk did not think so. In the heat of the 1848 campaign, others did, but significantly, in the aftermath of Polk's claim of executive privilege, the Senate demurred to the president, and Thomas Hart Benton—for the moment, at least—still consulted Polk on all pertinent matters.[14]

Meanwhile, Old Hickory continued to fret about what Sam Houston would do. No longer president of Texas, Houston was still, as Yell confided to Polk, "the power behind the throne, greater than the throne itself."

After Tyler's annexation decision, Jackson sent Houston a letter designed to remind him of the personal loyalties that Houston had long borne both to him and the union. "I congratulate you, I congratulate Texas and the United States," Houston's mentor wrote. "Glorious result in which you, General, have acted a noble part."

But Jackson was still not sure what Houston would do next. Finally, news that Houston had rejected Great Britain's overtures and set the wheels in motion for annexation reached the Hermitage. "General Houston has redeemed his pledge to restore Texas to the Union," Andrew Jackson Donelson reported to his uncle. Not only that, but Houston was on his way to the Hermitage to see his old chief and to ask Jackson's blessing on his son. Jackson immediately wrote to Polk with the news: "I knew British gold could not buy Sam Houston."[15]

Back in Texas, President Anson Jones called a special session of the Texas congress to vote on statehood and prepare a state constitution. As it turned out, the congress was presented with two documents to review. One was the House resolution proposing admission to the United States; the other was a treaty offered at the urging of Great Britain whereby Mexico would recognize Texas independence in return for a promise by Texas never to annex itself to another country. Significantly, even this proposed treaty left in doubt the exact boundary between Texas and Mexico.

Some in Texas, including Jones, still hoped for even more favorable terms from the United States and sought to use the Mexican proposal as a bargaining chip. But the rank and file of Texas had had enough delays. The Texas senate unanimously rejected the proposed treaty with Mexico, and then both houses of the Texas legislature unanimously voted for annexation by the United States.

On July 4, the special session ratified both the acceptance of statehood and the state constitution. All that remained was the perfunctory ratification by popular vote in October. Once the outcome of this vote and the state constitution were transmitted to the U.S. Congress, a final resolution was passed admitting Texas to the union as the twenty-eighth state. President Polk signed it on December 29, 1845, and Texas was finally and officially a part of the United States.

By then, one voice among the chorus that had sought the annexation of Texas was silent. On June 6, 1845, with blurry eyesight and a shaky hand, Andrew Jackson scrawled out what was to be his last letter. Marked "Confidential," it was addressed to the president of the United States, but it was clearly also to one of his most cherished associates.

"Be assured my friend," Old Hickory wrote to Polk, "that it is truly grateful to learn from you, that you have a united and harmonious cabinet. May it so continue to exist through your administration, is the prayer of your friend." Then Jackson went to great lengths to warn Polk of possible fraud in the Treasury Department. He urged Polk to investigate and as the lines of his letter became increasingly cramped and small, he abruptly closed by saying: "I can write no more, friendship has aroused me to make this attempt. Your friend, Andrew Jackson."

Two days later, a carriage carrying Sam Houston, his wife, Margaret, and two-year-old Sam junior, clattered up to the portico of the Hermitage. Their passage from Texas had been delayed for two days when their steamboat ran aground in the Mississippi. Arriving in Nashville on the evening of June 8, they hastened to the Hermitage, but they were three hours too late. At six o'clock that evening, the victor of New Orleans; the greatest hero in America; the man who had made himself and two others president of the

United States; and the man who, had he lived, might yet have made another president out of Sam Houston, was dead.

The first thing that Sam Houston did was to put his head on Old Hickory's lifeless chest. His next act was to sit down and write to Polk. "I have seen the corpse," Houston reported to his old Tennessee friend. "The visage is much as it was in life."

But much else had suddenly changed for both Houston and Polk. "A nation will feel this loss, as a nation has received the fruits of his toils," Houston continued. But if Houston felt the loss keenly, the occupant of the White House felt it even more so. Texas was safe, but now James K. Polk was truly on his own.[16]

CHAPTER 10

Standing Firm on Oregon

*F*ORTY YEARS AFTER the fact, with perhaps too much benefit of history and too aging a memory, the historian George Bancroft recalled a meeting with President Polk shortly after his inauguration. Bancroft was no casual visitor but was the same man who, as a delegate from Massachusetts to the 1844 Democratic convention, had plotted with Gideon Pillow and Cave Johnson to lead the northern charge for Polk's nomination. Bancroft's reward was to be secretary of the navy, and he accepted the post enthusiastically.

If Bancroft's memory was correct, Polk "raised his hand high in the air and bringing it down with force on his thigh" confided to Bancroft the "four great measures" of his administration. First, with Texas at last on the road to statehood, the "joint occupation" of Oregon had to be settled with Great Britain. Second, with the flanks of Oregon and Texas secure, the continent must be rounded out by the acquisition of California and "a large district on the coast." Third, the tariff, so onerous to the southern states, must be reduced to a revenue basis, and last, an independent treasury, immune from the banking schemes of recent years, must be established.[1]

To accomplish these goals, Polk was determined to spend whatever political capital he had. Having given his one-term pledge, he need not worry about saving any, and it is unlikely that he would have held anything back in any event. That simply had never been his style. Careful, calculating, sure to cover his flanks—particularly in having Old Hickory's blessing in any endeavor—Polk had nonetheless repeatedly demonstrated that in most things he kept his own close counsel and went at his own deliberate pace.

"I intend to be *myself* President of the United States," Polk told Cave Johnson before his inauguration, discounting the inevitable political rumors that he would be someone's pawn. Polk even said much the same thing to Andrew Jackson shortly before Jackson's death, when a dispute arose over the role Frank Blair and the Washington *Globe* would play in the Polk administration. "I must be the head of my own administration," Polk told his mentor, "and will not be controlled by any newspaper, or particular individual whom it serves."

Indeed, by the second month of Polk's presidency, the venerable *Globe* was sold and a new Democratic organ, the Washington *Union,* began publication. At the time, Polk's longtime friend Supreme Court Justice John Catron gave Old Hickory a candid and pointed assessment: "Our friend [Polk] is very prudent, and *eminently* firm regardless of consequences. He came here to be—THE PRESIDENT—which at this date is as undisputed as that you were THE GENERAL at New Orleans."[2]

Polk laid down a firm set of instructions for his Cabinet, the likes of which had never been seen before—or since. Polk required his six Cabinet appointees to sign an acknowledgment that they would support the principles and policies of the Democratic Platform as approved at Baltimore and amplified in his inaugural address. He promised to take "no part between gentlemen of the Democratic Party, who may become aspirants or candidates to succeed me in the presidential office" and in turn required that any Cabinet officer who chose to become a candidate must "retire from the Cabinet."

Further, Polk planned "to remain constantly in Washington" and expected his Cabinet to do the same. He strongly disapproved of the all-too-common practice of Cabinet officers "absenting them-selves for long periods of time" and leaving the management of their departments to chief clerks. Polk was determined to be a hands-on president, and he wanted a ready and willing hands-on Cabinet.[3]

The Cabinet Polk chose was representative both geographically of the country and politically of the Democratic party. James Buchanan of Pennsylvania became secretary of state, his personal reward for hard campaigning and managing the tariff issue in the Keystone State. Whether Buchanan would truly keep the "non-candidate" pledge remained to be seen. In accepting the appoint-ment, Buchanan merely told Polk that he could not control what others might do on his behalf and that "I cannot proclaim to the world that in no contingency shall I be a candidate for the Presi-dency in 1848." But if he were to be, Buchanan assured Polk, he would abide by Polk's wishes and resign.[4]

The Treasury Department went to Robert J. Walker of Missis-sippi, just as he had desired, although Polk first offered the post to Silas Wright. Polk appointed William Marcy of New York as secre-tary of war, but not without incurring some wrath from the Van Buren wing of the party in that state. After Wright declined the Treasury Department in order to remain as governor of New York, the Van Burenites promoted Benjamin Butler for that post or secre-tary of state. But those positions were already filled, and when But-ler declined the war department as beneath his dignity, it went to Marcy, who was not a Van Buren favorite.

For attorney general, Polk picked John Mason of Virginia, who had been Tyler's last secretary of the navy. Mason was also one of Polk's longtime friends, having attended the University of North Carolina and served in Congress with him. George Bancroft got New England's geographic slot and became secretary of the navy. That left the postmaster general to come from Tennessee.

While there were others in Polk's Tennessee circle who might have expected the appointment, it went to the ever-faithful Cave Johnson. In those days, the position of postmaster general— charged with making thousands of patronage appointments of local postmasters—frequently went to a party insider. No one was better versed in such matters than Cave Johnson.

After the turnstile Cabinet of Tyler, Polk's Cabinet would prove to be quite stable. Buchanan (presidential aspirations aside), Walker, Marcy, and Johnson would all serve the full four years of Polk's term. So would Mason, albeit in two different positions. Bancroft would leave only to become minister to Great Britain, his even greater desire.

On the legislative side, the new twenty-ninth Congress was composed of 143 Democrats, 77 Whigs, and 6 others in the House and—after Texas finally became a state—31 Democrats and 25 Whigs in the Senate. At first glance, these margins should have provided the new president with comfortable majorities, but that would not always be the case.

So, with a firm idea of what he wanted to accomplish, a Cabinet in place that was sworn to cordially cooperate in carrying out his policies, and a Congress composed of friendly though not necessarily subservient majorities, James K. Polk set about achieving the first objective of his presidency.

"*O*regon" had for some time been almost as open-ended a geographic description as "Texas." Great Britain based its claims to this area of the Pacific Northwest on the late eighteenth-century voyages of James Cook and George Vancouver and on the trans-Canadian journeys of Alexander Mackenzie—more than a decade before Lewis and Clark. American claims rested with Robert Gray's "discovery" of the mouth of the Columbia River in 1792 and Lewis and Clark's arrival there thirteen years later.

But the real exploration of the Oregon country occurred in the course of the fierce fur-trade competition between John Jacob Astor's American Fur Company and the British Hudson's Bay Company. Trappers and traders found Oregon rich not only in beaver pelts but also in fish, timber, and even farming opportunities. Russia, moving south from Alaska, and Spain, probing north from Alta (Upper) California, also found these attributes attractive.

As Monroe's secretary of state, John Quincy Adams negotiated the Treaty of 1818 with Great Britain that fixed the American-Canadian boundary east of the Rockies at the 49th parallel and provided for the joint occupation of the Oregon country for ten years.

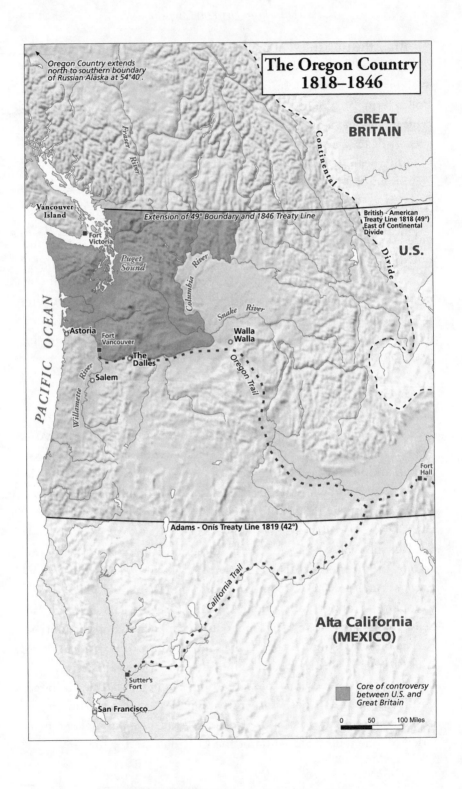

The Oregon Country
1818–1846

Oregon Country extends north to southern boundary of Russian Alaska at 54°40'.

GREAT BRITAIN

Continental

Fraser River

Vancouver Island

Extension of 49° Boundary and 1846 Treaty Line

British - American Treaty Line 1818 (49°) East of Continental Divide

Fort Victoria

Puget Sound

Columbia River

U.S.

Divide

PACIFIC OCEAN

Astoria

Fort Vancouver

The Dalles

Salem

Willamette River

Snake River

Walla Walla

Oregon Trail

Fort Hall

Adams - Onís Treaty Line 1819 (42°)

California Trail

Alta California (MEXICO)

Sutter's Fort

San Francisco

Core of controversy between U.S. and Great Britain

0   50   100 Miles

This meant that Oregon was essentially neutral ground and that each nation could make use of it without fortifying it and without prejudicing the other's claim.

The Adams-Onís Treaty the following year extinguished Spanish claims north of the 42nd parallel, the northern boundary of California. In 1824, Adams also completed an agreement with Russia that established the southern boundary of Alaska at latitude 54°40'. Russia and Great Britain agreed on the same boundary the following year.

All of this diplomatic wrangling meant that by 1825, Oregon could be said to be confined by the Russian boundary of Alaska at 54°40' on the north, the Spanish boundary of California at 42° on the south, the crest of the Rocky Mountains on the east, and the Pacific Ocean on the west. Spain and Russia had abandoned their claims, and Great Britain and the United States were left to divide the spoils. Faced with the expiration of the ten-year joint occupation agreement, both sides sat down to attempt to do just that.

They came remarkably close. The main point of contention focused not on the entire Oregon country but on an irregular rectangle of land between the Columbia River on the south and east, Puget Sound and the Pacific Ocean on the west, and the 49th parallel on the north. With the roily, windswept bar of the Columbia River affording no prospect of a safe anchorage in the south, both the United States and Great Britain were determined to control the calm, sheltered harbors of Puget Sound.

American negotiator Albert Gallatin and his British counterparts apparently flirted with the idea of splitting the difference then and there between the Columbia River and the 49th parallel. This would have left the United States with Grays Harbor on the Pacific but no anchorage on Puget Sound.

Gallatin's instructions from John Quincy Adams were quite specific on securing a position on Puget Sound, however, and when representatives of the Hudson's Bay Company balked at withdrawing from the Columbia, the two sides were at an impasse. Thus, Great Britain and the United States signed a treaty in 1827 that extended the joint occupation indefinitely and required either party only to give one year's notice prior to terminating it.

Despite the new treaty, some in the United States wanted to seize the initiative and promote the American settlement of Oregon as quickly as possible. They were part of an unorganized but increasingly influential Oregon lobby that included sailing captains, merchants, missionaries, whalers, and assorted entrepreneurs, who all wanted an American presence—an "American window on the Pacific"—through which to reach both Oregon's riches and the economic markets of the Far East.

One proponent of Oregon settlement was Congressman John Floyd of Virginia. He introduced a bill in the House of Representatives in December 1828 that called for the construction of forts throughout the territory and the award of land grants to American settlers.

A young congressman from Tennessee opposed Floyd's bill because it violated the joint occupation treaty by not giving the required year's termination notice. The question, the congressman said, was not "whether it was wise to make this treaty, but, having made it, what is its spirit and meaning?" On January 9, 1829, that congressman, James K. Polk, voted with the majority to defeat Floyd's bill.[5]

Without congressional encouragement, the 1830s saw only a trickle of American migration to Oregon. But this proved to be the missionary era. When the Methodist Church advertised for "two suitable men, unencumbered with families, and possessing the spirit of martyrs" to establish a mission among the Nez Percé, twenty-three-year-old Jason Lee and his nephew, Daniel Lee, answered the call.

In the spring of 1834, the Lees set out from Saint Louis with an Oregon-bound party of fur traders led by Nathaniel Wyeth. While Daniel Lee characterized him as "a perfect infidel," Wyeth nonetheless got them safely across the continent to the Hudson's Bay Company post at Fort Vancouver on the Columbia River opposite present-day Portland. There, Dr. John McLoughlin, the company's chief factor and effectively the ranking British subject in the region, welcomed them.

McLoughlin encouraged the Lees to build their mission about forty miles up the Willamette River, well to the south of the still contentious dividing line of the Columbia. This seemed like a British advantage at the time, but McLoughlin's haste to steer these Americans away from the north bank of the Columbia also led them into rich farming country.

By 1840, "reinforcements," as the missionaries called them, had come by sea and swelled their numbers to more than fifty, including many women and children. By the following year, one visitor to the Willamette mission (just north of present-day Salem) described its inhabitants as "more occupied with the settlement of the country and in the agricultural pursuits than in the missionary labors."

Meanwhile, other Protestant missionaries, with Marcus and Narcissa Whitman and Henry and Elizabeth Spaulding in the vanguard, had crossed the Rockies with fur trading contingents. The Whitmans established a mission at Waiilatpu (near present-day Walla Walla, Washington) and the Spauldings did likewise at Lapwai (near present-day Lewiston, Idaho). The Whitman mission in particular, situated where the rough passage over the Blue Mountains gave way to the wider plains of the Columbia, would soon provide a haven for more Oregon-bound travelers.

Narcissa Whitman and Elizabeth Spaulding were the first white women to cross the Rockies, and they soon became veritable advertisements for an entire generation of young American women. If Narcissa and Elizabeth could do it, well, the rush was about to happen.[6]

The key to the opening of the Oregon country lay on the Continental Divide in what is now south-central Wyoming. South of the rugged Wind River Range of the Rocky Mountains, the divide drops down to seventy-five hundred feet and meanders along the crests of rolling sagebrush-covered hills. The grade on both sides is comparatively gentle. Watercourses studded with cottonwoods boast of reliable water in either direction, eastward down the aptly named Sweetwater to the North Platte and westward down Pacific Creek toward the Green River. Never mind the difficulties that Lewis and Clark reported farther north, or the tortuous canyons that lock up the land in Colorado to the south, here was a veritable highway linking east and west.

This was South Pass, perhaps the most famous location in westward expansion west of the Mississippi. Its first documented crossing was in 1812 by Robert Stuart and a party of John Jacob Astor's trappers heading east. Mountain man Jedediah Smith is said to have "rediscovered" the pass in February 1824 while heading west. By the early missionary passages, South Pass was known as the one place along the Continental Divide guaranteed to provide a watered crossing suitable for wagons.

The first true wagon train to leave Westport Landing just west of Independence, Missouri, and roll toward South Pass was the Bidwell-Bartleson party of 1841. Led by mountain man Thomas "Broken Hand" Fitzpatrick, sixty-four men, women, and children crossed South Pass. Then, just east of Fort Hall and present-day Pocatello, Idaho, they made what would soon become a much-repeated decision: half of the group continued on to Oregon, the other half turned southwest toward California.

The following year, 1842, marked what is usually thought of as "the beginning of the covered wagon migration to Oregon." Dr. Elijah White, formerly with the Lee mission at Willamette, and Lansford Hastings, soon to be infamous for a faulty guidebook, shepherded a train of sixteen or eighteen wagons and 107 settlers westward. The wagons made it across South Pass, but most were abandoned at Fort Hall and sold to the Hudson's Bay Company.

Back in Washington that year, Secretary of State Daniel Webster and British envoy Lord Ashburton discussed the Oregon question as part of their negotiations to resolve the entire length of the American-Canadian border. Great Britain, however, was as unwilling in 1842 as it had been in 1827 to concede that critical rectangle between the Columbia River and the 49th parallel.

For its part, the United States was equally unwilling to do so, largely because a naval expedition led by Lieutenant Charles Wilkes had just returned from the North Pacific with fresh reports of both the hazards of the Columbia bar and the enticements of Puget Sound. So, while the Webster-Ashburton Treaty resolved boundary disputes between Maine and New Brunswick and reaffirmed the 49th parallel east of the Rockies, the Oregon country west of the mountains was still subject to joint occupation.

Then came the Great Migration of 1843. The economic designs of the Oregon lobby were bolstered by hundreds of ordinary families — some still smarting from the Panic of 1837 — who were lured westward by the promise of new lands and new opportunities. While its numbers would pale in comparison to the rush a scant half dozen years later, the 1843 migration found about one thousand people plodding along what would forever be called the Oregon Trail.

Westward the caravans creaked and groaned, past locations that were to become landmarks to the hordes who would follow: the spindly tower of Chimney Rock rising above the North Platte in western Nebraska, the rounded dome of Independence Rock near the mouth of the Sweetwater in central Wyoming — where a growing registry of names was carved into the rock — and of course, the gateway of South Pass.

The heavy Conestoga freight wagons of the East were too bulky for the rough terrain and long distances of the West, so lighter, more nimble "prairie schooners" were pulled by oxen. A dozen miles a day was considered a blistering pace.

In 1843, wagons made it all the way to the Whitman mission and down the Columbia to the Dalles, albeit over what one participant called "the roughest road I ever saw." From there, they floated down the Columbia on improvised rafts to the mouth of the Willamette. By one count, some 875 settlers made it all the way and swelled the population of the Willamette valley to about 1,500; all were Americans save for a few Canadian traders. John McLoughlin must have been having second thoughts.

That same year, while not shirking from an opinion on Texas, Henry Clay also offered his opinion on Oregon. "I think our true policy is to settle and populate our immense territory on the east of those [Rocky] mountains and within the United States," Clay declared, "before we proceed to colonize the shores of the Pacific; or at all events postpone the occupation of Oregon some thirty or forty years."

But that wasn't going to happen. In 1844, four major wagon trains left Missouri bound for Oregon and carried with them double the number of people in the so-called Great Migration. The floodgates were opening, and when it came to dealing with Great Britain over the issue of joint occupation, no one realized the value of American settlers on the ground better than John C. Calhoun.

While not a favorite of the North on most issues, upon his appointment as secretary of state, Calhoun found support in the northern press over his Oregon position. There was confidence that Calhoun "would not yield any part of Oregon" and would pursue "passive delay in Oregon to give American settlers more time to occupy the territory."

By the time Polk was inaugurated, another five thousand settlers were assembling in and around Independence and making ready to head west. Some would veer off the Oregon Trail near Fort Hall and strike for California, but most would end up in Oregon.

"Whoo ha! Go to it boys! We're in a perfect *Oregon fever*," exclaimed the Independence *Expositor*. And if there was any doubt that this fever was a family affair and not a male-dominated frolic, the proof came when the first official census was taken in 1849 after Oregon became a territory. It showed 5,410 males and 3,673 females; all but 298 were Americans.

Democratic congressman Andrew Kennedy of Indiana put winning Oregon in terms of simple mathematics. "Go to the West," Kennedy said in Congress in 1846, "and see a young man with his mate of eighteen; after a lapse of thirty years, visit him again, and instead of two, you will find twenty-two. That is what I call the American multiplication table." Here was the real winning of the west.[7]

𝐵ut sooner or later, the surge of population and the frenzy of flag-waving had to be made inviolate by international law. If southern sentiments during this period were largely in favor of the annexation of Texas, northern opinions, particularly in the states of the old Northwest Territory, were equally impassioned about acquiring Oregon—not just a part of it, but *all* of it. Senator E. A. Hannegan of Indiana was one who voiced the extreme view and said that should Polk stop short of 54°40′, it would be "a fall so profound—a damnation so deep that the hand of resurrection could not reach him."

While standing firm, Polk nonetheless seems to have been anxious to leave himself some room to maneuver. On their face, the words of the Democratic platform and Polk's inaugural seemed to leave no room for equivocation. "Our title to the *whole* [italics added] of the Territory of Oregon is clear and unquestionable," read the platform. Yet Polk's inaugural, while ostensibly reiterating that position, proclaimed: "our title to the country of the Oregon is 'clear and unquestionable,' " leaving out the word "whole." Was this merely an innocuous omission or—meticulous detail person that Polk was—a subtle attempt to provide for a fallback position, if necessary?[8]

The status of the diplomacy with Great Britain over the Oregon question that President Polk and Secretary of State Buchanan inherited from their predecessors, Tyler and Calhoun, was thus: British ambassador Richard Pakenham was on record as offering the Columbia River as the dividing line. Calhoun had countered with the 49th parallel—essentially, the same positions that the two countries had long espoused. In January 1845, considering the negotiations deadlocked, Pakenham proposed that the matter be submitted to arbitration. Calhoun refused, in the hope that the issue might still be settled directly.

After Polk's inaugural—with or without the word "whole"—Calhoun still professed delay as the best strategy and thought that the American policy should be "to be quiet, to do nothing to excite attention and leave time to operate."[9] In other words, westward ho, the wagons!

Polk refused to retain Calhoun as secretary of state but nonetheless considered appointing him as minister to Great Britain. When Calhoun—still among those eyeing the 1848 presidential race—declined to go abroad, Polk offered the post to several others and even had George Bancroft approach Martin Van Buren. The Red Fox replied that he did not think it appropriate for an ex-president to accept a foreign mission unless there was a crisis to resolve.

Polk finally settled on Louis McLane of Maryland, who had served Old Hickory in the same capacity and as secretary of state. If nothing else, McLane was of sufficient stature to signal that Polk was serious about resolving the Oregon question.

But the focal point of negotiations during the summer of 1845 proved to be Washington, not London. After Buchanan reiterated to Pakenham that the United States was unwilling to submit to arbitration, Pakenham repeated the request he had made of Calhoun the previous year and asked Buchanan to make a proposal to resolve the matter.

On July 12, 1845, after conferring at length with the president, Buchanan spelled out the Polk administration's position on Oregon in a letter to Pakenham. After an exhaustive recital of American claims to the entire territory, Buchanan nevertheless reported that Polk "found himself embarrassed, if not committed, by the acts of his predecessors" to seek a compromise. As such, the United States was willing to agree to the 49th parallel and allow Great Britain access to ports on Vancouver Island lying south of that line.

This was, of course, merely a restatement of Calhoun's previous offer, but it was also a far cry from the "whole" of Oregon pledge that many of Polk's supporters expected him to keep. Was Polk truly willing to compromise, or did he feel relatively certain that the British would reject the offer and come back with the line of the Columbia?

If the offer was accepted, Polk could tell the ardent 54°40′ crowd that he had been bound by his predecessor. If it wasn't, then Polk could fairly claim to be in a position to start over again from scratch, presumably advocating the "whole" of the territory. Pakenham soon made it easy for him to do the latter.

Pakenham's reply of July 29 showed some evidence that he had been bitten by the Calhoun bug of diplomatic indiscretion—forgetting that sometimes less is definitely better than more. In a letter that Polk characterized as "scarcely courteous or respectful," Pakenham went to extreme lengths to refute every claim to Oregon that Buchanan had advanced.

Significantly, the British minister made no counterproposal and rejected the American offer out of hand without submitting it to his government in London. Finally, Pakenham lectured Buchanan that the United States should make another offer "more consistent with fairness and equity, and with the reasonable expectations of the British government."[10]

Polk summoned Buchanan back to Washington from a summer vacation to draft a response. Buchanan seemed inclined to drag his feet—just as he had procrastinated in announcing his position on Texas annexation in the spring of 1844. Procrastination, however, was not in Polk's nature, and he may well have felt relieved that having attempted compromise, he could now wipe the slate clean and pin any future diplomatic intransigence squarely on John Bull.

In fact, the president felt so strongly about his government's reply to Pakenham—and admittedly may well have simply wanted to have his own version of events available for posterity—that he began to keep a diary. On the very day that he urged Buchanan to hurry up and prepare a response to Pakenham, Polk made his first entry in what would become an invaluable source of insight into his presidency and his character.

At the Cabinet meeting of August 26, 1845, Polk noted that the earlier American proposal of the 49th parallel had been made "first in deference to what had been done by our predecessors, and second with an anxious desire to preserve peace between the two countries." Polk seized on Pakenham's lack of a counterproposal and considered his own offer withdrawn. The ever-cautious Buchanan argued with the president at some length that at the very least their response should encourage a British offer. But Polk was adamant. If the British chose to make an offer, let them do so, with or without invitation.

When Buchanan fretted that war might result, Polk replied that "if we do have war it will not be our fault." But what about the possibility of a war with Mexico, Buchanan asked. Might it not be better to postpone any missive on Oregon until that matter was resolved?

Recognizing that it might well mean a war on two fronts, Polk was nonetheless not inclined to let one controversy rule the other. "We should do our duty towards both Mexico and Great Britain," he told Buchanan, "and firmly maintain our rights, and leave the rest to God and the country." According to Polk's diary, Buchanan groused in return that "God would not have much to do in justifying us in a war for the country north of 49°."

Buchanan wanted to delay, but Polk ordered that a response be drafted immediately, withdrawing the previous American offers of the 49th parallel. The president even urged his secretary of state to have the document on his desk the very next day. When the Cabinet convened in two special meetings on August 27 and 29 to consider revisions, Polk remained firm in not inviting another British offer and acquiesced only to the addition of Buchanan's expression of a wish for peace between the two countries.

At the last minute, Buchanan inserted two additional paragraphs with Polk's concurrence. One noted that while the United States refused to allow free navigation of the Columbia to the British, it would permit access to a port on the extreme southern tip of Vancouver Island (present-day Victoria, British Columbia).

The other showed that even Buchanan had a sense of humor. Tweaking Pakenham just a little, Buchanan noted that "a large and splendid globe now in the Department of State, recently received from London," showed the American boundary in the Northwest at the 54th parallel.

So, with Buchanan still grumbling that it was not "wise statesmanship to deliver such a paper in the existing state of our relations with Mexico," Polk urged him on his way, and Buchanan presented the American response to the British embassy on August 30, 1845.[11]

𝒫art of the reason for Polk's firm stand on Oregon was that much of the country was coming around to embracing the Oregon plank of the Democratic platform of 1844. History's shorthand has long associated the phrase "54°40' or Fight!" with the election campaign of 1844, but it really didn't catch on as a rallying cry to take all of Oregon until much later. By then, fifty-four forty conventions had been held in cities throughout the North, state legislatures had passed resolutions demanding all of Oregon, and newspaper editorials had trumpeted the unquestioned right of the American people to expand westward.

The most famous pronouncement of this sentiment was voiced by a journalist named John L. O'Sullivan, who coined two words to describe the national psyche. It was "the fulfillment of our manifest destiny," wrote O'Sullivan in the summer of 1845, "to overspread the continent allotted by Providence for the free development of our yearly multiplying millions."

Echoing this rapacious appetite, the New York *Morning News* proclaimed: "This national policy, necessity or destiny, we know to be just and beneficent, and we can, therefore, afford to scorn the invective and imputations of rival nations. With the valleys of the Rocky Mountains converted into pastures and sheep-folds, we may with propriety turn to the world and ask, whom have we injured."[12]

On October 22, 1845, amid this spirit of rampant nationalism, British ambassador Richard Pakenham presented himself at the home of Secretary of State Buchanan. Looking more than a little sheepish, Pakenham professed regret that the Americans' 49th parallel offer of July 12 had been withdrawn.

Truth be told, Pakenham had just received a reprimand from London. His boss, British foreign minister Lord Aberdeen, was furious with Pakenham for his unilateral and presumptuous response to Buchanan's letter. Aberdeen was even more upset that Polk had used the occasion to withdraw any offer and put the onus on the British for crafting a new plan. Where, Pakenham now pleaded with Buchanan, did that leave matters between the two countries?

Late that evening, Buchanan hurried over to the White House to consult with the president. Polk and Buchanan were already aware of Pakenham's predicament. Just the day before, they had received a confidential report from Louis McLane in London about Lord Aberdeen's frustration over Pakenham's response. Buchanan saw this as another opportunity to invite a British offer. Polk saw it as a sign of British weakness and continued to insist that the British government move first.

So the next day, when Pakenham arrived at the State Department for an official conference, he "seemed to be troubled" and uncertain "how to make a proposition as long as the American proposition remained withdrawn." Knowing well Polk's sentiments, Buchanan could offer Pakenham no comfort and merely told him "that what had occurred could not be changed." Even if Pakenham put a new offer on the table, Buchanan could guarantee nothing except that "it would be respectfully considered."

Polk had kept the ball squarely in Great Britain's court, despite the continued fussing of Buchanan that to do so was tantamount to war. "The truth is," Polk later confided to his diary, "Mr. Buchanan has from the beginning been, as I think, too timid and too fearful of war on the Oregon question, and has been most anxious to settle the question by yielding and making greater concessions than I am willing to make."[13]

𝒥f there was any weakness in Polk's resolve on pushing for all of Oregon at this point, it did not show in a wide-ranging conversation that he had the following day with Thomas Hart Benton. Old Bullion and Polk had been colleagues in Congress. Sarah Polk was on close terms with Benton's wife, Elizabeth, as well as his daughter, Jessie, whose only fault in her father's eyes was that she had eloped with a young army lieutenant named John Charles Frémont. In fact, Sarah Polk, usually in the company of the president, attended the same church as the Bentons, the First Presbyterian on Fourth Street.

The congenial Polk-Benton relationship had been strained by the entire affair at Baltimore. Polk had been piqued by Benton's hesitation on immediate annexation for Texas, and perhaps Benton, thirteen years Polk's senior, thought that he and not Young Hickory should have been next in line for the presidency.

It didn't help matters that Benton either misunderstood or was deceived by Polk's reported support for the Benton plan of renegotiating a treaty with Texas. Tyler's last-minute act made that issue relatively moot, however, and Benton found that he still had more in common with Polk than not. When Buchanan suggested that Benton come to the White House and consult on Oregon, Old Bullion jumped at the chance.

Receiving Benton at the White House, Polk found his fellow westerner's manner and conversation "altogether pleasant and friendly, and such as they had always been in former years when I was in Congress with him." Before their afternoon meeting was complete, these two expansionists—Jacksonian and Bentonian—had pretty much agreed on the next chapter of Manifest Destiny.

First, the United States would give Great Britain the required one-year notice to terminate the Oregon joint occupation agreement of 1827; second, U.S. laws would be extended over American citizens in Oregon; third, forts would be erected along the Oregon Trail and two or three mounted regiments raised to protect emigrants en route; and fourth, the federal Indian policy—which in that era usually meant forcible removal—would be extended to Oregon.

Polk told Benton that he intended to reaffirm the noncolonization clause of the Monroe Doctrine in his upcoming annual address to Congress. While Benton noted that such could hardly be expected to apply to the long-established British settlements along the Fraser River, he nonetheless agreed with the general principle. Certainly, Benton agreed with Polk's sentiments as they related to California.

Fearing that Great Britain "had her eye on that country and intended to possess it if she could," Polk told Benton that "in reasserting Mr. Monroe's doctrine, I had California and the fine bay of San Francisco as much in view as Oregon." Benton agreed that no foreign power should be permitted to colonize California any more than any power would be permitted to colonize Cuba should Spain fail to possess it.[14]

So, the two westward visionaries parted friends, and Polk continued to refine his first annual message to Congress. Not until the days of Woodrow Wilson in 1913 would presidents appear personally before a joint session of Congress and deliver what came to be called their State of the Union Address. Instead, Polk's message was hand-delivered in print on December 2, 1845.

Polk covered the pertinent issues of the day, but even his firm stand on Texas—recognizing its admission to the union as an accomplished fact not to be challenged by foreign powers—could not surpass his resolve on Oregon. Noting that all attempts at compromise with Great Britain had failed, the president recommended action on the points he had discussed with Benton, principally giving notice to terminate the joint occupancy agreement.

"At the end of the year's notice," explained Polk, "we shall have reached a period when the national rights in Oregon must either be abandoned or firmly maintained. That they can not be abandoned without a sacrifice of both national honor and interest is too clear to admit of doubt."

Then Polk went a bold step further. Alluding to past British and French influences in Texas and warning those governments away from any similar intrigues in Oregon, California, or anywhere else in North America, Polk became the first American president to reaffirm the Monroe Doctrine as a basic tenet of American foreign policy. He quoted Monroe's noncolonization clause—"the American continents . . . are henceforth not to be considered as subjects for future colonization by any European powers"—as continuing American policy.

Polk further insisted that whatever the European powers might think about "a balance of power," such "cannot be permitted to have any application on the North American continent, and especially to the United States. We must ever maintain the principle that the people of this continent alone have the right to decide their own destiny." In the words of Monroe Doctrine historian Dexter Perkins, Polk's brash statement—sometimes called the Polk Corollary to the Monroe Doctrine—"out-Monroes Monroe."[15]

𝒫olk's first annual message, particularly his strong stand on Oregon, was generally well received by Democrats and Whigs alike. But by the new year, at least one Democratic congressman, James A. Black of South Carolina, was very concerned about the pending debate in Congress over giving the one-year's notice. Fearing that it might split the Democratic party into northern camps in favor and southern camps opposed, Black took the unusual step of calling at the White House on Sunday evening, January 4, 1846.

Sarah, no doubt, was upset by this intrusion on a Sunday, and even Polk recorded in his diary that only Black's urgent insistence had gotten him to depart "from my established rule to see no company on the Sabbath." Black wanted Polk to use his influence to postpone a vote on the termination notice for several days until Black had brokered some sort of deal with the southern holdouts, including John C. Calhoun, once again a senator from South Carolina.

Polk was as firm as ever in replying that his position on giving notice was well known and that Congress should act on his recommendation without delay. Black apparently left somewhat calmed, but his visit provided Polk with one of his most often quoted statements on Oregon — even if it was self-quoted in his diary.

"I remarked to him [Black] that the only way to treat John Bull was to look him straight in the eye," the president recorded that evening, and "that I considered a bold and firm course on our part the pacific one; that if Congress faltered or hesitated in their course, John Bull would immediately become arrogant and more grasping in his demands."[16]

For the moment, James K. Polk was standing firm on Oregon.

CHAPTER 11

Eyeing California

$\mathscr{A}$T LEAST THE United States had some measure of legitimate title to Oregon. With Texas, it may or may not have had any legal claim, depending on how far one chose to imagine the boundaries of the Louisiana Purchase. In any event, thirty thousand American settlers in Texas soon made the point moot. But California; California was different. There, the United States could claim no right of discovery, no treaty of cession, no tidal wave of emigration. In California, Americans were operating solely on lust.

$\mathscr{S}$pain's claims to California went all the way back to Magellan and a succession of later expeditions north from Mexico. By the 1770s, the Spaniards had established a series of missions in California along what came to be called the Old Spanish Trail. These included San Diego in 1769 and San Francisco in 1776, the same year that thirteen British colonies across the continent were declaring their independence.

When the Adams-Onís Treaty of 1819 between Spain and the United States fixed the northern boundary of California at the 42nd parallel, it was not to extinguish American claims south of that line: the United States didn't have any. Rather, it was to transfer to the United States tenuous Spanish claims to the Oregon country north of that line.

Meanwhile, despite the Russian-American and Russian-British treaties fixing Alaska's boundary at 54°40', there was one Russian outpost well beyond those limits and deep in Spanish California. This was Fort Ross. The Russians founded it in 1811 some forty-five miles north of San Francisco Bay as an agricultural and hunting base. Reportedly, the Russians paid the Kashaya Native Americans some consideration for the land, but that didn't impress their Spanish landlords. The Spanish protested this Russian intrusion, but relations never deteriorated into open conflict.

In 1833, the Russians tried to purchase the nearby San Rafael and Sonoma missions directly in order to increase agricultural production, but the Spanish—technically now Californios or Mexicans after Mexico had declared its own independence—flatly refused.

When Czar Nicholas I finally gave the order to abandon Fort Ross in 1839, the post's manager first approached the Hudson's Bay Company and then the French about buying it. When neither expressed interest, the Russians turned to the Mexicans, but they were hardly willing to buy what they claimed was theirs by right.

So in 1841, the Russians negotiated a sale of the Fort Ross operation to John Sutter, a German who had already received a nearby land grant. The Mexicans were ecstatic. General Mariano Vallejo advised Governor Juan Bautista Alvarado: "The news I am going to give you is too good for me not to be persuaded that you will share my rejoicing. The Russians are going at last." But unknown to Vallejo, the Americans were coming.[1]

There was no better evidence that the Americans were eyeing California than the unexpected arrival of Commodore Thomas ap Catesby Jones in Monterey, the capital of the Mexican province of Alta (Upper) California. Jones was cut from the same cloth as Old Hickory. In fact, Jones made his reputation in 1814 in a mismatched fight on Lake Borgne between his flotilla of five tiny gunboats and the British invasion fleet attacking New Orleans.

Now, as commander of the five-vessel U.S. Pacific squadron, Jones had been operating out of Callao, Peru, under orders to protect American interests along the Pacific coast. In that age of laborious and frequently tardy communications, part of the job of any military officer was to anticipate.

In September 1842, Jones learned three pieces of information: the British Pacific squadron was sailing under sealed orders, the American consul at Mazatlán advised that war with Mexico appeared imminent over Texas, and a newspaper speculated that Mexico would cede California to Great Britain to pay certain debts. To Jones, this information meant that American interests in California had to be protected, and he set sail northward at once.

On October 18, 1842, a few hours out of Monterey, Jones issued a rather grandiose order to his command. It was "not only our duty to take" California, Jones declared, "but we must keep it afterwards, at all hazards." So, on the afternoon of October 19, Jones sailed into Monterey harbor onboard his flagship, U.S.S. *United States,* and anchored off the presidio. He then boldly sent one of his officers ashore to demand the surrender not just of the town but of all of Alta California—that part of California north of San Diego and Baja (Lower) California.

Juan Bautista Alvarado managed to convince Jones that it was beyond Alvarado's authority to surrender any more of California than Monterey, but with a garrison of only twenty-nine regulars under his command, he would do that immediately. The following day, one hundred fifty American sailors and marines landed to take possession of the presidio. They lowered the Mexican flag and raised the Stars and Stripes for the first time on the Pacific coast south of Oregon. With no legal right to the territory, Commodore Jones had nonetheless boldly asserted the old adage that "possession is nine-tenths of the law." There was only one problem. His anticipation had gotten the better of him.

Scarcely had Old Glory started to wave above Monterey than an American merchant produced recent newspapers that showed, however strained their relations might be, Mexico and the United States were not at war—nor had California been ceded to anyone.

Commodore Jones was forced to do a prompt about-face.

Down came the Stars and Stripes and up went the Mexican eagle again to an apologetic salute fired by the Americans. California had been under the American flag for only about thirty hours, but many thought that it was a good start.[2]

That same year, as it became clear that the negotiations around the Webster-Ashburton Treaty were not going to resolve the Oregon boundary question, President Tyler quietly discussed a sweeping tripartite agreement that addressed Oregon, Texas, *and* California. If nothing else, it showed that Tyler was thinking on a continental scale.

Great Britain was to get its wishes to all of the Oregon territory north of the Columbia River, including Puget Sound. Great Britain would then forgive Mexico's debt to Britain in exchange for Mexico's recognizing the independence of Texas and ceding that part of California north of the 36th parallel to the United States.

Great Britain would have Oregon north of the Columbia, and the United States would have its desired window on the Pacific from the mouth of the Columbia south to near Monterey, including San Francisco Bay. Mexico would receive much-needed international liquidity while retaining most of southern California and almost all of New Mexico. (The 36th parallel runs just north of Santa Fe.)

At one time, Tyler thought the odds of such a three-way deal were high. "Texas might not stand alone," the president told Secretary of State Webster, "nor would the line proposed for Oregon. [But] Texas would reconcile all to the [Oregon] line, while California would reconcile or pacify all to Oregon." Actually, it was shrewd thinking.

It is doubtful, however, that Mexico would have agreed to such a transaction in 1842, and Ashburton made it clear that Great Britain was not willing to broker it. By the time the "54°40' or Fight!" fever reached its peak in early 1846, even Tyler was backpedaling on what his intentions had been. "I never dreamed of ceding this country [Oregon between the Columbia River and the 49th parallel]," he told his son, "unless for the greater equivalent of California."

But had an agreement of this sort been reached in 1842 or 1843, Texas might never have become an issue in the 1844 presidential race, Tyler might even have been elected to a term of his own, and the Mexican-American War might not have been fought. Those are all speculations, but one assessment is certain. If such a deal for Oregon and California had been brokered in 1842, John Tyler would have largely resolved the continental borders of the United States.[3]

𝒯homas O. Larkin had been decidedly embarrassed by Commodore Jones's brash appearance in Monterey. He was the merchant who had produced the newspaper clippings. Larkin was one of the very few Americans not only in Monterey but in all California. In many respects, he was the vanguard.

Born in Massachusetts in 1802, Larkin was the quintessential businessman—well liked and well trusted. Larkin's half brother was a sea captain named John Cooper, who settled in Monterey in 1826 and quickly adopted all tenets of Mexican culture, marrying the sister of General Mariano Vallejo, converting to Catholicism, obtaining Mexican citizenship, and acquiring vast land grants in return. When Larkin followed Cooper and arrived in Monterey in 1832, he chose to do things the American way.

Larkin opened his first store with borrowed money, started a flour mill, and developed a brisk trade with the Boston ships that called. He also courted a young widow whom he had met on the voyage out. Rachel Holmes had gone to Hawaii searching for her sea captain husband, but when she learned for certain that he was dead, she accepted Larkin's letter of proposal and sailed for California. They were married as soon as Rachel's ship anchored at Santa Barbara, the first Protestant marriage in Catholic California. It was a sign that however much the Larkins interacted with Mexican culture, they and their offspring intended to remain American.

As Larkin's businesses flourished, the Larkin home became a requisite stop for many, if not all, of the Americans who passed through California. At first, most came by ship and sailed on, but that began to change in 1841 when the Bidwell-Bartleson party, the first wagon train to traverse the Oregon Trail, split up near Fort Hall. The Bidwell half came to California and stayed.

A handful of additional settlers followed, and on April 2, 1844, Larkin received word of his appointment as the first American consul in California, charged not only with promoting American trade, but also with protecting American interests. Essentially, Consul Larkin was the only representative of the American government west of the Rockies and south of Oregon, albeit still on Mexican soil.

Larkin was also a regular contributor of articles on California to newspapers in Boston and New York. In the aftermath of Commodore Jones's surprise visit, Larkin wrote to James Gordon Bennett at the New York *Herald:* "I imagine that you have never had a correspondent from the 'Far West.' In fact you have not found out as yet where the far famed 'Far West' is."

Larkin's subsequent articles changed that and encouraged the early trickle of emigrants into California. They came seeking the same new land and new opportunities that were luring people to Oregon. Indeed, similar reports had encouraged what seemed like half of Tennessee to head for Texas a decade or two earlier, and it wasn't long before "the Texas game" was on the minds of Mexicans and Americans alike in California.

Larkin's eastern correspondents soon asked him when there would be "enough wild Yankees in California to take the management of affairs in their own hands" and predicted that Americans there would soon be "sufficiently numerous to play the Texas game." In other words, they would make California part of the Union by hook or by crook—conquest, purchase, annexation, independent republic, or any combination thereof.[4]

California was barely mentioned during the campaign of 1844— Texas and Oregon fueled quite enough expansionist fervor—but once inaugurated, James K. Polk confided to George Bancroft that its acquisition was to be one of the four hallmarks of his administration. California, Polk vowed, was to be his own issue.

In championing the annexation of Texas, he had been making

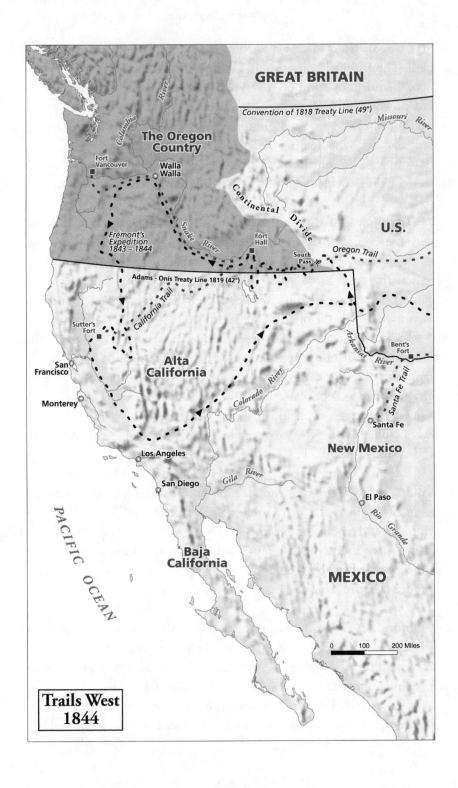

GREAT BRITAIN

Convention of 1818 Treaty Line (49°)

Missouri River

The Oregon
Country

Columbia River

Fort
Vancouver

Walla
Walla

Continental Divide

U.S.

Fort
Hall

Frémont's
Expedition
1843 – 1844

Snake River

South
Pass

Oregon Trail

Adams - Onís Treaty Line 1819 (42°)

California Trail

Sutter's
Fort

Arkansas River

Bent's
Fort

San
Francisco

Alta
California

Colorado River

Santa Fe Trail

Monterey

Santa Fe

New Mexico

Los Angeles

Gila River

San Diego

El Paso

PACIFIC OCEAN

Rio Grande

Baja
California

MEXICO

0   100   200 Miles

**Trails West
1844**

good the desires of Jackson and Tyler. In standing firm on Oregon, he was playing to a significant national sentiment. But Polk's seminal role in making California part and parcel of his continental vision and filling in the gap between Oregon and Texas put him squarely in the vanguard of the most ardent expansionists.[5]

In early June 1845, barely two months into his presidency, Polk's political mouthpiece, the Washington *Union,* sounded the president's expansionist charge for California in decidedly bold terms that made clear that the region would be an integral part of any future settlement with Mexico.

"For who can arrest the torrent that will pour onward to the West?" asked the *Union.* "The road to California will be open to us. Who will stay the march of our western people?" No one, was the *Union's* answer.

And while the United States was ostensibly still at peace with Mexico, the newspaper was not above providing a plausible scenario: "A corps of properly organized volunteers (and they might be obtained from all quarters of the Union) would invade, overrun, and occupy Mexico. They would enable us not only to take California, but to keep it."[6]

Even though Polk was determined to take California, over the course of his first summer in the White House, he got plenty of advice on the matter. The president had appointed his longtime confidant Robert Armstrong as U.S. consul in Liverpool. From there, Armstrong reported the long-standing speculation that Mexico had mortgaged California to Great Britain as security for its foreign debt.

Armstrong could not confirm the mortgage but told Polk that if the president had any reason to believe it, he should never settle the Oregon question short of 54°40′ unless Great Britain gave up any and all claims to land farther south. "England must never have California," Armstrong maintained, "and it seems to me advisable to make Oregon the bone of contention to prevent it. The whole country will sustain you on Oregon."

Indeed, boldness in Polk's actions, as Judge Catron had counseled so many years before, seemed to be now well advised on the international stage. "The expression of American interests has made

England recede from her Texian position," observed Alexander McCall of Virginia, but in return, "she will fix her eye upon California." That move had to be countered with another firm "expression of American interests."

Upon yet another rumor that Mexico was preparing an invasion of Texas, Congressman Stephen A. Douglas of Illinois, who was one of the staunchest "54°40' or Fight!" men, urged Polk: "The northern provinces of Mexico including California ought to belong to this Republic, and the day is not far distant when such a result will be accomplished."

Polk's old friend and emissary to Texas, Archibald Yell, was even more emphatic. "To make your administration bright and glorious," Yell urged from Arkansas, "we want a war with Mexico, and from present appearances we may also be blessed with an opportunity to give the Mexicans a drubbing, (which they have long deserved) and acquire Northern Mexico and Upper California, which has of late become indispensable to the government, to complete our defense and wants on the Pacific."[7]

But some of the correspondence that Polk received on California that summer was decidedly unsolicited and reeked of just the sort of attempts to curry patronage that Polk abhorred. In fact, Albert Fitz's letter of July 10, 1845, was more of a blatant "pay me or I tell the British" threat.

Fitz was one of those self-inflated characters who, having once served briefly as a special agent of the State Department, was now convinced that he alone held the balance of international power. Essentially, Fitz told the president that he had gathered confidential information on behalf of the United States, but had been paid only as a courier and not as a special agent. Fitz also alleged that the American government had broken its promise of future employment. Claiming that the British had approached him with an inviting offer, Fitz now demanded to be rewarded or else.

Great Britain was "eager for information, which I best may give," Fitz told Polk. "Texas and Oregon, and California, have aroused the distrust of far seeing British statesmen." If Fitz were to reveal "the secret acts and intentions of this Republic [the United States], as they were made known to me during 300 days of *special, secret, service,*" England would be most grateful and the information would "excite jealousy and distrust without bounds." To such black-mail, Polk made no reply.[8]

Far more in keeping with the president's continental vision — and in hindsight, quite prophetic — was a series of unsolicited letters he received from Charles Fletcher of Virginia, a clerk in the U.S. General Land Office who was traveling around the Great Lakes. At least six times during 1845, Fletcher wrote Polk promoting Fletcher's own plan to counter British designs on the Pacific coast and make Oregon and California secure.

The answer, Fletcher said, was a transcontinental railroad. Never mind that the Baltimore & Ohio Railroad reached no farther west than Cumberland, Maryland, or that the entire railroad mileage of the country was less than five thousand miles. Fletcher was emphatic. The fears of those who decried the Pacific as too far off were unfounded. "Let this railroad be finished," Fletcher predicted, "and all their arguments will vanish as the distance will be performed from the Pacific to Lake Michigan in ten days."

But that wasn't all. In addition to the railroad, Fletcher foresaw a telegraphic connection between "the capital and Astoria [Oregon] and the president can send an order to the mouth of the Columbia River after breakfast and receive an answer before dinner. These are not mere chimeras," Fletcher continued, "the inventions are already made and there is only wanting the power of government to assist individual enterprises to put them in use."

In yet another letter, Fletcher wrote from Buffalo, New York, in September 1845. He had just watched the steamship *De Witt Clinton,* named after the chief proponent of the Erie Canal, sail off toward the west. Fletcher predicted that it would not be long before "we shall see the locomotive 'President Polk' steaming away across the Rocky Mountains and meeting that great leviathan of the ocean, the steamship 'Star of the East,' just thirty days from Canton." Here was an expansionist visionary who made even Polk, Benton, and Douglas look nearsighted.

When Polk received this latest Fletcher missive, he scribbled the following note on the envelope. It summarized not only Fletcher's many letters but also an entire chapter of westward expansion yet to come. "An interesting essay, in relation to a railroad across the Rocky Mountains to the Pacific Ocean," the president wrote. "Wishes a charter granted to a company, with a grant of public land to aid them in constructing the road."[9]

𝒜ll of this California dreaming came to a head in October 1845, when Secretary of State Buchanan received a letter from the American consul in California. Thomas Larkin's dispatch, dated July 10, contained unsettling news. The Hudson's Bay Company had long furnished Californios with money and arms to deter the central Mexican government from asserting stronger control. These Californios were historically more receptive to amicable trading relations with the Hudson's Bay Company or arriving Americans — whether Larkin or recent overland emigrants — than was the central government in Mexico City.

Now, however, there were rumors that Great Britain was encouraging Mexico City to make a strong show of force in its northern provinces to counter such local autonomy. The Californios would resist this with "the last drop of their blood," Larkin noted, and wished to govern themselves.

Larkin also reported that Great Britain and France had both established consulates in California despite the fact that those offices did not appear to be transacting any commercial business. A French naval vessel had paid a call at Monterey, and a British man-of-war was expected soon. The situation was volatile.[10]

Buchanan discussed Larkin's report with Polk, and the president directed Buchanan to appoint Larkin a confidential agent of the State Department in addition to his duties as consul. Specifically, Buchanan advised Larkin that "should California assert and maintain her independence, we shall render her all the kind offices in our power, as a sister republic." That said, in a precursor to the strong Monroe Doctrine stand that Polk would articulate in his upcoming annual message, Buchanan also made it clear that the United States would "vigorously interpose" any European interference in California.

"The future destiny of that country [California] is a subject of anxious solicitude for the Government and people of the United

States," Buchanan wrote. "This government has no ambitious aspirations to gratify and no desire to extend our federal system over more territory than we already possess, unless"— hint, hint—"by the free and spontaneous wish of the independent people of adjoining territories." In other words, the government of the United States would gladly play "the Texas game" once again.

"Whilst the President will make no effort and use no influence to induce California to become one of the free and independent states of this Union," Buchanan concluded, "yet if the people should desire to unite their destiny with ours, they would be received as brethren, whenever this can be done without affording Mexico just cause of complaint."[11]

That was the official version—sufficiently respectful of Mexico in the event that the dispatch should fall into the wrong hands. It was entrusted to Commodore Robert F. Stockton, the same officer who had been in command of the U.S.S. *Princeton* on that tragic day on the Potomac. Stockton proceeded immediately to Norfolk, Virginia, and embarked for California via Cape Horn on board the frigate U.S.S. *Congress*. He sailed under sealed orders from Secretary of the Navy Bancroft that were not to be opened until his ship cleared the Virginia capes. Upon arriving in California, the commodore was to "do all in your power to conciliate the good feeling of the people of that place towards the United States."

If that failed, there was another option. Stockton was scheduled to take over command of the U.S. Pacific squadron from Commodore John D. Sloat, who was retiring—both in personality and from the service. Sloat's latest orders from Bancroft instructed the commodore to seize San Francisco and blockade Monterey if he were to "ascertain with certainty"—a reminder of Commodore Jones's indiscretion—that a state of war existed between Mexico and the United States. Stockton's new orders took that directive a step further. In the event of actual hostilities, the commodore was to disperse his forces—on land and at sea—to grab as much territory as he could.[12]

By sea around the horn, it would take Stockton at least six months to reach California. Time, Polk and Buchanan reasoned, was of the essence, and they quickly devised a backup plan calculated to reach Larkin sooner. Late in the evening on October 30, 1845, Polk received Lieutenant Archibald H. Gillespie of the United States Marine Corps at the White House.

Gillespie was given a copy of Buchanan's written instructions to Larkin and instructed to deliver them by way of the sea and a crossing of Mexico across the Isthmus of Tehuantepec. If questioned, Larkin's cover was that he was a representative of a Boston trading company who was undertaking the journey for his health. (How a crossing of the fever-ridden jungles of the Isthmus of Tehuantepec could be viewed as medicinal is an entirely different matter!)

But if Lieutenant Gillespie was a mere courier—no matter how clandestine—why did he meet with the president of the United States before departing? Even Polk was unusually circumspect in his diary and recorded only that he had "a confidential conversation" with Gillespie "on the subject of a secret mission on which he was about to go to California."

That there was more than just the letter to Larkin seems to be borne out by the president's observation that Gillespie's "secret instructions and the letter to Mr. Larkin . . . will explain the object of his mission." Apparently, Gillespie carried with him additional verbal messages for Stockton, Larkin, and one other agent of the United States government who just happened to be in the field, conveniently camouflaged as a surveyor.[13]

𝒥ohn Charles Frémont was, and remains, something of an enigma. To his defenders, Frémont will always be "the Pathfinder of the West," the quintessential explorer marching westward, ever westward. To his detractors, Frémont was an opportunistic bungler, a man who—had it not been for the political connections and journalistic talents of his wife and the dedicated services of his mountain man guides, including Kit Carson—might have simply marched off history's map.

As usual with someone who elicits such strong and divergent passions, the truth lies somewhere in between. Certainly, there is no denying that the West is covered with place-names—Frémont peaks, lakes, rivers, towns, and counties—that mark his paths.

John Charles Fremon, as his name was then spelled, was born in Savannah, Georgia, on January 21, 1813. His young mother, Anne Pryor, was legally married to a country gentleman more than forty years her senior, but it was her French teacher, Charles Fremon, who was the father of her firstborn. No divorce was ever granted, but Anne and Charles stayed together and had two more children before his untimely death in 1817.

According to Frémont family legend, in the course of their wanderings, the young couple, with baby John Charles in tow, was staying in a Nashville hotel when a bullet from the infamous Jackson-Benton gunfight came crashing through the wall.

The stigma of illegitimacy affected young Fremon deeply, but growing up in Charleston, South Carolina, he managed to rise above it. He adopted the spelling "Frémont," excelled at mathematics, and found a mentor in fellow South Carolinian Joel Poinsett, who was to become Van Buren's secretary of war. After Frémont learned his surveying skills on several railroad projects in the Appalachians, Poinsett secured his participation on Joseph Nicollet's 1838 and 1839 surveys of the country between the upper Mississippi and Missouri watersheds, in what is now western Minnesota and the eastern Dakotas.

As a twenty-eight-year-old lieutenant in the army corps of engineers, Frémont was in Washington in April 1841 working on maps and reports from these surveys when he graciously invited Senator Thomas Hart Benton and his family to watch the funeral procession of William Henry Harrison from his office window.

Benton and Frémont had recently become acquainted over their mutual western interests, but Frémont's real preoccupation was Benton's sixteen-year-old daughter, Jessie, who returned the officer's affections all too readily. When Benton discovered the mutual attraction, he promptly arranged for Frémont to spend the summer surveying on the Des Moines River. The absence did nothing to cool the ardor, however, and the couple was secretly married on October 19, 1841.

When the newlyweds confronted Jessie's father with the news, Old Bullion fumed and thundered, but soon reconciled to the fact that his strong-willed daughter would have her way. Much as Joel

Poinsett had already done, Benton set about keeping his new son-in-law in good stead with the army corps of engineers.

That summer of 1842, Lieutenant Frémont headed west along the faint traces of the Oregon Trail to document its cornerstone crossing of the Continental Divide at South Pass. In the process, he climbed a high peak in the Wind River Range—mountaineering historians will forever debate which one—and came home to Jessie that fall with enough adventures to fill a book.

Indeed, that is what happened. With the aid of Jessie's editorial direction, Frémont's report of what is routinely called his "First Expedition" was quickly published. It became not only a widely read adventure story—unfurling Old Glory atop some rocky snow-covered summit, no matter which one it really was, made for exciting reading—as well as an early guidebook for those heading west along the Oregon Trail.

Scarcely was the report published when Frémont was ordered on March 11, 1843, to head west once again. This time, he was charged with finding another crossing of the Continental Divide south of South Pass and continuing through the southern Oregon country to link his surveys with those of Charles Wilkes. In essence, Frémont was to map the void between the Rockies and the Sierra Nevadas.

Though ostensibly on a peaceful scientific expedition, Frémont requested Colonel Stephen Watts Kearny, the commander of the third military department at Jefferson Barracks, Saint Louis, to provide him with a mountain howitzer and five hundred pounds of artillery ammunition. Kearny was skeptical of the need, but because Frémont's connections to Senator Benton were so well known, Kearny reluctantly agreed. He did, however, report the matter to his superiors. By the time John J. Abert, the chief of the corps of engineers, wrote to Frémont questioning the requisition, Jessie saw to it that her husband was well westward.

Traveling up the Kansas, Republican, and South Platte rivers, Frémont visited two bastions of the fur trade on Colorado's high plains, Fort St. Vrain and Bent's Fort, and then angled northwest into the drainage of the North Platte. Contrary to the orders, he soon found himself again at South Pass and quickly learned what later surveyors would come to know: there is no easy pass through the Colorado Rockies.

So from Fort Hall, Frémont continued on to Oregon and in the process speculated that rather than there being one great river draining the heart of the American West, as had been long suspected, there was one great *basin* sucking in rivers from all points of the compass.

From Whitman's mission, Frémont's party continued down the Columbia and then in November 1843, despite the lateness of the season, headed south toward Klamath Lake to prove that no mythical San Buenaventura River drained westward from the Great Basin. At some point, Frémont crossed south over the 42nd parallel and entered Mexican territory.

By mid-January, the expedition was on the shores of Pyramid Lake. A few days later, on a river flowing eastward that Frémont would name after his guide, Kit Carson, Frémont determined to turn west and cross the towering barrier of the Sierra Nevada in the dead of winter. It was a grueling experience for man and beast, and somewhere west of present-day Bridgeport, California, they were forced to abandon Frémont's cherished howitzer, setting the stage for one of history's most celebrated treasure hunts. Six weeks later, Frémont and his advance group stumbled into Sutter's Fort, alive, but barely.

After recovering under Sutter's hospitality, Frémont took his party south through California's Central Valley in a grand circle around the Sierra Nevadas, crossing eastward back into the Great Basin via Cajon Pass and the Old Spanish Trail. By the time he finally returned to Saint Louis in August 1844, Jessie was frantic with worry, but there was little doubt that when it came to making maps of the West, her husband had become the acknowledged expert.[14]

Once again, the young couple—Jessie was still only twenty years old—spent a winter in Washington working on the expedition report. As befitting the geography it covered, this report of the second expedition was three times longer than the first and received even higher praise. In one of his last acts as a senator before joining Polk's Cabinet, James Buchanan made the motion to print an additional five thousand copies.

The Frémonts were in demand on the social circuit that winter, and while Jessie enjoyed the good graces of Sarah Polk, her husband and her father called on the president-elect to discuss the western landscape. Frémont described the Great Basin for Polk and noted his conclusion that the San Buenaventura and two other rivers thought to drain the Great Salt Lake existed only in the minds of earlier cartographers. But according to Frémont, Polk "found me 'young' and said something of the 'impulsiveness of young men,' and was not at all satisfied in his own mind that those three rivers were not running there as laid down."[15]

Nevertheless, these three men, Polk, Benton, and Frémont, shared an affinity for California. Frémont was quickly dispatched westward on his third expedition. His official orders called for him to return to the central Rockies, map the headwaters of the Arkansas, and return east the same year. But given his previous trip and his close ties to Benton, few were surprised when the fall of 1845 found Frémont not returning to Westport Landing but arriving instead at Sutter's Fort, having crossed the Great Basin and the Sierra Nevadas via Donner Pass.

Frémont's limited orders aside, Polk was well aware of the surveyor's wider itinerary. After the president's visit with Senator Benton on October 24, 1845, Polk noted in his diary that "some conversation occurred [with Benton] concerning Captain Frémont's expedition, and his intention to visit California before his return." Questions about how wide-ranging Frémont's discretion was to be on that visit and what possible actions Benton, or even the president, may have told Frémont to anticipate, would only add to the subsequent intrigue.[16]

𝒜mong those who were surprised—and a little dismayed—by Frémont's arrival in California was John Sutter. A few American emigrants coming out of the hills was one thing, but an American army "surveying" party whose self-important leader almost demanded to be resupplied was quite another. Sutter, whose own little fiefdom was conditioned on good relations with his Mexican neighbors, promptly informed Mariano Vallejo and Thomas Larkin of Frémont's arrival.

By January 27, 1846, Frémont and a small advance party reached Monterey. Like so many Americans before him, Frémont availed himself of the hospitality of Thomas and Rachel Larkin. The American consul even advanced the surveyor eighteen hundred dollars to ease the purchase of supplies from Sutter. When local Mexican officials questioned Larkin about why an American army officer was lodged in his house, Larkin assured them that Frémont had come only to rest his men and replenish supplies before pushing northward to Oregon.

Frémont received official Mexican permission to do so and established a small camp near San Jose. There, Frémont's party was reunited with a larger detachment led by mountain man Joseph Walker that had separated from Frémont in the Great Basin and circled the main Sierra Nevada to enter the Central Valley from the south. Suddenly, the Americans had an armed force of sixty men near Monterey. By Californio standards, those numbers made for a small army.

Frémont compounded the fears of local Mexican officials by acting quite rudely in his dealings with them and then moving his entire command south from San Jose—back toward Monterey—rather than retiring northward toward Oregon as he had been requested to do. When more letters of protest reached him, Frémont complicated the situation by establishing a fortified camp atop Gavilan Peak (Hawks Peak) and raising the American flag. Mexican general José Castro called out his militia and moved forward with about two hundred men to dislodge the Americans.

All of this was a little too strong a playing of "the Texas hand" even for Thomas Larkin, and he quickly tried to defuse the crisis. Meanwhile, the question that Larkin had to be asking himself was, What in the world was Frémont trying to prove? It seemed that even Frémont didn't know the answer to that. For all of Larkin's role as the American consul, he could only assume that this famous son-in-law of one of the country's most powerful United States senators had his instructions from the highest levels.

As it turned out, the potential confrontation at Gavilan Peak evaporated on the night of March 9, 1846, when Frémont quietly abandoned his makeshift fortification and slowly started north for

Oregon. He was in no hurry, however, and he spent considerable time in the Sacramento Valley.

Some American settlers there saw him and his armed force as their ticket toward independence. John Sutter saw it as just the opposite, and he warned General Castro about Frémont's seemingly erratic movements. "Flitting about the country with an armed body of men," Sutter later recalled, Frémont "was regarded with suspicion by everybody."

And Larkin was to have no respite, either, for even as Frémont distanced himself from Monterey, the equally pompous Lieutenant Archibald H. Gillespie landed in town on April 17, 1846. Gillespie promptly delivered to Larkin a copy of Buchanan's letter to him of the previous October. The original was still on its way via Commodore Stockton, but Larkin now learned that one way or the other, his consular duties put him square in the midst of American intrigue in California. "The pear is near ripe for falling," Larkin reported to American businessman William Leidesdorff in Yerba Buena (San Francisco) a few days later.[17]

Meanwhile, Lieutenant Gillespie hurried north with personal letters for Frémont from Jessie, as well as letters from Benton and Buchanan. Doubtless Gillespie's assertion to Larkin that he had come directly from the president of the United States and needed to reach Frémont only heightened Larkin's impression that these two were the ultimate insiders. Certainly, family letters hardly demanded Gillespie's personal rush northward.

Two weeks later, in the early dawn of May 9, 1846, on the southern shores of Upper Klamath Lake, Lieutenant Gillespie rode into Frémont's camp. What conversations occurred between the two young army officers remain a mystery. What seems almost certain, however, is that each thought the other to be more of an insider than he really was. Frémont was impressed that the president of the United States had sent a messenger across the continent to find him. Gillespie was under the impression that the son-in-law of Thomas Hart Benton was on the scene with far more than a passing interest in the developing internal politics of California.

"I saw the way opening clear before me," Frémont would later write. "War with Mexico was inevitable; and a grand opportunity now presented itself to realize in their fullest extent the far-sighted views of Senator Benton, and make the Pacific Ocean the western boundary of the United States. I resolved to move forward on the opportunity."[18] Little did Frémont know how convoluted his path would become.

CHAPTER 12

Mission to Mexico

𝒠VEN AS JAMES K. POLK went about the Oregon and California goals of his administration, there was still considerable uncertainty about whether or not the United States would have to fight for Texas. Sam Houston would soon arrive in Washington as one of the new state's first senators; meanwhile, Mexico was hardly appeased. And even if Mexico did acquiesce to the annexation, the nagging question of its boundary with Texas had never been resolved. Was the Texas border the Nueces River or the Rio Grande?

Many in Texas had resolutely claimed the Rio Grande as their western boundary as far back as 1836. As the Texas congress convened in the summer of 1845 to approve the joint resolution of annexation, Polk was determined to stand by those claims.

On the same day that he ordered American army and naval units into Texas in anticipation of annexation, Polk advised Andrew Jackson Donelson that he would "maintain the Texas title to the extent which she claims it to be, and not permit an invading enemy to occupy a foot of the soil east of the Rio Grande."

Brigadier General Zachary Taylor, who was in command of the

army units moving into Texas from Fort Jesup, Louisiana, was told in no uncertain terms that "the Rio Grande is claimed to be the boundary between the two countries." In deploying his troops, Taylor was ordered "to approach as near the boundary line, the Rio Grande, as prudence will dictate."

Prudence momentarily halted Taylor at Corpus Christi at the mouth of the Nueces River and at San Antonio, but that did not stop Polk from continuing to voice the more expansive claim. "General Taylor at the head of our whole western forces is on the march to the western frontier," the president advised Robert Armstrong in Liverpool, "and will occupy the country on the Rio Grande."

There seems little doubt that Polk was firmly committed to this position, although some of his tougher statements may have been political posturing for the benefit of Mexico. In the same letter to Armstrong, Polk confided that he had "little apprehension of war" but wanted the United States to be "fully prepared to protect and defend Texas against the aggressions of Mexico if she shall make such."

It is also very clear that Polk would not be swayed from his continental vision and that he saw the pieces of Oregon, California, and Texas as interrelated. On August 29, 1845, the very day that Polk approved the final draft of Buchanan's letter withdrawing a compromise offer on Oregon, the president expanded Taylor's orders in Texas.

Any crossing of the Rio Grande by a Mexican army in force was to be regarded as an act of war. If Taylor deemed it advisable, he was to attack first and not wait to be attacked. And in that event, while Taylor was not authorized to penetrate any great distance into Mexico, the general was nonetheless charged with taking Matamoros on the south bank of the Rio Grande and any other Mexican positions along the river.[1]

*B*ut for all of his posturing and military preparations, Polk was also seeking a peaceful resolution with Mexico—particularly if it could be accomplished in a way that had most of California and New Mexico dropping into the American orbit. Mexico had severed diplomatic relations with the United States in March 1845 when Juan Almonte stormed out of Washington in response to Tyler's signing the joint resolution for annexation. Secretary of State Buchanan soon recalled the American minister, who had not been helping matters by carrying on a "needlessly angry correspondence" with the Mexican foreign minister, and then set about finding a new person to do the administration's bidding.

Polk and Buchanan's goal appeared to be a fresh start in rebuilding relations between the two countries by appointing someone "unknown to the Mexicans and against whom they have no personal prejudice." Unfortunately, the man they chose fit neither requirement.

His name was William S. Parrott, a sometime dentist from Virginia who spoke fluent Spanish and who had been engaged in extensive business dealings in Mexico over the years. As such, Parrott was both known and despised in Mexico because he was among the Americans aggressively pursuing commercial claims against the Mexican government for goods previously sold to it.

Polk had a long history of dispatching trusted lieutenants to do his bidding when the stakes were high. Cave Johnson, Gideon Pillow, and Archibald Yell come to mind. Nevertheless, Polk agreed with Buchanan on this appointment and commissioned the self-serving Parrott to return to Mexico City as a secret agent. Parrott was to convince the Mexican government of the benefits of restoring some measure of diplomatic relations.

If Parrott found a receptive audience, he was to reveal his official capacity and announce that the United States would gladly send a minister to Mexico as soon as there was an expression that he would be received. Buchanan's instructions to Parrott also made it quite clear, however, that the annexation of Texas was a done deal and "can never under any circumstances be abandoned."[2]

𝒯he major problem with any mission to Mexico, however, was that the political situation south of the Rio Grande was convoluted at best. For almost two decades, Antonio López de Santa Anna had cast a huge shadow across the Mexican landscape, but not without facing bitter rivalries and ever-changing loyalties. Santa Anna had

come to prominence in 1829 at the age of thirty-five when he successfully repulsed an attempt by Spain to reclaim the country.
Hailed as a hero, Santa Anna was elected president of Mexico in
1833, but he soon dissolved the congress and declared himself dic-
tator.

In 1836, Santa Anna marched north to quell the American up-
starts in Texas and presided over the siege of the Alamo. After Sam
Houston literally caught him napping at the battle of San Jacinto,
Santa Anna signed a treaty recognizing Texas independence, but
both Santa Anna and those who came to power in Mexico City in
his absence soon repudiated it.

Returning to Mexico, Santa Anna spent three years in the political wilderness while Anastasio Bustamante served as president.
Then Santa Anna once again rushed to the forefront to thwart a
French occupation of Veracruz in a dispute over Mexico's foreign
debt. In the process, he lost the lower half of his left leg but endeared himself to the Mexican people.

By 1841, Santa Anna was once again president of Mexico,
counting among his allies General Mariano Paredes y Arrillaga, the
commander of troops in the northern part of the country. But the
chronic problems of an empty national treasury, fractious internal
friction, a civil war in Yucatán, and continuing border strife over
Texas remained no matter who was president. When many Mexicans, including General Paredes, had finally had enough of Santa
Anna's self-indulgence — reburying his severed limb with elaborate
pomp and ceremony was just one example — Paredes issued a revo-
lutionary *pronunciamiento*, protesting both Santa Anna's excesses
and his high level of taxation.

Santa Anna moved north to challenge Paredes with an army
that had questionable loyalties, and in his absence, José Joaquin
Herrera was named interim president late in 1844. Santa Anna
sailed away to Cuba soon afterward, supposedly banished from
Mexico for life.

Herrera was left to run a government with Paredes looking over
his shoulder and questioning every move he made. It didn't help
matters that Herrera tended to attract moderates who might have

been willing to reach some accommodation over Texas, while Paredes became the champion of the *puros* who saw Texas as just the first
grab of a rampant American imperialism.[3]

𝒮ecret agent William Parrott sailed south for Mexico into this sea
of political instability. Ironically, he left New York on the same vessel bearing the departing Mexican minister. As might have been expected, Parrott was not warmly received upon his arrival at
Veracruz, and he appears to have kept a low profile for several
months.

Nonetheless, by late August 1845, Parrott wrote Buchanan that
it was his firm belief that Mexican foreign minister Manuel de la
Peña y Peña was receptive to receiving an envoy from the United
States. Someone "possessing suitable qualifications for this court,"
Parrott maintained, "might with comparative ease, settle, over a
breakfast, the most important national question." But Parrott also
warned that any negotiations would have to be conducted quietly
lest the opposition to Herrera's government trumpet them as a sign
of weakness.[4]

Buchanan presented Parrott's communication to the full Cabinet meeting on September 16, 1845. All members agreed that "it
was expedient to re-open diplomatic relations with Mexico," but
that they should be kept secret so that the British, French, and
other foreign ministers in Washington would not "take measures to
thwart or defeat the objects of the mission."

Polk made very clear in his diary that evening exactly what
those objects were to be. "One great object of the mission," the president claimed, "would be to adjust a permanent boundary between
Mexico and the United States" that would include the purchase of
California and New Mexico. Polk proposed that the boundary be
the Rio Grande as far as El Paso and then the 32nd parallel west to
the Pacific. Guessing that this territory might be had for "fifteen or
twenty millions," the president nonetheless acknowledged privately
that he was "ready to pay forty millions for it."[5]

To carry out this delicate mission, Polk now chose as his special
envoy John Slidell, a native of New York who had moved to New

Orleans to practice law in 1819. Old Hickory had appointed Slidell the U.S. attorney for the eastern district of Louisiana during his first term. Elected to the House of Representatives in 1843, Slidell was willing to resign his seat in order to embark on Polk's mission, and from all appearances he could be counted on to exercise discretion and unswerving presidential loyalty.

But no sooner had Polk decided to dispatch Slidell than Buchanan presented the Cabinet with recent New Orleans newspapers that suggested Mexican officials would not be nearly as receptive to an American envoy as Parrott had boasted. Polk directed Buchanan to ascertain through formal channels—in this case the American consul in Veracruz, John Black—whether or not Slidell would be received.[6]

This additional exchange of letters took time, and it was November 6, 1845, before Polk received a response from Black that Mexico was indeed willing to talk. Three days later, William Parrott showed up in Washington and reiterated the same view. Despite Peña y Peña's warning that Parrott was anathema to most Mexican officials, Polk nonetheless immediately proceeded to appoint Parrott secretary of the American legation and send him back to Mexico City. But in moving ahead with John Slidell, Polk and Buchanan, unwittingly or not, committed an even graver diplomatic faux pas.

Peña y Peña's letter to Black inviting negotiations specifically called for Polk to appoint a commissioner charged with full authority to resolve all matters. Instead, Polk appointed Slidell a full-fledged ambassador—in diplomatic language, an envoy extraordinary and minister plenipotentiary.

The latter was predicated on the restoration of full diplomatic relations between the two countries—something that the weak Herrera government was in no position to accept without some face-saving measure. Whether this was a deliberate attempt by Polk and Buchanan only to appear to negotiate in good faith seems doubtful, but it does seem out of character for both men to have made this error.

In any event, Buchanan gave Slidell a detailed list of instructions and a shopping list for possible negotiation scenarios. First and most preferable to the Polk administration, Mexico would accept the Rio Grande boundary and cede New Mexico and at least as much of California as would include both Monterey and San Francisco. In return, the United States would assume all American commercial claims against Mexico—judged to be about five million dollars—and pay an additional twenty-five million dollars. If Mexico insisted on retaining Monterey, the additional compensation fell to twenty million dollars.

If Mexico was unwilling to cede California, Slidell was still authorized to assume the American claims and pay five million dollars for the Rio Grande boundary and all of New Mexico north of El Paso. Finally, Slidell's last-ditch effort was to secure the Rio Grande boundary to its headwaters in exchange for an American assumption of claims. This would have had the effect of transferring all of present-day New Mexico and southern Colorado east of the Rio Grande, including Santa Fe, to the United States.

Polk, too, wrote to Slidell, and while he claimed to have "but little to add" to Buchanan's instructions, he was again very clear in stating his objective. "I will say however," the president emphasized, "that I am exceedingly desirous to acquire *California,* and am ready to take the whole responsibility, if it cannot be had for less, of paying the whole amount authorized by your instructions. If you can acquire both *New Mexico* and *California,* for the sum authorized, the nation I have no doubt will approve the act."[7]

But how did Polk manage to reconcile his stated goal of California with the last-ditch option of just the Rio Grande boundary in Slidell's instructions? Quite likely, he simply assumed that should Mexico agree to settle the Texas boundary only at the Rio Grande, Larkin, Frémont, and Gillespie would see to it that "the Texas hand" was played out in California. It might take a little longer than if Slidell could arrange a one-stop shopping trip, but it would happen in due course.

*W*hen Slidell arrived in Veracruz on November 29, 1845, the Herrera government was on the verge of collapse. Slidell's mission was hardly a secret. Paredes was loudly accusing Herrera of being too soft in the face of American aggression, and the slightest sign of conciliation on his government's part was likely to bring it down.

"A few months more and we shall have no country at all," wrote *La voz del pueblo* as it gave full details of Slidell's intended purchase and urged the people to resist it. Peña y Peña refused to see Slidell and used as his excuse Slidell's full diplomatic rank rather than his appearing as a mere commissioner.

That left Slidell little to do but wait expectantly for a likely change in government. Writing to Polk on December 29, Slidell confessed that "a war would probably be the best mode of settling our affairs with Mexico, but the failure of the negotiation will be very disagreeable and mortifying to me." He also reported that troops loyal to Paredes were within three leagues of the capital.

On January 2, 1846, Herrera's government fell, and Slidell looked around to see if he might be accorded a better reception from the new Paredes government. But Paredes had come to power in large part on a platform of blustering anti-Americanism, and he was hardly about to sit down and suddenly appear conciliatory.

Slidell waited expectantly for another two months, but the Paredes government finally notified him on March 12, 1846, that he would not be received. "Be assured," Slidell advised Buchanan as he packed his bags for the United States, "that nothing is to be done with these people, until they shall have been chastised."[8]

That was indeed the opinion to which Polk was coming, reluctantly or not. Upon learning of the Herrera government's initial rejection of Slidell, Polk ordered General Taylor to advance from Corpus Christi—something Taylor had already received the discretion to do—and assume a position on the Rio Grande. In the dead of winter—even winter in south Texas—Taylor was slow to do this, and in the meantime, another unlikely soldier of fortune presented himself to Polk at the White House.

He was Colonel Alexander J. Atocha, a Spaniard who was nonetheless an American citizen and one of those holding claims against the Mexican government. In other words, he, like William Parrott, had a vested interest in a peaceful settlement, in which their claims against an empty Mexican treasury would be converted into U.S. dollars. Atocha had an interesting proposition, and Polk, usually not one to fall for a fast-talker—he had, after all, had plenty of experience with Lean Jimmy Jones—appears to have nibbled at the bait.

Atocha purported to be on friendly terms with Santa Anna, currently in exile in Cuba. If Santa Anna should be able to return to Mexico, Atocha hinted, he might well return to power. Then, in order to raise funds and credit for his new government, Santa Anna might be willing to make a cession of certain northern lands in exchange for cash and an assumption of claims. Atocha expressed surprise that an American naval squadron had been withdrawn from Veracruz in order to benefit the Slidell mission and that Taylor had so far advanced only to Corpus Christi. The only way to deal with Mexico, Atocha asserted, was with a show of force.

Polk went to great lengths in his diary to record his conversations with Atocha—the president saw him twice more three days later—and reported his suggestions to the Cabinet. Treasury Secretary Walker was inclined to send an agent to confer with Santa Anna. Buchanan was adamantly opposed both to that suggestion and to Atocha's bravado that Slidell's purchase offers were best delivered from the deck of an American warship in Veracruz harbor.

Momentarily, Atocha faded into the background. He would return some months later to renew his proposal as a shadowy agent of Santa Anna, but in the meantime, his assertion that the United States should deal firmly with Mexico may have hardened Polk's resolve that he was doing the right thing. The truth was, of course, that having long felt at the end of an American bayonet, Mexico was only repulsed all the more by what it considered American arrogance.[9]

Some historians have questioned Polk's sincerity in dispatching John Slidell to Mexico. They claim that Polk was determined to have war with Mexico and that Slidell's mission was simply diplomatic window dressing so that the United States could be said to have exhausted all reasonable avenues short of war.

As evidence that Polk and Buchanan were purposely argumentative, these commentators cite the dispatch of a full-fledged minister, the return of the offensive Dr. Parrott, and the up-front American statement that the annexation of Texas was a settled fact, the latter despite Peña y Peña's warning of Mexico's need to exact adequate reparation. (There might, after all, have been some face-saving gesture toward Mexico that in no way would have changed the fact that Texas was now part and parcel of the United States.)

But if Polk was so determined on war, why was he so infatuated with Colonel Atocha's proposition? The better reading suggests that Polk was indeed determined—not to have war with Mexico, but rather to have Texas to the Rio Grande and also New Mexico and California. If this could be accomplished short of war, so be it, particularly because it was far from certain at this point that the debate over Oregon would be resolved without war. Polk was not averse to war with Mexico, but all of his public and private positioning suggests that he saw war as only one of many means of achieving his territorial goals.[10]

On April 7, 1846, the president received word in Washington that the Paredes government had refused to receive Slidell and that the envoy had demanded his passport and was returning home. Polk was determined to apply to Congress for—in his words to Slidell of five months earlier—"the proper remedies," but decided to wait until Slidell returned to Washington and briefed him in person. In reality, however, since he had already ordered Zachary Taylor forward to the Rio Grande, events half a continent away were increasingly beyond Polk's control.

The Polk administration's man on the scene on the Rio Grande was definitely far more soldier than diplomat. Zachary Taylor was born on November 24, 1784, in Virginia, but even then his father, Richard, was in the process of moving to lands near Louisville, Kentucky. Young Zachary would always consider himself a farmer, but he also became a lifelong soldier, receiving his commission as a first lieutenant in 1808 at the age of twenty-three.

Taylor saw only one major engagement during the War of 1812, but he was marked as a man to stand firm when his staunch defense saved the small frontier post of Fort Harrison on the Wabash. Later, his service record became a roll call of the frontier, from the Black Hawk War in Wisconsin to the Seminole War in Florida. By the Florida campaigns, Taylor had won a brevet promotion to brigadier general and acquired the nickname "Old Rough and Ready" for his willingness to share the hardships of his troops.

Along the way, one of his daughters, Sarah Knox Taylor, fell in love with a young officer in his command named Jefferson Davis. Taylor knew the hardships of army life only too well, and he opposed the marriage. Davis's solution was to resign from the army and elope, but tragically, Sarah died within months of setting off for the Davis plantation in Mississippi.

By the spring of 1844, with tensions mounting over the annexation of Texas, General Taylor was ordered to Fort Jesup to take command of the Corps of Observation. This force had been formed to monitor the uneasy situation with Mexico and to stand ready to assist Texas should it be invaded. Once annexation was assured, Taylor moved some four thousand troops forward to Corpus Christi and—per Polk's orders of January 13, 1846—advanced to the Rio Grande in March to construct Fort Texas opposite Matamoros.[11]

Reinforcements quickly arrived on the Mexican side of the Rio Grande, and on April 12, General Pedro de Ampudia sent Taylor a letter demanding that the Americans immediately withdraw to behind the Nueces. This Taylor refused to do, and instead he asked his naval counterparts to blockade the mouth of the Rio Grande, effectively isolating Matamoros from the gulf.

At least some officers among Taylor's command had their doubts about their mission. "We have not one particle of right to be here," Colonel Ethan Allan Hitchcock confessed in his diary. "Our force is altogether too small for the accomplishment of its errand. It looks as if the government sent a small force on purpose to bring on a war, so as to have a pretext for taking California and as much of this country as it chooses."[12]

An uneasy standoff continued between the two forces, and in the interim, General Mariano Arista arrived to take command on the Mexican side. Brash and boastful with a bushy beard of red hair, Arista had refused to support Paredes's revolution against Herrera and seemed to have been left to his own devices in the north. Arista promptly informed Taylor that he was of the opinion that war had begun and that he intended to prosecute it.

Taylor's response was to reinforce his patrols. In the early morning of April 25, 1846, Captain Seth Thornton led two companies of dragoons (essentially heavily armed cavalry or mounted infantry) some twenty-five miles upstream on the north bank of the Rio Grande to investigate reports of large numbers of Mexican cavalry crossing the river. Arriving at a small ranch, Thornton's patrol stopped to investigate a stockade of chaparral. While they were inside, a force of several hundred Mexican cavalry surrounded them and cut off their retreat. In the fight that followed, eleven American dragoons were killed and twenty-six others were captured, including Captain Thornton.

In announcing the skirmish to Washington the next day, Taylor was matter-of-fact: "Hostilities," Old Rough and Ready reported, "may now be considered as commenced."[13]

"American Blood upon American Soil"

$\mathcal{T}$HREE DAYS AFTER the attack on Thornton's patrol, President Polk discussed what he termed "the Mexican question" with his Cabinet. Given the two- to three-week delay in communications from the Texas frontier, all were ignorant of recent events there and Taylor's pronouncement that hostilities had begun. Nonetheless, while they waited for John Slidell to arrive in Washington, there was growing concern that after the refusal of the Paredes government to receive him, the only effective recourse was war.

It was now Polk's opinion, and the unanimous opinion of his Cabinet as well, that the president should follow through with his plan to send a message to Congress "laying the whole subject before them." In doing so, Polk proposed to recommend that "measures be adopted to take redress into our own hands for the aggravated wrongs done to our citizens in their persons and property in Mexico." With no report of military hostilities yet in hand, Polk's mention of "wrongs" could refer only to the various commercial claims against the Mexican government. He requested that Buchanan "prepare from the archives of the Department of State a succinct history of these wrongs as a basis of a message to Congress."[1]

On Sunday, May 3, 1846, as was his custom, the president attended the First Presbyterian Church with Sarah and two of their nieces. That evening, despite his aversion to Sunday callers, he requested a meeting with Thomas Hart Benton. Old Bullion cheerfully called at the White House and listened as Polk reviewed the state of relations with Mexico. When Polk asked for Benton's views, the senator replied that he had not completely made up his mind, but advised delay until the Oregon question was resolved.

Benton did express "a decided aversion to war with Mexico if it could be avoided consistently with the honor of the country." Polk assured Benton that there was ample cause for war, but that he, too, was "anxious to avoid it if it could be done honorably." Polk again pledged not to do anything until Slidell arrived, but impressed upon Benton that he simply "could not permit Congress to adjourn without bringing the subject before that body."[2]

On May 5, the Cabinet held its regular Tuesday meeting. The subject of Mexico and "the possibility of a collision between the American and Mexican forces" was again a chief topic of conversation, although no dispatch had been received from General Taylor since that dated April 6 — *before* General Ampudia's demand that the Americans withdraw to behind the Nueces.

The following evening, dispatches from General Taylor dated as late as April 15 arrived. There was still no report of an "actual collision," although Polk confided to his diary that "the probabilities are that hostilities might take place soon." Vice President Dallas, who, as was then the custom, did not attend Cabinet meetings, Secretary of State Buchanan, Secretary of War Marcy, and Polk's one-time convention foe Senator Lewis Cass of Michigan met with the president to discuss the situation and "the condition of our army."[3]

On Friday morning, May 8, the wait for John Slidell was over. Buchanan and Slidell arrived at the White House, and after a few minutes together, Buchanan retired and left Polk to confer alone with Slidell for about an hour. Slidell repeated his previously expressed views "that but one course towards Mexico was left to the

United States." Polk concurred and assured Slidell that he would be making a communication to Congress about Mexico very soon.

The next morning, the Cabinet held its regular Saturday meeting. Polk distinctly asked the Cabinet's advice on whether or not he should send a message to Congress on the following Tuesday asking for a declaration of war. Secretary of State Buchanan, Secretary of the Treasury Walker, Secretary of War Marcy, Attorney General Mason, and Postmaster General Johnson all replied in the affirmative. Only Secretary of the Navy Bancroft dissented, saying that he would support a declaration of war only in the event of a hostile attack by Mexico.

So the president of the United States and his Cabinet, minus one lone dissenter, prepared to ask Congress to declare war on Mexico. At this point the only true grievances known to the president and his Cabinet were the approximately five million dollars of commercial claims owed by the Mexican government to American merchants. The far more pressing reason for war was the Mexican government's unwillingness to allow the United States to leverage those claims into a real estate deal for its northern provinces of California and New Mexico.

Before the Cabinet adjourned, Polk directed Buchanan to make copies of all correspondence with Slidell, and Marcy to do the same with any orders and reports between his department and General Taylor. These were to be submitted to Congress as backup to Polk's request for a declaration of war. It is relatively certain that had Polk's request and this documentation been submitted as planned, some measure of protracted debate would have occurred in both houses. Certainly, Senator Benton, stated friend of the administration though he may have been, would have asked some pointed questions.

But that was not to be. At about 6:00 P.M. on the evening of May 9, 1846—four hours after the Cabinet had adjourned—the president was handed the dispatches from General Taylor reporting the Thornton encounter and declaring hostilities to have commenced. Polk had his smoking gun. Suddenly, this matter was no longer about American commercial interests and a lust for territory. The national honor that both Polk and Benton held dear—and indeed had learned so much about from Old Hickory—had been stained with American blood.[4]

After working all day on Sunday, save for attending church with Sarah, Polk sent his request for a declaration of war to Congress at around noon on Monday, May 11. Justifying the causes that existed prior to this notice, Polk noted that "the redress of the wrongs of our citizens naturally and inseparably blended itself with the question of boundary. The settlement of the one question in any correct view of the subject involves that of the other."

The government of Mexico had "solemnly pledged" the previous October to receive and accredit an American envoy, the president went on, but two Mexican governments had "refused the offer of a peaceful adjustment of our difficulties. . . . The cup of forbearance had been exhausted even before the recent information from the frontier of the Del Norte."

But now things were very different. "After reiterated menaces," the president declared, "Mexico has passed the boundary of the United States, has invaded our territory and shed American blood upon American soil. She has proclaimed that hostilities have commenced, and that the two nations are now at war." That phrase, "American blood upon American soil," resounded like the shot of a cannon across the Capitol and would come back to haunt the president in the months ahead.[5]

But it made for an easy congressional decision. After all, who among the 282 congressmen and senators would dare to resist this reported insult to American arms and this call to battle? The answer was, not very many.

On the evening of May 11, scarcely five hours after Congress had received the president's message, John Slidell had the dubious privilege of reporting back to Polk that his war message had passed the House of Representatives by a vote of 174 to 14. John Quincy Adams was among those voting no.

Garrett Davis of Kentucky challenged the president's claim that "the war was begun by Mexico" and asserted that "it is our own President who began this war." But Davis nonetheless was caught up with the overwhelming majority and voted for the bill. He did so "with hearty alacrity," he said, in order to support the call for men and supplies in the bill, while "at the same time protesting against its falsehoods."⁶

In the Senate, it took all of another day. Predictably, Thomas Hart Benton was among those not immediately persuaded. Polk had invited Benton to review his war message on the morning of May 11—just prior to submitting it to Congress—in the hope of gaining his support. Benton not only told the president that he disapproved of marching troops to the Rio Grande, but he also implied that he did not think that American territory legally extended west of the Nueces.

Old Bullion called on Polk again at the White House that same evening and asked about the number of men and the amount of money that would be required to defend the country. Polk replied, in language that would be used again by future presidents in future conflicts, that "no more men would be called out and no more money expended than would be absolutely necessary to bring the present state of hostilities to an end," but at the moment it was impossible for him to say what those numbers would be.

When Polk held up the quick action of the House of Representatives as evidence that the country was on the right track, Benton huffed that in the nineteenth century, war should not be declared without a much fuller discussion than had been heard in the House. Buchanan and Marcy were also present for this evening meeting and engaged Benton in some debate. For his part, Polk soon realized that they weren't going to change Old Bullion's mind. The president "abstained from engaging further in the conversation" and pondered going to war without the support of his party's chairman of the Senate Military Affairs Committee.

Convening at noon on Tuesday, May 12, the Senate debated the president's war message while senators on both sides of the aisle had their say. Benton pleaded that peace was still possible and that "the door was open for an adjustment of our difficulties." John C. Calhoun spoke at great length against the declaration. But the charge of American blood upon American soil fueled indignation that was impossible to quiet.

When the Senate vote was finally taken at around six-thirty that evening, Benton joined the majority in voting overwhelmingly for war by a vote of 40 to 2. Three senators abstained, including Calhoun, who may somehow have thought that by taking no position, he was keeping his presidential options alive for 1848.

Benton, however, put his finger squarely on the landslide result. Many affirmative votes were given by members "extremely averse to this war," Old Bullion growled—no doubt counting himself among that number—who nonetheless had acted out of a feeling of "duress in the necessity of aiding our own troops." In a broader sense, the hurried passage of the president's war bill marked a watershed in the power of a president to declare war in support of his foreign policy.[7]

The following afternoon, May 13, 1846, a congressional delegation called on the president and presented him with the act declaring war against Mexico. Polk read it in the presence of the congressmen and then signed it. Afterward, he met with Secretary of War Marcy and General Winfield Scott to discuss troop dispositions and the many volunteers to be raised.

In what would be but the first of many adversarial encounters with his generals, Polk found Scott's plan for the troops from each state incomplete, and he requested "a more formal report." The president also offered Scott command of the army, although as the country's senior general it seemed to be Scott's prerogative. Polk recognized this but noted, "I did not consider him in all respects suited to such an important command."

That evening at a special Cabinet meeting, there was other dissension in the ranks. Buchanan presented a draft of his proposed dispatch to American missions abroad announcing the declaration of war. The secretary of state proposed to inform foreign governments that "in going to war we did not do so with a view to acquire either California or New Mexico or any other portion of the Mexican territory." Polk for his part was incredulous. What Cabinet meetings had Buchanan been attending for the past year?

What made Buchanan weak-kneed was his continuing preoccupation with the possibility that Great Britain or France or both might declare war to prevent the United States from acquiring California. Polk dismissed these concerns out of hand and retorted that he would "stand and fight until the last man among us fell in the conflict" before he would make such a statement as Buchanan suggested.

Polk again declared his disdain for foreign meddling on the continent and repeated his previous assertion that "there was no connection between the Oregon and Mexican questions." Before he would give a pledge renouncing any territorial claims, he would let the war that Buchanan feared with Britain come and "would take the whole responsibility."

Buchanan continued the debate for some time, although the rest of the Cabinet strongly supported the president. Finally, after a discussion that Polk called "one of the most earnest and interesting which has ever occurred in my Cabinet," Buchanan was ordered to strike his territorial disavowal. In its place, Polk scribbled a paragraph for him to insert. "We go to war with Mexico," Buchanan's dispatch to American missions now read, "solely for the purpose of conquering an honorable and permanent peace."[8]

Once more it appeared that James K. Polk had followed the advice that his old Tennessee friend, Justice John Catron of the United States Supreme Court, had written him back in the days of his fight for the speakership of the House of Representatives. "Go for the expedient and for success—give and take—but *act,* and that quickly and boldly."[9]

In the evolution of American presidential power, it is difficult to overstate the transition that occurred on May 13, 1846. The framers of the Constitution specifically reserved the power to declare war for the legislative branch. While chief executives had routinely defended American interests abroad with military means as early as Jefferson's actions against the Barbary pirates in 1801, Congress took its war-making powers very seriously.

The American declaration of war against Great Britain in June 1812 had been a congressional affair. Architect of the Constitution that he was, President James Madison knew full well where the power to declare war was lodged. In the spring of 1812, Madison agonized over sending a war message to Congress, doing so only after considerable pressure from war hawks in the House of Representatives led by a young Henry Clay.

The House debated four days before passing the measure 79 to 49, and even then, Congressman Josiah Bartlett of New Hampshire judged "the business was too hasty." The Senate took four times as long before finally voting to declare war on June 17, 1812, by a margin of 19 to 13. It would prove to be far and away the closest war vote in American history.[10]

Thirty-four years later, not only did James K. Polk almost demand that Congress recognize that a state of war already existed, but also he left little doubt that those who failed to respond to his charge would be branded as cowards. The House of Representatives took only two hours to debate the president's message before passing a declaration of war. The Senate took a day more before passing it.

The next time that an American president asked Congress for a declaration of war, the response was largely the same, although William McKinley was far more reluctant than Polk in presenting his request. On April 25, 1898, two months after the battleship *Maine* was sunk in Havana harbor—there is still some debate over the cause—Congress rushed to pass McKinley's war message by large margins.

"By God, don't your President know where the war-declaring power is lodged?" one senator thundered to Assistant Secretary of State Rufus Day when McKinley appeared to drag his feet in the hope of some last-minute settlement. But that was the last time that Congress would attempt to take the lead or even seriously assert its constitutional war powers.[11]

Woodrow Wilson's war message of April 2, 1917, to a special session of Congress prior to the United States' entry into the First World War, was approved by the Senate 82 to 6 on April 4, and by the House of Representatives 373 to 50 in the early hours of April 6. The Second World War, of course, is in another category. After the undeniable action of Japan at Pearl Harbor and the subsequent declaration of war on the United States by Germany, only Congresswoman Jeannette Rankin of Montana voted against the two war messages delivered by Frankin D. Roosevelt. After the Second World War, despite extensive military operations in Korea, Vietnam, and the Middle East, Congress has never again exercised its constitutional power to declare war.

The point as it relates to James K. Polk is this: all the fears that the Whigs had voiced about Old Hickory being a military chieftain and exercising dictatorial powers had proven unfounded. The truth is that by the time Jackson sat in the White House, the temperament of his earlier years had moderated. He may have threatened to hang John Calhoun over the nullification crisis, but even Old Hickory backed off when it came to the attempts of his administration to acquire Texas. His protégé, however, pulled no such punches.

By backing up his policy aims—Texas to the Rio Grande—with an American army in a position where it was almost certain to become embroiled in some incident, Polk showed exactly the decisiveness that some had feared of Old Hickory. By using that incident to shame the American Congress into declaring war to further those policy aims, Polk changed the character of the American presidency.

From a chief executive who merely reported the facts to Congress, as Madison had done, and then asked it to do its legislative duty, Polk made the president the decision-maker, subject only to Congress's coerced acquiescence. Given the enormous accumulation of presidential power post-Polk, this transition may not seem significant. But in 1846, Polk's strong executive leadership was the click that sent the pendulum of the war-making power swinging away from Congress and toward the executive branch.

*M*eanwhile, unbeknownst to those in Washington, General Taylor had already fought two battles on what the American Congress had overwhelmingly declared to be American soil. After the loss of Thornton's patrol on April 25, Old Rough and Ready looked around and found his position at Fort Texas decidedly exposed. Defensively, it might withstand a considerable siege, but the bulk of Taylor's equipment and supplies were unprotected thirty miles to his rear at Port Isabel on the Gulf Coast.

Thornton's debacle was evidence that the Mexicans had crossed the Rio Grande in force above his position, and when Taylor received intelligence that an even larger force was assembling to cross below Matamoros, the danger of being caught by a two-prong pincer movement became obvious. Somehow, Taylor needed to protect his supply base at Port Isabel and at the same time resupply Fort Texas. So, on May 1, leaving Major Jacob Brown and five hundred men of the 7th Infantry regiment to hold Fort Texas, Taylor moved out with the remainder of his army and three hundred wagons and headed back toward Port Isabel.

General Anastasio Torrejón's sixteen-hundred-man cavalry unit—part of which had ambushed Captain Thornton—was indeed making a wide circle westward in an attempt to get between Port Isabel and Taylor's position at Fort Texas. General Arista and several thousand infantry likewise crossed the Rio Grande below Matamoros, but with only two boats at their disposal, the operation took far longer than expected. By the time Torrejón and Arista moved toward each other to close the trap north of Fort Texas, Taylor and his column, having made a forced march of thirty miles over two days, were back at Port Isabel.

Among the young officers in Taylor's command who were getting their first taste of combat were Lieutenant Braxton Bragg, whose light artillery battery had been delegated to the defense of Fort Texas, and Lieutenant Ulysses S. Grant, who was now at Port Isabel. On the afternoon of May 2, the sound of artillery fire from the south announced to those at Port Isabel that Arista had laid siege to Fort Texas. "For myself, a young second-lieutenant who had never heard a hostile gun before," Grant wrote years later, "I felt sorry that I had enlisted."

Both Taylor and Arista knew that Taylor had no choice but to reinforce Port Isabel and then return to the aid of the 7th Infantry at Fort Texas with the bulk of his command. This Taylor began to do on the afternoon of May 7 after having his adjutant issue an order that the general wished to remind his battalions of infantry that "their main dependence must be in the bayonet."

By noon the following day, Taylor's command of some two thousand men and three hundred wagons now laden with supplies had returned about two-thirds of the way to Fort Texas. At a pond

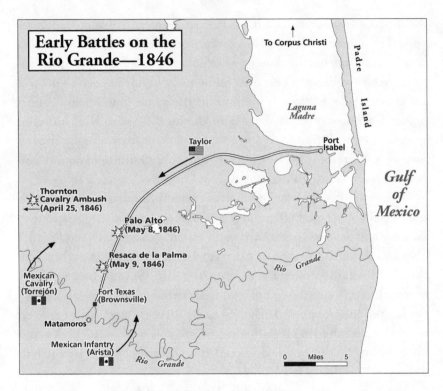

Early Battles on the Rio Grande—1846

at Palo Alto, they encountered Arista's troops, some thirty-three hundred, drawn up in a double line a mile in length across the Matamoros road. The Mexican position was well anchored and offered no hope of turning its flanks. The Americans paused to fill their canteens in the pond and then deployed in their own line across the road about seven hundred yards in front of the Mexican position.

Bayonets, Taylor had said, would win the day, but it proved to be just the opposite. Mexican artillery opened fire but had no explosive shells; their lead cannonballs merely struck the sandy ground and bounced along with little destruction. Taylor's artillery, with exploding shells, soon did considerably more damage to the Mexican line. Arista pondered a frontal charge, but thick chaparral between the opposing lines was not conducive to such a maneuver.

Instead, Artista sent Torrejón's cavalry against Taylor's right flank. When this attack was repulsed—again largely by artillery— Arista tried a similar assault on Taylor's left and his exposed wagon train. This attack also failed. After the Americans made a short-lived cavalry attack of their own upon the Mexican wagons, a fire sparked by artillery rounds caused such dense smoke across the battlefield that both sides broke off the battle.

The brief encounter was hardly decisive. The Mexicans still blocked the road to Matamoros, but 92 men had been killed and 116 wounded by Taylor's artillery fire. The Americans, on the other hand, had had only 9 men killed and 44 wounded. Among the fatally wounded, however, was Captain Sam Ringgold, who had been one of the principal architects of the practice of assigning small companies of light "flying" artillery—usually four mobile six-pounders—to infantry regiments. They had proven their worth at Palo Alto.

By dawn the following morning, Arista had withdrawn to a stronger position about five miles to the south. He chose a line of bluffs and ravines formed by an old channel of the Rio Grande at a place called Resaca de la Palma. Taylor, still outnumbered, now faced the decision of once more advancing or waiting for reinforcements from a call for volunteers he had made to the governors of Texas and Louisiana. But Old Rough and Ready seems to have been confident in the skills of his regular forces and, after a conference with his officers, gave the order: "Gentlemen, you will prepare your commands to move forward."

Once more, Taylor's column marched south down the road toward Matamoros, but this time Taylor left his cumbersome wagon train behind under a rearguard of dragoons and artillery. When his scouts reported Arista's army again deployed across the road, Taylor chose to ignore the Mexican flanks—in part because of the dense chaparral cover—and concentrate on forcing the road in the Mexican center.

The general first ordered an artillery battery to the front in an attempt to blast a hole in the Mexican line. When that position became exposed and was almost overrun by Mexican cavalry, Taylor turned to his own cavalry and sent a company commanded by Captain Charles May charging down the road toward the Mexican artillery positions. Mounted by fours, May's troopers stormed down the road—by one account with May's "long black hair flying in the breeze"—and quickly carried the Mexican guns.

But Mexican infantry immediately moved to counter this sudden assault, and May was forced to turn around and gallop back to the safety of Taylor's lines. In exasperation, Old Rough and Ready turned to his regiments of infantry and ordered Colonel William G. Belknap of the 8th Infantry, "Take those guns and by God keep them."

Belknap did so and also captured Mexican general Rómulo Díaz de la Vega. General Arista rushed forward to plug this hole in his center, but his forces were too spread out, and when they saw the vaunted Mexican 2nd Brigade fall back along the Matamoros road, most joined in the retreat. Arista reported casualties of 154 men killed, 205 wounded, and 156 missing. American casualties were comparatively light, with 49 dead and 83 wounded. Suddenly seasoned by battle, young "Sam" Grant wrote to his sweetheart, Julia Dent, "I think you will find that history will count the victory just achieved one of the greatest on record."

By nightfall, the Mexican army was streaming back past Fort Texas and across the Rio Grande. Taylor followed and in due course rejoined the defenders of Fort Texas, only to learn that the commander of the 7th Infantry, Major Jacob Brown, had been hit by an artillery shell and killed while inspecting his positions four nights earlier. Taylor promptly renamed the post Fort Brown. The city of Brownsville would grow up around it. Arista continued a slow retreat west to Monterrey, and on May 18, Taylor crossed the Rio Grande and occupied Matamoros.[12]

$\mathscr{W}$hen news of Taylor's victories at Palo Alto and Resaca de la Palma reached Washington, the town went giddy with celebration. Barely was the ink dry on the declaration of war, and then here was news that seemed to boast the invincibility of American arms. Never mind that in retrospect these battles would be seen as relatively minor engagements and that all Taylor had managed to do was make good the American claim to the Rio Grande.

More than a few observers thought that the whole thing might be over by the end of summer and that in addition to the Rio Grande boundary's being secure, Polk's dream for California and New Mexico might be achieved as well. Even Polk's war message had offered his hope that hostilities might end quickly, and he had pledged "to renew negotiations whenever Mexico shall be ready to receive propositions or make propositions of her own."

By the end of May, John Black, the American consul in Mexico City, reported to Buchanan his view that the Paredes government "would eagerly embrace the first chance whereby they might have an amicable arrangement of all differences."

Secretary of the Navy Bancroft expressed similar optimism. "If Mexico makes peace this month," Bancroft speculated in late May, "the Rio Del Norte and the parallel of 35 [approximately present-day Bakersfield, California, to Albuquerque, New Mexico] may do as a boundary. After that 32, which will include San Diego." But all this talk of peace while grabbing as much territory as possible was decidedly premature.[13]

CHAPTER 14

54°40' or Compromise!

$\mathcal{N}$OW OLD HICKORY'S boy definitely had a war on his hands. The question was, would he have to fight another over Oregon? On that issue, we left James K. Polk standing firm, wanting all of Oregon and brashly asserting—if only to himself—that the only way to treat John Bull was to look him straight in the eye.

Countless history texts to the contrary, the battle cry of "54°40' or Fight!" had not been raised during Polk's election campaign. But in the winter of 1845–46, the same expansionist fervor that had earlier promoted the annexation of Texas now resounded about acquiring all of Oregon.

On November 6, 1845, Polk's unofficial Democratic mouthpiece, the Washington *Union*, published an editorial captioned "The Whole of Oregon or None." This pronouncement was reprinted in pro-Oregon newspapers throughout the country, and its title was modified slightly into the slogan "All of Oregon or None."

In his first annual message to Congress a month later, Polk reported on the failure of negotiations with Great Britain and reiterated "our title to the whole Oregon Territory." Polk urged Congress to give the one-year notice required to terminate the joint occupation agreement of 1827.

During that year of notice, Polk recommended Congress also take steps, "without violating this convention," to extend the protection of American laws and jurisdiction over its citizens in Oregon. (Great Britain had done so in regard to its subjects in the jointly occupied territory as early as 1821.) Perhaps because he had been reading so much about transcontinental railroads and telegraphs from his earnest correspondent Charles Fletcher, the president also noted that "an overland mail is believed to be entirely practicable." He suggested "the importance of establishing such a mail at least once a month."[1]

Throughout December 1845, Secretary of State Buchanan badgered the president with a series of what-ifs related to the stagnant Oregon negotiations. For his part, Polk generally refused to engage in speculation and maintained that it was up to the British to make the next move. Polk would neither propose nor solicit another offer.

When Buchanan advised that the British ambassador, Richard Pakenham, was then likely to request that the matter be put to arbitration, the Cabinet unanimously determined to reject such a proposition. When Pakenham indeed made an arbitration proposal a week later, all Cabinet members stood by their decision.

But by the close of 1845, Polk had also received a letter from his old friend Aaron Brown, recently elected governor of Tennessee, urging him to give Great Britain a chance to "ease off" and save face in the Oregon negotiations. Brown advocated the transfer of the negotiations to the American ambassador in London, Louis McLane, and "some *fresh* negotiator on the part of Great Britain."

This Polk was not about to do—preferring to oversee things firsthand through Buchanan. Still, Polk may have considered Brown's advice that any new twist in the negotiations might—in Brown's words—"enable Great Britain to take some more favorable position toward an adjustment than she can now do without seeming to *back out*."[2]

The "twist" that Polk seems to have secretively begun to consider was that if the British were to submit another offer—no doubt falling short of Polk's publicly declared "whole of Oregon"—he might nonetheless submit the matter to the Senate for its *advice* prior to seeking its constitutionally mandated *consent*.

This strategy, which would focus the political fallout on the Senate, may have first been suggested to the president by Senator William Allen of Ohio, the chairman of the Foreign Relations Committee, on Christmas Eve, 1845. Allen soon felt the heat of the "all of Oregon or none" movement that was being fanned throughout the Northwest and got swept along with it. He came to regret his moderate suggestion, but Polk would take Allen's strategy to heart a few months later.

In the meantime, on February 9, 1846, the House of Representatives passed a resolution giving notice to Great Britain terminating the joint occupancy agreement. The Senate was an entirely different story. There, a lengthy and hard-fought debate dragged on and on.

The "all of Oregon" crowd in the Senate resolutely opposed any amendments that hinted of compromise short of 54°40'. On the other side, the moderates included Thomas Hart Benton, who had long made clear to Polk that he felt American claims north of the 49th parallel were sketchy at best. John C. Calhoun, having abandoned the policy of "passive delay" that he'd advocated as secretary of state, also favored a compromise along the 49th parallel.

This muddle continued until March 4, when Senator William H. Haywood of North Carolina created a stir by purporting to speak for the president on the Senate floor. Haywood claimed that Polk would "probably ask the Senate for its previous advice in case of a British offer to compromise at the forty-ninth parallel."

The only person more irritated than the staunch 54°40' men at this apparent wavering in the president's "all of Oregon" position was Polk himself. He quickly countered that "no one spoke *ex cathedra* for me," that his views had been laid out in his annual message, and that he had "authorized no one to express any other opinions."

But once again, the shrewd politician in Polk showed himself. Having made those pronouncements, Polk did not specifically disavow Haywood's representations of his views. He was keeping his options open.[3]

———

*N*ow a nineteenth-century version of a media blitz occurred in Washington. Suddenly, the figures "54°40′" (or simply "54 40") appeared all over town. "In the course of two or three nights," reported a newspaper correspondent, "these cabalistic figures were written apparently four or five thousand times upon the windows, doors, street-corners, houses, public buildings, stores and fences of the different avenues and streets of the city."

Senator Jacob W. Miller of New Jersey observed these numbers chalked "on doorways and fences . . . from one end of Pennsylvania Avenue to the other." He facetiously suggested that these new notices "might perhaps overcome the weight of official records, and our title to '54 40' be made 'clear and indisputable' by party resolutions, by dinner toasts, by wax stamps, and by chalked doors and fences."

The exact phrase "54°40′ or Fight!" seems to have evolved out of this frenzied Senate debate — not with the "all of Oregon" faction but with the moderates who took issue with them. Senator George Evans of Maine lambasted those who favored "54°40′ at all hazards." Senator Alexander Barrow of Louisiana spoke of the men who advocated "54°40′, war or no war." And Old Bullion Benton decried the folly of "54°40′ or war."

Then on March 11, Senator Reverdy Johnson of Maryland, who had read Henry Clay's letter declining an invitation to speak before the 1844 Whig convention, referred to senators William Allen and Edward Hannegan as the "hotspurs of the Senate" and gentlemen who "were all for 54, 40 or fight." There it was at last: "54°40′ or Fight!"

A few weeks later, the Saint Louis *Republican* reported that the 1846 wave of emigrants heading for Oregon was flying banners reading "Oregon 54°40′ — all or none" and proudly proclaiming that they were willing to fight for it. Then, on April 8, things got really bizarre. The Philadelphia *Dollar Newspaper* suggested that the abbreviation "P.P.P.P." should stand for "Phifty-Phour Phorty or Phight." Strangely enough, it was in this form that the most widely remembered slogan of Polk's presidency swept the country in the year of its origin — 1846, *not* 1844.[4]

*𝒜*s the Senate debate on giving notice dragged on, Polk wrung his hands over what seemed to him to be both an unnecessary and an imprudent delay. How could he appear to stand firm before the British lion when his own United States Senate was debating in public the deep divisions between those proponents of 54°40′ and the moderates who appeared satisfied at 49°? Viewing the action from the diplomatic gallery, Richard Pakenham must have smiled more than a few times.

And the Senate, for all its internal debate and Polk's repeated assertions that his views remained as he had laid out in his annual message, was still far from certain what the president's final position would be. Even John J. Crittenden, a staunch Whig and friend of Henry Clay, recognized the president's dilemma.

"If he don't settle and make peace at forty-nine or some other parallel of compromise, the one side curses him," Crittenden wrote, "and if he yields an inch or stops a hair's breadth short of fifty-four degrees forty minutes, the other side damns him without redemption. Was ever a gentleman in such a fix?"[5]

On the evening of April 9, Thomas Hart Benton made another call on the president at the White House. Once again, Old Bullion lobbied Polk for the senator's way out of the fix. Repeating his views that American title was best to the Columbia and the British to the Fraser River valleys, Benton advocated the 49th parallel as the "proper line of settlement." In fact, Benton wanted to make an offer of 49° part of the notice of termination.

Begrudgingly, Polk agreed to "consider" doing so, but he told Benton that any "notice should be given speedily." Polk thought that its delay in the Senate kept Great Britain from making *any* new offer. After all, why should that country make an offer? The United States Senate might end up voting for 49° without Great Britain's doing anything.

Polk insisted that Great Britain make the first move. "Great Britain was never known to do justice to any country—with which she had a controversy," the president had written to A.O.P. Nicholson the week before, "when that country was in an attitude of supplication or on her knees before her." Take that, John Bull![6]

———

$\mathcal{F}$inally, on April 16, 1846, the Senate passed a resolution giving Great Britain the required one year's notice of termination. It was not, however, "a naked notice"—as Polk termed it—such as had been passed by the House, but rather one that contained conciliatory language introduced by Reverdy Johnson. Its preamble now expressed the hope that despite the notice, the United States and Great Britain might reach an "amicable settlement of all their differences and disputes in respect to [Oregon]."

Rather than a conference committee to resolve the two versions, Polk thought it "safest for the House to concur with the Senate" and not risk further delay. "The long delay in the Senate and our divided councils in Congress," Polk wrote in his diary, "have added greatly to the embarrassments of the question.

"The truth is," the president continued, "that in all this Oregon discussion in the Senate, too many Democratic Senators have been more concerned about the presidential election in '48, than they have been about settling Oregon either at 49° or 54°40'. 'Forty-eight' has been with them the great question, and hence the divisions in the Democratic party."[7]

On April 23, both houses of Congress approved the Senate version of the termination notice. Polk signed it five days later, and off it went by steamer to Louis McLane in London for presentation to the British government. While not the point man in the Oregon negotiations, McLane had nonetheless done a good job of keeping communications open with British Foreign Secretary Lord Aberdeen and advising Buchanan in return that the British lion had not taken kindly to Polk's "whole of Oregon" statement in his annual address.

The British government had indeed been waiting for the Senate to resolve itself before submitting any new offer, but to McLane's credit, he had taken advantage of recent letters and newspaper reports predicting the action to convince Aberdeen to be prepared to instruct Pakenham promptly in making another offer. Consequently, when the official notice of termination, with its preamble hoping for an "amicable settlement," reached London on May 15, it took the British government only four days before a compromise offer was en route to Pakenham by steamer from Liverpool.

Hearing well the sentiments expressed by the moderates in the United States Senate, the British offer called for the 49th parallel, but with a southern jog to give all of Vancouver Island to the British. Originally, the offer also insisted on the perpetual free navigation of the Columbia for British subjects, something Polk was adamantly opposed to as a source of perennial friction. Only at the last moment did McLane convince Aberdeen to limit navigation rights to the Hudson's Bay Company. In doing so, he may have saved the day.

By now, war between the United States and Mexico was a certainty. The British did not know that as yet, and some historians have speculated that if they had, Aberdeen's government might not have been so quick to make any offer, preferring to see how the chips fell.

But Great Britain was in close communication with Mexico and well aware of the simmering debate over Texas. It seems unlikely that the war news, when it reached London on May 29, came as much of a surprise or did much to alter Britain's long-standing wish to resolve the Oregon question. Rather, it was on the American side of the Atlantic that the war footing with Mexico produced a sudden rush to accept the British proposal and avoid two wars on two fronts.

Buchanan presented the new British offer to Polk's Cabinet on June 6. Now Polk had to decide whether he would indeed submit the treaty to the Senate for its advice before asking its consent. Attention immediately focused on the navigation rights on the Columbia, and Polk doubted that he could agree to such terms because they would still leave considerable British influence south of the 49th parallel. But with a Cabinet full of lawyers, he need not have worried.

Treasury Secretary Walker and Secretary of War Marcy advised that the current Hudson's Bay charter expired in 1859. It was the opinion of both Cabinet members that the rights reserved to the company under the proposed treaty would not extend beyond the term of the present charter, even if it was renewed. Thus, any British navigation rights on the Columbia would expire in 1859.

With this loophole discovered, Polk polled his Cabinet and found all but one in favor of submitting the treaty to the Senate for its advice. Incredibly, the holdout was Secretary of State Buchanan, the very Anglophile who had tiptoed around offending Great Britain ever since he had assumed office. Buchanan suddenly sounded like the most ardent of expansionists and claimed that "the 54°40' men were the true friends of the administration and he wished no backing out on the subject."

The president was outraged. "I felt excited at the remark but suppressed my feelings and was perfectly calm," he later recorded. Buchanan carried on in the same vein in meetings over the next three days, at several points refusing to have any hand in drafting the cover letter submitting the treaty to the Senate and—in Polk's recollection—becoming outwardly belligerent about the matter.

Finally, it dawned on Polk that much like some members of the Senate, Buchanan was really playing to '48 and not 54°40'. Among Buchanan's likely rivals for the 1848 Democratic nomination was Lewis Cass, who had gotten "more intimately connected with the Fifty-four Forties" than even Cass had designed, and this was Buchanan's way of staking out similar ground. Buchanan wasn't going to be the candidate who had given up half of Oregon.

With Buchanan's political posturing recognized, Polk drafted his own submittal letter and sent the proposed treaty to the Senate on June 10. "My opinions and my actions on the Oregon question were fully made known to Congress in my annual message of the 2nd of December last," the president wrote. But "the magnitude of the subject" now compelled Polk to seek the Senate's advice before he either accepted or rejected the offer. If the Senate should advise acceptance, the president would follow its advice. Otherwise, he would reject the treaty and stand firm for all of Oregon.

Two days later, to no one's surprise, the Senate advised acceptance by a vote of 38 to 12. When Polk submitted it again for formal ratification on June 18, the Senate gave its consent 41 to 14. Suddenly, the battle cry of "54°40' or Fight!"—so closely associated with James K. Polk—had become the political reality of "54°40' or Compromise."[8]

After the ratification vote, the Washington correspondent of the New York *Tribune* asked rhetorically, "Where now is the watchword of the four Ps 'Phifty-Phour Phorty or Phight'?" A spoof reply came from the New Orleans *Tropic:* " 'Phifty-Phour Phorty or Phight' has now phortunately phallen to phinal phlat phooted phixing at 'Phorty-nine' without the 'Phight' against a phoreign phoe."

But not all sections of the country brushed off the defeat so casually. The Cleveland *Plain Dealer*—in the heart of "54°40′ or Fight!" country—blamed the defeat on "a traitorous alliance of Southern Democrats with Tory Whigs. . . . Had the president showed 'Phight' to Great Britain," the *Plain Dealer* went on, "as valiantly as he showed 'Phifty Phour Phorty' to the people of this country, we should have had the whole of Oregon ere now."[9]

For Polk, however, it truly was a political win-win. He had maintained his position for "all of Oregon," and by asking the Senate's advice before submitting the treaty for ratification, he had placed the onus of any compromise on that body. He would be the man who had won Oregon south of 49°; Congress would take the responsibility for forfeiting that portion north of 49°. Hard-core expansionists continued to think that Polk had fallen short of his campaign pledge, but the vast majority of Americans considered the acquisition of the better half of Oregon without a shot to be a brilliant coup, particularly because there was now a war on another border.

There were also political wars to be fought on the domestic front. While much of Polk's attention—and that of later historians—focused on his foreign policy, two of the four goals of his administration that Polk had confided to George Bancroft at the beginning of his term were decidedly domestic. These were the reduction of the tariff to a revenue basis and the establishment of an independent treasury. Here, too, the president would have to accept some measure of compromise.

In the summer of 1845, Secretary of the Treasury Robert J. Walker took the lead in producing a voluminous—and some thought far too scientific—analysis of the tariff as a revenue-producing tool. Walker's report attempted to show "at what rate duties on various articles would produce the maximum revenue—or, in other words, beyond what point duties became high enough to reduce the volume of imports and hence the amount of revenue."

When Polk put Walker's findings forward as the standard for establishing revenue tariff rates, it was only inevitable that the percentages that Walker had assigned to certain categories of goods would come under political attack. This was particularly true in Buchanan's home state of Pennsylvania. There, the coal and iron interests remembered all too well Polk's persuasive hints in the well-circulated Kane letter during the 1844 campaign that a revenue tariff could afford reasonable incidental protection. Where was it? they now asked.

While every commodity and industry had its protectionist champions, there were some goods on Walker's list that certain congressmen thought shouldn't be there at all. Ohio Democrat Jacob Brinkerhoff and a dozen Buckeye colleagues threatened to vote against the Walker tariff bill unless tea and coffee were excluded. "It was the poor man's refreshment when he came home from his work" Brinkerhoff maintained, "and it was often the poor woman's only luxury."

Still riled over the president's compromise on Oregon, Brinkerhoff went on: "Now, we must pay for a war for southern conquest, after you have given away millions upon millions of acres of our own territory at the North. . . . We can defeat your bill, and will defeat your bill." To Walker's regret, the administration counted votes and agreed to remove tea and coffee duties from the tariff bill.[10]

But the bill's passage was still not assured. For a time in the summer of 1846, it looked as if Congress might adjourn for the session without taking up the tariff or any other domestic matter. Worn out by the lengthy debates over Oregon and having done their duty in declaring war on Mexico, many congressmen were eager to leave town. Some were opposed to Polk's domestic agenda in any manner, and others were eager to join the volunteer armies marshaling for what was presumed to be nothing but glory in Mexico.

In the end, it was the war with Mexico—and the need to pay for it—that convinced Congress to stay in session by a very narrow vote. In this era before income taxes, it was the revenue from the tariff that would pay for the war or anything else. Thus, on July 3, 1846, after considerable debate, the House passed what was officially the Tariff Act of 1846 by a vote of 114 to 95. The only Pennsylvania Democrat to vote with the president in the affirmative was a thirty-two-year-old representative named David Wilmot, whom the president would soon have occasion to hear from again.

Polk called the tariff bill "vastly the most important domestic measure of my administration" and found the House action "highly gratifying," but there was still the Senate. There the drama was to be even greater.

When Senator James Semple of Illinois, one of the most disgruntled of the 54°40′ men, decided to go home, Polk sent the reliable Cave Johnson to the Baltimore & Ohio Railroad station to intercept him and hurry him to the White House for a late-evening round of presidential persuasion. Semple agreed to stay and support the tariff, but in the final maneuvering for a vote, Vice President George Dallas was forced to break a tie and declare in favor of the president's tariff, much to the chagrin of his home state of Pennsylvania. Thus, Polk and Walker's largely free trade revenue tariff became law, and it remained so without major changes until 1857.[11]

𝒽aving stayed in session and dispensed with the tariff, the Congress next looked to Polk's proposal for an independent treasury. The president preferred the term "constitutional treasury" and maintained that it had never been the intent of the framers to put government money in banks outside of the government's immediate control. Polk, of course, had been one of Old Hickory's foot soldiers in Jackson's long-running campaign against a national bank.

Essentially, Polk's treasury plan—here, too, the principal architect was treasury secretary Robert Walker—was for the government to hold its own funds in newly constructed vaults and not deposit funds in a national corporation nor in individual state banks. Further, all transactions with the national treasury were to be done on a hard-money basis.

"To say that the people or their government," Polk observed in his first annual message, "are incompetent or not to be trusted with the custody of their own money in their own Treasury, provided by themselves, but must rely on the presidents, cashiers, and stock-holders of banking corporations, . . . would be to concede that they are incompetent of self-government."[12]

Martin Van Buren had gotten a similar independent treasury plan passed in 1840, but after Harrison's election, the Whigs repealed it. Whig efforts to reestablish a national bank instead failed, however, under Tyler's veto, not once but twice. The Polk-Walker plan for an independent treasury passed the House by a straight party line vote of 122 to 66 in April 1846 and then went to the Senate Finance Committee, where it proceeded to gather dust.

As the summer went by, Polk became increasingly impatient and leaned on the committee chair, Dixon Lewis of Alabama, and Thomas Hart Benton, who was a committee member, to move the matter along, stressing that it was as important as the tariff for his administration. They finally did so. On the day after the tariff vote, the Senate approved the independent treasury bill by a party line vote of its own, 28 to 25.

In retrospect, it was somewhat ironic that a subject that had been Andrew Jackson's leading domestic issue for a decade, and that had caused John Tyler to split with the Whig party, should now be passed with so little emotion. In the end, the tariff and other legislation overshadowed it, and even some Whigs were said to be in favor, although they dared not vote as such. Polk did not even record its passage in his usually thorough diary. Nonetheless, the Independent Treasury Act of 1846 remained in effect until 1913, when the current Federal Reserve System was created.[13]

Quite suddenly, James K. Polk had achieved the twin domestic measures of his administration. But Congress had also come up with a few ideas of its own. Chief of these was the Rivers and Harbors Bill. In truth, it was one of the largest pieces of pork barrel legislation yet to come before the American Congress.

As with the issue of a national bank, Polk had allied himself early on with Old Hickory on the issue of internal improvements. Government support for such projects as roads, canals, and railroads was anathema to Jacksonian Democrats. That was the way that Henry Clay and his Whigs proposed to spend the common man's money.

Still, many Democrats in the Northwest thought that they were due some assistance from the public trough. John Wentworth of Illinois even came up with the later oft-repeated premise that "Congress should initiate as many projects as possible, thus forcing later Congresses to complete them in order to prevent the earlier appropriations going to waste."

Pro-improvement Democrats minced no words in warning their Democratic colleagues that such federal support of local projects was vital to their reelection. "Let gentlemen say that it was Democratic to withhold all appropriations for these great western rivers;" they warned, "let them say that it was pure Whiggery to make them; and they would find a rather stale and barren account of representatives from the valley of the west in the next Congress."

Though solicited for his opinion, Polk merely noted his past opposition to internal improvement bills and said that he would "remain uncommitted until called to act." On March 20, 1846, by a vote of 109 to 90, the House passed an appropriation of $1,378,450 (then an enormous amount, considering that the entire national debt was only about $17 million) for forty distinct and separate projects, many of them small harbors on the Great Lakes.

The Senate took its time with this measure, too, in part to keep northwestern Democrats solidly behind the tariff bill as their quid pro quo. Indeed, when the Senate passed the Rivers and Harbors Bill 34 to 16 on July 24—four days before the tariff vote—those Democrats still firmly against such internal improvements quietly hoped for a presidential veto. Polk waited until after both the tariff and treasury bills had been signed into law before showing his hand.

On August 3, the president returned the Rivers and Harbors Bill with his veto message. Noting that many of the projects were of a local character far beyond what could be considered essential to the nation's commerce, the president could find no constitutional power to construct works of internal improvements within the states. "To call the mouth of a creek or a shallow inlet on our coast a harbor," he wrote, "can not confer the authority to expend the public money in its improvement."

Then, in a statement ever so prescient of future legislative actions, Polk declared: "Should this bill become law, the principle which it establishes will inevitably lead to large and annually increasing appropriations and drains upon the Treasury, for it is not to be doubted that numerous other localities not embraced in its provisions . . . will demand, through their representatives in Congress, to be placed on an equal footing with them."[14]

If there was irony in the way that the independent treasury bill quietly passed after two decades of monetary battles, Polk's veto of the pork barrel Rivers and Harbors Bill set the stage for far greater irony in the future. The Democratic party of Jefferson, Jackson, and Polk, with its opposition to federally funded internal improvements, would become the party of Franklin D. Roosevelt and the New Deal and Lyndon Baines Johnson and the Great Society.

It had been a busy final two weeks of the first session of the twenty-ninth Congress, but it wasn't over quite yet. With the Oregon crisis resolved and his domestic agenda well in hand, Polk now felt that he needed some financial leverage to get diplomatic negotiations reopened with Mexico. He decided to ask Congress for what amounted to a presidential "slush fund" upon which he might draw for an immediate down payment to Mexico in the event a treaty could be signed that included his desired territorial acquisitions.

Polk's primary motivation had its genesis in the intrigue of the conversations the president had had the previous February with the shadowy Alexander Atocha. The day that Polk signed the declaration of war, Secretary of the Navy Bancroft issued orders to Commodore David Conner's squadron in the Gulf of Mexico to blockade all Mexican ports. But there was a curious loophole: "If Santa Anna endeavors to enter the Mexican ports, you will allow him to pass freely."

Polk was in fact so intrigued by Atocha's proffered scenarios of Santa Anna's return to power that he dispatched Commander Alexander Slidell Mackenzie (by no small coincidence the Spanish-

speaking brother of John Slidell who had taken the additional sur-
name) to Cuba to meet with the exiled leader. Santa Anna was told
that he might pass the American blockade unmolested, and that the
United States would welcome his return to Mexico in the hope he
would effect a rapid end to the hostilities. The United States wanted
land; Santa Anna would need cash; it seemed—to Polk at least—
a ready-made solution.

Mackenzie met with Santa Anna on July 6, 1846, and reported
back to Buchanan that the ex-ruler was indeed receptive. After all,
how could he be anything but, if it was his ticket back to Mexico?
Santa Anna even suggested—as Atocha had earlier—that the
United States could aid Santa Anna most by continuing to support
Taylor's position on the Rio Grande and the naval threats along the
Gulf Coast.

Polk, usually more sensitive to history than he appears to have
been on this occasion, apparently failed to remember that Santa
Anna had used the threat of a foreign invasion to assume power
once before and to rally his country against the French. If the
would-be Napoléon of Mexico didn't keep his word about peace
and the northern provinces, Polk would look a little foolish.

But for now, it was worth the gamble. On August 8, 1846, Santa
Anna sailed from Havana for Veracruz in the company of Manuel
Rejon, Juan Almonte, and Alexander Atocha. On the very same
day, Polk sent a message to the House of Representatives asking for
an appropriation of two million dollars "to provide for any expenditure which it may be necessary to make in advance for the purpose
of settling all our difficulties with the Mexican Republic."[15]

Polk had already cleared the way in the Senate by consulting
with Benton and other members of the Foreign Relations Committee, but because this was an appropriations bill, it had to originate
in the House. James McKay of North Carolina, the chairman of the
House Ways and Means Committee, introduced a bill that afternoon making the requested appropriation "for the purpose of defraying any extraordinary expenses which may be incurred in the
intercourse between the United States and foreign nations."

That was plenty vague, but everyone understood "foreign nations" to mean Mexico and, conceivably, "extraordinary expenses"

might even cover any required inducements to Santa Anna. On that note, the House adjourned for dinner with sentiment appearing to favor the bill's passage.

Two days earlier, however, the House had voted to establish a territorial government for the newly won Oregon country. Northern and western Democrats had added an amendment that copied the language of the Northwest Ordinance of 1787 and decreed that "neither slavery nor involuntary servitude shall ever exist in said Territory." It had caused little fuss and had been approved 108 to 43 with even four southern Whigs and three southern Democrats voting in the affirmative.

Somewhere over the course of the evening's dinner—with the House of Representatives spread out over Capitol Hill boardinghouses, hotels, and saloons—someone suggested that it might be a good idea to adopt a similar antislavery position over all lands that might be acquired from Mexico. As the House reconvened, the idea quickly gained support, particularly from Great Lakes Democrats miffed over the president's veto of the Rivers and Harbors Bill and from protectionist Democrats equally upset by the passage of the tariff bill.

The person selected to introduce the antislavery amendment to the two-million-dollar bill was David Wilmot of Pennsylvania. After the two-hour limit on debate expired, what would forever be called the Wilmot Proviso was adopted by the House and the special appropriation then passed by a vote of 85 to 79.

But suddenly, the lines drawn were no longer Democrat versus Whig, but rather northerner versus southerner. Free-state Democrats supported the bill 52 to 4; slave-state Democrats opposed it 0 to 50. Two southern Whigs from Kentucky voted for the bill despite sectional pressure, and eight northern Whigs voted against it because they were opposed to *any* new territories, slave or free.

"After an excited debate in the House," Polk wrote in his diary, "a bill passed that body, but with a mischievous and foolish amendment to the effect that no territory which might be acquired by treaty from Mexico should ever be a slave-holding country. What connection slavery had with making peace with Mexico it is difficult to conceive."

On the morning of August 10, less than an hour before both houses of Congress were scheduled to adjourn for the session, the Senate took up the House appropriation bill with its Wilmot Proviso glaring at one and all. Dixon Lewis of Alabama promptly moved to strike the proviso and apparently had the votes to do so.

But then, John Davis, a Whig from Massachusetts, took the floor—and refused to yield it. His filibuster continued until the Senate was gaveled adjourned without taking a vote. The Senate had also failed to act on the bill for the territorial government of Oregon.

Polk was furious. "Had there been time, there is but little doubt the Senate would have struck out the slavery proviso and that the House would have concurred," the president professed. "Senator Davis, however, resorted to the disreputable expedient of speaking against time and thus prevented the Senate from acting upon it. . . . Should the war be now protracted," the president continued, apparently failing to grasp fully the sectional earthquake that had just occurred, "the responsibility will fall more heavily upon the head of Senator Davis than upon any other man."[16]

𝒥ames K. Polk had compromised on Oregon and had won the better part of it. He was prepared to do whatever was necessary to protect Texas and complete the acquisition of New Mexico and California. But the one escalating controversy that he could no longer ignore was slavery. No matter how Polk tried to rationalize it—call slavery part of the constitutional compromises not to be disturbed, assert that the topic had no place on the political stage, or defend slavery as some specious southern institution—it was a tide that he could not control.

Slavery. It would gnaw and gnaw and gnaw. And now, although only the House of Representatives had agreed to the Wilmot Proviso, the debate over slavery and its extension had become a key component of Mr. Polk's territorial acquisitions.

ANDREW JACKSON

Andrew Jackson, "Old Hickory," spent his remaining political capital and his last ounces of physical strength to see James K. Polk elected president.
National Portrait Gallery, Smithsonian Institution

Artist Ralph Earl, who fre-
quented Jackson's Hermitage,
painted these portraits of
James and Sarah Childress
Polk around 1830.
James K. Polk Home

This image of James K. Polk was made in 1838 by the artist Charles Fenderich while Polk was speaker of the House of Representatives. It was widely copied and circulated during Polk's governorship of Tennessee and after his nomination for the presidency. For many, it was the first image they saw of Polk.

James K. Polk Home

MARTIN VAN BUREN.
President of the United States.

Martin Van Buren was Jackson's first political heir. When Van Buren's stance on the annexation of Texas exasperated Old Hickory, Jackson summoned Polk to the Hermitage.

National Portrait Gallery, Smithsonian Institution

Frequently unsung, President John Tyler stalwartly laid the groundwork for Polk to acquire Texas and much of the American West. *National Portrait Gallery, Smithsonian Institution*

MATTY MEETING THE TEXAS QUESTION.

This political cartoon, captioned "Matty Meeting the Texas Question," was a satire on the great debate over the annexation of Texas. Benton and Calhoun offer Martin Van Buren "Texas," caricatured as an ugly warmongering hag. Van Buren is reluctant to embrace the issue despite Jackson's prodding. Meanwhile, Polk and Dallas watch, and Polk says, "What say you Dallas? She's not the handsomest Lady I ever saw but that $25,000 a year—Eh! it's worth a little stretching of Conscience!" (The presidential salary was $25,000 annually.) *Library of Congress LC-USZ62-791*

For most of his political life, Henry Clay aspired to the presidency. He rarely doubted his own abilities to move an audience with impassioned rhetoric or written word.
National Portrait Gallery, Smithsonian Institution

Another Jackson protégé, Sam Houston left Tennessee for Texas, but remained loyal to Jackson and the Union when it counted.
National Portrait Gallery, Smithsonian Institution

Sarah Childress Polk, 1803–1891, G.P.A. Healy painting, 1846.
James K. Polk Home

James Knox Polk, 1795–1849, G.P.A. Healy painting, 1846.
James K. Polk Home

Polk judged Secretary of State James Buchanan an able man but was frequently frustrated by his changing positions and unwavering ambition to be president himself.

This first photograph of a president's Cabinet was taken by John Plumbe, Jr., in 1846. Seated from left to right are Attorney General John Y. Mason, Secretary of War William L. Marcy, the president, and Secretary of the Treasury Robert J. Walker. Tall and balding Postmaster General Cave Johnson and a dapper Secretary of the Navy George Bancroft stand behind them. Secretary of State Buchanan was absent. *James K. Polk Home*

GEN. WINFIELD SCOTT.

Winfield Scott was at the center of the American military for half a century. His Whig politics and fixation with personal glory did nothing to endear him to Polk. *National Portrait Gallery, Smithsonian Institution*

Zachary Taylor was a career military officer who was most comfortable in his life as a planter. But when the Whigs came calling with presidential whispers, Taylor responded. *National Portrait Gallery, Smithsonian Institution*

Missouri's Thomas Hart Benton was every bit the expansionist that Polk was, but Benton tempered his views on Oregon and California. Benton later went to war with the president over his son-in-law's conduct in California. *National Portrait Gallery, Smithsonian Institution*

John Charles Frémont might have emerged from his California campaigns an untarnished hero, but his vaunting ambition got the better of him and put the Benton-Frémont clan on a collision course with Polk. *National Portrait Gallery, Smithsonian Institution*

Gideon Pillow was one of the few people to hold considerable sway over Polk no matter how the political chips fell.
James K. Polk Home

SELF-INFLATING PILLOW.

This cartoon by Nathaniel Currier was published during Pillow's court-martial. Pillow's attempts at self-promotion in the "Leonidas" letter are punctured by a sword labeled "Truth," held by Winfield Scott, who exclaims, "Heavens what a smell!" *Library of Congress LC-USZ62-11404*

This reproduction of a Mathew Brady daguerreotype of Polk was taken near the end of his presidency and clearly shows the strains of his years in office. *Library of Congress LC-USZ62-1491*

James and Sarah planned to retire to Polk Place, once the home of Felix Grundy, in Nashville. Polk spent less than two months there before his untimely death; Sarah wore her widow's black there for another forty-two years. *James K. Polk Home*

The Polk Home in Columbia, Tennessee, is the only surviving home associated with James and Sarah Polk, although they never lived there. The home belonged to Polk's mother, who survived her son. *James K. Polk Home*

James K. Polk gave his full measure to the presidency, and Sarah Childress Polk gave her full measure to him. This daguerreotype of the couple was taken in 1849 as his term was coming to an end. *James K. Polk Home*

CHAPTER 15

To Santa Fe and Beyond

*T*HAT JAMES K. POLK was bound and determined to acquire New Mexico and California for the United States is best evidenced by two actions that Polk took within forty-eight hours of sending his war message to Congress. First, on May 12, 1846, the president asked Secretary of the Navy Bancroft to review the orders given the Pacific squadron over the past year. These included instructions to Commodore Stockton from the previous October that in the event of war with Mexico, he was to seize California ports and as much territory as he could. Bancroft calculated that Stockton would soon hear the war news and do just that.

The following day Polk took the second step. After conferring with Secretary of War Marcy and General Winfield Scott, Polk dispatched a special messenger to Fort Leavenworth on the Missouri frontier with orders for Colonel Stephen Watts Kearny and his regiment of dragoons to ride west at once for Santa Fe, New Mexico. The messenger also carried an urgent requisition calling upon the governor of Missouri to raise a thousand volunteers and send them west in support.

Polk's immediate plan was for Kearny to protect the annual caravans of American traders making their way along the Santa Fe Trail. Then, with volunteer reinforcements close behind, Kearny was to occupy Santa Fe and be in a position to strike westward into California before winter. While not entirely ignoring Taylor's position on the Rio Grande, the president nonetheless told Marcy and Scott that the first movement of American forces "should be to march a competent force into the northern provinces and seize and hold them until peace was made."

Two weeks later, Polk advised his Cabinet that his purpose was "to acquire for the U.S. California, New Mexico, and perhaps some others of the northern provinces of Mexico, whenever a peace was made." In making that determination, the president had the counsel of Thomas Hart Benton, who produced the reports of his son-in-law's prior expeditions and assured Polk that Kearny's force could reach California via a southern route before the worst of winter.[1]

*A*s it turned out, Colonel Stephen Watts Kearny was to become more than a little disgruntled with Senator Benton's famous son-in-law. Almost fifty-two years old, Kearny was a no-nonsense, by the book, regular army officer who had first served in the War of 1812. By coincidence, Kearny and Winfield Scott had been together as young officers at the Battle of Queenston Heights during an American attempt to invade Canada. After American militia refused to cross the Niagara River to support the regulars, the British counterattacked, and Kearny and Scott were among those taken prisoner.

After the war, Kearny stayed in the army and served throughout the Mississippi and Missouri frontiers, including a tour as the first commandant at Jefferson Barracks just south of Saint Louis. In the course of these assignments, he came to know Thomas Hart Benton quite well and married Mary Radford, the stepdaughter of explorer William Clark. In 1836, Andrew Jackson signed Kearny's commission as a full colonel, and he was posted to Fort Leavenworth to command the First Dragoons, which was known as something of an elite unit.

Initially from Fort Leavenworth and later as commander of the Third Military District headquartered at a much-expanded Jefferson Barracks, Kearny sat astride the two great avenues of westward expansion, the Oregon and Santa Fe trails. In 1845, Kearny led 280 dragoons all the way to South Pass and then returned along the eastern Rockies via Bent's Fort and the Arkansas River. Called "a demonstration of force," the exercise was calculated to discourage Sioux, Cheyenne, and Arapaho from attacking the increasing number of wagon trains on both trails.[2]

On May 26, 1846, while at Fort Leavenworth, Kearny received news of the declaration of war and his initial orders charging him with seizing New Mexico. A week later, Secretary of War Marcy sent Kearny more detailed instructions and left no doubt as to the colonel's ultimate objective.

"It has been decided by the President to be of the greatest importance in the pending war with Mexico," Marcy directed in orders marked "Confidential," "to take the earliest possession of Upper California. An expedition with that view is hereby ordered, and you are designated to command it."

Six months later, unforeseen circumstances in California would cause Kearny's orders of June 3, 1846, to be carefully scrutinized. But as he read them at Fort Leavenworth, they appeared to be sweeping in nature and to afford Kearny total authority in the lands he traveled. Kearny was to "conquer Santa Fe," provide for the "safe possession of it," and then with the remainder of his command "press forward to California."

The route by which Kearny would enter California was left to his discretion. But, continued Marcy, "we are assured"—probably by Thomas Hart Benton, relying on Frémont's reports—"that a southern route . . . is practicable; and it is suggested as not improbable, that it can be passed over in the winter months, or, at least, late in autumn." Almost wishfully, Marcy added: "It is hoped that this information may prove to be correct."

As to Kearny's future coordination with Commodore Stockton and the United States Navy, Marcy expected that by then the navy would be "in possession of all the towns on the sea coast, and will cooperate with you in the conquest of California." If Kearny needed more help, he was authorized to muster into the service of the United States "Mormon emigrants en route to California" and such

Americans then in the region "as you may think useful to aid you to hold the possession of the country."

In both New Mexico and California, Kearny was charged with establishing temporary civil governments. "It is foreseen that what relates to the civil government will be a difficult and unpleasant part of your duty," Marcy continued, "and much must necessarily be left to your own discretion." That comment would prove to be a gross understatement.

Polk and Marcy were reposing considerable trust in Stephen Watts Kearny and giving him wide authority and discretion to complete his mission. And just to make certain that Kearny would outrank Commodore Stockton or any other officer that he was likely to encounter west of Fort Leavenworth, Kearny, after thirty-four years in the army, was awarded a brevet as a brigadier general. The appointment was effective, Marcy told Kearny, "as soon as you commence your movement towards California."[3]

𝒷rigadier General Kearny's first stop was Santa Fe via the Santa Fe Trail. For the better part of two decades, the Santa Fe Trail, linking Independence, Missouri, with Santa Fe, New Mexico, had been the key commercial artery into the land that Polk was now determined to make the *American* Southwest. After crossing the plains of eastern Kansas, the trail ran west up the Arkansas River and then southwest across the dry arroyos at the heads of the Cimarron and Canadian rivers. Looping around the southern end of the Sangre de Cristo Mountains, it descended to the plaza at Santa Fe.

One of the biggest drawbacks to this route was a lack of water between the Arkansas River and the Sangre de Cristos. Charles Bent, one of the Santa Fe Trail's earliest traders, offered an alternative to this waterless stretch by promoting what came to be called the Mountain Branch. This route continued west up the Arkansas, swung south across Raton Pass, and met up with the main trail again near what later became Fort Union. The Mountain Branch was longer and involved a climb over 7,754-foot Raton Pass, but the odds of going thirsty were greatly reduced.

In 1832, Charles Bent and his brothers began construction of an outpost just downstream from where the Mountain Branch left the

Arkansas. In a few short years, Bent's Fort became the gateway not only to Santa Fe but also to much of the Southwest. Sooner or later, everyone who was anyone in the history of the region passed through Bent's Fort, and many a traveler lifted a mug or two of Taos whiskey behind its adobe walls to celebrate the occasion.[4]

Kearny quickly determined that, given the distances involved crossing the plains, the concern for forage for such a large number of horses, and the various times that his units would be ready to march, Bent's Fort would be the logical point of rendezvous. The new brigadier general was well known to the Bent brothers from his years on the Missouri frontier as well as from his visit to their post the previous year. Whether the Bents looked upon this mass influx as simply good for business or as the vanguard of great changes for their trading empire is debatable.

Two companies of the First Dragoons left Fort Leavenworth bound for Bent's Fort as early as June 6, 1846. Another company followed the next week. Two companies of the volunteer First Missouri Mounted Regiment, under the command of lawyer-turned-soldier Alexander W. Doniphan, were ready to leave by June 16. By the end of the month, Kearny reported that more than fifteen hundred men were on the march, along with hundreds of wagons and four twelve-pound and twelve six-pound howitzers.

Kearny himself rode out of Fort Leavenworth on June 30 with two remaining companies of the First Dragoons. His last communication to Washington before his departure did not report good news. From Charles Bent, Kearny had learned that New Mexico governor Manuel Armijo was expecting the arrival of three to five thousand troops from Mexico to aid in the defense of his capital.[5]

Among the officers on Kearny's staff was a young lieutenant on loan from the corps of topographical engineers named William H. Emory. His duties included making a preliminary survey of the terrain over which Kearny's little Army of the West passed.

"The road from Santa Fe to Fort Leavenworth," Emory soon recorded, thinking far ahead, "presents few obstacles for a railway, and if it continues as good to the Pacific, will be one of the routes to be considered over which the United States will pass immense quantities of merchandise into what may become, in time, the rich and populous states of Sonora, Durango, and Southern California."[6]

As Kearny headed for Bent's Fort and leapfrogged ahead of his other units, he did his best to impart some order of military discipline and preparedness among his new soldiers. "As a military man," wrote one recent volunteer about Kearny, "we find him just strict enough to keep us all in order, but not in the least oppressive. He is, however, fond of rapid marching and keeps us at it steadily."

If there was the slightest doubt in Kearny's mind about the urgency of his mission, it was removed when James W. Magoffin, a seasoned Santa Fe trader, caught up with the general at Bent's Fort late in July. Magoffin had come from Washington, where his close ties to Senator Benton had gotten him interviews with the president and Secretary of War Marcy. Both seemed to think that Magoffin might prove a useful intermediary with the Mexican government in Santa Fe.

Marcy gave Magoffin a letter of introduction to Kearny and it stressed that those in Washington were eagerly awaiting word from him. "The President desires your opinion, as early as you are in a situation to give it," Marcy wrote, "of the practicability of your reaching California in the course of this autumn, or in the early part of next winter. I need not repeat the expression of his wishes that you should take military possession of that country as soon as it can be safely done."[7]

Magoffin proved to be a valuable emissary. Accompanied by Captain Philip St. George Cooke and twelve dragoons, Magoffin rode from Bent's Fort to Santa Fe in advance of the main army and presented Governor Armijo with a message from Kearny. Carefully avoiding any mention of the grand sweep of his orders, Kearny merely informed the governor that he had come to assert the long-held claim of Texas to New Mexico east of the Rio Grande, including Santa Fe and Taos.

Armijo bristled and issued a proclamation calling on New Mexicans to resist the invaders, but as the Army of the West crossed the pinyon-studded slopes of Raton Pass and moved south, it met no opposition. In the end, Armijo decided not to contest even Santa Fe, and he fled to Albuquerque. Consequently, on the warm afternoon of August 18, 1846, General Kearny led his Army of the West into the plaza of Santa Fe unopposed and halted before the venerable Palace of the Governors, the symbol of Spanish and then Mexican rule for more than two centuries.

The remaining New Mexican officials bade the general welcome, and as the Stars and Stripes was quickly raised above the plaza, Kearny declared his intention to take possession of the province in the name of the United States. By then, there was little that his reluctant hosts could do but offer their conquerors refreshments of wine and brandy.

Lieutenant Emory reported that "we were too thirsty to judge of its merits, [but] anything liquid and cool was palatable." Within a week, Kearny's further pronouncements made it clear that the American claim was to all of New Mexico and not just that portion east of the Rio Grande.[8]

When the news reached Polk that Kearny had "taken possession of Santa Fe without firing a gun or shedding blood, and had proclaimed New Mexico to be . . . a part of the United States," the president expressed nothing but satisfaction. "General Kearny," Polk noted in his diary, "has thus far performed his duty well."

Kearny's orders from Polk and Marcy authorized him next to establish temporary civil governments, and this Kearny did with gusto, calling on Alexander Doniphan and several other lawyers to draft what came to be called the Kearny Code. But when the general proclaimed the code to be the basic law of New Mexico, declared the territory to be a part of the United States, and even arranged for the election of a territorial delegate to Congress, he may have overstepped his bounds.

A few months later, buoyed by midterm elections that cost the Democrats thirty-five seats in the House and gave the Whigs a 115-to-108 majority, Congress prepared to ask harder questions about Polk's conduct of the war. Strict constructionists were aghast at Kearny's wide-ranging discretion and demanded to see the orders given to military commanders for the establishment of local governments in any captured territory. Only Congress, they maintained, could properly annex territory and provide for its governance, even if the Senate had recently failed to take such action related to Oregon.

Polk was forced to concede that in some respects General Kearny had "exceeded the power of a military commander over a conquered territory." Polk and Buchanan finally agreed that in responding to Congress, the president must disapprove the more far-reaching pronouncements of Kearny's work, though without censuring the general, who, Polk thought, "had misconceived the extent of his authority, but who had, no doubt, acted from patriotic motives." But by then, Kearny had appointed Charles Bent governor of New Mexico Territory and was well on his way to California.[9]

𝒮tephen Watts Kearny left Santa Fe on September 25, 1846, with some three hundred troops of the First Dragoons. Behind him, the tide of volunteers streaming into New Mexico threatened to overflow Santa Fe. Alexander Doniphan and his First Missouri regiment of about one thousand men were momentarily left to garrison the town and subdue Apache warriors who had been raiding to the south. Upon the arrival of Colonel Sterling Price and the twelve hundred volunteers of the Second Missouri, Price took over garrison duties, and Doniphan and his command started down the Rio Grande to capture El Paso.

Along with Price's Missourians came the Mormon emigrants en route to California whom Polk's orders to Kearny had instructed him to recruit. Numbering about five hundred men, this was the famous Mormon Battalion, the only unit of the U.S. Army ever designated by religion. It had been mustered into service at Council Bluffs, Iowa, on July 16, 1846, from among the Latter-day Saints, with the understanding that in exchange for assistance in the conquest of the Southwest, the Polk administration would provide army jobs and look favorably upon the Saints' further westward migration.

Polk was eager to have these emigrants—recently driven out of Illinois toward points yet uncertain—operating with the United

States and not against it. Such service, he believed, would "conciliate them, attach them to our country, and prevent them from taking
part against us."

Certain Illinois politicians had lobbied Polk to block the Mormons' exodus westward altogether, but the president felt strongly
that "the right of emigration or expatriation was one which any citizen possessed." As to the religious character of the debate, Polk declared: "I could not interfere with them on the ground of their
religious faith, however absurd it might be considered to be; that if
I could interfere with the Mormons, I could with the Baptists, or
any other religious sect; and by the constitution any citizen had a
right to adopt his own religious faith."

But that didn't mean that Polk was not nervous about any one
sect's holding a numerical advantage in California or elsewhere.
When a regiment of non-Mormon volunteers was raised in New
York and sent by sea to California, they had to agree—at Senator
Benton's suggestion—to accept discharge in California and remain
there as permanent residents, lest the territory be overwhelmed
with Mormons. In one of the least candid assertions of his political
career, Polk told New Yorkers critical of his expansionist plans for
California that these settlers would actually end up in Oregon.[10]

Kearny was well on his way down the Rio Grande when he
learned of the arrival of the Mormon Battalion in Santa Fe. Its commander had died en route, and General Kearny ordered Captain
Philip St. George Cooke to return to Santa Fe and assume command. Cooke preferred to be in the vanguard with Kearny, but he
did so, appeased with the rank of lieutenant colonel and the understanding that he would hurry the battalion along toward California
as quickly as possible. Later, Cooke described their trek west as "a
leap in the dark of a thousand miles of wild plain and mountains."

On October 6, 1846, just south of Socorro, as Kearny's advance
detachment prepared to leave the stately cottonwoods along the Rio
Grande and strike toward the stark headwaters of the Gila, a cloud
of dust appeared out of the west. Apaches were still a concern, and
the column prepared for an attack. But the dust proved to be the
veteran scout and mountain man Kit Carson and a party of sixteen

men bound for Washington with urgent dispatches from California. As it turned out, their news would confound, far more than enlighten, General Kearny's next moves.[11]

*M*eanwhile, far to the south on the Rio Grande, Old Rough and Ready Zachary Taylor was intent on completing his mission in northern Mexico. But by the end of the summer, Taylor was not forthcoming enough for Polk in grand military strategy and the logistical requirements of his army.

"General Taylor, I fear, is not the man for command of the army," the president fumed; "he is brave but he does not seem to have resources or grasp of mind enough to conduct such a campaign." Of course, it didn't help their relationship any that Taylor was not completely immune from the whispers of certain Whigs that here was a general in the image of William Henry Harrison to lead them back to the White House.[12]

Taylor had told Polk and Winfield Scott that an attack upon Mexico City was impractical from his theater of operations—five hundred miles of mountainous terrain, a tenuous supply line, and far too many unruly volunteers were among his reasons. Instead, Taylor proposed—and Polk and Scott initially agreed—that his operations be confined to securing the northern provinces of Nuevo León, Coahuila, and Chihuahua, essentially that part of northern Mexico between the Sierra Madre Oriental and the Rio Grande. Initially, this meant seizing Monterrey, the provincial capital of Nuevo León.

To advance on Monterrey, Taylor moved ninety miles up the Rio Grande from Matamoros and established a supply depot at Camargo. The summer weather was miserably hot and humid, and while little Mexican resistance was encountered, upward of one-third of Taylor's command was on the sick list from dysentery and assorted fevers. By mid-August 1846, the Americans were moving south from the Rio Grande toward Cerralvo and, eventually, Monterrey, ninety miles distant from the river.

Reaching the pleasant orchards and green fields of Cerralvo on August 25, Taylor learned that General Pedro de Ampudia was once again commanding the Mexican Army of the North and would

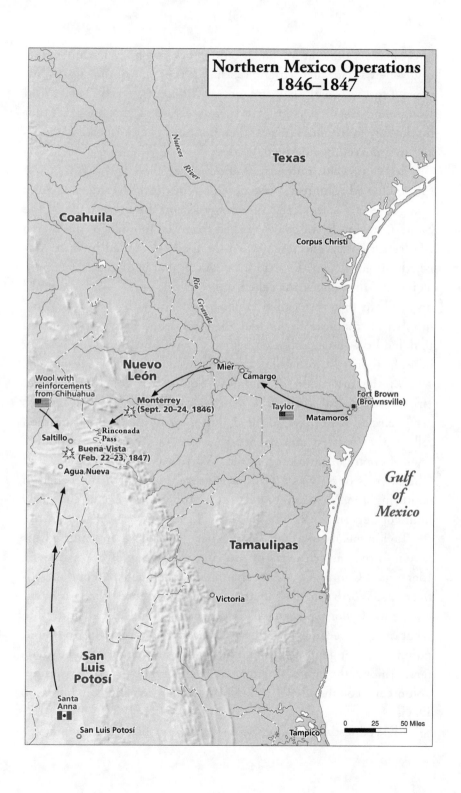

Northern Mexico Operations
1846–1847

Texas

Coahuila

Nueces River

Rio Grande

Corpus Christi

Nuevo León

Mier

Camargo

Wool with reinforcements from Chihuahua

Monterrey
(Sept. 20–24, 1846)

Taylor

Fort Brown
(Brownsville)

Saltillo

Rinconada Pass

Matamoros

Buena Vista
(Feb. 22–23, 1847)

Agua Nueva

Gulf
of
Mexico

Tamaulipas

Victoria

San
Luis
Potosí

Santa
Anna

San Luis Potosí

Tampico

0   25   50 Miles

likely make a stand at Marin, about twenty-five miles from Monterrey. When Taylor met with no resistance there, he optimistically advanced to the broad plain in front of Monterrey itself. There, Old Rough and Ready was greeted by a twelve-pound cannonball that hit directly in front of him and then bounced over his head. Monterrey, it appeared, would be defended.

Taylor's forces, numbering about three thousand regulars and four thousand volunteers, assembled on the northeast side of the city in a grove of pecan trees. Monterrey sat on the north bank of the Santa Catarina River as it emerged from the foothills of the Sierra Madre Oriental. The town was principally defended by an unfinished cathedral near the road from Marin that had been turned into a citadel—the Americans called it the "Black Fort"—and a redoubt on a hill to the west called Independencia. With about the same number of troops as Taylor had, General Ampudia was determined to defend the town, although he had received orders to retreat fifty miles farther west to Saltillo, the provincial capital of Coahuila.

On the afternoon of Sunday, September 20, 1846, Brevet Brigadier General William J. Worth, leading one wing of Taylor's army, circled west to avoid the defenses of the Black Fort and then fell on the western approaches to Monterrey, cutting Ampudia's lines of communication to Saltillo. Worth's assertion to Taylor that "the town is ours" was a little premature, but Worth succeeded in capturing the Mexican battery atop Independencia in the early hours of September 22.

Taylor meanwhile had feinted here and there and pushed his way into the eastern parts of the city, where one of his engineers, Lieutenant George G. Meade, had made a detailed map of the fortifications. Worth's encircling attack had some sense of military acumen, but Taylor's piecemeal deployment of individual units into what quickly became street fighting hardly squared with the reputation for great generalship that he would later enjoy in some quarters. Among the units so engaged was a regiment of Mississippi volunteers commanded by Taylor's former son-in-law, Jefferson Davis.

By Wednesday evening, September 23, rather than organizing a counterattack at one prong of the American army or the other, General Ampudia penned a letter to Taylor suggesting that his dwindling garrison be allowed to evacuate the city. Taylor initially refused, but met with Ampudia in person the following morning. The two generals agreed that Ampudia would surrender the city and within a week retire westward across Rinconada Pass toward Saltillo.

Not only did Taylor's generosity permit Ampudia's army to escape largely intact to fight again, but Taylor also agreed to an eight-week armistice. Old Rough and Ready did so, in part, to refresh his own troops. But he also thought, in his words, "it would be judicious to act with magnanimity towards a prostrate foe, particularly as the president of the United States had offered to settle all differences between the two countries by negotiation."[13]

That magnanimous sentiment seemed to square with Polk's views earlier in the summer, but by autumn it had become obvious that the battles and diplomatic overtures to date were only the beginning—not the beginning of the end. On September 19, the president received word that for all his intrigue with Colonel Atocha and the forbearance of the American navy in permitting Santa Anna to return to Mexico, the Americans had been double-crossed.

Santa Anna had indeed managed to push Paredes aside and assume tenuous control of the Mexican government, but his new foreign secretary, Manuel Rejon, now refused Buchanan's offer to reopen peace negotiations. Santa Anna felt too strongly about the causes of the war, Rejon reported in an apparently deliberate snub of Polk, to focus on the future.

But rather than delivering an absolute "no," Rejon cagily suggested that a final decision on negotiations might be made when the Mexican Congress convened in December. Meanwhile, Santa Anna was even then planning to rally an army at San Luis Potosí and oust Taylor from the northern provinces.

In the wake of Santa Anna's double cross, Polk had hardened his views, although Taylor, half a continent and three weeks away, could hardly be blamed for not knowing it. The result was that when Taylor's special messenger reached Washington on Sunday,

October 11, 1846, with news of the victory at Monterrey, Polk was furious that Taylor had agreed to an armistice that enabled a Mexican army to escape and prepare to fight again.

Taylor, the president observed, "had the enemy in his power and should have taken them prisoners, deprived them of their arms, discharged them on their parole of honor, and preserved the advantage which he had obtained by pushing on without delay further into the country." The following day, the Cabinet concurred that Taylor had committed "a great error."[14]

Two days later, on October 13, orders went out to Taylor to give the Mexicans "requisite notice that the armistice is to cease at once, and that each party is at liberty to resume and prosecute hostilities without restriction."

These instructions reached Taylor on November 2, only a couple of weeks before the armistice was due to expire anyway on its own terms. But what really put Old Rough and Ready in a foul and defensive mood was that there was no word of thanks from the Polk administration for his capture of Monterrey. "Damned, ungrateful Democrats," Taylor may well have muttered under his breath.

Then, too, there was the recent requisition of troops from his command to take part in an expedition to capture the province of Tamaulipas immediately east of Nuevo León and to the south of Matamoros. This was Polk's response to Santa Anna's double cross, and Polk hoped that more military pressure on the northern provinces would in turn persuade the Mexican Congress—in the unlikely event that it dared to act independently of Santa Anna—to reopen peace negotiations.[15]

But if Taylor thought that Polk had changed the rules on him in criticizing the armistice at Monterrey, Old Rough and Ready was soon to have occasion to run afoul of the president in an even bigger way. Part of the problem was that decisions were being made relatively quickly in Polk's White House. It took six to eight weeks to send an order or a request for information to Taylor and get his reply, and by the time the communication was complete, it frequently looked as if the general was not keeping up with the momentum.

Before the news of Monterrey reached Washington, Taylor was

initially assigned a substantial role in the proposed Tamaulipas campaign against Tampico, a seaport on the gulf about two hundred fifty miles south of the mouth of the Rio Grande. Polk and his Washington war planners hoped that this port might provide a base of operations where the Americans could avoid the deserts south of Monterrey and from which they could advance either directly west on San Luis Potosí or southwest to Mexico City.

From a dispatch to Taylor that was intercepted, Santa Anna learned of the planned attack on Tampico and chose to withdraw the garrison there and save it to fight another day. Consequently, the U.S. Navy sailed into Tampico harbor unopposed on November 12. But by now, it had dawned on the planners that any advance on Mexico City from Tampico would still have to cross the rugged Sierra Madre.

Later, when Taylor moved eastward from Monterrey and captured Victoria, the mountainous provincial capital of Tamaulipas, he saw the movement as part of the original war plan of anchoring a defensive line along the Sierra Madre while awaiting negotiations with Mexico. Polk, having by then decided that the waiting game was not accomplishing anything, saw Taylor's move as the general's belated and halfhearted participation in the Tampico operation.

Writing in his diary, Polk was increasingly critical of Taylor: "He is evidently a weak man and has been made giddy with the idea of the presidency. He is most ungrateful, for I have promoted him, as I now think beyond his deserts, and without reference to his politics. I am now satisfied that he is a narrow minded, bigoted partisan, without resource and wholly unqualified for the command he holds."[16]

There is ample evidence that Taylor reciprocated Polk's feelings. Taylor fumed all the more when he was instructed to advance no farther than Monterrey and provide still more troops to support the administration's latest designs against Veracruz.

So, with little regard for the occupant of the White House, Old Rough and Ready chose to pick and choose among his orders. He determined that occupying Saltillo—although it was fifty miles beyond Monterrey—was in keeping with his original orders of maintaining a defensive line along the Sierra Madre. Taylor's main problem in that regard was that he was short of troops—until, that is, he unexpectedly got help from another direction.

Brigadier General John Ellis Wool and his column of about three thousand regulars and volunteers had originally struck west from San Antonio in late September and headed for Chihuahua in yet another prong of Polk's plan to capture Mexico's northern provinces. Wool's command included a young captain in the topographical engineers named Robert E. Lee and a volunteer regiment of Arkansas cavalry commanded by Polk's longtime friend and political ally Archibald Yell.

But after crossing the Rio Grande, the closer that Wool got to Chihuahua, the more this wide, arid region south of El Paso seemed to be a backwater, both economically and militarily—at least when compared to Taylor's activities farther east. Wool suggested to Taylor in early November that if he went on to Chihuahua "all that we shall find to conquer is distance" and asked permission to move eastward instead and support Taylor in his operations around Saltillo. Taylor, having lost more troops than he could spare to the machinations against Tampico and Veracruz, readily agreed.

By now, Santa Anna was ready to put his own plan into effect. Assembling troops from central Mexico, Ampudia's largely intact army from Monterrey, and the garrison from Tampico, Santa Anna gathered a formidable force of some twenty thousand troops at San Luis Potosí. His plan was to drive north across an imposing two hundred miles of desert and smash Taylor at Saltillo, opening the way for some of his troops to retake Monterrey and push on to the Rio Grande.

Santa Anna himself would return to the south in time to repulse any American attack at Veracruz. Only then, with the invader pushed back, would he perhaps negotiate. (And California? California had always been too distant from Mexico City to receive much attention.)

Wool's command joined Taylor's on December 21 at Agua Nueva, about twenty miles south of Saltillo on the road from San Luis Potosí. Neither Taylor nor Wool had quite planned it that way, but Wool had come scurrying to Taylor's defense after receiving what proved to be an erroneous, or at least a premature, report that Santa Anna was moving north in force.

Old Rough and Ready, too, had hurried to the scene from his Victoria operation. A few days later, there was another report of an approaching army, but Captain Robert E. Lee soon "discovered that rows of white objects glimmering in the moonlight were not the tents of an enemy army, as reported, but a flock of bedded sheep."

For his part, Old Rough and Ready was still not convinced that Santa Anna was capable of mounting an attack in force across the inhospitable terrain north of San Luis Potosí. Taylor's view changed on the morning of February 21, 1847, when various patrols, including a major force of dragoons led by Lieutenant Colonel Charles May, galloped into Agua Nueva and reported that Santa Anna's army of some twenty thousand was on their heels. If Taylor had obstinately pushed forward from Monterrey in defiance of Polk or in the hope of sparking another battle to bolster his reputation, he was about to get more than he had bargained for.[17]

*T*aylor was initially determined to stand and fight on the broad plain at Agua Nueva, but this would have left his troops—outnumbered as they were at least three to one—sorely exposed to Mexican cavalry. Wisely, General Wool prevailed upon Taylor to withdraw some distance to Angostura Pass just south of the little hacienda of Buena Vista.

The pass was a natural defensive position that afforded Santa Anna's army only three possible means of attack. The Mexicans could move directly up the main San Luis Potosí–Saltillo road through a narrow canyon, eastward against Taylor's left flank via a ridge called "the plateau," or still farther east along a long ridge that made a wide circle toward the American rear at Buena Vista.

For a time, Taylor feared that Santa Anna might not attack here at all but rather circle west and occupy Saltillo in an attempt to cut the American supply lines. In hindsight, Santa Anna probably should have done just that. But if Wool indeed saved Taylor's reputation—and perhaps his army—by counseling a defensive retreat to Angostura Pass, there was no one to whisper similar advice to Santa

Anna. Encouraged by the American retreat from Agua Nueva—and apparently willing to ask the near impossible from exhausted and thirsty men who had just struggled across a sunbaked desert—Santa Anna ordered an advance straight up the San Luis Potosí–Saltillo road.

This attack on the late afternoon of February 22, 1847, made no headway, and a similar Mexican thrust against the plateau resulted in little better. Momentarily, the Mexicans fell back. Taylor positioned the Second Indiana and Second Illinois volunteer regiments on the plateau to counter the attack he thought would be renewed in the morning, and then he rode north six miles to Saltillo. Old Rough and Ready was still nervous that Santa Anna was planning a wide sweep around his right flank.

The next morning, Santa Anna took plenty of time organizing his elaborate infantry and cavalry units. His three-to-one advantage might have been even greater had Santa Anna not lost so many men on his death march from San Luis Potosí. As it was, approximately five thousand entrenched Americans faced about fifteen thousand advancing Mexicans.

When the day's attack finally began, it was a combined assault against both the narrows on the road and the plateau. An artillery battery and the First Illinois held firm at the narrows, but when the commander of the Second Indiana inexplicably ordered a retreat along the plateau, other volunteer regiments followed, and soon there was a gaping hole in the American left flank.

About this time, Taylor arrived back on the scene from Saltillo. The sound of the guns had persuaded him that Santa Anna was still coming straight at him. One report quotes General Wool as greeting Taylor with a dismayed, "General, we are whipped." Taylor supposedly replied, "That is for me to determine."

Taylor quickly ordered Jefferson Davis to take his Mississippi Rifles, who had been with him at Saltillo, and plug the hole. Davis's regiment rushed into the breach, rallied the retreating troops, and with considerable help from "flying artillery" units, managed to regain some ground.

Next, Santa Anna turned to the third avenue of attack and sent Mexican lancers riding hard for Buena Vista up the far eastern ridge. Among the American cavalry units that charged into the fray to counterattack were four companies of the Second Dragoons led by Lieutenant Colonel Charles May and the First Arkansas Cavalry Regiment led by Colonel Archibald Yell.

Close behind the lancers, Santa Anna committed his last division to the long eastern ridge in an attempt to encircle the American position on the plateau. Once more, Taylor sent Davis and his Mississippi Rifles, along with the Third Indiana, to stem the tide. The regiments formed an inverted *V* and held their fire until the Mexicans were within seventy yards of the lines. The force of a volley halted the Mexican advance, and only an improper use of a white flag, which momentarily interrupted the American fire, permitted the remaining Mexican soldiers to return to their lines.

Now it was Taylor's turn to push too far. Seeing the Mexicans retreat, and perhaps annoyed over their use of a white flag to cover their withdrawal, Old Rough and Ready—or perhaps it was Wool—ordered an advance down the plateau. But when only six companies of the First Illinois responded, they were suddenly terribly exposed. The Mexicans counterattacked with a renewed vengeance. The Second Kentucky, led by Lieutenant Colonel Henry Clay Jr., the son of the defeated Whig presidential candidate, rushed to aid their comrades, as did the Mississippi Rifles and several batteries of flying artillery.

Finally, it was the steady pounding of Taylor's artillery—both canister and grapeshot—that turned the tide for the last time. At one point, a legend—probably born more in Taylor's subsequent presidential campaign than on the field at Buena Vista—had Old Rough and Ready calmly surveying the scene and remarking almost casually to Braxton Bragg of his artillery, "A little more grape, please, Captain Bragg."

That much is speculation, but what does seem certain is that whatever his political or administrative sins, Zachary Taylor was a cool head once under enemy fire. It is also certain that at Buena Vista, artillery had again saved the man who had once exhorted his troops to rely on the bayonet.

Ironically, among the artillery officers with Bragg that day was Lieutenant George H. Thomas, who had charge of a six-pounder.

One war later, these two officers would be among the many from this campaign who would face off as generals in a far more horrific struggle. In September 1863, Thomas, still wearing Union blue, would again stand firm, repulse an attack by Bragg's Confederates, and make his reputation as the "Rock of Chickamauga."

Others would not live to see that conflict or even the end of the present one. Among those to fall in the last hours at Buena Vista were Polk's staunch Democratic friend Archibald Yell and Henry Clay Jr., who valiantly fought to cover the retreat of his Second Kentucky. The horrors of war transcend the strife of politics.

Old Rough and Ready had been very, very lucky. His unauthorized advance south from Monterrey and his tenuous hold on Angostura Pass were quickly forgotten. In the wake of some thirty-five hundred Mexican casualties—five times the American number—and Santa Anna's retreat back to San Luis Potosí, Taylor once again looked like an untarnished hero. "No result so decisive could have been obtained by holding Monterrey," the general reported to Washington.[18]

Polk had another opinion. When the adjutant general asked permission to order all military units to fire a salute in honor of Taylor, the president quickly demurred, publicly saying that no such thing had been done for Jackson after New Orleans and that he declined to set a precedent.

"The truth is," Polk huffed privately to his diary, "the indomitable bravery of our army saved General Taylor, and not his good generalship, at the battle of Buena Vista. Had that battle been lost, he would have been condemned by the whole country for this rashness in violation of his orders in taking the advanced position he did."[19]

And while the battle of Buena Vista signaled the end of major fighting in northern Mexico, Mr. Polk's increasingly unpopular war dragged on.

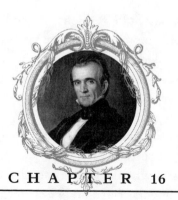

C H A P T E R 16

Mr. Polk's War

ƊESPITE THE NEAR unanimity of the congressional vote to declare war, a good part of the country was skeptical of—if not outright hostile to—the Polk administration's war program. This
opposition was strongest in New England, where expansion in any
direction had traditionally been viewed as a dilution of that region's
national influence. In New England, this particular expansion by
Mr. Polk into the Southwest was seen by many as a grand plot to
further that dilution not only by the admission of more states but by
the abhorrent addition of more *slaveholding* states.

Domestic protest over unpopular wars was not something born
in the twentieth century. On the leading edge of opposition to the
government's policy in 1846 was a twenty-seven-year-old New
England poet and would-be literary critic who had yet to make his
reputation. His name was James Russell Lowell, and in a series of
letters called *The Biglow Papers,* Lowell blasted slavery in general and
asserted in particular: "They jest want this Californy, so's to lug new
slave states in."

Lowell's fellow Bay State resident Henry David Thoreau spent a night in jail for refusing to pay his state taxes in protest of the war. Thoreau's friends bailed him out, but a year after the war vote—with no end in sight—the Boston *Daily Atlas* minced no words in calling the conflict "Mr. Polk's War."[1]

Throughout his entire political career, James K. Polk was routinely undaunted by opposition to the policies he was determined to implement or defeat—whether free trade, the annexation of Texas, or internal improvements. But that is not to say that Polk was entirely immune from political pressure. The president was well aware—particularly after the Whig victories in the midterm elections—that congressional support for the war was not guaranteed. Many congressmen in both parties voted appropriations to fund the call-up in troops but did not support the war itself. Polk, therefore, was under increasing pressure to bring about a speedy resolution.

In his second annual message to Congress, in December 1846, Polk devoted the majority of his words to chronicling "the injuries we had sustained" from Mexico and rehashing relations with that nation since the Louisiana Purchase. He defended the administration's intrigue in abetting the return of Santa Anna to Mexico and optimistically noted, "It remains to be seen whether his return may not yet prove to be favorable to a pacific adjustment of the existing difficulties."

Then, contrary to his private goals, Polk again vowed publicly: "The war has not been waged with a view to conquest, but, having been commenced by Mexico, it has been carried into the enemy's country and will be vigorously prosecuted there with a view to obtain an honorable peace."[2]

"Into the enemy's country" meant Taylor's advance beyond the Rio Grande and Kearny's march to Santa Fe and beyond. But by then it also meant Polk and his Cabinet had decided that only a strike at the heart of Mexico would bring Santa Anna to the peace table. With Tampico ruled out as too far removed, the "where" was relatively easy to determine. The initial target and key access point to Mexico City would be Veracruz, on the Gulf Coast. Who was to command this expedition was far more complicated, even though the choice of General-in-Chief Winfield Scott appeared obvious.

Born in Virginia in 1786 and trained as a lawyer, Winfield Scott had been in the Richmond courthouse watching Aaron Burr's trial for treason in the summer of 1807 when news of the *Chesapeake-Leopard* Affair prompted him to join the local militia. By the following spring, Scott was commissioned a captain in the regular army and ordered to New Orleans with a company of artillery. There, he got himself crosswise with his commanding officer, Brigadier General James Wilkinson, the other key player in the Burr conspiracy. Publicly branding both Burr and Wilkinson as traitors and branding the general in particular a liar and a scoundrel did not bode well for Scott's career.

But, if anything, Winfield Scott was always resilient. Entering the War of 1812 as a reprimanded captain, he quickly vaulted to lieutenant colonel in the Second Artillery and earned notice for his initiative at Queenston Heights. The following year, Scott took part in the capture of Fort George, and in 1814 as a brigadier general led an ill-advised advance at Lundy's Lane that nonetheless came to be regarded as valiant.

By the war's end, Scott was not quite twenty-nine years old and a brevet major general. He would remain in that rank for twenty-seven years until John Tyler removed the brevet designation and appointed him general-in-chief in July 1841.

After Polk's war message, it was both prudent and expected that Polk should seek Scott's counsel and advice. The problem was that these two egotistical polar opposites—the thin, reticent scholar certain that he was always right and the robust, outgoing soldier equally certain that he was right—had never liked each other. Nor, it appears, did they try very hard to find any reason to change their opinions.

Scott, nine years older than Polk, had already served as a general officer under eight presidents. The only one he seems to have held in any awe was Old Hickory, although that did not keep Scott from being an ardent Whig. Scott's political appetite had always been as strong as his taste for good food, and the general assumed that sooner or later he would occupy the White House himself. (Scott had been a candidate for the Whig presidential nomination in 1840 but had quickly faded under Henry Clay's presumptive campaign and Harrison's ultimate win.)

While Zachary Taylor's Whig leanings out on the Rio Grande were one thing, Winfield Scott had spent two decades cultivating his political philosophy among the eastern establishment. Scott was a die-hard Whig and—Polk seems to have decided early on—that was all that the president needed to know. Polk, after all, valued or damned party affiliation with a fervor approaching religious conversion.[3]

Nonetheless, on the same day that Congress declared war, Polk appointed Scott supreme commander of whatever forces would take the field against Mexico, including Taylor's. Polk assumed that Scott would head for the Rio Grande posthaste. Scott assumed that he would spend the summer in Washington crafting a comprehensive strategy and seeing to the logistics of a greatly expanded army.

Sensing Polk's immediate displeasure, Scott wrote Marcy an imprudently phrased letter saying that he was determined to secure himself against "the most perilous of all positions: A fire upon my rear, from Washington, and a fire, in front, from the Mexicans." Then the news of Taylor's victories at Palo Alto and Resaca de la Palma reached Washington, and suddenly it didn't seem so urgent to Polk that Scott rush to the front. The president left Taylor in command in the field and relegated Scott to administrative duties in Washington.

Scott attended to this work during the summer of 1846 and then in September petitioned Secretary of War Marcy for the principal field command. Without explanation, but assuredly with Polk's concurrence, Marcy turned him down. When news reached Washington a short time later that Taylor had covered himself with more glory at Monterrey—no matter how undeserved—Scott was beside himself. He had to get into the fray.

And truth be told, Polk and Marcy needed Scott as much as the general wanted to be center stage in the coming campaign. As Scott spent the fall honing the plan for an ambitious amphibious landing at Veracruz, Polk and his cabinet tried to find anyone but Scott who was qualified to lead it.

"I have strong objections to General Scott," the president confessed, "and after his very exceptionable letter in May last, nothing but stern necessity and a sense of public duty could induce me to place him at the head of so important an expedition. Still, I do not well see how it can be avoided."

So, on November 19, 1846, Polk met with Scott at the White House and once again conferred upon him what amounted to the supreme command of U.S. troops in Mexico. According to Polk, the general "was so grateful and so much affected that he almost shed tears." The president requested that Scott make a report on what forces he planned to leave with Taylor and what units he planned to take with him to Veracruz, and Scott departed, "apparently the most delighted man" the president had "seen for a long time."[4]

But even as Scott departed Washington—this time with plenty of haste—Polk was promoting a plan whereby Congress would create the rank of lieutenant general (three stars to Scott's two) and supersede Scott with a good Democratic general. Polk's candidate was none other than Thomas Hart Benton, and Old Bullion seems to have suggested the idea himself.

Benton's military credentials were open to question, service with Old Hickory against the Creek and a commission as colonel in the Missouri militia notwithstanding. But what Benton proposed, and what Polk really seems to have been after, was a reliable political ally to supervise his Whig generals in the field and also to be in a position to negotiate a peace treaty on the spot.

Curiously, Benton, who had once professed a decided aversion to war with Mexico if it could be avoided, now advocated a full-scale assault on Mexico City. He told the president, "ours were a go-ahead people, and that our only policy either to obtain a peace or save ourselves was to press the war boldly." That much Polk intended to do even if he had to rely on Whig generals.[5]

Congress would have to act on the creation of any super-rank, and in the meantime, news of the proposal rankled Scott as but one more political attack on his rear. But with the go-ahead from Polk and Marcy, Scott threw himself into implementing the seaborne assault on Veracruz. The general-in-chief left New York late in November 1846 and headed first to the mouth of the Rio Grande, where he hoped to confer with Taylor.

But Old Rough and Ready had no desire to meet Scott face-to-face and by design was off on his own excursions to Victoria and Saltillo. Taylor was none too pleased that Scott had written him that he was "not coming, my dear General, to supersede you," but nonetheless planned "to take from you most of the gallant officers and men whom you have so long and so nobly commanded."

Scott gathered up those units from Taylor's command that he found along the Rio Grande—mostly William Worth and David Twiggs's regulars and Robert Patterson's volunteer infantry, about nine thousand men—and headed for Lobos Island south of Tampico to rendezvous with six thousand more troops from the United States. By March 7, 1847, Scott and his new army were off the proposed beachhead at Collada just south of Veracruz.

While Scott and his division commanders were inspecting the landing site with Commodore David Conner, their vessel veered too close to shore and drew cannon fire from the Mexican shore batteries. Several shells splashed close, and a direct hit would have decimated Scott's staff and the current campaign, and also could have conceivably changed the history of the Civil War. On board with Scott that day as junior officers were George G. Meade, Robert E. Lee, Joseph E. Johnston, and P.G.T. Beauregard.

Two days later, William Worth's division led the first wave of fifty-five hundred men ashore against only minimal resistance. By evening, Scott had twelve thousand men on the beach. (Military historian John S. D. Eisenhower called it "the largest amphibious invasion yet attempted in history.") These troops quickly encircled Veracruz, and after a heavy bombardment, the town surrendered on March 27.[6]

"This was joyful news," Polk recorded in his diary in a rare burst of emotion two weeks later when the word reached Washington. But Veracruz was the tip of the proverbial iceberg. It was to be only a base of operations from which to carry the fight to Mexico

City, and in this effort the Americans would once again confront Santa Anna.

On the very day that Scott landed at Veracruz, Santa Anna stumbled back to San Luis Potosí after his defeat at Buena Vista. Early reports tried to cheer Mexico into believing that the battle had been a Mexican victory, but half of the twenty thousand men that Santa Anna had started north with two months before had died in battle, starved to death, or deserted. Only the horror of a foreign invader on Mexican soil could wipe away the stigma of Buena Vista and cause the Mexican populace to rally once more around Santa Anna.

Two roads diverged from Veracruz toward Mexico City: the National Highway to the north and the Orizaba Road to the south of the 18,700-foot volcanic giant of Orizaba. Santa Anna correctly surmised that Scott would take the route of the National Highway, because it was in better condition and perhaps because it followed the historic path of Cortez against the Aztecs.

By mid-April, Santa Anna had gathered together about twelve thousand troops and forty-three pieces of artillery and spread them across a narrow pass just south of the town of Cerro Gordo. His right flank was protected by the Rio del Plan, and any American advance would have to come straight up the road or along a series of ridges to the east. Uncannily, the positions and terrain were similar to Buena Vista, but with reverse roles.

The opening moves proved much the same, too. Twiggs's division probed the Mexican artillery positions between the river and the road and then prepared to move east via the higher ridges. Two solo scouting excursions—one by Captain Beauregard and the other by Captain Lee—showed the way using a rough trail around El Telegrafo Hill and into the Mexican rear.

By April 17, Scott and his other divisions had arrived on the field, and he gave orders for the attack. Twiggs would lead the main assault around Santa Anna's left flank, while Brigadier General Gideon Pillow, commanding a brigade of Tennessee and Pennsylvania volunteers, would apply pressure on the artillery batteries in the center.

It was no secret that Gideon Pillow was Polk's general—a

Democratic insider among a host of Whigs. Polk's longtime political ally may have called himself a general after his strategy at the 1844 Democratic convention, but in the hills of Mexico, he seemed to be out of his element. Upon receiving his orders to charge artillery with bayonets—albeit on the flank—Pillow protested furiously to Scott that it was "a desperate undertaking" and that he expected to leave his bones there.

Scott was unmoved by such theatrics, and the attack began. But Pillow's protestations only got louder and then devolved into shouting matches with his regimental commanders. By the time Twiggs's division had cracked the Mexican left and essentially won the battle, Pillow's regiments had made two unsuccessful attacks and seen their general "going down the hill in our rear" not to be "seen or heard from until the whole engagement was over."[7]

In making his report to Washington, however, General Scott was very sensitive to Pillow's ties to the White House. He graciously reported to Secretary Marcy: "Brigadier General Pillow and his brigade twice assaulted with great daring the enemy's lines of batteries on our left; and, though without success, they contributed much to distract and dismay their immediate opponents."[8]

But the die had been cast for greater friction to develop between Pillow and Scott as the American army ground onward toward Mexico City. Meanwhile, Santa Anna, his carriage riddled with bullets, escaped south from Cerro Gordo toward the village of Orizaba to plot his next move.

𝒫resident Polk received the news of the fall of Veracruz as Scott's army was advancing on Cerro Gordo. Even though Congress had not acted on Benton's proposal to create a super-rank of lieutenant general, Polk was determined to send a high-level civilian diplomat to be at Scott's side and thus ready to negotiate just as soon as the Mexicans showed any willingness to do so. Again, however, the complicated question was "Who?"

With a bevy of Whig generals in the field, Polk's first requirement was that the peace commissioner be a Democrat. But his appointee could not be too prominent a Democrat. "Such is the jealousy of the different factions of the Democratic party in reference to the next presidential election towards each other," the president cautioned, "that it is impossible to appoint any prominent man or men without giving extensive dissatisfaction to others, and thus jeopardizing the ratification of any treaty they might make."

So initially Polk favored sending James Buchanan. He assumed that a Cabinet officer would give gravity to the mission and that the secretary of state would be seen as the president's man despite his own presidential aspirations.

Despite Buchanan's abilities, Polk's relationship with his secretary of state was the most contentious of any among his generally compliant Cabinet. Polk was frequently frustrated by Buchanan's contrarian positions and his on-again, off-again desire to leave the Cabinet for the Supreme Court. Indeed, one cannot but wonder whether Polk wasn't just looking for a good reason to get Buchanan out of town.

But Polk acknowledged — and Buchanan quite readily agreed — that given Mexico's refusal to receive a commissioner, Buchanan couldn't simply join Scott and then wait around "with no assurance whether the Mexican authorities would agree to negotiate." So Buchanan suggested a more dispensable man than he presumed himself to be. That person was Nicholas P. Trist, the chief clerk of the State Department.

Trained as a lawyer, Trist was fluent in Spanish. His Democratic pedigree seemed secure in that he was married to a granddaughter of Thomas Jefferson and had served a brief stint as Andrew Jackson's private secretary in the White House. Polk quickly agreed with Buchanan's recommendation and summoned Trist to his office the very same day. But once again, the man who had so often sent well-known personal confidants on critical political errands now placed the resolution of the gravest crisis of his presidency in the hands of someone he scarcely knew.

Polk planned to invest Trist secretly with plenipotentiary powers and dispatch him to Scott's headquarters with a working draft of a peace treaty. If Santa Anna — or whoever might be in power — found it acceptable, Trist could show his full credentials and conclude the agreement. If the Mexicans agreed only to appoint commissioners and negotiate, Trist was to report accordingly and

Buchanan would be sent to take over. The matter of secrecy was so important that Polk stressed it at length to Trist, and also summoned the deputy clerk charged with copying the draft of the treaty and personally swore him to secrecy.[9]

On April 13, 1847, Buchanan submitted a draft of the proposed treaty to the regular Tuesday meeting of the Cabinet. It called for a boundary along the Rio Grande upstream to the 32nd parallel (just north of El Paso) and then straight west to the Pacific, reaching the ocean some fifty miles south of San Diego. Another article provided for a perpetual right of transit across the Isthmus of Tehuantepec. (As witness to the importance the Polk administration placed on future Pacific trade, Secretary of the Treasury Walker advocated the isthmus as more significant than the cession of New Mexico and California.) In consideration for both, Buchanan proposed the assumption of American claims and the payment of fifteen million dollars.

Polk expressed the hope that this boundary and concession might be obtained for that price, but wanted Trist authorized to pay more "if he found that to be the only obstacle in concluding the treaty." But how much more? "I was willing to make the consideration double that sum ($30,000,000)," the president said, "if the cession could not be obtained for a less sum, rather than fail to make a treaty."

Buchanan balked at Polk's largesse, but Polk told him that another twelve months of war would cost much more. The remainder of the Cabinet sided with the president, and Buchanan left to modify Trist's instructions. But when the secretary of state returned to the White House that evening with another draft, he exhibited his usual contrary strain by having amended the Tehuantepec rights paragraph. Instead of an up-front payment, Buchanan proposed that five million dollars be withheld until Mexico had constructed a canal or railroad across the isthmus and made the rights more valuable.

Ever the careful politician covering his flanks, Polk retorted that such a stipulation might be construed by some in Congress as making internal improvements in a foreign country and would thus be decidedly inconsistent with his usual stand on such matters. So

Buchanan redrafted Trist's instructions, and the treaty as Polk wanted it and Trist left Washington on the morning of April 16, 1847, with full powers to conclude a peace.[10]

In Polk's eyes, secrecy was paramount. What the president seems to have feared most was the Whig editors of the *National Intelligencer.* They were busy promoting the presidential prospects of Zachary Taylor, and the president worried that if they found out about Trist's mission, they would likely do their best to sabotage it. It didn't help the president's humor any that he had learned just four days before that John C. Calhoun—Democrat though he purported to be—was flirting with endorsing Taylor.

Then, for all his secrecy, Polk did what by twenty-first-century standards seems counterintuitive. If news of Trist's mission was to be kept from the Whig press at all costs, Polk nonetheless told Thomas Ritchie, the editor of the Democrats' own mouthpiece, the Washington *Union,* the whole story. "I did this in the strictest confidence," the president claimed, "because it was necessary that he should know it in order to shape the course of his paper in reference to it."[11] Spin, it seems, has been around politics a long, long time.

What happened, of course, was that Polk's web of secrecy held for less than seventy-two hours. On April 20, the New York *Herald* published a letter signed merely "Maheeko," which disclosed Trist's departure and his mission—in Polk's words—"with remarkable accuracy and particularity."

The letter was in fact so accurate and detailed that the president was certain "that the writer must have obtained information on the subject from someone who was entrusted with the secret." Polk was livid. "I have not been more vexed or excited since I have been president than at this occurrence," he protested.

Polk confronted Buchanan and immediately blamed the deputy clerk in the state department—a Whig—for the leak. Buchanan vouched for the clerk, and Polk found it equally impossible that "any of my Cabinet have betrayed my confidence." That left Ritchie of the *Union,* but he, too, assured the president that "he had not as much as alluded to or hinted the matter to any human being." Unless Trist had indiscreetly boasted of the importance of his mission, someone in the president's inner circle was not telling the truth.

It appears that Polk did not come right out and accuse Buchanan himself of the indiscretion, but by reading between the lines of his diary, one can see the thought seemed to have weighed heavily upon his mind. Calling the disclosure of Trist's mission "a great outrage upon me," the president told Buchanan, "I had found that almost everything that transpired in the Cabinet got into the newspapers, that I had been annoyed no little by it, and that I intended to put an end to it."[12]

$\mathscr{B}$ut the real fireworks started when Nicholas Trist arrived in Veracruz on May 6, 1847, and communicated with General Winfield Scott, who was busy advancing beyond Cerro Gordo. If the diplomat and the general had met in person at the outset, the following two months of rancor and backbiting might have been avoided. Trist, however, was reportedly feeling poorly. He chose to remain temporarily in Veracruz and to forward to Scott through a special military detachment Buchanan's sealed letter to the Mexican foreign minister, Marcy's instructions to Scott, and Trist's own hastily written cover letter.

Trist's cover letter to Scott has not survived, but from subsequent events, it is credible to speculate that its tone was far from ingratiating. Marcy's instructions were written with the assumption that Trist would brief Scott on the full background of his mission and the draft of the treaty. Accordingly, Marcy only advised Scott directly that should Trist inform him under certain circumstances that "further active military operations should cease," Scott was to regard Trist's directive as emanating from the president. Finally, there was the matter of the sealed communication to the Mexican foreign minister that Scott was instructed to pass on without knowledge of its contents.

For starters, the very appearance of a diplomatic envoy in Mexico caught Scott by surprise. Always suspicious that there was a conspiracy brewing against him, Scott had weathered his initial choppy relations with Polk and had even managed to stay relatively calm through the rumors that the president was going to appoint a lieutenant general to supersede him. But now, here was the chief *clerk* of the state department purporting to tell the general-in-chief how and when to conduct military operations. Pompous Scott went bombastic.

"I see," Scott immediately fired back at Trist, "that the Secretary of War proposes to degrade me, by requiring that I, commander of this army, shall defer to you, the chief clerk of the Department of State, the question of continuing or discontinuing hostilities." Such was a military question, Scott declared, and the safety of his army demanded that Scott, and Scott alone, be the one to make the determination when hostilities would cease.

Trist received this communication while en route to Scott's headquarters at Jalapa. He paused to write a five-thousand-word rebuttal. It included the pointed observation that Scott's orders did not originate with Marcy but "from him, who, if the constitution of the United States be anything but an empty formula, is 'the commander-in-chief' of 'this army,' and of the whole armed force of the United States."

Small wonder that when Marcy received letters from Scott about his conflict with Trist, the secretary of war—who knew Scott well and Trist somewhat—exclaimed in frustration: "I fear Scott and Trist have got to writing. If so, all is lost!"[13]

The president was even more frustrated. Scott's reaction simply reinforced Polk's opinion that the general was a Whig not to be trusted, despite his groveling prior to departing for Mexico. As for Trist, Polk had to wonder how someone so highly recommended by Buchanan could become such a loose cannon so quickly. Trist was supposed to have given Scott copies of both the draft treaty *and* the missive to the foreign minister—which reiterated that hostilities would not cease until a treaty was signed—which would have avoided all of this.

"Between them the orders of the Secretary of War and the Secretary of State have been disregarded," Polk grumbled; "and the danger has become imminent that because of the personal controversy between these self important personages, the golden moment for concluding a peace with Mexico may have passed." The president ordered Buchanan and Marcy to write their respective charges and strongly condemn their conduct.[14]

*I*f Trist had an excuse that he didn't feel well during this exchange, it didn't help Scott's demeanor that at the very same time Trist appeared on his flank, the general was losing a goodly part of his army—not to Mexican firepower but to volunteer departures. The enlistments of the one-year volunteers who had rallied to Polk's May 1846 call to arms were expiring, and the vast majority had seen enough and were opting to go home. Seven volunteer regiments totaling more than three thousand men marched out of Jalapa for Veracruz on the very day that Trist landed there.

Suddenly down to only seven thousand effective troops, Scott nonetheless sent Worth's division to occupy Puebla, just seventy-five miles from Mexico City. Worth did so without a fight on May 15, and Scott joined him there with most of his troops on May 28. Within a week, the general had abandoned all positions between Veracruz and Puebla and essentially cut his supply lines to the coast in order to concentrate his forces for an attack on the capital. Trist also arrived at Puebla, although the two men still refused to meet personally.[15]

But at Puebla, Scott's rapid advance inland ground to a halt. The reasons were many. He needed more troops; there was confusion over Trist's role; and no one was quite sure whether Santa Anna was marshaling forces for a grand last stand, offering to surrender, or merely continuing the diplomatic sleight of hand for which he was well known. The last thing that Scott could afford, however, was a stalemate. And for a while during the long summer of 1847, that is exactly what Mr. Polk's war looked like it might become.

*W*hile Polk pondered this possibility, the president took the only trips of his presidency beyond the immediate vicinity of Washington, save for a week he and Sarah spent on the Chesapeake shore in August 1846 and another week he spent in Pennsylvania in August 1848. Late in May 1847, the couple left Washington to attend graduation ceremonies at Polk's alma mater, the University of North Carolina.

Aside from a twenty-mile carriage ride between Raleigh and

Chapel Hill, most of their journey was by rail, so much had this transportation conveyance revolutionized travel in the dozen years since Old Hickory's first presidential train ride. What the Polks probably did not realize was that their brief stops before crowds at railroad depots along the route were inaugurating a century-long tradition of presidential whistle-stops.

Less than a month later, Polk embarked on a two-week tour of Philadelphia, New York, and New England. Sarah did not go on this trip. Instead, she accompanied her niece, Johanna Rucker, home to Tennessee. Johanna had lived at the White House and become a surrogate daughter. Save for a week in the summer of 1848 and a trip by Sarah to New York City after the 1848 election, it was the only time that the Polks were separated during his presidency.

Among the president's party heading north was John Appleton, the chief clerk of the navy department, whom Polk asked to keep a journal of the trip. In Appleton's first paragraph, he recorded that the president's "journey was undertaken with no political purpose," but the truth was that James K. Polk had rarely done anything in his entire adult life that had not had a political purpose.

No doubt part of his motivation was—as Polk expressed it—to see "a section of my country in New England which I had never before visited." But the president was also keenly aware of the increasingly divisive sectionalism gripping the country. Earlier in the year, Congress had finally voted three million dollars for Polk's treaty negotiation "slush fund," but only after the Wilmot Proviso banning slavery in new territories had again been included by the House.

The Senate passed the three-million-dollar bill without the proviso, and enough votes shifted in the House to accept the Senate version. But the extremely close votes were occasioned not so much along party lines as between north and south. For a southern president to visit New England was a strong statement that Old Hickory's union still lived.

And New England received the president in exactly that way. To suppose that the region was unanimously opposed to "Mr. Polk's war" is as erroneous as the supposition of regional unanimity against "Mr. Madison's war" during the War of 1812. Regional politics were more complex and opinions far more mixed than that. Even Boston turned out to welcome Polk enthusiastically.

There was only one incident that Polk chose to record himself from the entire two-week tour and it *was* highly political. An obvious stop might have been with former president Martin Van Buren at his home at Kinderhook south of Albany. But the invitation from Van Buren was delivered verbally by Benjamin Butler only as the president arrived in New York. Polk declined. "If Mr. Van Buren really desired me to visit him," the president noted, "he would have written to me inviting me to do so," and not postponed a verbal message to so late a period.[16]

Van Buren was still smarting over the 1844 convention and Polk's independence in not consulting him more closely over his Cabinet appointments. Indeed, from his lair at Kinderhook, the Red Fox had not completely given up hope that somehow he might still win a second term in the White House.

No wonder then that, with some of the public opposing the war, with Whig generals having visions of grandeur, and with the Democratic party from former presidents to his own secretary of state fixating on 1848, Polk had delighted in the cheers of his tour. No sooner had the president returned to Washington, however, than there was plenty more fire on Polk, from one of his oldest and closest allies.

CHAPTER 17

Old Bullion's Son-in-Law

$\mathcal{T}$HE POLITICAL INFIGHTING among Zachary Taylor, Winfield Scott, and the Polk administration paled beside the controversy that Thomas Hart Benton's bullheaded son-in-law ignited in California. When General Stephen Watts Kearny greeted Kit Carson south of Santa Fe on October 6, 1846, no one could have foreseen that the decision Kearny made that day would hold such ominous ramifications for President Polk, Senator Benton, John C. Frémont, and for Kearny himself.

Kit Carson told Kearny an amazing story. After meeting Lieutenant Archibald Gillespie on the shores of Upper Klamath Lake the previous spring, Captain Frémont had rounded up his band of mountain man explorers and headed back south to the vicinity of Sutter's Fort. Rumors were rampant that Mexicans were massing to drive American settlers from the Sacramento Valley and perhaps even build a fort at Donner Pass to prevent the influx of more immigrants.

How much Frémont instigated what happened next has always been debated, but in the early hours of June 14, 1846, a group of

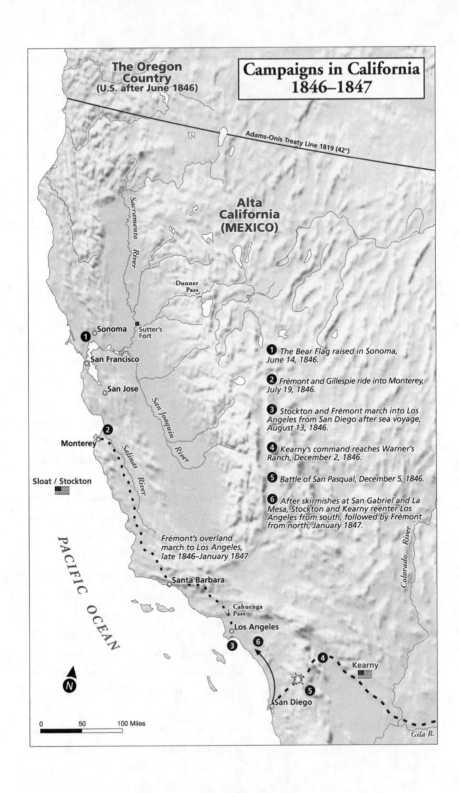

The Oregon Country
(U.S. after June 1846)

Campaigns in California
1846–1847

Adams-Onís Treaty Line 1819 (42°)

Alta
California
(MEXICO)

Sacramento River

Donner Pass

Sonoma ●1 ■ Sutter's Fort

San Francisco

San Jose

San Joaquin River

Monterey ●2

Salinas River

Sloat / Stockton ▭

PACIFIC OCEAN

Frémont's overland
march to Los Angeles,
late 1846–January 1847

Santa Barbara

Cahuenga Pass

Los Angeles

●3 ●6

San Diego

●5

●4 Kearny ▭

Colorado River

Gila R.

❶ The Bear Flag raised in Sonoma,
June 14, 1846.

❷ Frémont and Gillespie ride into Monterey,
July 19, 1846.

❸ Stockton and Frémont march into Los
Angeles from San Diego after sea voyage,
August 13, 1846.

❹ Kearny's command reaches Warner's
Ranch, December 2, 1846.

❺ Battle of San Pasqual, December 5, 1846.

❻ After skirmishes at San Gabriel and La
Mesa, Stockton and Kearny reenter Los
Angeles from south, followed by Frémont
from north, January 1847.

N

0   50   100 Miles

thirty-two Americans led by Ezekiel Merritt rode into the town plaza at tiny Sonoma, just north of San Francisco Bay. They went to the home of Mariano Vallejo and took him prisoner, despite the fact that Vallejo was not on active military duty, no Mexican soldiers were stationed at Sonoma, and Vallejo himself was generally sympathetic to American interests.

Before the day was done, William L. Todd, a cousin of Mary Todd Lincoln, took a piece of brown cloth and drew a broad red stripe at the bottom, a star and a ferocious grizzly bear at the top, and the black words "California Republic" in the middle. This bear flag was raised in place of the Mexican flag in the town plaza amidst cries of independence, although exactly what that meant, no one was quite certain. By the Fourth of July, however, Frémont and his exploring party were at Sonoma, intermingling with the "Bear Flaggers" for a decidedly American celebration.[1]

Meanwhile, the American navy had once again landed at Monterey, California. Prior to Commodore Robert F. Stockton's anticipated arrival, the American Pacific squadron was still under the command of John D. Sloat. Hearing of the initial border clashes along the Rio Grande, but with no solid news that a formal declaration of war had occurred, Sloat sailed north from Mazatlán to Monterey per his standing orders to counter any possible British advances.

Well aware of the faux pas of Thomas ap Catesby Jones in rushing to raise the Stars and Stripes at Monterey four years earlier, Commodore Sloat casually anchored his flotilla of four ships in Monterey harbor and went ashore to pay a courtesy call on General José Castro. As he did so, Sloat kept glancing out to sea for any sign of a British man-of-war. Before any appeared, he learned what had transpired in Sonoma.

Given the apparent roles of Frémont and Gillespie, Sloat concluded that they had acted on explicit orders from Polk. In turn, Sloat demanded that Castro surrender Monterey. Castro did so and fled south. Sloat then sent a detachment to seize Yerba Buena (San Francisco).

Learning of Sloat's actions, Frémont and Gillespie assumed that Sloat had acted on his own explicit orders. They took comfort that

Sloat's conquests gave official credence to their own. Frémont and Gillespie subsequently rode into Monterey on July 19 at the head of 160 horsemen and asked Sloat to muster their troops into the American army as the California Battalion. Then, when it dawned on Sloat that Frémont's role was not nearly as well defined as the commodore had thought, Sloat was only too happy to turn over his command to the newly arrived Commodore Stockton and sail away from California as quickly as possible.

Stockton had none of Sloat's qualms and not only praised Frémont's efforts but also set about conquering the rest of California. Stockton dispatched one ship to Yerba Buena, kept another at Monterey, and sailed with two others, the frigate *Congress* and sloop of war *Cyane*, to attack the southern towns.

Frémont's California Battalion went to San Diego on board the *Cyane*—Kit Carson was among those to get seasick—and raised the American flag there without firing a shot. Stockton and the *Congress* called at Santa Barbara and performed a similar flag raising. Then, leaving a garrison of sixteen men at Santa Barbara, Stockton sailed on to San Pedro, the port for the little village of Los Angeles.

When Stockton summoned Frémont to march north from San Diego and join him in attacking Los Angeles, the defending forces of General Castro retreated through the San Bernardino Mountains toward Sonora, Mexico. Consequently, on August 13, 1846, Stockton and Frémont marched into Los Angeles to the accompaniment of a brass band. Their entry, Frémont recalled, had "more the effect of a parade of home guards than of an enemy taking possession of a conquered town."

Four days later, Stockton finally received official word of the declaration of war against Mexico, and he issued a proclamation declaring California a possession of the United States. It was this triumphant news—the capture of Polk's coveted California with scarcely the firing of a shot—that Carson carried east with him.[2]

Hearing all this from Kit Carson in the hot New Mexican desert, General Kearny faced a critical decision. His orders appeared clearcut. If successful in New Mexico—which he had been—Kearny was to "press forward to California" and "establish temporary civil governments" as he had done in New Mexico.

Among the great debate that would soon ensue were the lengths to which Kit Carson went to advise Kearny that Commodore Stockton had already established some measure of civil government in California. What was more, on September 2, 1846, Stockton, acting as governor of the newly conquered territory, had designated John C. Frémont, by now a lieutenant colonel, military commandant and had promised to appoint him governor in his stead when Stockton sailed away later in the fall.

It is doubtful that this fact—whether or not Carson explicitly communicated it to Kearny—had any bearing on the general's decision to press westward. At the core of his decision—as for any good military officer—were his orders. "California" and "civil governments," they read, and Kearny was first and foremost one to follow orders. Second, as a longtime friend of Frémont and the extended Benton family, Kearny might well have planned—as Carson in fact later claimed that Kearny had said—to make Frémont governor himself, much as he had just installed Charles Bent in Taos.

Consequently, with apparently no hesitation or foreboding, Kearny determined to continue to California. He even prevailed upon Carson to return with him as his guide. But with California militarily secure—or so it appeared—there was little reason to take three hundred dragoons along. They might be useful once there, but the logistics of feeding and watering so large a force while en route across largely unknown desert were daunting. Besides, the troops might be more useful in New Mexico as part of Alexander Doniphan's planned campaign against Chihuahua.

So Kearny kept Lieutenant William H. Emory of the engineers and about one hundred officers and dragoons with him and ordered the remainder of his force back to Santa Fe. This plan seemed sound as Carson led Kearny's reduced force westward across the arid Gila River country. But on November 23, 1846, at the confluence of the Gila and Colorado rivers, the Americans captured a Mexican messenger bound from California to Sonora. His papers announced the unsettling news that California had not gone as quickly or as quietly into the American column as Carson's dispatches had indicated.

If Thomas O. Larkin and certain leading Californios had been allowed to play a more active role, a California republic on the model of Texas in 1836 might have provided a peaceful transition to U.S. control. But Commodore Stockton rejected such a notion, and this opened the door for a widespread Californio revolt. After all, Stockton and Frémont had not defeated Castro's forces so much as these forces had dispersed to fight another day. That day came even as Carson rode eastward bearing news of the early American victories.

What lit the powder keg was Lieutenant (now Captain—everyone got a promotion when their side was winning) Archibald Gillespie's less than enlightened administration of Los Angeles. Had any "proper and prudent person been left here," Thomas Larkin confided to his wife, "this disturbance would not have happened." Even the Americans agreed that Gillespie had "punished, fined and imprisoned who and when he pleased without any hearing." Larkin told his wife that he had seen "that trouble was coming on California" as early as May or June "by that badly acted affair at Sonoma, [begun] and ended in wrong."

Consequently, Captain José Maria Flores forced Gillespie's forty-eight-man garrison in Los Angeles to surrender in late September. Next, Flores quickly captured the small American garrisons left at Santa Barbara and San Diego. Back in Monterey, Stockton immediately summoned Frémont and his California Battalion, which had returned to the vicinity of Sutter's Fort, to hasten back to Monterey and again sail for southern California.

When Frémont replied that he would march overland instead— like Carson, he, too, had never gotten his sea legs—Stockton went ahead by himself and landed troops at San Pedro. They were promptly foiled in any attempt to move inland on Los Angeles, however, and Stockton had to be content with recapturing San Diego and making its fine harbor his base of operations. With American control in the south reduced to San Diego, and Californio forces operating at will, General Stephen Watts Kearny was riding into a wide-open war with only about one hundred troops.[3]

Fortunately for Kearny, the numbers on both sides during this campaign were quite small, but that did not mean that the fighting would not be fierce. On December 2, 1846, Kearny's small command reached Warner's Ranch, about sixty miles east of San Diego, and confirmed the report that only San Diego remained in American hands in the south. With Mexican forces under Andrés Pico marshaling to block Kearny's advance, he sent a message to Stockton at San Diego asking for reinforcements.

Two days later, as Kearny continued his cautious march westward, who should come to his aid with thirty-nine men and a four-pounder but the blundering Captain Gillespie. Stockton also sent word that if Kearny deemed it prudent, he should take advantage of the opportunity to attack Pico and about one hundred men at the Indian village of San Pasqual.

Having eaten their share of dust and seen little glory in almost a thousand miles since Santa Fe, Kearny's officers were champing at the bit and "extraordinarily desirous to meet the enemy as soon as possible." When an American patrol accidentally alerted Pico to the proximity of Kearny's command near midnight on the evening of December 5, Kearny resolved to roust his sleeping dragoons and attack immediately.

The Americans rode by twos down a narrow trail into the valley of San Pasqual. By one account, upon reaching the plain, Kearny's order to "Trot" was incorrectly repeated as "Charge!" and all bedlam broke loose. Some of Pico's horsemen feigned a retreat only to wheel around and charge forward with superb horsemanship and deadly lances.

Kearny was in the thick of things, as was Captain Gillespie, who urged his troops to "Rally, men, for God's sake, rally! Show a front, don't turn your backs." But Gillespie's efforts only attracted a more frenzied Mexican onslaught as some of the attackers recognized him as the despotic ruler of Los Angeles.

Casualty rates were appallingly high on both sides, by one account twenty-one killed and twenty wounded—more than 30 percent—on the American side alone. Three of Kearny's officers were among the dead, and he himself suffered a nasty lance wound to the groin and a saber wound to the buttocks. Nevertheless, Kearny doggedly continued his advance until he found a defensible position around what is still called Mule Hill. By December 7, Pico received reinforcements and enveloped the Americans with a tight siege. Once again Kearny sent a desperate plea to Stockton for assistance.

Supposedly, Stockton sent a message back declining to provide any, but that may well have been a ruse to put Pico off guard in case it was intercepted—which it was. The fact remains that as Kearny prepared to fight his way out of Mule Hill in the early hours of December 11, a sentry's challenge of "Who goes there?" was answered by a relief column of eighty marines and one hundred sailors. The following afternoon in a pouring rain, a tattered and begrimed Stephen Watts Kearny led his First Dragoons into San Diego in a far less regal procession than he had led into Santa Fe.[4]

𝒞ommodore Stockton proved a gracious host and even offered his own quarters to the wounded general. Technically, even though most of the troops in the field were attached to Stockton's naval units, Kearny was now the ranking officer in the theater of operations, and by some accounts Stockton seems to have initially recognized this.* Certainly, Kearny showed Stockton his orders, and Stockton was well aware of the large discretionary power these orders invested in the general.

But Kearny was still recovering from his painful wounds and was hardly at his best. When an immediate attack on Los Angeles was deemed advisable, Kearny encouraged Stockton to lead the way, providing considerable grist for future debates about who had supreme command of the assault. Nonetheless, Kearny, Stockton, and about five hundred dragoons, sailors, and marines marched northward, and after minor battles—skirmishes, really—at San Gabriel and La Mesa, the Americans recaptured Los Angeles early in January 1847.

---

*It was frequently a little confusing, but in the nineteenth-century American navy, the commander of a flotilla was designated "commodore" no matter what his rank in the permanent grades. Stockton was a captain by naval rank, which was equivalent to a colonel in the army and hence subordinate to Kearny's brevet rank of brigadier general. The rank of commodore was equivalent to that of brigadier general.

During all of this, the question was repeatedly asked, where were Colonel Frémont and his vaunted California Battalion? Frémont had taken his time marching overland from the Sacramento Valley. Upon entering Los Angeles, General Kearny even sent a messenger riding in search of Frémont to warn him that certain troops recently engaged under Flores and Pico might still pose a hostile force.

But as it turned out, Kearny needn't have worried. Acting under authority as Stockton's duly appointed military commandant, Frémont had negotiated with Andrés Pico what came to be called the Treaty of Cahuenga. Essentially, it granted Californios a sweeping general amnesty despite the fact that Frémont's superior—whether Stockton or Kearny—was only a few miles away. The result was that on January 14, 1847, John C. Frémont once again rode into Los Angeles looking every bit the conqueror. Even Stockton wasn't pleased by this initiative.

What followed set the stage for one of the most celebrated courts-martial in the history of the United States Army. Before it was over, the celebrated "Pathfinder of the West" would stand accused of insubordination, and two of the most powerful men in the country—the president and the senior senator from Missouri—would stand on opposite sides.

Friction between Commodore Stockton and General Kearny increased after the capture of Los Angeles. Then, on January 22, 1847, Stockton sailed for Mazatlán, much as he had been trying to do since before the Californio uprising. But before Stockton did so, he—just as he had promised almost five months earlier—appointed John C. Frémont "governor and commander-in-chief of the territory of California until the President of the United States shall otherwise direct."

General Kearny thought that his own orders were evidence of the president's directing otherwise, and Kearny expected Frémont, who signed his letters to Kearny as "Lieutenant Colonel, United States Army," to acknowledge the same. But Frémont insisted on deriving his authority and position from the rather dubious continuing authority of Commodore Stockton. Kearny expected Frémont to follow his orders. Frémont said no. Not just no, but emphatically no. Here was a blatant case of insubordination.[5]

It seems quite likely that had John C. Frémont simply saluted Stephen Watts Kearny and acknowledged both Kearny's orders and his authority in the military chain of command, Kearny may well have appointed Frémont governor of California and returned east in the spring of 1847 as planned. Different though they were in personality, Kearny and Frémont were of the same Missouri circle that emanated from the hub of Thomas Hart Benton. In fact, *both* owed their presence in California to Benton, the senator having recommended Kearny for the Army of the West command and having always championed his son-in-law's western excursions.

Much has been written—quite erroneously, it seems—about a high degree of personal enmity existing between Kearny and Frémont, stemming from Frémont's dramatic requisition of the mountain howitzer from Kearny for his second expedition in 1843. The truth is that Frémont did most things with an exaggerated dramatic flair—frequently to his detriment.

Kearny correctly reported the howitzer requisition to his superiors, whereas without a personal acquaintance with Frémont and the Benton clan, another officer might not have provided the weapon at all. And in fact, one of Kearny's first letters upon arriving in Los Angeles was directed to Old Bullion, assuring the senator and his daughter that her young cavalier was "perfectly well and has gained great credit."

The other flag often waved in Frémont's defense is that Kearny and the military establishment held a grudge against him because, in Benton's words, Frémont had committed the sin of entering the military "without passing through West Point," and had then compounded it by becoming "distinguished."

That criticism may have held some water among the cadre of younger West Pointers who watched Frémont's subsequent court-martial with a certain amount of glee, but there is no evidence that Kearny himself felt that way. Kearny, after all, had not gone to West Point and had spent almost his entire career on the western frontier well removed from any cadre of eastern elitists.

What in the world, then, had young—he was still barely thirty-four—John C. Frémont been thinking? While there are many partisans on both sides, the spurious conspiracy theories involving the mountain howitzer and West Point were nurtured by the Frémont-Benton faction well after the fact. They were put forth to brush aside Frémont's actions in California—actions that can only be called what they were: military insubordination occasioned by vaunting ambition.

If Frémont at this point had any hope of retaining his title and eluding the noose that was tightening around his neck, it was that orders would arrive with Stockton's replacement that would approve the commodore's actions and hence Frémont's own. But that was not to be. The navy was rotating commodores of its Pacific squadron with extraordinary speed. The next orders for Stockton announced the pending arrival of his replacement and also advised him that military operations on land and the administration of the civil government were under the direction of the senior army officer in the theater.

The next orders for General Kearny reached him in San Francisco on February 13, 1847, and reiterated the same thing. Complimenting Kearny for his success in New Mexico, Winfield Scott ordered him to erect suitable fortifications in Monterey and San Francisco bays; muster into the army such California volunteers as he could find; and as the senior officer of the land forces, perform the duties of civil governor. In other words, Kearny was to carry out the orders that the general had previously shown to both Stockton and Frémont and that they had chosen to ignore.[6]

News of the command controversy in California reached President Polk in late April 1847. At the time, his relationship with Thomas Hart Benton had never been better. Old Bullion enjoyed easy access to the White House to discuss both diplomatic and military matters, and the president genuinely valued his advice.

Their joint effort to create the rank of lieutenant general for Benton had not been adopted by Congress, but Polk had offered Benton an appointment as a major general instead. Still hoping to achieve the intent of the broader plan, Benton attached two conditions to his acceptance—first, that he be given supreme command of the army in Mexico, and second, that he also be invested with full diplomatic powers to conclude a peace treaty.

When Polk realized that he could not promote a new major general ahead of four senior officers—despite his professed willingness to recall both Taylor and Scott to solve half of the problem—Benton declined the appointment. This was more a matter of political reality than any great friction between Old Bullion and Polk, and the president reiterated that had Congress created the super-rank, "I should have selected General Benton for that important command."

The Polks and the Bentons were also close socially. They routinely attended the same Presbyterian church. On March 18, 1847, James and Sarah were honored guests in the Benton home for the marriage of Old Bullion's eldest daughter, Eliza, to William Carey Jones of New Orleans. Polk even did the honors of escorting the bride to the supper table.[7]

But now there was the first hint that opposite sides were about to be taken. "An unfortunate collision has occurred in California between General Kearny and Commodore Stockton in regard to precedence in rank," Polk recorded privately on April 30, 1847. "It appears," he continued, "that Lieutenant Colonel Frémont refused to obey General Kearny and obeyed Commodore Stockton."

A few days after reading their correspondence, the president was "fully satisfied that General Kearny was right, and that Commodore Stockton's course was wrong." Indeed, he thought that both Stockton and Frémont had "acted insubordinately and in a manner that is censurable." Yet Polk also expressed the hope—perhaps out of deference to Benton—that "so rigorous a course" as a court-martial would not be pursued.[8]

A month later, Jessie Benton Frémont called at the White House. Jessie had known the Polks since she was a little girl and was particularly well acquainted with Sarah, but this time she appeared with Kit Carson in tow and asked to see the president. Carson had finally arrived in Washington after doubling back to California with Kearny.

"Mrs. Frémont seemed anxious to elicit from me," Polk noted, "some expression of approbation of her husband's conduct, but I evaded making any." That evening, Carson called again by himself, and he and the president talked at length about California and "the collision." In truth, Polk reiterated in his diary, "I consider that

Colonel Frémont was greatly in the wrong when he refused to obey the orders issued to him by General Kearny."

About a month after Polk completed his New England tour, Senator Benton returned from a summer visit to Missouri and he, too, had a conversation with Polk in which he sought the president's approval of Frémont's conduct. Polk was too astute to fall into that trap, even when Benton hinted that he might call for a full Senate investigation into "this whole California business."

This was Benton's not so subtle way of pressuring Polk, but as others had learned to their detriment, James K. Polk was not one to be bullied. Polk simply told Benton that the president "had nothing to fear from the most searching investigation," and while he hoped it would not be necessary to convene a court-martial, he would "have no objection to the fullest and broadest investigation." There it was. The frost was suddenly on the Polk-Benton friendship. It would only grow colder.[9]

Meanwhile, General Kearny had established a civil government in California and had turned it over to his subordinate, Colonel Richard B. Mason. On May 31, 1847, Kearny set out for Washington. John C. Frémont, who might well have had Mason's job but for his own self-importance, was ordered to follow him. Frémont rode not in the van as the pathfinder and a conqueror of California but in a separate detachment trailing General Kearny's main command. By the time the caravan reached Fort Leavenworth, Frémont was officially notified that he was under arrest and ordered to report to the adjutant general in Washington.

On the morning of September 11, 1847, Kearny arrived in Washington and immediately went to pay his respects to the president. The Cabinet being in session, Polk asked the general to call again, which Kearny did five days later. Polk and Kearny talked at length about California, but "no conversation took place in relation to his recent difficulty" with Stockton and Frémont. Polk did not introduce the subject and "was glad that [Kearny] did not."[10]

Two days later, Polk learned that Frémont had also been in Washington but had departed hastily to see his dying mother in South Carolina. In Frémont's absence, however, the Benton circle began to apply more pressure on Polk. William Carey Jones, who had married Eliza Benton in the president's presence only months before, called to say that Frémont desired a speedy trial to clear his name. Old Bullion, who was dusting off his legal skills and preparing to defend his son-in-law in person, again requested a broader investigation.

And Jessie Benton Frémont sent her own letter to the president imploring him to "see the manifest injustice to Mr. Frémont of letting his accusers escape from the investigation of the charges they have made against him." Jessie asked that Kearny and his officers be made to "stand the trial as well as himself."

When Frémont arrived back in Washington a week later—tragically, his mother had died just hours before he'd arrived at her bedside in Charleston—he went directly to the White House to call on the president. Decorum prevented him from directly discussing his plight. "Colonel Frémont is under arrest," Polk noted after the visit, but "made no allusion to that fact or to his case while in conversations with me."[11]

In the afternoon of Frémont's visit, Polk felt the symptoms of a chill and by the following day was too ill to attend church. Whatever the ailment was, it lingered, and both the president and Mrs. Polk were quite sick for a prolonged period during late September and early October 1847. They slept poorly for many nights, and on several occasions, Polk expressed grave concern for his wife.

By the time that Polk resumed his normal routine of receiving callers, it was October 18 and almost a month had passed since he had last opened his doors to the public. "Quite a number came in, all of whom but three were seeking office," and one of those was begging money. Showing his wit, Polk "concluded that if no persons had called in that time who had more important business than those who called today, the public had lost nothing by my absence from office."[12]

But now the Benton lobbying became intense and even downright rude. Old Bullion returned to Washington from another trip to the West on October 21 and called at the White House the next morning. If Polk would not broaden the investigation, Benton threatened to pursue courts-martial against Kearny and three of his key officers.

Three days later, the senator's son, John Randolph Benton, presented himself before Polk and demanded an appointment as a lieutenant in the regular army. When the president explained that it was his policy to give preference to those enlisted men who had served in Mexico, young Benton got loud and obnoxious and stormed out of the president's office muttering an oath. (Needless to say, there was no Secret Service in those days.) One observer who witnessed the scene thought the young man was drunk.

Young Benton's new brother-in-law, William Carey Jones, was an applicant for a chargé d'affaires position, but Polk was not favorably inclined toward him because until recently Jones had been the editor of a Whig newspaper. Presciently, Polk had predicted six months before, when Senator Benton had first pushed Jones's case, "if I do not appoint Mr. Jones, it will be the cause of a violent outbreak of opposition to me by General Benton." Now the cause wasn't just one son-in-law but two, plus Benton's son.

"I have always been upon good terms with Colonel Benton," Polk wrote later, "but he is a man of violent passions and I should not be surprised if he became my enemy because all his wishes in reference to his family and their appointments to offices are not gratified, and especially if I do not grant his wishes in reference to Colonel Frémont's trial."

But Polk was adamant in his course: "I will grant [Benton] no favors or privileges which I would not grant to any other officer, even though I should incur his displeasure and that of his friends by refusing to do so."[13]

That is exactly what happened. Frémont's trial began on November 2, 1847, at the Washington Arsenal. Thomas Hart Benton and William Carey Jones appeared as counsel for the accused. Polk insisted that he knew of "no reason why this case should produce more interest or excitement than the trial of any other officer charged with a military offense," but realized that "Senator Benton is resolved to make it do so."

Frémont's defense team went so far as to argue that Kearny's initial orders did not apply in California because he had been instructed to establish civil governments only "should you conquer" California. Stockton and Frémont claimed that "you" applied to Kearny personally and maintained—apparently overlooking the Californio revolt—that *they* had conquered California before Kearny's arrival.

After three months of drama, a military court of thirteen officers found John C. Frémont guilty of all charges of insubordination, principally mutiny, disobedience of orders, and conduct prejudicial to the public service. He was sentenced to dismissal from the service, although a majority of the judges recommended clemency.

Now the fate of Old Bullion's son-in-law lay with the president. Polk had made it quite clear that he would do his duty without regard to Benton's friendship, but he was also one to appreciate results. Rightly or wrongly, Frémont had had a hand in securing California and accomplishing one of the key goals of Polk's presidency. What would the president do?

At the regular Saturday Cabinet meeting of February 12, 1848, Polk expressed doubt "whether the facts as proved amounted to the legal definition of mutiny." There seemed to be little doubt, however, about the disobedience and prejudicial conduct charges. Nonetheless, the Cabinet agreed that Frémont—whose previous exploits had made him the darling of the press—should not be dismissed from the service. The central question became whether the president should approve or disapprove the findings of the court.

This was such a politically charged matter that Polk postponed the decision a day and called a rare Sunday evening Cabinet meeting to resolve it. After some sharp debate—Buchanan in particular was highly critical of Kearny's role—Polk determined to approve the court's findings but not dismiss Frémont from the service.

If Polk saw this as a way to appease Benton and still do his duty—he was, after all, following both the court's decision and its leniency recommendation—the president was mistaken. Benton and Frémont would never be appeased over a matter so entwined with honor. It was not clemency they sought, Jessie Benton Frémont vowed, but "justice."

When Polk advised Frémont that "in consideration of distinguished services" he should "report for duty with his regiment," the would-be governor of California responded that he would resign from the army unless the conviction was overturned. Polk chose not to reply. A month later, Frémont tendered his resignation and headed back to California as a private citizen.[14]

The evening that Polk signed his decision in the Frémont case, he and Sarah entertained their old adversary Henry Clay at the White House for the first time. "The party was an exceedingly pleasant one," the president noted, "and I was much gratified to have it in my power to pay this mark of respect to Mr. Clay." But among the forty or so guests, Thomas Hart Benton was conspicuously absent.

Old Bullion was immovable. "I meet Colonel Benton almost every Sabbath at church," Polk recorded in his diary several months later, "but he never speaks to me as he was in the habit of doing before the trial of Colonel Frémont."

Almost a year later, the situation had not changed. "From the day I approved the sentence of the court-martial in Colonel Frémont's case," Polk recalled, "Colonel Benton, for no other cause than that I dared to do my duty, has been exceedingly hostile to me. He has not called on me, nor have I spoken to him for more than twelve months."[15]

The Polk-Benton relationship was dead. And while Polk viewed it as he viewed most relationships—as political and not personal—its demise would be draining for both men. For Benton, the energy he expended in Frémont's defense may have sapped him of the personal determination and political allies essential to a run for the presidency on his own in 1848. For Polk, it meant that he had lost a powerful ally in Congress and that the antiwar Whigs who had swept into office in the midterm elections would increasingly put him on the spot.

CHAPTER 18

A President on the Spot

*T*HERE IS AMPLE evidence that James K. Polk set his sights on the presidency early in his political career. His first election to Congress, his desire for the Speaker's chair, and his pursuit of the vice presidential nomination in 1840 were only way stations along the road to the top. But once in the White House, Polk found the prize far more burdensome than glorious. Even as he managed to accomplish his primary goals, political strife was fierce; office seekers incessant; and the job itself—at least as Polk micromanaged it—physically taxing on his relatively weak constitution.

"I am fifty-two years old today, this being my birthday," the president mused on November 2, 1847. "I have now passed through two-thirds of my presidential term, and most heartily wish that the remaining third was over, for I am sincerely desirous to have the enjoyment of retirement in private life."[1] But the remaining sixteen months would be even more trying.

*O*n December 7, 1847, Polk sent his third annual message to the opening session of the thirtieth Congress. It was not as well received as his prior two. Among the reasons was the growing antiwar sentiment that had manifested itself in the most recent congressional elections. The Democrats had retained control of the Senate, but their majority in the House of Representatives was gone. There the Whigs held a narrow advantage of 115 to 108. Among the new Whig faces was a freshman congressman from the seventh district of Illinois named Abraham Lincoln.

It didn't help Polk's cause that the president could report no change in relations with Mexico. Yet once again, Polk made his case that Mexico had commenced the war, that the United States was the aggrieved nation, and that the country had been compelled to repel the invader in self-defense. But by now there were many skeptics, Lincoln among them.

On December 22, 1847, the new congressman from Illinois introduced what came to be called his "spot resolutions." They asked eight specific questions of the president. Lincoln minced no words and directly challenged Polk to "establish whether the particular spot on which the blood of our citizens was so shed was or was not at that time *our own soil.*"

Indeed, Lincoln and his fellow Whigs became quite adept at criticizing Polk and the war itself, while resolutely voting appropriations for supplies and support of the troops in the field. In January 1848, the Whig-controlled House voted on a resolution that praised General Taylor and his officers and men "for their indomitable valor, skill and good conduct" at the battle of Buena Vista almost a year earlier. It should have passed with the same degree of unanimity as the vote to declare war, but by a vote of 85 to 81 the Whigs added a clause that the war had been "unnecessarily and unconstitutionally begun by the President of the United States." Lincoln was among those voting in the majority.

Nine days later, Lincoln rose to defend that vote and to press his challenge to the president. "Let the President answer the interrogatories I proposed," Lincoln said dramatically, as if he were back in an Illinois courtroom. "Let him answer fully, fairly, and candidly. Let him answer with facts and not with arguments. Let him remember he sits where Washington sat, and so remembering, let him answer as Washington would answer."[2]

When none other than Lincoln's friend and law partner, William Herndon, questioned Lincoln's strident opposition to Polk's actions, Lincoln reminded Herndon that the war powers were vested in the legislative branch by the Constitution and to permit Polk such power would place the president "where kings have always stood."

"Allow the President to invade a neighboring nation, whenever *he* shall deem it necessary to repel an invasion," Lincoln lectured Herndon, "and you allow him to do so, *whenever he may choose to say* he deems it necessary for such purpose—and you allow him to make war at pleasure."[3]

Part of Lincoln's opposition stemmed from Polk's increasing use of executive privilege. Prior to the midterm elections, Polk rarely refused to supply Congress with information about his executive actions. One case when he refused involved his instructions to General Kearny for the conquest of California. Since the campaign was barely under way, Polk did not want to jeopardize its success by publicizing it or "excite the jealousy of England or France, who might interfere."

But as antiwar sentiment increased and the new Whig majority in the House flexed its muscles, it demanded more and more information. Lincoln and his colleagues now wanted to ascertain the extent of Polk's war aims and his instructions for negotiating with Mexico—both to John Slidell prior to the declaration of war and to Nicholas Trist more recently. How far, the opposition wanted to know, did Polk intend to go with territorial conquests, and how hard had he tried to negotiate a peace?

Prior congressional requests for executive branch information were traditionally made with the "customary and usual reservation" that the release of such information was not inconsistent with national interests. With their new majority, however, the Whigs were suddenly asking for information on the war without this reservation. Polk bristled, saying "the call of the House is unconditional" and refused to supply the "instructions and orders" because the negotiations were not yet complete. Nor did Polk ever respond to Lincoln's spot resolutions.[4]

Lincoln's bulldog attacks played well among his fellow Whigs in

Congress, but his political enemies in generally pro-war, pro-expansionist Illinois made the most of them. Labeled a traitor by his Democratic opponents and faced with an uphill race, Lincoln chose not to run for reelection in 1848. The far greater irony is that a scant dozen years later, the same Abraham Lincoln who challenged the presidential power of James K. Polk would unilaterally exercise greater executive power when faced with preserving the union that Jackson and Polk both held so dear.

So how was the war going? For a time it appeared that the biggest battle west of Veracruz might be between the ever-pompous Winfield Scott and Polk's equally self-important emissary, Nicholas Trist. Certainly, their relationship had gotten off to a rocky start. Then, at Jalapa, Trist became violently ill, quite possibly from the scourge of yellow fever. Scott, who was always a very compassionate fellow despite his personal ego, took it upon himself to send several jars of guava marmalade to the ailing diplomat.

Unbeknownst to Scott, guava marmalade was Trist's favorite, stemming from his days as the American consul in Havana. That broke the ice. By the time Scott and Trist finally met in person a short time later, they quickly formed a mutual admiration society. Trist was soon writing to Buchanan that Scott's "fidelity and devotion" could not be surpassed when it came "to the restoration of peace." For his part, Scott hastily wrote Secretary of War Marcy and asked him kindly to disregard Scott's earlier tirades against Trist. Onward, then, to Mexico City.[5]

Reinforcements for Scott began arriving at Puebla in July 1847, among them a forty-five-hundred-man force commanded by Gideon Pillow. Despite his indecision at Cerro Gordo, Pillow was now a major general thanks to his friend the president. Another contingent of about twenty-four hundred men marched into Puebla on August 6 under the command of Brigadier General Franklin Pierce. He, too, was a loyal Democrat and Polk ally and had turned down Polk's offer to be attorney general, after John Mason moved to secretary of the navy, in order to serve in Mexico.

When Scott finally moved west from Puebla along the National Highway toward Mexico City, his army comprised about fourteen

Campaigns in Mexico 1847

1 *Scott captures Veracruz, March 29, 1847.*

2 *Battle of Cerro Gordo, April 18, 1847.*

3 *Battle of Churubusco, August 20, 1847.*

4 *Battle of Molina del Rey, September 8, 1847.*
Pillow storms Chapultepec, September 13, 1847.

5 *Scott enters Mexico City, September 14, 1847.*

Gulf of Mexico

Jalapa

Veracruz

Mexico City

Iztaccihuatl
17,342 ft
(5286 m)

Puebla

National Highway

Pico de Orizaba
18,855 ft
(5747 m)

0   25   50 Miles

thousand troops in four divisions. To oppose him, Santa Anna had rallied some twenty-five thousand men, but at least half of them were last-minute volunteers. Santa Anna stationed the bulk of these troops at El Peñon, a position astride the National Highway east of Mexico City, and assumed that Scott would continue to follow this road into the capital.

Mexico City lay at the heart of the Valley of Mexico, a circular depression some hundred miles in circumference and seven thousand feet in elevation. A rim of even higher mountains surrounded it. Much of the valley floor was covered with lakes and marshes that made any approach by a large army problematic.

When Scott's troops reached the pass on the northern slopes of the 17,342-foot volcano of Iztaccihuatl and descended into the valley, they were indeed following in the footsteps of Cortez. Scott expected Santa Anna to defend this area, but the Americans crossed unopposed. Scott then faced a decision in front of the Mexican defenses at El Peñon. Should he attack head-on as at Cerro Gordo, or try some other maneuver?

After receiving advice from his engineers, including Captain Robert E. Lee, Scott chose to leave one division temporarily in front of El Peñon and circle west with the remainder of his army to come at the capital from the south. This move took Santa Anna by surprise and he was slow to counter it.

By August 18, 1847, after a muddy slog, the Americans had concentrated near San Augustin just south of the Churubusco River. A large lava flow some five miles wide and three miles deep offered protection from the troops that Santa Anna was belatedly massing along the river, but the lava flow also hampered any forward advance.

Finding the main route north to Churubusco on the eastern side of the lava flow heavily defended, Scott sent most of his army westward along a crude road hacked out of the lava under Captain Lee's direction. Emerging from the bleak terrain on the afternoon of August 19, the Americans came under artillery fire about the time Gideon Pillow arrived on the scene as the senior commander.

Perhaps to make up for Cerro Gordo, Pillow rushed an attack, and his haste almost resulted in one of his brigades being cut off from the main force. Persifor F. Smith, a steady soldier who lacked all the flair and controversy of both Pillow and Scott, came to the rescue with his own brigade and by the following morning was leading the main American assault northward.

Learning of this success, Scott turned Worth's division around and sent it back along the eastern side of the lava flow to converge in a pincer movement at the bridge crossing at Churubusco. By nightfall on August 20, the Americans had swept up to the very gates of Mexico City, and Santa Anna was counting his losses behind the city's last defenses. Some four thousand Mexicans had been killed or wounded, another three thousand captured. American casualties numbered over one thousand.[6]

Scott might well have stormed the gates then and there and entered the capital, but he paused and offered Santa Anna a temporary cease-fire. The gesture was conditioned upon Santa Anna's peace commissioners negotiating in good faith with Scott's newfound friend, Nicholas Trist.

When Polk heard that yet another Whig general had granted an armistice, no matter how temporary or contingent on negotiations, the president was not pleased. He professed that Scott should have pressed the Mexican government "to an immediate decision upon the terms of peace which Mr. Trist was authorized to offer," and if these terms were refused, he should have taken the city without delay. Polk feared that Santa Anna agreed to the armistice "only to gain time to reorganize his defeated army for further resistance."

At the time, Scott's pause seemed well advised, because the British legation and certain American residents had reported that an assault on the capital would only provoke more opposition. Scott and Trist also worried that if key government officials were driven away, there would be no one left with authority to negotiate, thus prolonging matters still further.

In the end, Polk was right. The Mexican commissioners rejected Trist's terms and broke off negotiations, thus breaching the terms of the armistice. All the pause had accomplished was to permit Santa Anna to consolidate his defenses and require Scott to make one final costly attack.

On September 8, Worth's division attacked Molino del Rey, a cluster of stone buildings housing a flour mill and, reportedly, a cannon foundry. These buildings stood just west of the fortress of Chapultepec, which controlled the western approaches to two causeways that led across marshlands to the western gates of the capital.

Molino del Rey was taken—it turned out there was no cannon foundry—but with 116 U.S. soldiers dead and 671 wounded. This was more than Taylor had lost at Monterrey. Rather than dampen Mexican morale, the defenders' dogged defense and retreat to the walls of Chapultepec served to heighten it.

Three days later, Scott assembled his officers and debated pressing the attack against Chapultepec or opting for an apparently less defended route via the San Antonio gate. Robert E. Lee spoke in favor of this southern approach. Most of the engineers agreed with him, as did many of the generals. Only Captain P.G.T. Beauregard argued for a direct assault against Chapultepec from Molino del Rey.

The only voice that really mattered was Scott's, and he, too, decided on the western approaches against Chapultepec. Many on his staff were stunned and—given the ferocious defense at Molino del Rey—feared defeat. Even Scott is said to have admitted privately that he had misgivings. (Military historian and Scott biographer John S. D. Eisenhower speculates that Scott's determination to attack from the west through Chapultepec may have been swayed by a desire to justify the costly assault on Molino del Rey.)

So, on the morning of September 13, after a lengthy artillery bombardment, Gideon Pillow's division led the way against the fortress of Chapultepec. Once again, names that would resound in a future conflict were scattered across the field, including Lieutenant James Longstreet, who was wounded in the action, and George Pickett, who charged forward with the regimental colors of the 8th Infantry.

Among the defenders, none were more heroic than the young cadets of the military college. They and other defenders engaged in hand-to-hand combat as the Americans put scaling ladders against the walls of the castle of Chapultepec and swarmed inside. One cadet came to symbolize Mexico's resistance and became a legend when he wrapped himself in the Mexican flag and leaped to his death off a high wall rather than surrender.

The battle was costly to both sides, but within three hours it was over. Worth's division passed through Pillow's position and pressed the attack along the causeways. By evening, Santa Anna had evacuated Mexico City, and by about noon on the following day, September 14, 1847, General Winfield Scott rode into the city square of the capital of Mexico.[7]

With that, the worst of one war was supposed to be over. But unbeknownst to Scott, the fire in his rear, about which he was always so paranoid, was about to get hotter. The instigator—Scott partisans would be quick to call him a culprit or worse—was one of President Polk's best friends, Gideon Pillow. And while coming at it with a far different point of view from Abraham Lincoln's, Pillow, too, was about to put his president on the spot.

There was no question that Gideon Pillow owed his position in the American army to his political connections. Cave Johnson may have called him a "great general" on the convention floor at Baltimore, but heretofore, the battles that Pillow had fought had been legal or political, not military. Nevertheless, when Congress set about expanding the army with volunteers and providing for new brigadier generals, Pillow was determined to be one of them. Naturally, he wanted to command the volunteer regiment being raised in Tennessee.

Both Pillow and Aaron V. Brown—who had recently married Pillow's sister, Cynthia, after the death of Brown's first wife—wrote letters to Polk asking that Pillow be given the appointment. What with Cave Johnson's prior blessing, Polk could hardly fail to heed the wishes of his most trusted Tennessee triumvirate.

So high was Polk's own opinion of Pillow—even before his magic touch at Baltimore—that the president probably needed little convincing. "I have great confidence in Pillow," the president acknowledged when Pillow was in Mexico, "but he is young in the service and the country does not know his merits as well as I do."

Indeed, while General Pillow suffered the disdain of the West Point cadre as much as any other volunteer general, he seems to have acquitted himself well enough. If one overlooks his tenuous actions at Cerro Gordo and his tactical faults on the road to Churubusco, there was still plenty of honor with which to return home and stoke a political career. The basic facts of his stalwart attack on Chapultepec are not in question, and he suffered a nasty ankle wound in the thick of things.

What got Gideon Pillow into trouble—and caused him to make trouble in turn for everyone else—was that he came to proclaim rather loudly that his actions alone had won the war in Mexico. Writing to his wife, Mary, after Churubusco, Pillow bragged, "I can only say my part was far more brilliant and *conspicuous* than I myself, in my most sanguine moments ever hoped for." But even that was probably true, and the statement was, after all, meant only for family consumption.

After his attack on Chapultepec, Pillow told Mary that she had for a husband "a gentleman, who has now the name in the army of the '*Hero of Chapultepec*' " and that "I know I am not mistaken when I say it will give my name a place in history which will live while our Republic stands." Pillow closed this letter by telling Mary that even she might consider him vain and egotistical, but such apprehension did not keep him from writing similar thoughts to correspondents outside the family circle.[8]

Even before Chapultepec, Pillow met with James L. Freaner, a correspondent for the New Orleans *Daily Delta.* The political general gave Freaner a written account of the Churubusco campaign that not only had Pillow leading the entire assault on Mexico City but also minimized the role of Persifor Smith and largely ignored Winfield Scott.

Freaner recognized the account for the puff piece that it was and simply set it aside. But then Pillow's adjutant, Archibald W. Burns, took the manuscript, made a few changes, signed the fictitious name "Leonidas," and mailed it directly to the *Daily Delta,* where it appeared on September 10, 1847.

Six days later, a similar letter appeared in the New Orleans *Daily Picayune.* Among other claims, the letters reported that "Pillow was in command of all the forces engaged" and that "General Scott gave but one order." Leonidas even compared Pillow to Napoléon at Ulm.

In the meantime, Pillow had submitted his official reports for the actions at both Churubusco and Chapultepec to General Scott. They were written in a similar style and in an only slightly moderated tone. Scott was miffed, but merely asked Pillow to modify the reports and correct obvious errors about who gave what orders when and to whom. A few days later, however, when copies of the New Orleans newspapers reached Mexico City, Scott's legendary temper began to boil.

It didn't help the Scott-Pillow relationship that President Polk's favorite general was not above routinely flaunting his relationship with the president. Pillow thought that he should have been included in the peace negotiations that Scott and Trist were finally pursuing, and he wrote personal letters to Polk criticizing all of Scott's and Trist's actions. Because Pillow's reports underscored the political biases that Polk had long held against the Whig general, the president gave them high credence.

Then there was the matter of the howitzer trophies. Two captured guns had been taken off their carriages after Chapultepec and placed in Pillow's personal baggage wagon. Taking such souvenirs was decidedly against army regulations, and Pillow later claimed that this was done without his knowledge or consent. But Scott, who was increasingly upset over the fabrications in Pillow's battle report and the Leonidas letters, was not convinced of Pillow's veracity. Pillow, in turn, demanded that Scott convene a court of inquiry to clear his name.

Scott did so, and the court found the majority of the blame to rest on Pillow's subordinates. But it also concluded that Pillow knew that the howitzers had not been removed from his wagon as quickly as they should have been. The inference was that Pillow had been in no hurry to return them.

With his reputation already suffering among regular officers—mostly because they found Pillow's accounts of his exploits so hilariously inflated—Pillow appealed the court's decision over the head of General Scott and directly to Secretary of War Marcy. He also wrote privately to his chief benefactor and told Polk that Scott was intending to brand him with an attempt "to embezzle the public property" if the president did not intervene.

For Scott, this blatant disregard for the military chain of command was the last straw. On November 22, 1847, Scott ordered Pillow to consider himself under arrest and ordered a court-martial.

But Pillow was not to be alone. Scott also found himself at odds with Brigadier General William J. Worth, who had served as Scott's aide in the War of 1812 and who had even named his son Winfield Scott Worth. Scott had recently taken exception to some of Worth's decisions in occupied Puebla, and Worth became upset and promoted his own Leonidas-type letter to the Pittsburgh *Post*.

It was signed "Veritas" and praised Worth, not Scott, for the critical decision to circle south of Mexico City rather than advancing directly against El Peñon. When Worth's chief of artillery, Lieutenant Colonel James Duncan, revealed himself to be the author of the Veritas letter, Scott brought charges against all three: Pillow, Worth, *and* Duncan.

When Scott issued orders sternly reminding all officers of long-standing regulations prohibiting the publication of private letters that detailed military operations, Pillow complained directly to Polk that these "assassin-like tactics" were aimed only at him, Worth, and Duncan. Scott had not enforced the regulations earlier, Pillow charged, because all prior letters for publication had "*praised* and *glorified* Scott himself."[9]

When Polk received news of what he again termed "unfortunate collisions," he did not question Pillow's version, particularly after Pillow also in effect tattled on Scott and Trist for making an advance payment—a bribe as it were—to Santa Anna to induce the peace process.

Polk put the blame for everything squarely on Scott. "A most embarrassing state of things exists in the army," the president fumed, "all produced by General Scott's bad temper, dictatorial spirit, and extreme jealousy lest any other general officer should acquire more fame in the army than himself."

This was exactly the presidential response that Pillow had hoped to elicit. And by asking that the courts-martial be held in the United States and broadened to investigate Scott's conduct as well, Pillow hoped to give Polk the perfect opportunity to recall Scott to Washington, thus opening the way for a Democratic general—perhaps Pillow himself—to take command in Mexico.

"The whole affair," Pillow told Mary, "will produce much excitement and newspaper discussion at home, but it will prove ultimately great to my advantage. . . . The [effect] of this proceeding will place me more prominently and more favorably before the nation."[10]

*W*hat is particularly interesting about this entire affair is the tremendous influence that Gideon J. Pillow held over James K. Polk. For years the president had been a shrewd judge of men. He had been almost immune from the political pressure of a steady onslaught of office seekers. He had routinely put principles and duty first—as recently as in the strangely similar case of Benton and Frémont. But beginning with Pillow's defense of Polk's younger brother, through the nomination fight at Baltimore, and throughout the Mexican campaigns, in Polk's eyes Gideon Pillow could do no wrong. And for Gideon Pillow, Polk would use the full powers of his presidency.

On January 3, 1848, Polk's Cabinet unanimously agreed to recall Winfield Scott. Ten days later, after some discussion about an appropriate successor, Secretary of War Marcy issued formal orders removing Scott from command and replacing him with a good Democrat, Major General William O. Butler. Marcy's orders also released Pillow, Worth, and Duncan from arrest; reduced the charges against Worth; and permitted Pillow to question Scott's own conduct in his pending court-martial, during which Pillow was only too pleased to serve as his own attorney.

Not everyone agreed with Polk's unimpeachable regard for Pillow. "That an idiot monkey," Lieutenant D. H. Hill raged, "could cause the greatest Captain of the age [Scott] to be disgraced upon the very theatre of his glory will not be credited by posterity." And anti-Pillow sentiment went so far through the army that even an army wife in Matamoros, Helen Chapman, ventured, "General Pillow will find that his petty little attorney tricks for notoriety are out of place with Army men."

Eventually, the charges against both Worth and Duncan were dropped, and Pillow was left to face two counts: violating general regulations in having written or procured to be written the Leonidas letter, and conduct unbecoming an officer and a gentleman stemming from his feud with Scott.

Initially, the court-martial convened in Puebla, Mexico, on March 13, 1848, then moved to Mexico City, and concluded in Frederick, Maryland, the following June. When Pillow's adjutant, Archibald Burns, took responsibility for the Leonidas letter, Pillow was cleared of that charge, although the lawyer in Pillow took pains to tell Polk that "all statements of fact" in the letter "proved to be true."[11]

After that, the remaining charge quickly became a battle between Scott and Pillow over who did what, when, and where. Pillow was relentless in his courtroom attack, theatrical in his manner.

Scott—his own theatrics aside—struggled on the public stage. Finally, the court decided that "no further proceedings against General Pillow" were warranted.

Polk approved the conclusion, but "did not concur with the Court in all their findings and inferences from them," feeling that they did not "do [Pillow] full justice." When Polk subsequently promoted two members of the court—Nathan Towson to brevet major general and William Belknap to brigadier general—Scott observed that the promotions were "for their acceptable services in shielding Pillow and brow-beating Scott."[12]

Even before these findings, Polk had instructed Marcy to confirm Pillow's appeal from Scott's decision in the howitzer case and make certain that it was made "clear that [Pillow] did nothing for which he deserves the slightest censure." When the full case was closed, Polk's opinion had not changed: "General Pillow is a gallant and highly meritorious officer, and has been greatly persecuted by General Scott, for no other reason than that he is a Democrat in his politics and was supposed to be my personal and political friend."

In his memoirs, Scott described Pillow quite differently. According to Scott, Polk's friend was "amiable and possessed of some acuteness, but the only person I have ever known who was wholly indifferent in the choice between truth and falsehood, honesty and dishonesty;—ever as ready to attain an end by the one as the other, and habitually boastful of acts of cleverness at the total sacrifice of moral character."[13]

Given those extremes, one can only wonder whether Polk and Scott, who were both so sound in their judgment on so many other matters, were not both wrong in some degree. In the end, it seems that Pillow had managed to put both of them on the spot.

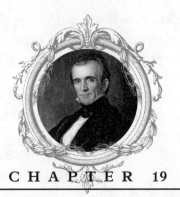

CHAPTER 19

Securing the Spoils

$\mathcal{G}$IDEON PILLOW'S EFFORTS to distract attention from his own questionable conduct by accusing Winfield Scott and Nicholas Trist of offering bribes in pursuit of peace were not entirely without merit. Barely had Scott and Trist patched up their feud when they eagerly embraced some form of inducement to jump-start negotiations. Such a monetary requirement by Mexico had, in fact, been hinted at since Colonel Atocha's earlier visits with the president.

Prior to the advance on Mexico City, General Scott was of the opinion that even the occupation "of twenty of the principal places in this Republic" would not force Mexico to sue for peace without some personal inducement to "the principal authorities in this miserably governed country." Indeed, Scott told his new friend Nicholas Trist: "We have both learned, through the most unquestionable channels, that this is invited and expected as an indispensable condition precedent to any negotiation."

Even the expected amounts were well advertised. Ten thousand dollars was to go in advance to one man—very probably Santa

Anna himself—and another million dollars was to be paid and divided among others upon the signing of a treaty.

Scott paid the initial ten thousand dollars out of the army's contingency fund, but not before he held a council with his senior officers and got various degrees of approval. By one account, Gideon Pillow—his later protestations to the contrary—strongly supported the transaction. Other generals expressed approval of the motive but not the method, and some thought the entire matter a diplomatic affair best left to Trist without involving the army.[1]

How much Scott's down payment and the pledge of additional funds influenced Santa Anna is open to question. Scott's advance into the Valley of Mexico and the victory at Churubusco may well have played an even greater role. The result, however, was that Santa Anna appointed Mexican peace commissioners, and they first met with Trist on August 27, 1847, during Scott's post-Churubusco armistice.

Much to his surprise, Trist found that the Mexican position was essentially the same as Colonel Atocha had advanced to Polk six months earlier. In fact, from the proposals that the Mexican commissioners put forth, it would have appeared to an outside observer that the commissioners were dictating terms after a Mexican army had landed at Baltimore and knocked on the gates of Washington instead of the other way around.

Mexico proposed to relinquish Texas north of the Nueces River, but with a neutral zone closed to settlement between it and the Rio Grande. The commissioners refused to cede New Mexico or most of Upper and Lower California, and only begrudgingly expressed a willingness to take cash for lands north of the 37th parallel. This would have given the United States San Francisco but not Monterey. Any right of passage across the Isthmus of Tehuantepec was flatly refused.

(The Mexican commissioners themselves balked at presenting some of Santa Anna's more outrageous demands. These included the cancellation of all debts against Mexico simply in consideration of negotiations taking place, and payment for all damages caused by the American army in Mexico.)

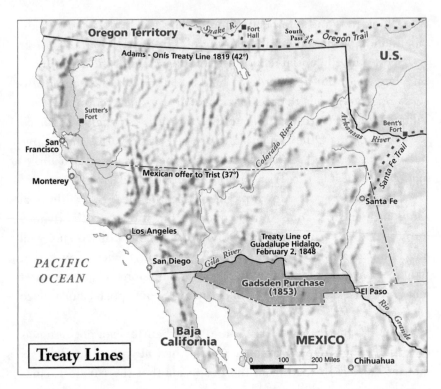

To his credit, Trist did not throw up his hands in outrage. Perhaps he should have. Instead, he offered to withdraw the American claims for Lower California (Baja) and the Tehuantepec transit rights in exchange for a cash payment for Upper California and New Mexico. But then, rather than standing firm on the core matter, Trist agreed to submit the question of the Nueces boundary—instead of the Rio Grande—to Washington for further consideration.

The Rio Grande boundary, of course, was the one point that had been written in blood in Trist's instructions. It had been the basic tenet of Polk's foreign-policy actions since he announced in the spring of 1844 that he was for the annexation of Texas. Where had Trist been when Polk had declared two years later that American blood had been shed on American soil?[2]

As it happened, at the very same moment that Trist was finally negotiating and making his faux pas about the Nueces, Polk was discussing with his Cabinet whether Trist should be instructed to demand even more territory than his original instructions required.

Polk was increasingly annoyed by the slow course of the war, mounting military expenses, and growing antiwar sentiment. The president announced, "If Mexico continued obstinately to refuse to treat, I was decidedly in favor of insisting on the acquisition of more territory."

Three days later at his next Cabinet meeting, Polk posed two distinct questions. As far as he knew, "the Mexican Government had continued stubbornly" to refuse to negotiate. Given that, should the dollar amounts offered be reduced and more territory demanded?

Secretary of State Buchanan spoke in favor of reducing the cash offer from thirty million dollars to fifteen million and extending the settlement line from the Rio Grande to the Gulf of California southward from 32° at least another half degree — about thirty-five miles. (Buchanan's reason for this apparently minor move would become clear soon enough.)

Secretary of the Treasury Walker and Attorney General Nathan Clifford were for taking the state of Tamaulipas, including its port of Tampico. Clifford also expressed the opinion that if Scott took Mexico City and "the Mexicans still refused to make peace," Trist should be recalled.

For the moment, Polk was inclined to keep Trist at his post and follow Secretary of the Navy Mason's advice that to change Trist's instructions when he might already have a treaty in hand under the original set "would embarrass the administration in approving and ratifying it." Consequently, the Cabinet agreed to postpone its discussion until the next round of communications from Mexico arrived. In the interim, Polk was left to "sincerely hope that a treaty of peace may have been concluded and signed."[3]

*W*hen the next dispatches from Mexico arrived in Washington, they began one of those frustrating exchanges of delayed instructions, belated ideas, and misunderstood motives that was exacerbated by the slow communications of the times. On September 14, 1847, Polk and Buchanan learned from Trist that peace negotiations had begun, but also that Scott had granted a temporary armistice. Polk fretted about the effectiveness of the armistice and waited patiently for more news.

Nothing further arrived until October 2, when the State Department—with no word from Trist—received a detailed account of the initial negotiations from a Mexican newspaper. It recounted the Mexican demands and reported that Trist had offered to refer the matter of the Nueces boundary to Washington.

Polk and Buchanan simply did not believe it. Buchanan called the Mexican terms "a mere mockery" and wrote Trist that "we do not believe there is any truth in the assertion of the Mexican commissioners" that Trist had waffled on the Rio Grande as a boundary.

Meanwhile, Polk was in the throes of a dire three-week illness. He managed to visit his office only briefly on October 4, but nonetheless resolved that day to recall Trist, because it was now clear that Mexico would not accept the proposed treaty as delivered. Having Trist remain expectantly on the scene might do more harm than good.

"Mexico," the president said, "must now first sue for peace, and when she does we will hear her propositions." Any future proposals to reopen negotiations were to be forwarded by General Scott directly to the president.[4]

Barely had Buchanan sent off Trist's recall when a September 4 dispatch from Trist arrived in Washington on October 21. It confirmed that Trist had indeed been doing more harm than good. "I can never approve a treaty or submit one to the Senate, which would dismember the State of Texas," Polk scrawled in his diary after learning that Trist's retreat from the Rio Grande was indeed fact. "Mr. Trist," the president declared, "has managed the negotiation very bunglingly and with no ability."

"As this fact is now placed beyond a doubt," Buchanan wrote Trist on October 25, "the President has instructed me to express to you his profound regret that you should have gone so far beyond the carefully considered ultimatum to which you were limited by your instructions."

Trist was clearly in great disfavor, and Buchanan told Trist that Polk had directed him "to reiterate your recall." So eager now was Polk to get Trist out of Mexico that Buchanan sent a third recall notice through the British embassy in case the other communications should fail to reach him.[5]

In the meantime, Trist had not been idle. When Santa Anna resigned as president after the American occupation of Mexico City, the steady Manuel de la Peña y Peña, as head of the supreme court, had become interim president.

By way of the British legation in Mexico City, Trist sent the interim government an October 20 letter that was backdated to September 7. It simply ignored the end of the armistice and purported to be a reply prior to the breakdown in negotiations.

Peña y Peña's government responded favorably, but by the time commissioners were reappointed, another change in Mexican government had occurred, and General P. M. Anaya was president and Peña y Peña his foreign-relations minister. By now, Trist had received his recall notice from Buchanan, and everyone in Mexico City knew it.

Considering Buchanan's tone, one would think that Trist would simply have packed his bags and followed his orders to return to Washington posthaste. Indeed, that appears to have been his initial reaction. After writing Buchanan an argumentative defense of his referral of the Nueces issue, Trist wrote his wife, Virginia, saying, "I have bid adieu *forever* to official life." He asked her to inform Buchanan that he would not resume his duties at the State Department because the secretary of state would "soon see the impossibility of this, or my having *anything* to do with Mr. Polk."

Such a violent reaction against Polk by a fellow protégé of Old Hickory's might have been occasioned by a touch of yellow fever. The real cause, however, may have been the machinations of Polk's chief informant, Gideon Pillow, who sought to undermine Scott. Say to Buchanan, Trist went on to tell Virginia, "that a baser, villain, and dirtier scoundrel does not exist out of the penitentiary, nor in it, than General Pillow."

But then the relatively positive changes in the government in Mexico City—changes that Polk and Buchanan had no way of knowing about—gave Trist second thoughts. Quite suddenly, the Mexican government and the British legation were both urging Trist to stay and complete a treaty. General Scott urged the same thing, desiring that he and Trist should be the ones to wrap things up—*that* would show Pillow!

Trist responded with typical ego. "If the present opportunity be not seized *at once*," he told the British attaché, Edward Thornton, "all chance for making a treaty *at all* will be lost for an indefinite period—probably forever." If anything, Trist's assertion that only he could make things work made him sound a lot like his despised foe, Gideon Pillow.

Writing again to his wife on December 4, Trist advised Virginia by way of a family cipher: "I will make a treaty, if it can be done, on the basis of the Bravo [Rio Grande], by 32°; giving 15 millions besides the 3 millions cash [for claims]."

Two days later, Trist wrote Buchanan a massive sixty-five-page tome that announced his intention to ignore Buchanan's recall instructions. Trist criticized the president for sabotaging the peace process and desiring a further war of conquest. Then, knowing full well that Pillow was Polk's knight-errant, Trist also went to great lengths to lambaste Pillow as being totally devoid of character. With that, whatever bridges Trist might have once had to the Polk administration were burned.[6]

𝒯wo thousand miles away in Washington, the ongoing drama was once again being acted out based on months-old information from Mexico. Polk and Buchanan were under the expectation that Trist, having received his recall orders, was now bound for Washington, not ensconced in the Mexican capital writing a sixty-five-page manifesto.

On December 7, 1847, as part of his third annual message, Polk reported to Congress on the failure of Trist's mission and his subsequent recall. The president defended Trist's original instructions to demand considerable Mexican territory as the only way Mexico could satisfy "the just and long-deferred claims of our citizens against her and the only means by which she can reimburse the United States for the expenses of the war."

But Polk also tried to calm certain Whigs and northern Democrats by downplaying a growing movement for all of Mexico. Even his own secretary of the treasury, Mississippian Robert J. Walker, had told a recent Cabinet meeting that he was for "taking the whole of Mexico, if necessary." Emphasizing that the burden was now on

Mexico to sue for peace, Polk reiterated to Congress that it was never his objective "to make a permanent conquest of the Republic of Mexico or to annihilate her separate existence as an independent nation."[7]

Four days later, Polk received Pillow's letter of October 28 recounting the bribery intrigues of Scott and Trist. The president expressed "in the strongest terms my condemnation of such conduct" and began the discussions with his Cabinet that would lead to Scott's recall. As for Trist, Polk continued to assume that he was already on his way home.

Then on January 4, 1848, Polk heard what he termed "most surprising" news. It was rumored that Trist was still in Mexico City and had renewed the peace negotiations on his own. Buchanan's recall instructions had indeed authorized Trist to return with any treaty that might have been signed prior to receiving the recall, but otherwise, Buchanan had specifically instructed him to suspend all negotiations immediately. "He may, I fear," sighed Polk, "greatly embarrass the Government."

The next day, Virginia Trist called at the State Department and, as requested by her husband, showed Buchanan the message in cipher that, despite his recall, Trist intended to offer Mexico a treaty on the terms of his original instructions. "His conduct astonishes both the Secretary of State and myself," Polk recorded after Buchanan hastened to the White House with the confirmation.

But this reaction was mild compared to the president's response when Trist's sixty-five-page missive reached Washington on January 15. Calling it "the most extraordinary document I have ever heard from a diplomatic representative," Polk termed it "arrogant, impudent, and very insulting to his Government, and even personally offensive to the President." In one of those relatively rare outbursts of anger, Polk said that he had "never in my life felt so indignant," and he ordered Buchanan to send "a short, but stern and decided rebuke."

Polk's plan now was to invest Scott's replacement, General William O. Butler, with the diplomatic power to conclude a treaty as well as with command of the army. Interestingly enough, this joint role was exactly what Senator Benton had wanted for himself, what had been withheld from Winfield Scott, and what was now finally to be given to Butler as the country's ranking *Democratic* general. Should Nicholas Trist still be around army headquarters when these orders arrived, Butler was also told "to order him off, and to inform the authorities of Mexico that he had no authority to treat."[8]

*B*y the time these orders reached Mexico City, it was too late. Trist's deed had already been done. Once again, the Mexican government had changed hands, and three commissioners had been appointed to negotiate with Trist. This time, the American who was now a private citizen without portfolio made it clear that not only were certain terms nonnegotiable, but also that time was of the essence. No doubt anticipating the rebuke from Washington or, more likely, the arrival of an authorized diplomat, Trist told his Mexican counterparts that the treaty had to be completed by February 1, 1848.

As it was, it took until February 2 for all details to be agreed upon and copies completed in both English and Spanish. While the negotiations had been held in the capital, the Mexican commissioners requested that the official signing take place at the nearby town of Guadalupe Hidalgo, and by that name the treaty came to be called.

Under the terms of the Treaty of Guadalupe Hidalgo, the Rio Grande—which had gotten Trist into such trouble—was recognized as the boundary of Texas, from the Gulf of Mexico to El Paso. New Mexico and Upper California were ceded to the United States for fifteen million dollars. The United States also agreed to assume the payment of those claims previously liquidated against Mexico— some $2 million, plus accrued interest—and pay up to $3.25 million for similar claims that had yet to be settled.

The boundary between Upper California and New Mexico and the Mexican states of Baja California, Sonora, and Chihuahua was to be decided with precision by a joint boundary commission. Generally, it was to run westward from near El Paso to the western boundary of New Mexico, north along it to the Gila River, and down the middle of the Gila to its confluence with the Colorado.

Trist, for whatever criticisms would later be leveled against him, had ensured the inclusion of San Diego by running the boundary at an angle (rather than on a parallel of latitude) from the Colorado-Gila confluence to a point just south of the desired port. He had also reduced the total compensation from the thirty million dollars authorized in his original instructions to fifteen million. The only point he did not acquire—which had been discretionary—was the right of transit across the Isthmus of Tehuantepec.

Once the treaty was signed, Trist hurried a copy to Washington with James L. Freaner, the correspondent for the New Orleans *Daily Delta* who had refused to print Gideon Pillow's infamous Leonidas letter. Freaner made record time and arrived in Washington on the evening of February 19, 1848. By 9:00 P.M., Buchanan had called at the White House and placed the treaty in the president's hands.[9]

"Mr. Trist has acted very badly, as I have heretofore noted in this diary," Polk recorded after hearing the salient points, "but notwithstanding this, if on further examination the treaty is one that can be accepted, it should not be rejected on account of his bad conduct."

To discuss the particulars, the president summoned his Cabinet to a Sunday evening meeting. Secretary of War Marcy, Secretary of the Navy Mason, Postmaster General Cave Johnson, and Attorney General Nathan Clifford advised that the president accept Trist's work and send it to the Senate for ratification. Secretary of the Treasury Walker, still fanning the "all of Mexico" movement, was opposed, as was James Buchanan.

Buchanan now advocated increased territorial claims in proportion to his increasing presidential ambitions. Perhaps with an eye toward southern votes, Buchanan declared that he would not be content with anything less than a line along the crest of the Sierra Madre Orientals, which at a minimum would have acquired the additional states of Nuevo León and Tamaulipas.

In response, Polk rather pointedly reminded Buchanan of Buchanan's attempt on the night of the declaration of war to assure foreign governments that the United States had no territorial goals. Polk had rejected Buchanan's language then, and until recently Buchanan had lagged far behind the expansionist consensus of the

Cabinet, whether worrying about Great Britain's reactions over Oregon or opposing Scott's final advance on Mexico City. Polk was certain that the presidential bug was to blame for this sudden change in Buchanan's opinions.

No decision was made Sunday evening, and when the Cabinet met again at noon on Monday, Buchanan was still opposed. Nonetheless, Polk assigned his own reasons for immediately submitting the treaty to the Senate. He was doubtful of gaining more territory, particularly when the proposed boundaries essentially conformed to Trist's instructions. And he was fearful that further negotiations might drag on and on.

But the real reason for Polk's decision lay at the other end of Pennsylvania Avenue. "A majority of one branch of Congress is opposed to my administration," said the president. "They have falsely charged that the war was brought on and is continued by me with a view to the conquest of Mexico; and if I were now to reject a treaty made upon my own terms . . . the probability is that Congress would not grant either men or money to prosecute the war."

If that happened, what James K. Polk feared most was that the resulting withdrawal of troops from Mexico might jeopardize the prizes of California and New Mexico he had already won. With or without Buchanan, the treaty would go to the Senate.

Polk understood Buchanan's motives. The secretary of state wished the whole responsibility for the treaty's submission to rest with the president. That way, Polk observed, "if [the treaty] was received well by the country, being a member of my administration, he would not be injured by it in his Presidential aspirations, . . . but if, on the other hand, it should not be received well, he could say, 'I advised against it.' "[10]

So, on February 23, 1848, without the blessing of his secretary of state, Polk had his private secretary deliver the Treaty of Guadalupe Hidalgo to the Senate for its advice and consent. In his brief cover message, the president noted, "it was not expected that Mr. Trist would remain in Mexico" or continue to negotiate. But he had, and because the resulting treaty substantially conformed to Trist's instructions, the president felt it his duty to submit it to the Senate "with a view to its ratification."

The one exception that the president made was to recommend that the Senate delete Article X, which dealt with prior Mexican land grants in Texas and the ceded territories. Trist had had no instructions on this point, and while deleting the article would lay the foundation for centuries of future litigation, neither Polk nor anyone in his Cabinet saw its relevance to ending the current conflict. Polk also attached to his transmittal copies of the instructions to John Slidell and Nicholas Trist that he had previously withheld under the claims of executive privilege, which had so annoyed Abraham Lincoln.[11]

As the Senate quickly moved to debate the document that would impact almost a third of the future continental United States, there was plenty of irony. The first moment came when John Quincy Adams collapsed at his desk in the House of Representatives two days before Polk's submission. The sixth president of the United States lingered on the couch in the Speaker's room for two days before dying on the very evening that the treaty was delivered to the Senate.

In recent years, Adams had questioned Polk's war aims and increasingly painted issues in terms of abolitionism. But it could not be forgotten that long before the Treaty of Guadalupe Hidalgo, John Quincy Adams had rejoiced in his own extension of American claims to the Pacific by the Adams-Onís Treaty.

"The first proposal of [the boundary to the Pacific] in this negotiation was my own," Adams recorded in his diary in 1819, "and I trust it is now secured beyond the reach of revocation." Almost thirty years later, Polk had embraced that proposal and was determined to make it inviolate from Puget Sound to San Diego.

When the Senate resumed deliberations after Adams's funeral, the treaty debate made for some unlikely allies, among them Whig Daniel Webster and Democrat Thomas Hart Benton. Webster, despite his interests in Pacific commerce, declared that New Mexico and California taken together were "not worth a dollar." He and fourteen fellow Whigs attempted an amendment that would have returned all territory west of the Rio Grande to Mexico.

Benton, too, was opposed to the treaty as presented. He objected to Trist's acting without authority and again proposed—as he had done before Tyler's decision on Texas—that a formal commission be appointed to negotiate with Mexico. Presumably, Benton saw himself playing a leading role as head of the Senate Foreign Relations Committee.

Polk worried that Benton's true opposition stemmed from other factors. With John C. Frémont's court-martial just concluded, Polk found it "difficult, upon any rational principle, to assign a satisfactory reason for anything Colonel Benton may do." Then, too, there was Benton's long-held view that the Nueces, not the Rio Grande, was the true boundary of Texas. Regarding this view, Polk speculated that Old Bullion was "apt to think that nothing is done properly that he is not previously consulted about."

There was also Senator Edward A. Hannegan of Indiana, who was still bemoaning the demise of 54°40'. If Webster wanted no territory, Hannegan wanted all of it. Hannegan and ten other Democrats, mostly from the West and South and including Sam Houston and Jefferson Davis, proposed an amendment that would have added the Mexican states of Chihuahua, Coahuila, Nuevo León, and Tamaulipas—essentially Buchanan's line at the Sierra Madre and then some—to the acquired territory.

Such dissension within Democratic ranks just fueled Whig opposition further. "If the Democratic party were united in favor of the treaty," Polk noted as he worried about the final vote, "I doubt whether a single Whig would vote against it." As it was, the president was convinced that far too many of both parties were focused on the presidential election and not the interests of the country.

"If the treaty in its present form is ratified," the president declared, "there will be added to the U.S. an immense empire, the value of which 20 years hence it would be difficult to calculate, and yet Democratic and Whig Senators disregard this, and act solely with the view to the elevation of themselves or their favorites to the presidential office."[12]

Before the final vote, there was even an attempt by Senator Roger Sherman Baldwin of Connecticut to include Wilmot Proviso language excluding slavery from any acquired territory. But on March 10, 1848, with the tenth article eliminated as the president had requested, the Senate ratified the Treaty of Guadalupe Hidalgo by a vote of 38 to 14, four more votes than the required two-thirds. The vote was far more sectional than it was along party lines. Twenty-six Democrats and twelve Whigs voted in the affirmative, and an equal number of Democrats and Whigs—seven each—voted in the negative.

Now all that remained was to rush the treaty back to Mexico and trust that the Mexican Congress would accept its amended form and accord it a similar ratification. To undertake this assignment, Polk chose Senator Ambrose H. Sevier, a loyal Democrat of Arkansas, but the senator became violently ill just as he was due to leave Washington. In desperation, Polk turned to his attorney general, Nathan Clifford, and prevailed upon him to undertake the mission, with Sevier to follow.

Polk was so pleased with Clifford's appointment to the mission to Mexico that one almost senses that the president wished he had chosen his attorney general as the emissary in the first place. As if declaring that there would be no more loose cannons like Nicholas Trist, Polk characterized Clifford as "perfectly familiar with all my views" and "a very discreet, sensible man."

Clifford arrived in Mexico City with the amended treaty on April 11. Senator Sevier, having recovered quickly, was only four days behind him. Together, their work was efficient and anticlimactic. The Mexican constitution required the approval of both houses of the legislature. This was achieved by a vote of 51 to 35 in the Chamber of Deputies on May 19 and, after three days of debate, a vote of 33 to 4 in the Senate.

While it was not a proud moment for Mexico, moderates recognized that "not to ratify the treaty would have meant continued American military occupation, a prolonged financial disaster for the Mexican government, and the probable loss of additional territory." In the end, most took the view of Peña y Peña: "It was a treaty of recovery rather than of cession" and it had to be done.[13]

𝒯he final irony of the Treaty of Guadalupe Hidalgo was that having gained legal title to almost one million square miles, the United States soon realized that the boundary line had been drawn a little too far north to suit budding transcontinental railroad dreams. Remember Buchanan's attempt to add another half degree—some thirty-five miles of land in southern New Mexico? Among his reasons were the reports of General Kearny and his chief topographer, Major William H. Emory.

Kearny wrote, "if a tolerable wagon road to [the Gila's] mouth from the Del Norte is ever discovered, it must be on the south side" of the river. Along this southern side, Emory found that his contemplated railroad route to Santa Fe did indeed "continue as good to the Pacific." But by fixing the Gila River itself as the nation's boundary through much of what is now southern Arizona, the Treaty of Guadalupe Hidalgo had left this strip in Mexican hands.

Thus in 1853, when Secretary of War Jefferson Davis in particular was focusing on a southern transcontinental railroad corridor, James Gadsden was sent to Mexico to negotiate for as much territory as could be had south of the Gila. Who should now be president of Mexico once again but Santa Anna, proving if nothing else that he was one of the great survivors of history. And once again, there were hints that only well-placed "inducements" could effect a transaction.

Gadsden negotiated without making any, and for fifteen million dollars—reduced to ten million dollars when ratified by the American Senate—Mexico ceded New Mexico's Mesilla Valley and the southern watershed of the Gila to the United States. Article 8 of the treaty also guaranteed the United States the long-desired right of transit for a proposed "plank-and-rail road" across the Isthmus of Tehuantepec and authorized the United States "to extend its protection to the route" whenever it felt justified in doing so.

These rights were never exercised—because plans developed for a Panamanian railroad and canal farther south—but they remained in effect until a 1937 treaty concluded between Mexico and the United States as part of President Franklin D. Roosevelt's Good Neighbor Policy.[14]

𝒯he signed copy of the Treaty of Guadalupe Hidalgo reached Washington on the afternoon of July 4, 1848. The president had just returned to the White House from ceremonies laying the cornerstone of the Washington Monument. Polk summoned Buchanan and directed that an official proclamation be prepared immediately, because he wanted to sign it on Independence Day.

Two days later, Polk reported to Congress that the ratification by both parties was complete and that "the war in which our country was reluctantly involved, in the necessary vindication of the national rights and honor, has been terminated."

As to the results, Polk told Congress: "The extensive and valuable territories ceded by Mexico to the United States constitute indemnity for the past, and the brilliant achievements and signal successes of our arms will be a guaranty of security for the future, by convincing all nations that our rights must be preserved." Indeed, the president concluded, "the results of the war with Mexico have given to the United States a national character abroad which our country never before enjoyed."[15]

What Polk did not say—and what perhaps the Jacksonian in him simply refused to consider—was that any "guaranty of security for the future" was most in jeopardy not from some foreign power but from within. The "national character abroad" was increasingly sectionalized at home. The ticking time bomb, of course, was the question of slavery.

The more immediate question for James K. Polk during the early months of 1848 had been whether or not he would seek another term. With the Treaty of Guadalupe Hidalgo, the four main objectives of his presidency had been realized: Oregon was resolved with Great Britain, the tariff was reduced to a revenue basis, an independent treasury was in place, and now California and the Southwest were secure. Despite his pre-election vow to seek only one term, would Old Hickory's boy run again?

CHAPTER 20

The Whigs Find Another General

THE BATTLES THAT Major General Zachary Taylor fought in northern Mexico in 1846 and February 1847 were hardly grand military conquests. At Palo Alto and Resaca de la Palma, Taylor slugged out an advance to relieve the garrison at Fort Brown. At Monterrey, he owed his victory far more to Worth's enveloping tactics than to his own blunders in urban warfare. And at Buena Vista, save for the steadfastness of Jefferson Davis's Mississippi Rifles and a few well-placed artillery pieces, Taylor might well have lost the field. But by the time the Whig press got done telling his story, Zachary Taylor was a general wearing the mantle of Washington and Jackson.

Remembering their success with William Henry Harrison as a war hero in 1840—albeit three decades after Harrison's little affair at Tippecanoe—the Whigs were determined to find another general to run for president in 1848. Here was Taylor, fresh from the battlefields, self-effacing, and looking every bit the cross between Jackson's daring and Harrison's log cabin simplicity. Never mind that Taylor had spent a considerable part of his military career tending to plantations in Kentucky and Louisiana and was in fact a man of some wealth, or for that matter that his politics were largely undefined.

On the other hand, Polk's opinion of Taylor was very well defined. Old Rough and Ready was a man about whom Polk had always had his doubts. When Polk's Cabinet debated between Taylor and William O. Butler as a replacement for Winfield Scott in Mexico early in January 1848, many seemed to favor Taylor. Polk reminded them, however, of "the trouble he had given and our dissatisfaction with him at the time we were reluctantly compelled to send Scott to supersede him." When Polk gave this opinion, "the dissenting members of the Cabinet were silent, and did not express their assent to my views. I, however, made my decision on this point absolute."[1]

So, Taylor would not go to Mexico City, but as the bandwagon carrying him toward the Whig presidential nomination gathered speed, the question on many minds was whether James K. Polk — his prior one-term pledge to the contrary — would agree to run for reelection to oppose him.

As the maneuvering on the Treaty of Guadalupe Hidalgo proved, the Democratic party was badly splintered with presidential motives and would-be candidates. When it came to speculation about Polk's seeking another term, some Democratic leaders feared that he would run and quash their own chances, while others begged him to run to save the party. The president, it seemed, was either a threat to individual ambitions or the last hope for party unity.

As the Democratic convention prepared to convene in Baltimore late in May 1848, Polk received a veritable parade of delegates and congressmen who called at the White House and begged him to run again. The president found such expressions of support truly "gratifying to me," but steadfastly maintained that he was not a candidate.

Indeed, despite Polk's arduous pursuit of the presidency throughout his political career, there is no evidence to suggest that he ever contemplated reversing his one-term pledge. As in so many other things, James K. Polk determined a course and stuck with it.

As early as December 1845, when Senator Benton worried that

Polk might be a candidate again, the president confided to his diary:
"My mind has been made up from the time I accepted the Baltimore
nomination, and is still so, to serve but one term and not to be a candidate for re-election."

Over a year later, in the afterglow of the early victories in Mexico and before antiwar dissent at home had grown so loud, Polk was
of the same mind. "I will do my duty to the country," the president
wrote, "and rejoice that with my own voluntary free will and consent I am not to be again a candidate. This determination is irrevocable."

And even with his four principal goals—Oregon, California, a
revenue tariff, and an independent treasury—achieved, the size of
the United States almost doubled, and a divisive war waged and
won, Polk refused to be swayed from his decision. He met privately
with Cave Johnson a few days before the Democratic convention
opened and gave Johnson a letter for him to read to the convention
before the presidential balloting. Once again, the president reiterated that he would not to be a candidate for reelection.[2]

The truth was, even without his pledge of serving but one term,
James K. Polk had by now had more than enough of the presidency. Never a robust individual, he had given it his all and had
paid the price personally. Polk's presidential diary is filled with references about how tired he was at the end of the day; what little
time he had for leisure; and how poorly he frequently felt, usually
from some measure of gastrointestinal distress.

Sarah worried about his health as she had always done and took
a dominant role in running the domestic side of the White House.
She also joined her husband in presiding at the evening receptions
that were usually held twice a week. In those days, anyone could
call at the White House, both at these receptions and during certain open office hours, and lobby discreetly—or sometimes not so
discreetly—for an issue, a political appointment, or a personal favor.
Job seekers were the worst, in Polk's view, and he found their incessant interruptions far more annoying than his Whig opponents
in Congress.

The White House executive staff was minuscule in those days.
It is best measured by the fact that when the president's chief aide,

his private secretary, was absent from Washington, the president borrowed a temporary replacement from one of the other executive departments. Of course, it didn't help the presidential job load that Polk was by nature a hands-on manager.

"The public have no idea of the constant accumulation of business requiring the President's attention," Polk wrote as his term was coming to an end. "No President who performs his duty faithfully and conscientiously can have any leisure. If he entrusts the details and smaller matters to subordinates, constant errors will occur. I prefer to supervise the whole operations of the Government myself rather than entrust the public business to subordinates, and this makes my duties very great."[3]

All these factors, combined with Polk's frequent assertions, leave little doubt that Polk was truly sincere when he said that he looked forward to his retirement. By his own hand, he would be a one-term president and become the first chief executive to refuse to run for a second term.

And while pressured from various quarters to do so, Polk resisted any thought of attempting to name his successor. He remained steadfastly neutral and "refused to lend his influence to any aspirant." Buchanan may well have thought he deserved the president's support from the traditional stepping-stone of the State Department, but he and the president had argued too many times for that. In fact, part of the Polk-Buchanan friction over the years stemmed from Polk's view of his Cabinet as public servants, not aspiring politicians.

Silas Wright of New York, whom Polk highly respected and might have favored, was dead of a sudden heart attack at the age of fifty-two. Reconciling with Benton or Calhoun was now out of the question. Franklin Pierce was a Polk protégé, but their bonds did not begin to approach the relationship between Polk and Old Hickory. Van Buren's name was still on the lips of antislavery New Yorkers, but that issue aside, Polk was long past any affection for, let alone allegiance to, the Red Fox.

Among the front-runners for the 1848 Democratic nomination, that left Lewis Cass, whom Polk had bested at the 1844 convention. Cass had spent most of Polk's term as a senator from Michigan and been loudly among the 54°40′ crowd. While taking no public position, Polk nonetheless confided to his diary early in 1848 that Cass had given his administration "an honest and hearty support, and if he is the nominee I will support him with great pleasure." In fact, the president went on to write, "there is no other whom I would support with more pleasure."[4]

𝒮o, with Polk's hopes for a successor expressed only privately, the Democrats opened their convention in Baltimore on May 22, 1848. Immediately, there was turmoil from New York, as the Empire State sent two different sets of delegates. One group was the pro–Van Buren, antislavery faction, who were called "Barnburners," because "in the manner of the Dutch farmer who burned his barn to destroy the rats," they were determined to stamp out slavery at any cost. The more moderate "Hunker" faction was generally inclined to support Polk's expansionism and oppose such restrictions as the Wilmot Proviso.

The division in New York did not bode well for Democratic unity. On the first day of the convention, the credentials committee decided to bar both sets of delegates unless each agreed to support the nominee of the convention. The Hunkers promised to do so, but the Barnburners refused to give an answer. The credentials committee then tried to avoid making a decision between the two warring factions and gave seats to *both* delegations. Predictably, this pleased no one. The Barnburners, who were under instructions from Van Buren to walk out in the unlikely event Polk was renominated, chose to walk out in any event.

The convention proceeded to ballot among the favorites of Lewis Cass, James Buchanan, and Levi Woodbury of New Hampshire before Cass received the requisite two-thirds on the fourth ballot. To balance the military popularity of the expected Whig nominee, the Democrats chose General William O. Butler, Polk's replacement for Scott, as their vice presidential nominee.[5]

When the Whigs whooped and hollered their way into Philadelphia two weeks later—among the delegates was Abraham Lincoln—there were only two serious obstacles to Zachary Taylor's nomination. The lesser of the two was a challenge from Taylor's fellow general, Winfield Scott.

There was no doubt that Scott wanted to be president. He had sniffed the Whig nomination in 1836 and 1840 and would carry the party's banner in 1852 in its last hurrah. But in 1848, Taylor was too well connected with party stalwart John J. Crittenden, and Scott too bogged down in the Pillow court-martial. Scott garnered some complimentary votes but ran a weak third.

That left the man who had been Crittenden's favorite in prior years. Yes, it was true. Although seventy-one years old, Crittenden's fellow Kentuckian, Henry Clay, was determined to make his fourth run for the White House. Past loyalties aside, Crittenden simply did not think Clay could win and had been promoting Taylor since the general's much-publicized advance to the Rio Grande.

Ex-president John Tyler, who saw Henry Clay in the summer of 1847, may have said it best: Clay was "as old as his gait indicates. Can it be that he looks to '48? Is the fire of ambition never to be extinguished?"

The answer was no. On the first ballot in Philadelphia, Clay received 97 votes—many from New York—against Taylor's 111. Winfield Scott was a distant third with 43. The second ballot told the tale of the convention, as Taylor gained seven votes and Clay slipped to 86. Clay's camp called a recess to stem the tide, but on the third ballot the following day, Taylor received 133 votes—eight short of the required simple majority. Clay's decreased further to 74.

By the fourth ballot, most of Clay's supporters had smelled inevitable defeat and rallied to Taylor. Old Rough and Ready was nominated with 171 votes, against 60 delegates still stalwart for Scott and only 32 hanging on for Clay.

But total harmony was not to be. Charles Francis Adams was as adamant against slavery as his father, John Quincy, had been. He had pledged to bolt the convention if the nomination went to the slaveholding Taylor, and now he walked out, taking some of the pro-Clay New York Whigs with him.

Abolitionist Charles Allen of Massachusetts stayed but opposed the traditional call to make the nomination unanimous. Then, proving that the Democrats were not the only party to be vexed by sectional issues, Allen proposed the adoption of the Wilmot Proviso. His motion was quickly ruled out of order, since even to consider it would have splintered Taylor's support in the South.

General Taylor, who was far away in Louisiana, had voiced no vice presidential preference, so the balloting for the second slot was wide open. Fourteen names were put forward, but the field quickly came down to Abbott Lawrence of Massachusetts—who was rumored to be willing to contribute $100,000 to the campaign if nominated—or Millard Fillmore of New York, a former congressman and current state comptroller.

Fillmore proved acceptable to both Taylor and Clay supporters, and he won handily on the second ballot, 173 to 87. Fearing further dissension, the Whigs made no attempt to adopt a party platform and simply adjourned to the innocuous campaign cry of "Peace, Prosperity, and Union."

As it turned out, Taylor played the role of the reluctant candidate "summoned" to the office to the hilt. Ever-expanding telegraph lines carried the news of his nomination to Memphis and then a steamboat raced down the Mississippi with flags flying and whistle blaring. But when convention chairman John Moorhead did not receive an acceptance from the nominee by the end of June, Moorhead wrote Taylor a second time.

In those days, most mail was sent collect with the recipient paying the postage. It turned out that Taylor had given the Baton Rouge postmaster strict instructions not to deliver any postage-due mail. Thus, Moorhead's notification ended up in the dead-letter pile until it was finally retrieved by Taylor and answered in mid-July.

Upon hearing of this excuse for the delay, William Seward of New York wryly wrote to Thurlow Weed: "The Candidate was very Rough and quite Unready, in refusing a nomination for the Presidency from a Whig convention because it was not *post paid*!" (By coincidence, it was Polk's postmaster general, Cave Johnson, who initiated the concept of the prepaid postage stamp. That way, the post-office department got paid even if the recipient refused the letter.)[6]

The Whigs left Philadelphia hoping for party unity. "By many, and often, it has been said they would not abide the nomination of Taylor," Lincoln wrote to Herndon. "But since the deed has been done, they are fast falling in." The same could not be said for the Democrats. The schism in New York ran too deep.

Before June 1848 was out, the disaffected Barnburners met in Utica, New York, and proposed to run ex-president Martin Van Buren against both Taylor and Cass. By the time that this third-party movement met in Buffalo in August, it had garnered a constituency throughout the North and had attracted the antislavery factions of the Democratic and Whig parties, as well as the remnants of Birney's Liberty party.

Few things showed the depth of antislavery sentiment in the North better than the heretofore-unthinkable alliances that were created. Under a banner of "Free Soil, Free Speech, Free Labor, and Free Men," the new Free-Soil party nominated Old Hickory's handpicked successor, Martin Van Buren, for the presidency. Then it turned to the son of Jackson's old foe and put Charles Francis Adams in the vice presidential slot.

To Polk, who himself had been the beneficiary of a third party's siphoning off Whig votes in 1844, the desertion of the Barnburners from the Democratic party to lead the Free-Soil movement amounted to nothing short of political treason. "This is a most dangerous attempt to organize geographical parties upon the slave question," Polk fumed. "It is more threatening to the Union than anything which has occurred since the Hartford convention in 1814. Mr. Van Buren's course is selfish, unpatriotic, and wholly inexcusable."[7]

The 1848 campaign entwined the debate over the expansion of slavery with the question of what governmental status was to be extended to the newly acquired territories of California and New Mexico, as well as to Oregon. Despite Polk's continuing pleas, Congress still had not authorized a territorial government for the latter, even though its annexation had been settled in 1846.

When it came to slavery in these new territories, Polk was convinced that "the only means of allaying the excitement" of Van Buren's third-party bid, and what the president termed "the distracting subject of slavery," was to extend the well-established Missouri Compromise line of 36°30′ to the Pacific. Enacted in 1820, the compromise prohibited slavery in Louisiana Purchase territories north of the southern boundary of Missouri, but required runaways who ventured north of the line to be returned to their owners.

Throughout the summer of 1848, Congress hotly debated territorial government bills for California, New Mexico, and Oregon. When the Senate finally passed a single bill organizing territorial governments for all three on July 27, the measure recognized provisional antislavery laws already passed in Oregon and prohibited slavery in that territory.

But in California and New Mexico, the Senate left the slavery question to be decided by a rather vague process of court appeals that seemed to promise that a southern-leaning U.S. Supreme Court would ultimately uphold slavery there. The House promptly tabled this effort and passed its own bill limited to the organization of the Territory of Oregon.

Now Polk faced a dilemma. It was clear that in the tumult of the presidential campaign, Congress was not going to resolve the slavery question in California and New Mexico—both would have to wait for some measure of government. As to Oregon, Polk might simply have signed the bill and hastened to appoint territorial officials without further comment.

But the president felt compelled to make it clear that he was signing an Oregon territorial bill prohibiting slavery only because Oregon lay well north of the Missouri Compromise line. Over Buchanan's objections, Polk insisted on transmitting a lengthy message to Congress along with the signed bill that essentially said that his signature on the Oregon measure should in no way be construed as favoring similar antislavery restrictions south of that line.

"Had [Oregon] embraced territories south of that compromise," Polk observed, "the question presented for my consideration would have been of a far different character." The question of slavery did not "embrace merely the rights of property," the president noted, "but it ascends far higher, and involves the domestic peace and security of every [southern] family."

Some have offered this statement as evidence of Polk's determination to extend slavery, but this seems unlikely. Read in the context of his total career, it seems far more likely that—careful politician that he was—the president was simply striving for balance and trying to accord the South some measure of compromise that he deemed essential to preserving the union. Perhaps the best evidence of this interpretation is that he concluded his message with a lengthy quote from George Washington's Farewell Address warning against "geographical discriminations."

Even if Polk had been making one of the strongest pro-South statements of his presidency, it failed to appease John C. Calhoun and other states'-rights southerners. They urged the president to veto the Oregon bill on the grounds that *any* antislavery provisions were beyond the constitutional powers of Congress.

Nonetheless, Polk signed the Oregon bill on the morning of August 14, just before Congress was scheduled to adjourn at noon. His appointments of James Shields of Illinois to be territorial governor and Joe Meek to be territorial marshal were also hastily approved. (Shields would decline and be replaced with Joseph Lane of Indiana.) Ironically, however, in the rush to adjournment, the president's message that he had intended as a call for unity was not read to the House.[8]

Perhaps an even greater irony was that no sooner had Congress adjourned than Senator Thomas Hart Benton—still smarting over the Frémont court-martial—penned an inflammatory letter to the people of California. Since Congress had failed to provide a territorial government for them, Benton urged Californians "to meet in convention" and form their own government, in effect ignoring the civil government that had been put in place by Kearny.

Polk termed the letter "extraordinary," and since it was to be delivered to California by Frémont himself, Polk thought "the inference is plain enough" that Benton was suggesting that Californians make his son-in-law governor of any independent government they might form. Polk directed Buchanan to write his own letter to Californians advising them that they had no right to "abrogate their de facto government and form one of their own" and promised to make action on territorial status for California a priority when Congress reconvened in December.[9]

𝓜eanwhile, Polk's expansionist appetite had not been completely satisfied. Acquiring the island of Cuba had intrigued Americans since before the revolution. Colonial troops had helped Great Britain capture the island from Spain during the French and Indian War only to have it returned after the peace treaty. Had it not been for the Gulf of Mexico, Jackson might well have continued his Florida adventures to the gates of Havana.

Since the second Adams presidency, it had been the policy of all major political parties that control of Cuba could not be permitted to pass to a strong maritime power that could use it to dominate the Caribbean. Spain no longer qualified as a naval power and was a safe landlord, but French and British designs on the island were another matter.

John O'Sullivan, who had articulated the cry of "Manifest Destiny," called on the president in May 1848 and urged the purchase of Cuba from Spain. Polk heard out O'Sullivan and expressed no opinion in return, but nonetheless confided to his diary that "I am decidedly in favor of purchasing Cuba and making it one of the States of the Union."

But when O'Sullivan called again on the president in early June, his Cuban scheme was decidedly aggressive. Half a century before Teddy Roosevelt and his Rough Riders, O'Sullivan suggested that discharged American troops then in Mexico should detour to Cuba on their return to the United States and engage in the same sort of intrigue that Frémont had promoted in California.

This was a little too blatant for Polk, and he told O'Sullivan that "if Cuba was ever obtained by the U.S. it must be by amicable purchase, and that as President of the U.S. I could give no countenance to such a step, and could not wink at such a movement."

But that did not keep the president from making an overture to the Spanish government in Madrid. How important Cuba was deemed, as compared to recent acquisitions from Mexico, is evidenced by the fact that with the president's blessing, Buchanan instructed the American minister to Spain, Romulus Saunders, to offer up to a hundred million dollars for the island. Only when Spain proved an unwilling seller was the matter postponed for half a century. Meanwhile, Polk had Secretary of War Marcy issue strict orders to troops in Mexico that there were to be no soldier-of-fortune forays into Cuba.[10]

All of these matters left the president feeling decidedly worn-out. Polk had been sick for most of June, and after Congress adjourned in August, he took one of the rare vacations of his presidency. Sarah was occupied at the White House entertaining guests from Tennessee, but Polk escaped the summer heat of Washington and went by rail and coach to Bedford Springs, Pennsylvania. He professed that the spring water improved his digestive system, and after a week there he appeared somewhat rejuvenated.

On the return to Washington, Polk and his traveling companions, nephew Samuel P. Walker and Dr. Jonathan Foltz, stopped over at Berkeley Springs, in what was then Virginia, for a night and chanced into Strother's Hotel, one of two hotels in town. As it turned out, Strother was an ardent Federalist, whom Polk termed "very vindictive."

When it came time to arrange carriage transportation back to the Baltimore & Ohio Railroad station, a distance of two and a half miles, Polk was told that all seats were filled and that Strother proposed to send him by regular stage to Hancock, a distance of six miles. "This, I did not like," remarked the common-man Jacksonian in a rare demand for special treatment.

Three young travelers graciously offered their seats to the presidential party, but Polk "declined to accept them, stating that I had been badly treated by the landlord, but that I would not put them to any inconvenience; that during my absence from Washington I had no other or greater privileges than any other citizen, and that I would take care of myself."

Fortunately, one of the town's leading Democrats came to the president's rescue with a suitable carriage, and after a tersely worded parting with Strother, Polk departed for the railroad station in proper presidential style and arrived back at the White House that evening.[11]

His respite was deserved but short-lived, as he threw himself into the presidential campaign and did what he could to promote the Democratic cause. High on his agenda was replacing certain Barnburners who held patronage appointments in New York and who had defied the party and rallied to Van Buren's banner. Chief of these was Benjamin F. Butler, the U.S. attorney for the southern district of New York.

Despite the approaching end of his term, Polk was still besieged by office seekers. Some, as Polk wrote, "were old customers, having called repeatedly before." Others presented themselves begging for both office and money. "One of these," the president noted, "was a stout-looking young man, in good health, and I gave him neither."

Among those to call seeking an office during the campaign was Lewis Cass Jr., son of the Democratic presidential candidate. Young Cass sought an appointment as chargé d'affaires in Rome and apparently saw no conflict between that and how it might be used against his father. "I am a friend of his father and anxiously desire his election," Polk wrote, "and I am sure I should have seriously injured [Cass] if I had gratified the wishes of his son."[12]

While Polk held himself above participating directly in the campaign—such would be decidedly unpresidential, and Polk had repeatedly emphasized the public service and public trust aspects of his office above all others—the Polk inner circle from Aaron Brown to Cave Johnson did their utmost for the Democratic cause. There was, however, one name conspicuously missing.

After all that James K. Polk had done for him, Gideon Pillow was reluctant to get involved in the 1848 campaign. As recently as July, Pillow had made a frantic visit to the White House just days after the end of his court-martial to ensure that the president would complete his promotion to major general. Blaming it on his ankle wound and ignoring the pleas of Cave Johnson to "bestir yourself in the great and good cause," Pillow "refused his friends" and excused himself from the campaign.[13]

𝒪n November 2, 1848, the president observed his fifty-third birthday. "Upon each recurrence of my birthday," he wrote, "I am solemnly impressed with the vanity and emptiness of worldly hon-

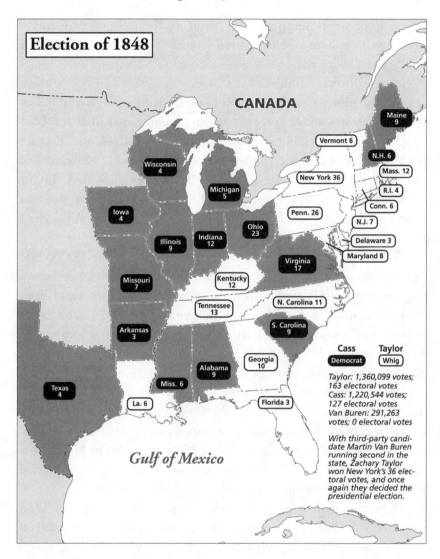

Election of 1848

CANADA

Maine 9

Vermont 6

N.H. 6

Wisconsin 4

Mass. 12

New York 36

R.I. 4

Michigan 5

Conn. 6

Iowa 4

Penn. 26

N.J. 7

Ohio 23

Illinois 9

Indiana 12

Delaware 3

Maryland 8

Missouri 7

Virginia 17

Kentucky 12

Tennessee 13

N. Carolina 11

Arkansas 3

S. Carolina 9

Texas 4

Alabama 9

Georgia 10

Miss. 6

La. 6

Florida 3

Gulf of Mexico

Cass   Taylor

Democrat   Whig

Taylor: 1,360,099 votes;
163 electoral votes
Cass: 1,220,544 votes;
127 electoral votes
Van Buren: 291,263
votes; 0 electoral votes

With third-party candi-
date Martin Van Buren
running second in the
state, Zachary Taylor
won New York's 36 elec-
toral votes, and once
again they decided the
presidential election.

ors and worldly enjoyments, and of the wisdom of preparing for a future estate." Five days later, the country prepared for its own future course by electing the next president of the United States.

November 7, 1848, was the first instance when the states all cast presidential ballots on the same day. That fact, plus the growing network of telegraph lines in the four years since Polk's election, made for speedy election returns. "Information received by the telegraph and published in the morning papers of this city and Baltimore," Polk wrote the next day, "indicate the election of General Taylor as President of the United States. Should this be so, it is deeply to be regretted."

It proved true. Thanks to the desertion of the Red Fox and his band of Barnburners, Taylor won New York State with a plurality of 218,603 votes (48.2 percent) against a combined total for Cass and Van Buren of 234,828. Once again, as in 1844, the Empire State's 36 electoral votes decided the outcome. Tied at 127 electoral votes and with the number of states almost evenly divided, Taylor and Cass watched New York drop into Taylor's column to give him a commanding 163 to 127 electoral college victory. The Whigs had put another general in the White House.

Tennessee, despite its favorite-son Democrat in the White House, voted for the Whig candidate for the fourth presidential election in a row. (It would do so again in 1852.) Martin Van Buren carried no states but polled a nationwide total of 291,263 votes (9.8 percent) among fifteen northern states. It was enough to ensure that the issue of slavery would not go away and would become increasingly sectionalized.

If there was a saving grace for the Democrats, it was that General Taylor had no coattails. In fact, the Democrats held the Senate and recaptured the House by a slim three-vote margin. But the outgoing president was not charitable in his assessment of his successor. "Without political information and without experience in civil life," Taylor was "wholly unqualified for the station."

Then the man who had always held party first, but who nonetheless had always seemed able to remain above party control, gave his benediction. Having been "elected by the Federal party and by the various factions of dissatisfied persons who have from time to time broken off from the Democratic party, [Taylor] must be in their hands and be under their absolute control." The thought made Polk shudder for the future of the union.[14]

CHAPTER 21

Homeward Bound

𝒯HE ELECTION OF Zachary Taylor did not deter James K. Polk from finishing the last four months of his term with the same zeal and dedication that he had brought to the previous forty-four months. At the core of his efforts remained his determination to provide governments for the territories of California and New Mexico and to rise above the increasingly bitter divisions brought about by the debate over slavery.

On December 5, 1848, the president submitted his fourth and final annual message to Congress. He went to great lengths to recount the present state of the union and the successes of his administration, but one sentence buried in a long paragraph filled with numbers of square miles and acres said it best. "The Mississippi," Polk reported, "so lately the frontier of our country, is now only its center."

Polk also took it upon himself to assert the president's power to veto congressional legislation. Although he had exercised the veto power sparingly, Polk had nonetheless come under criticism that these vetoes somehow stifled the will of the people. Not so, the president maintained. Rather, he said, "the President represents in the executive department the whole people of the United States, as each member of the legislative department represents portions of them."

Far from apologizing for the constitutional veto powers given the president, Polk strongly affirmed them and advocated their use at a level that even Old Hickory had not espoused. "The mere passage of a bill by Congress," Polk argued in support of presidential participation in the legislative process, "is no conclusive evidence that those who passed it represent the majority of the people of the United States or truly reflect their will." Conveniently, Polk seemed to have forgotten that he himself had been elected by less than 50 percent.[1]

Two days later, the president got a firsthand look at samples of the metal that would quickly put to rest any arguments that California was half a continent too far to be part of the United States. Secretary of War Marcy called at the White House and showed Polk specimens of California gold dug from near John Sutter's fort.

Even Polk, the Jacksonian expansionist, could not have predicted that within two short years upward of one hundred thousand immigrants would stream across the continent and give California the statehood he wanted for it. Prescient politician that he was, however, Polk might have predicted that when that new state sent its first two elected senators to Washington, one of them would be Old Bullion's son-in-law, John Charles Frémont.

But as 1848 turned to 1849, the issue of admitting California to the union was tightly entangled with the debate over slavery. Certainly, Polk was inherently a southerner who seems to have accepted the institution of slavery as a given even as he steadfastly hoped that it might remain outside the realm of politics.

If Polk wrestled personally with the evils of the institution and how one man's ownership of another squared with Jacksonian democracy, he left no record of it. What he did wrestle with was the consequences of the resulting political debate on the institution he valued above all others—the federal union.

"The agitation of the slavery question is mischievous and

wicked, and proceeds from no patriotic motive by its authors," Polk wrote in late December 1848. "It is a mere political question on which demagogues and ambitious politicians hope to promote their own prospects for political promotion. And this they seem willing to do even at the hazard of disturbing the harmony if not dissolving the Union itself."

Polk believed that the Whigs and their Federalist predecessors had "from the commencement of our history been opposed to the extension of our [geographic] limits." Polk feared that the influx of people into California and the immediate need for some form of government might lead to an independent government if "Congress adjourned without acting on the subject."

The admission of California, Polk told his Cabinet, rose above ordinary party considerations. "We have a country to serve as well as a party to obey," he lectured, as he desperately sought some form of middle ground.

But there were extremists on both sides and Polk knew it. "I feared there were a few Southern men who had become so excited that they were indifferent to the preservation of the Union. I stated that I put my face alike against Southern agitators and Northern fanatics and should do everything in my power to allay excitement by adjusting the question of slavery and preserving the Union."

In the end the extremists on both sides prevailed. Polk and southern moderates supported the admission of California as a free state because its geography was simply not conducive to slavery, but southern extremists fought them on principle alone and opposed the admission of *any* free states.

When Stephen Douglas's select committee reported a bill to make California a state and give New Mexico territorial status, Polk encouraged southern members to support it. But now northern extremists attacked and objected that under the existing Missouri Compromise line such action would make slavery legal in New Mexico no matter how economically unprofitable.

With the clock ticking down to March 4 on this session of Congress, critics of the Douglas bill sought to prevent debate on it by urging the greater necessity of passing the general appropriations bill. Then Isaac Walker of Wisconsin offered an amendment in the Senate

to join the controversial territorial government bill with the appropriations bill. Acquiescing to slavery in New Mexico territory, the
Walker amendment barely passed the Senate, but the House voted its
own version of a joint appropriations–territorial government bill with
Wilmot Proviso language *excluding* slavery from New Mexico.

The result was an impasse. Polk vowed to veto any application
of the Wilmot Proviso to territory south of the Missouri Compromise line even if it meant vetoing the entire appropriations bill. On
March 2, the House rejected the Senate's Walker amendment version, and a conference committee reported no progress on getting
the Senate to remove the amendment from its version of the appropriations bill.

As the lights of Congress burned well past the time set for adjournment, Polk went to the Capitol, as was the presidential custom
on the last day of the session. He was prepared to sign or veto as
necessary, but still the debate raged. Finally, at four in the morning
on March 4, Polk retired to his hotel for some rest. Two hours later,
a committee of Congress appeared in the parlor and reported that
both the Walker and the Wilmot Proviso versions of the territorial
bill had been removed from the appropriations bill.

Polk was spared having to veto the entire appropriations bill in
order to defend slavery south of the Missouri Compromise line. The
result, however, was that while the appropriations bill was saved,
no measure of government was extended either to California or
New Mexico. Those matters would have to wait for another Congress and another president.[2]

Although Polk was preoccupied with the California debate,
among the last-minute bills presented to him was one to create the
Department of the Interior. Polk was skeptical. He found the bill
long and complicated and had little time to examine it in detail. He
feared "its consolidating tendency" and thought that it would cen-
tralize power over public lands in the federal government to the
detriment of the states, where he thought it belonged.

Not knowing how right he would be regarding the nation's future land-use policies, Polk nonetheless signed the bill because he
could find no constitutional objections and because there was no
time to prepare a responsible veto message. So, instead of being

heralded as the father of the Department of the Interior, Polk made certain to leave a record of his doubts so that "my signature of the bill may not hereafter be regarded as conclusive evidence that I was in favor of the measure."[3]

Meanwhile, president-elect Zachary Taylor had arrived in Washington late on the evening of February 23 and checked into Willard's Hotel. The general and Polk had never met. Given the friction between them over the Mexican campaigns, neither held the other in particularly high esteem.

At the regular Saturday Cabinet meeting the next morning, Buchanan asked the president whether it might be proper for the Cabinet to call on Taylor. Polk took strong exception to this and said that if his Cabinet called on the general "before he called on me, I should feel that I had been deserted by my own political family."

This seemed to satisfy everyone but Buchanan, who huffed that he was determined to call on Taylor despite the president's feelings. Before Buchanan could do so, Taylor eliminated any embarrassment for those concerned. He sent word to Polk via Jefferson Davis, now a senator from Mississippi, that Taylor was momentarily indisposed from his travels but would be pleased to call upon the president at the White House on Monday.

Taylor did so about noon in the company of Davis and some other friends and was graciously received by the president and the first lady. Polk invited Taylor to dinner the following Thursday, and Taylor accepted. Thus, despite political differences, the stage was set for a cordial transition of power. It might not have occurred so amicably had Buchanan rushed to call on Taylor and had Taylor assumed from this gesture that Polk was not inclined to receive him. Established etiquette required the president-elect to call upon the sitting president, and both Polk and Taylor seemed to understand that.

If the whole matter seems rather petty, the president put his finger on what he thought was the root of it. "Mr. Buchanan is an able man," Polk confided to his diary, "but is in small matters without judgment and sometimes acts like an old maid."[4]

The dinner the Polks gave for Taylor on March 1 consisted of about forty people of both political parties. Sarah Polk assigned herself the delicate role of sitting between General Taylor and his defeated opponent, Lewis Cass. The president escorted Sophia Dallas, the wife of the vice president, to the table because the vice president was occupied presiding over a late-night session of the Senate. Others in attendance included vice-president-elect Millard Fillmore, Jefferson Davis, all of Polk's Cabinet and their wives, and longtime Polk friends Supreme Court Justice John Catron and his wife, Matilda. According to Polk, "not the slightest allusion was made to any political subject."[5]

*D*uring these last days in office, the president also tended to a variety of personal matters. Two years before, Aaron Brown had served as Polk's agent in purchasing a suitable retirement home for the president and Sarah in Nashville. Fittingly, it was the old home of his first mentor, Felix Grundy. The Polks renamed it Polk Place and its renovation was nearing completion. Sarah had made a trip to New York with her nieces after the November election to arrange final furnishings, and now she supervised the packing of their other belongings and the president's books and papers.

Polk also took the opportunity to execute a new will. He left the bulk of his estate to Sarah, including a life interest in Polk Place. Recognizing Sarah's devotion during "all the vicissitudes" of his public and private life, Polk acknowledged her "prudence, care and economy" in acquiring and preserving his property. He gave her full discretion to dispose of their assets at her death between her relations and his and expressed a wish only that they be distributed "as equally as practicable" between their two sets of blood relatives. In this, he seems to have assumed without question that he would be the first to die.

But then Polk added language that can only be termed highly discretionary. "Should I survive her," he wrote, "unless influenced by circumstances which I do not now foresee, it is my intention to emancipate all my slaves, and I have full confidence, that if at her death she shall deem it proper, she shall emancipate them."

Polk didn't direct that his slaves be freed; he didn't direct Sarah to free them; he merely said that it was his present intention to do so. Was the master politician simply hedging his bet for posterity?

If the forces of abolition prevailed, history could judge him accepting of these forces. But should the economic system of which he was a part prevail, he—and Sarah, too—could maintain what was a significant part of their wealth.[6]

*A*fter the final flurry of congressional action in the wee hours of Sunday, March 4, the president and Sarah attended church services in Washington for the last time. They were given a fond farewell, and it was a fitting benediction on their four years of national service.

"I feel exceedingly relieved that I am now free from all public cares," Polk wrote. "I am sure I shall be a happier man in my retirement than I have been during the four years I have filled the highest office in the gift of my countrymen."[7]

Now there occurred one of those interesting political footnotes. By law, Polk's presidential term ended at noon on March 4, but the date was a Sunday, and Taylor wanted the inauguration festivities scheduled for Monday, March 5. The question became who was president of the United States on Sunday, March 4, after the stroke of noon?

Some have argued that Polk simply served one additional, and by all accounts quiet, day. Others, including the historian of the United States Senate, maintain that Taylor became president at noon on March 4 even if he didn't take the oath of office until the following day.

Partisans of David R. Atchison, however, claim that he served the country as president for one twenty-four-hour span. Atchison was a Democratic senator from Missouri, and as president pro tempore of the Senate, he was next in line to the presidency behind the president and vice president. Supposedly, he succeeded to the "vacant" office for a day, with or without the benefit of an oath. It makes a great tidbit, but the fallacy in Atchison's claim is that his Senate office, and thus his place in the line of succession, *also* expired at noon on March 4.[8]

Atchison himself apparently gave no thought to the situation, and on a cold and blustery Washington morning, March 5, 1849, with a stiff wind blowing in from the Potomac, Zachary Taylor left Willard's Hotel. In an open carriage drawn by four matched grays, he drove to collect James K. Polk from his rooms at the Irving Hotel, and they rode together down Pennsylvania Avenue to the Capitol.

If Polk's recollection is correct, in the course of the ride, the conversation turned to California and Oregon, and the outgoing president understood his successor to say that both "were too distant to become members of the Union" and that it would be better for them to establish independent governments. This was exactly the Whig disdain for expansion that Polk had long feared, but the truth of the matter was that Taylor's subsequent position on the admission of California was close to Polk's.

Perhaps it was Taylor's inaugural address that left Polk to assume the worst. According to the man once heralded as the Democrats' best stump speaker, Old Rough and Ready delivered it "in a very low voice and very badly as to his pronunciation and manner."

When Taylor was finished, the Chief Justice of the Supreme Court administered the presidential oath and James K. Polk, the ex-president, advanced to Zachary Taylor and shook his hand, saying, "I hope, sir, the country may be prosperous under your administration." Privately, though, Polk had come to find Taylor "a well meaning old man," but also "uneducated, exceedingly ignorant of public affairs, and . . . of very ordinary capacity."[9]

As Zachary Taylor settled into his first evening in the White House, James and Sarah Polk departed the city that had been their home for more than half of their twenty-five years of married life. Their return to Tennessee was to be a roundabout tour of the Deep South characterized by boisterous welcomes and grand banquets. Everywhere they went, Polk was hailed as a hero, but what he needed most was rest.

Near midnight on Inauguration Day, Buchanan, Marcy, Mason, and the latter two's wives saw the Polks to the southbound boat despite the late hour and a damp and chilly night. By three the next morning, James and Sarah were cruising down the Potomac toward the railroad connections on the Virginia shore. At Fredericksburg, the ex-president stepped to the rear of the cars and acknowledged the first of many throngs of well-wishers. From there,

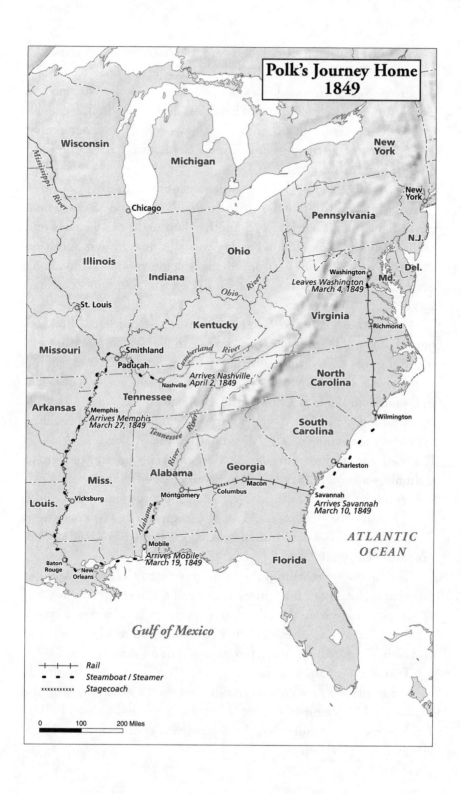

**Polk's Journey Home
1849**

Wisconsin

Michigan

New
York

New
York

Chicago

Pennsylvania

Illinois

Ohio

N.J.

Indiana

Mississippi River

Ohio River

Washington
*Leaves Washington
March 4, 1849*

Md.

Del.

St. Louis

Kentucky

Virginia

Richmond

Missouri

Smithland

Cumberland River

North
Carolina

Paducah

Nashville

*Arrives Nashville
April 2, 1849*

Arkansas

Memphis

*Arrives Memphis
March 27, 1849*

Tennessee

Tennessee River

Wilmington

South
Carolina

Georgia

Charleston

Miss.

Macon

Alabama

Columbus

Savannah

Louis.

Vicksburg

Montgomery

*Arrives Savannah
March 10, 1849*

Alabama River

**ATLANTIC
OCEAN**

Baton
Rouge

New
Orleans

Mobile

*Arrives Mobile
March 19, 1849*

Florida

Gulf of Mexico

─┼─┼─┼─ Rail

• ─ • ─ • Steamboat / Steamer

xxxxxxxxxxxx Stagecoach

0   100   200 Miles

it was south through Richmond and Petersburg to Wilmington, North Carolina, where Polk had agreed to a day of festivities.

From Wilmington, James and Sarah went by steamer to Charleston for another round of banquets and toasts. Polk termed it "not only a warm, but an enthusiastic welcome," and noted that "every mark of distinction and respect, without regard to political divisions, was paid to me."

By March 10, after passing under a canopy with the inscription "The Old Palmetto State bids thee farewell," they took a steamboat leg to Savannah, Georgia, and another late night of speeches and salutes. Blissfully, the following day was a Sunday, when Sarah eschewed travel. The day afforded them some rest in a Savannah hotel after a Presbyterian service in the morning and an Episcopal service in the afternoon.

"We had a dusty and fatiguing ride on the railroad," Polk reported of the 180 miles between Savannah and Macon on the Central Railroad of Georgia. But the fact that he could cover such a distance in a single day was evidence of how railroads had changed the country in the four years of his administration.

After a day in Macon—Sarah was so fatigued that she declined to attend the evening's ball—they boarded the Macon and Western Railroad for a short distance and then went by stagecoach to Columbus after a night's layover en route. Even that stop at a private residence found four or five hundred people assembled and a huge banquet spread out. After the requisite ball, James and Sarah—both still chilled from an afternoon rainstorm—did not retire until nearly 2:00 A.M.

The following morning, they continued into Columbus and endured another day of festivities. The accolades were gratifying, but by the time they rode the Alabama Railroad into Montgomery the next evening, the ex-president was "suffering from [a] violent cold and cough" and was "greatly fatigued and quite unwell."

Taking the steamer *Emperor* down the Alabama River to Mobile seemed to promise a welcome respite, but on the second day on the boat a deck passenger died of what was reported to be cholera. There were also rumors that the disease was common in both Mobile and New Orleans.

One of the scourges of the nineteenth century, cholera was a highly contagious intestinal disease caused by bacteria and usually transmitted in food or water contaminated by those afflicted. It caused acute diarrhea and vomiting and resulted in the loss of body fluids leading to extreme dehydration, shock, and death. While some measures of quarantine were employed after a general outbreak, there was then almost no understanding about the relationship between preventive cleanliness and good health.

Polk, who had a long history of suffering from chronic diarrhea and gastric discomfort, was always fearful that his intestinal distress was the onset of cholera. Had he known of the outbreaks prior to leaving Washington, he might have opted for the more direct northern route and forgone the celebratory tour, but now he was "too far on my journey to change my route."

Mobile meant another series of receptions and dinners, and then on March 20, the Polks sailed for New Orleans and arrived at the Lake Pontchartrain landing early the next morning. Considering the cholera outbreak, Polk was determined to pass through New Orleans as quickly as possible, but the local reception committee came on board and—with assurances that the city was healthy—implored him to stay because of their extensive preparations. "Perceiving that I could not carry out my resolution to pass immediately through the city without seeming to act rudely," Polk "yielded to their wishes."

The first order of welcome was "a sumptuous breakfast," but Polk found the French style of cooking suspect. He "took a cup of coffee and something on my plate to save appearances, but was careful to eat none of it." As soon as an opportunity arose, the ex-president discreetly asked a servant to bring him a piece of corn bread and a slice of broiled ham instead.

A grand procession through the city followed, after which the Polks again tried to depart. Told that doing so before the huge public dinner that evening would mortify the better half of New Orleans, Polk again relented "against my own wishes and better judgment."

Not until the following evening, after yet another tiring day of events, did the Polks manage to board the steamboat *Caroline E.*

Watkins for the journey upriver to Nashville. Utterly worn-out though he was, Polk acknowledged that the journey thus far had been "a triumphal march" and that "the cordial welcome which has been extended to me by thousands of my fellow-citizens, without distinction of political party, far exceeds anything I had anticipated."

But the specter of cholera was following him upriver. At Baton Rouge just before noon on March 23, Polk received a salute and briefly went ashore while Sarah remained on board to receive local dignitaries. It was difficult to say which was the safer course, as a passenger succumbed to cholera that same day. The next day at Natchez, Polk was not persuaded by the preparations of the town fathers and declined to go ashore. He did likewise the following day at Vicksburg, as he continued to experience severe intestinal distress.

At Vicksburg, his path crossed one final time with that of Henry Clay. A steamboat bearing the would-be president had preceded the ex-president's vessel upriver and upon arriving off Vicksburg had been mistaken for Polk's. Clay's boat was given a lively cannon salute, which prompted Clay to observe, "I hope, gentlemen, I am not stealing Mr. Polk's thunder." Assured that there was plenty of powder for both, Clay went on his way and Polk's arrival was welcomed by a similar barrage.

Upriver at Memphis, it was two of Polk's own nephews who met his boat and pleaded with their uncle to step ashore and partake in the planned ceremonies. Polk reluctantly did so, but returned before the meal. Meanwhile, three more deaths from cholera were reported on board, along with other cases that had not been fatal.

Finally, on March 28, after a fitful night, James and Sarah summoned a physician from Paducah, Kentucky. Although he did not diagnose the ex-president's distress as cholera, the Polks made plans to leave the steamboat that afternoon at Smithland, Kentucky. All of the boats coming upriver from New Orleans were reporting numerous cholera deaths and Polk was "well satisfied" to leave the river.

For four days James and Sarah hunkered down in a hotel in Smithland. Learning of their situation, Sarah's brother, Dr. William R. Rucker, arrived from Murfreesboro and provided medicine and much-needed moral support. Finally, on April 2, almost a month after their departure from Washington, the Polks steamed up the Cumberland River to be met on the Nashville levee by a crowd of admirers, including their old friend and best man, former governor Aaron Brown. Polk Place was still not finished, so they checked into the Verandah House, but at least their homeward journey was done.[10]

$\mathcal{B}$ack home in Nashville, Polk seemed to rally, although he remained quite exhausted. His first order of concern was to visit his aging mother in Columbia. The outpouring from their old neighbors delighted Sarah and him, and Gideon Pillow once more pushed himself into the spotlight by giving the official welcome in the town square. But it was the house at the corner of Market (now West Seventh) and High streets to which he hurried.

"I can perceive that time has made its impression on her since I saw her, though I was glad to find her in good health," Jane Knox Polk's fifty-three-year-old firstborn offered of his seventy-two-year-old mother. No doubt she saw quite a change in him—his photograph taken just before leaving the White House shows the toll—and the mother was in much better health than the son was.

James and Sarah spent ten days with his mother in Columbia, went back to Nashville briefly to check on the progress on Polk Place, and then made a similar visit to Sarah's family in Murfreesboro. Returning to Nashville on April 24, they found Polk Place still not finished, but "two or three rooms had been fitted up so that we could occupy them." They resolved "to take possession of the house at once and superintend the arrangements necessary to put it in order."

For a time, this task seemed to improve Polk's general health, and he found the exercise of supervising the work about the house and grounds agreeable. By the end of May, the house was coming together and Polk bought a pair of bay carriage horses and took Sarah on a three-mile ride to Aaron Brown's home to test them.

But cholera was still in the air. Several neighbors were afflicted and Polk deemed it prudent to remain at home the following day. Then on the next day, June 2, 1849, the diary that Polk had kept so meticulously since the Oregon crisis in the summer of 1845 came to an abrupt end. His last entry described a carriage drive to visit friends eight miles out of town and an afternoon devoted "to arranging my library of books in presses which I had caused to be made to hold them."[11]

Thirteen days later, barely ensconced in his new home of Polk Place, James Knox Polk was dead at fifty-three. His ex-presidency of 103 days remains the shortest in history. In the end, cholera was the likely cause of death, but the stress and strain of the presidency had lowered his resistance to any foe.

As Polk faded, his elderly mother rushed from Columbia to be at her son's bedside. She watched as the man who as a baby had been denied baptism in the Presbyterian Church amidst his grandfather's antics now chose on his deathbed to receive the sacrament from the Methodist Church.

At twenty minutes before five on the afternoon of June 15, 1849, James Knox Polk breathed his last. Reportedly, his final words were "I love you, Sarah, for all eternity, I love you."[12] Even if this utterance was embellished, there was nothing in Polk's life to suggest that the sentiment behind it was not true.

Sarah Childress Polk, an accomplished and influential first lady well ahead of her time, would wear widow's black for the rest of her life. Sarah would live at Polk Place and be as much a shrine to his memory as the house itself was.

Polk's funeral was held at the McKendree Methodist Church in Nashville and his body temporarily interred at the Nashville city cemetery while a tomb was prepared at Polk Place. A.O.P. Nicholson, who had once been tempted to desert the Polk banner, supplied the lines on Polk's tombstone:

> *By his public policy he defined, established, and extended the boundaries of his country. He planted the laws of the American union on the shores of the Pacific. His influence and his counsels tended to organize the national treasury on the principles of the Constitution, and to apply the rule of freedom to navigation, trade, and industry.*[13]

Applying the rule of freedom for all men would be left to his successors.

CHAPTER 22

A Presidential Assessment

$\mathcal{D}$ESPITE THE LAURELS bestowed on James K. Polk during his triumphant journey home in the spring of 1849, his presidential reputation was quickly eclipsed by the growing tumult of civil war. The first major Polk biography—besides his campaign biography of 1844—was published the year after his death. Written by John S. Jenkins, it gave Polk little credit for the territorial acquisitions of his administration and assigned a pro-slavery motive to his expansionism.

This bias against Polk's accomplishments continued after the Civil War. James Schouler's multivolume history of the United States concluded its account of the Polk administration by noting that whatever its fruits, both sweet and bitter, "the gatherer of those fruits was very soon forgotten."

It might have been different if George Bancroft, America's historian and Polk's first secretary of the navy, had followed through with his plan to write the definitive history of the Polk administration. Bancroft had full access to the Polk papers and to Sarah. Nothing came of the project because of Bancroft's advancing years,

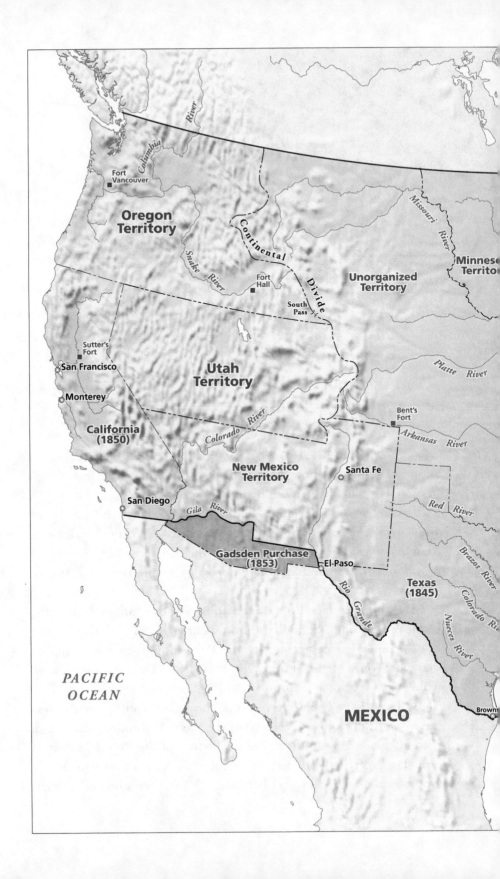

**Polk's Legacy
1850**

CANADA

Maine

Vt.

N.H.

Wisconsin
(1848)

Michigan

New
York

Mass.

Boston

Conn. R.I.

Mississippi River

Iowa
(1846)

Chicago

Pennsylvania

New
York

Illinois

Ohio

N.J.

Indiana

Ohio River

Washington

Del.

Md.

St. Louis

t
venworth

Kentucky

Virginia

Missouri

Cumberland River

Nashville

North
Carolina

Tennessee

Arkansas

Tennessee River

South
Carolina

Georgia

ATLANTIC
OCEAN

Louisiana

Alabama

Miss.

g River

New
Orleans

Florida
(1845)

Gulf of Mexico

except a postscript to Polk's entry in *Appleton's Cyclopaedia of American Biography.*

"Viewed from the standpoint of results," Bancroft wrote, the Polk administration was "perhaps the greatest in our national history, certainly one of the greatest." The editors merely opined that even forty years after Polk's death, "it may still be too soon to judge [his public career] with entire impartiality."[1]

But how had Polk's contemporaries fared?

Henry Clay was to have one last moment on the national stage. With tempers flaring over slavery, Clay crafted the Compromise of 1850. California was admitted as a free state. The rest of the Mexican Cession was organized as the territories of Utah and New Mexico without mention of slavery. Slaves might be brought into those territories, but, as Clay told his northern colleagues, their geography was not conducive to the plantation system and nature was on the side of the abolitionists.

To appease the South, a more stringent fugitive slave law was enacted, and while the slave trade was banned from the District of Columbia, slavery itself was not. Finally, Clay's potpourri settled the boundary between Texas and the New Mexico Territory well east of the Rio Grande in exchange for federal assumption of Texas's pre-annexation debts.

The debates on Clay's compromise saw the passing of three congressional giants. John C. Calhoun, who would be dead before the measures were passed, resolutely refused to yield any point to the North. Daniel Webster weighed in on the side of the union. Within three years, Webster and Clay were also dead.

Zachary Taylor, despite his Inauguration Day comments to Polk about the distance to California, championed its admission as well as that of New Mexico as a state, much to the chagrin of Taylor's southern supporters. Old Rough and Ready died in office sixteen months after his inauguration. He, too, may have been the victim of cholera or some other intestinal malady. His vice president, Millard Fillmore, became the last of the four Whig presidents—three and a half, if one counts John Tyler's true colors.

And what of Tyler? James K. Polk would be called the president who doubled the size of the United States, but John Tyler had given him a pretty fair start by his tenacious pursuit of Texas. On the brink of the Civil War, Tyler emerged from retirement to chair a national peace convention in an effort to preserve the union. When that proved unsuccessful, Tyler reluctantly urged Virginia to secede. He was subsequently elected to the Confederate House of Representatives, but died before taking office.

The Whigs denied Millard Fillmore his renomination in 1852 and turned instead to Winfield Scott, albeit not until the fifty-third ballot. James Buchanan, Lewis Cass, William Marcy, and Stephen Douglas all vied for the Democratic nomination that year before it went to Franklin Pierce of New Hampshire. A former senator and general whom Polk had long recognized as a rising star, Pierce was an acceptable compromise to most factions, just as Polk had been eight years earlier.

Once again, northern antislavery forces refused to support their party's nominees, but Pierce handily beat Scott and the splinter groups with almost 51 percent of the popular vote. A year younger than Polk had been at his election, forty-eight-year-old Pierce appointed William Marcy secretary of state, Jefferson Davis secretary of war, and James Buchanan ambassador to Great Britain.

Thomas Hart Benton had approached Polk's presidency with some suspicion and a feeling that the office should have been his own, but the two were natural allies, and Polk initially benefited from Benton's counsel on Oregon and the war with Mexico. That relationship unraveled in the wake of Frémont's court-martial. Blood—in this case Jessie's and her devotion to Charles—was definitely thicker than water.

Old Bullion returned to Washington in December 1850 for the final session of the thirty-first Congress, and among the bills he introduced was one for the construction of a railroad from Saint Louis to San Francisco. But Benton the unionist was increasingly out of step with pro-slavery sentiments in Missouri, and he was defeated for reelection to the Senate early in 1851. Undeterred, he won election to the House of Representatives and died in Washington in 1858.

That Old Bullion's son-in-law, John Charles Frémont, should

receive the 1856 Republican presidential nomination was a commentary both on the national-hero status associated with explorers in that era and on the neophyte nature of the Republican party. The antislavery group had its cause; what it needed was a well-known figure to lead it. The rallying cry of "Free Soil, Free Men, Frémont!" fit the bill.

Frémont's Democratic opponent in 1856 was James Buchanan, finally the nominee of his party after almost two decades of trying. By then, Buchanan was well past his prime, and the prospects of civil war — postponed but not extinguished by the Compromise of 1850 — made the nomination rather hollow. Buchanan was the choice of the party because by serving Franklin Pierce in London for the previous three years, he had managed to avoid the bitter round of debate about slavery in the territories that Stephen Douglas had reopened with the Kansas-Nebraska Act.

Buchanan was elected president with 45.4 percent of the popular vote to Frémont's 33.0 percent, in large measure because Millard Fillmore siphoned off 21.6 percent to his American party, or Know-Nothing movement, which was rabidly anti-immigrant and anti-Catholic. Lewis Cass became Buchanan's secretary of state.

Even amidst the furor of domestic matters, Franklin Pierce and James Buchanan continued to press expansionist policies. Pierce said in his inaugural address that his foreign policy would "not be controlled by any timid forebodings of evil from expansion." His administration negotiated a treaty of annexation with Hawaii that was never signed because of a change in Hawaiian rulers, and Buchanan, as president, offered Russia as much as five million dollars for Alaska.

Both moves were ahead of their time. The Alaskan purchase was dropped after the Russian minister informed his government that given the poor relations between Buchanan and Congress, no treaty sponsored by the president was likely to win Senate approval. Apparently, that was the case. When Buchanan's minister to Mexico negotiated rights-of-way for two railroad routes across Mexico — one from the lower Rio Grande to Mazatlán and the other from Nogales to Guaymas — the Senate rejected it 18 to 27.[2]

Sam Houston never gave up his own interest in the presidency, but his efforts to win the Democratic nomination in 1852, 1856, and 1860 fell far short. He remained in the Senate until 1859, when he was elected governor of Texas. But the man who had followed his mentor, Old Hickory, and brought Texas into the union was destined to preside over its secession. When that happened in 1861, Houston resigned the Texas governorship and died heartbroken by the carnage two years later.

Andrew Johnson, one of the Immortal Thirteen of Polk's governorship and never a close Polk ally, was himself elected governor of Tennessee in 1853 and again in 1855. The legislature sent Johnson to the U.S. Senate in 1857, where he opposed secession and was the only southern senator not to resign at the outset of the Civil War. Depending on which part of Tennessee one was in, Johnson was either a hero (East Tennessee and the Cumberland Plateau) or a traitor (Middle and West Tennessee).

Lincoln picked Johnson as his vice president in 1864 in a gesture to heal wounds, but Lincoln's subsequent death and Johnson's impeachment by the Radical Republicans in Congress set reconciliation back at least a generation. In 1875, the Tennessee legislature again elected Andrew Johnson to the U.S. Senate, the only ex-president to serve there.

Gideon Pillow courted the vice presidential nomination in 1852 in much the same way that Polk had stalked it in 1844. As a major general and war hero, Pillow thought a Pierce-Pillow ticket—or even a Pillow-Pierce ticket—was possible. But after Franklin Pierce got the nomination, the convention turned not to Pillow but to Senator William R. King of Alabama to balance the ticket. Later, in 1857, Pillow failed to win a U.S. Senate seat.

In 1862, as commander of Confederate troops at Fort Donelson, Pillow became entwined in a controversy far exceeding that day at Cerro Gordo. The result was that Pillow escaped Grant's encirclement and left Simon Buckner to accede to Grant's unconditional surrender.

But nothing, it seemed, could humble the high regard Pillow held for himself. In 1873, he wrote Grant, now president of the

United States, and sought an appointment for himself to the U.S. Supreme Court, noting, "I suppose there is no Southern lawyer, who would be more acceptable to the Southern people."³

Many of the young officers of the American army who had cut their teeth fighting in Mexico wound up as generals fighting each other. Among them were Robert E. Lee, P.G.T. Beauregard, and Braxton Bragg for the South and Ulysses S. Grant, George G. Meade, and George McClellan for the North. By then, Polk's critic, Abraham Lincoln, and Taylor's savior at Buena Vista, Jefferson Davis, sat in opposing presidential mansions.

Perhaps the greatest political survivor of all was Santa Anna. In 1853, the self-styled Napoléon of the West was inaugurated as president of Mexico for the fourth and final time. Two and a half years later, he was exiled again. After the disruptive decade of French intervention in Mexico, Santa Anna returned to Mexico in 1874 and died in Mexico City two years later, a full forty years after his troops had started so much by storming the Alamo.

𝒜nd what of the political legacy of James K. Polk? His reputation began its rise from near obscurity in 1910 when his presidential diary was published. Written contemporaneously with events, it opened a long-closed window on the motives and machinations of his administration. In 1922, Eugene McCormac relied heavily on Polk's diary to publish a detailed political biography of Polk.

By 1945, Polk's Democratic heir, Franklin D. Roosevelt, had taken the executive powers of the presidency—in both foreign affairs and domestic matters—to a level that made even the assertive, hands-on Polk look like a caretaker. In 1948, just before Harry Truman whistle-stopped his way to a come-from-behind victory, Arthur M. Schlesinger asked fifty-five leading historians to rate the American presidents—not on lifetime achievement but on performance in the White House.

To the surprise of many in the general public, James K. Polk was ranked number ten in a list of twenty-nine and qualified for the "near-great" category. When Schlesinger repeated the poll in 1962, Polk finished eighth in a field of thirty-one. His was easily the least-recognized name among the well-known high scorers of Washington, Jefferson, Jackson, Lincoln, the two Roosevelts, and the more recent names of Woodrow Wilson, who finished fourth, and Harry Truman, who placed behind Polk at number nine. In 1996, Arthur M. Schlesinger Jr. made a third survey, and among thirty-nine presidents, Polk held steady at number nine, still in the "near-great" category.[4]

There are three key reasons why James K. Polk deserves recognition as a significant and influential American president. First, Polk accomplished the objectives of his presidential term as he defined them; second, he was the most decisive chief executive prior to the Civil War; and third, he greatly expanded the executive power of the presidency, particularly its war powers, its role as commander in chief, and its oversight of the executive branch.

Few presidents have come to office with as specific a set of goals as Polk enumerated at the beginning of his term: resolve the joint occupation of Oregon, acquire California, reduce the tariff, and establish an independent treasury. Polk accomplished three of these by 1846, and while it took a war to acquire California, with its resolution also came most of the American Southwest. Simply put, Polk did what he set out to do.

As to his assertiveness as president, there is the obvious comparison to be made with his mentor. Polk never achieved the huge popularity or the enduring fame of Andrew Jackson, but Old Hickory owed that more to the power of the Battle of New Orleans than to his record in the presidency. Yes, Jackson, with Polk as his minion, opposed a national bank and refused federal dollars for internal improvements, but he also came up short in annexing Texas and experienced plenty of political turmoil among his Cabinet and with his first vice president, John C. Calhoun.

Of course, the other comparison to be made between Old Hickory and Polk is that after his defeat in the disputed election of 1824, Jackson won two terms by wide margins. Polk squeaked into the White House by five thousand votes in New York state, but that did not keep Young Hickory from acting as though it were a mandate.

Polk was determined from the outset, as he said, "to be *myself* president of the United States." Polk's career was shaped by his support of Jackson, and in the end, Jackson used his last influences to make Polk president. But Polk came to the White House with a stronger determination than Jackson had to use its powers—whether to acquire California, declare war on Mexico, or stand on principle against Thomas Hart Benton. This determination made James K. Polk the most assertive chief executive prior to Abraham Lincoln.

When it came to war powers, James Madison had wrung his hands in 1812 and vacillated on how and when he should approach Congress about declaring war. By contrast, Polk aggressively planned to make war against Mexico even before news of the attack on Taylor's forces reached Washington. When Polk's war message finally reached Congress, it asked for congressional concurrence that a state of war already existed rather than a deliberation about whether or not one should be declared.

When it came to being commander in chief in that war, Polk directed the strategies of his generals to an extent that was rivaled among nineteenth-century presidents only by Abraham Lincoln. And even Lincoln did not fully grasp the reins as commander in chief until after he had given General George McClellan wide discretion and acquiesced to McClellan's ponderous Peninsula Campaign.

From the beginning of the Mexican War, as Taylor was fighting on the Rio Grande, Polk made certain that Kearny was dispatched not just to New Mexico but onward to California, and he made sure that similar California orders were issued to the navy. Polk consulted routinely with Secretary of War Marcy and was the chief architect of the nation's military policy.

Too often, it could be argued, Polk's decisions as commander in chief were colored by strong partisanship—for example, holding Whig generals Taylor and Scott suspect from the start and remaining blindly loyal to Gideon Pillow. But in the end, with the war successfully concluded, it is hard to argue with the final results.

Then there is the matter of presidential oversight of the executive branch. Somewhat tongue in cheek, Arthur M. Schlesinger Jr. wrote in *The Imperial Presidency* that Polk was "the only President who clearly died of overwork." There is no doubt that Polk was what would later be called a micromanager. He held twice-weekly Cabinet meetings and used them to direct and monitor the affairs of government.

As Polk was quick to claim himself, "I have made myself acquainted with the duties of the subordinate [Cabinet] officers, and have probably given more attention to details than any of my predecessors."

Not only was Polk's hands-on style in evidence with the communications that emanated from the state and war departments, but it was also in evidence in domestic affairs. At Polk's direction, Treasury Secretary Walker prepared what was essentially the first executive budget and brought its supervision under the president and not the House Ways and Means Committee.

Finally, there was Polk's assertion in his last annual message that more than a representative of a governing party, "the President represents in the executive department the whole people of the United States."[5]

Those three standards—accomplishing one's stated programs, exercising assertive executive leadership, and assuming accountability for the actions of the executive branch—are good benchmarks against which to judge any president.

Despite his accomplishments and lasting influences, if the general public has heard of James K. Polk today, they are likely to associate him with the campaign slogan of "54°40' or Fight!" and the political label of a dark horse. The first is simply erroneous; the Oregon slogan came into usage well after his election campaign. But what about the "dark horse" label?

Given the political credentials of some of Polk's successors, the dark horse label seems best justified for Polk only if one defines it narrowly as one who is not his party's apparent nominee. Prior to Polk's nomination in 1844, the heir apparent to the presidency— solidly established through the office of secretary of state, save for the popular generals Jackson and Harrison—had gotten his party's nomination and won the election.

To say that Polk was not his party's apparent nominee in 1844 is definitely true. But it does not follow that he was a political unknown or even that he suddenly vaulted onto the national stage. After fourteen years in Congress—four of them as Speaker of the House—and after being governor of Tennessee, a vice presidential hopeful in 1840, and Andrew Jackson's appointed political heir, James K. Polk was an experienced national politician.

The dark horse label does not fit Polk as readily as it fits some of his successors. Franklin Pierce, for example, was not considered by the Democrats in 1852 until the thirty-fifth ballot and did not win until the forty-ninth ballot. Nor does the label fit Polk as well as it does last-second compromise candidates who went on to win the presidency with little prior national exposure, notably Rutherford B. Hayes, James A. Garfield, and Warren G. Harding. And for that matter, what about the Republican nominee in 1860, a one-term congressman from Illinois who emerged from the pack in a brokered convention on the third ballot?

Label Polk a dark horse if you will, but far from being a flash from the back of the pack, Old Hickory's boy came to the presidency far better prepared and qualified than many of his successors. The best evidence of that is in the record that he forged.

*O*ne standard American history text said of James K. Polk: "His mind was not of the first order, for he lacked imagination and was too tense and calculating to allow his intellect free rein."[6] But an intellect that not only imagined but also achieved a continental vision for the United States can hardly be said to have been bridled.

If one gives Polk credit for lobbying the passage of the Texas resolution just before his inauguration, in four years' time he increased the territorial size of the United States by 38 percent, nearly doubling it. Polk, the slaveholder, did not give much thought to the consequences of such expansionism on indigenous Native Americans or Mexicans. That ignorance may well be debated on moral grounds, but it cannot take away Polk's stunning political achievement.

The irony, of course, is that in the early years of the twenty-first century, a tidal wave of Hispanic immigration continues to sweep northward from Mexico, not only into the provinces that James K.

Polk wrested from Mexico one hundred sixty years ago, but throughout the United States. It is a tidal wave of population and culture as inexorable as that which rolled into Texas in the 1830s, into Oregon in the 1840s, and into California in the 1850s. Whatever else history is, it is not static.

EPILOGUE

Sarah

ℐN SCRUTINIZING JAMES K. Polk's presidential record, it is an error to overlook the integral role that Sarah played in his presidency. Much as James did with the presidency, Sarah took the role of first lady to a new level.

Aside from her social graces, Sarah's long involvement with her husband's political campaigns, her in-depth knowledge of the issues and personalities of Washington, and her unrivaled role as presidential confidante all made her a powerful and influential first lady. In the century between Dolley Madison, who was still the grande dame of Washington society during the Polk administration, and Edith Wilson—who assumed extraordinary presidential prerogatives during her husband's illness—Sarah has no rival.

With the death of James Knox Polk, Sarah Childress Polk began the longest widowhood of any first lady—forty-two years. For later presidential widows who made it their remaining life's work to keep alive the memory of their husbands, Sarah set a standard they could only hope to emulate. Polk Place, with the presidential tomb on its lawn, became Sarah's shrine to the man who had

spared himself no personal hardship in the performance of his duties and who had given his every effort for his country.

When that country was torn apart by civil war, Polk Place became a neutral ground, respected both by Northerners who heard
the echoes of Polk's fervent prayers for union and by Southerners
who held its departed master among their stalwart forebears.

When the first Union army to occupy Nashville advanced on
the city early in 1862, much of the populace cowered or fled in ter-
ror. One of the committee appointed to meet the invaders reportedly asked Sarah Polk, "What shall I say to General Buell for you?"
Her reply was typical of Sarah. "Tell him I am at home," replied the
matron of Polk Place. Hat in hand, General Don Carlos Buell quietly called to pay his respects several days later.

When the carnage of four years of battle was over and the nation that Polk and his mentor, Jackson, had championed was re-
born, the Tennessee legislature resumed its annual pilgrimages to
Polk Place. "You were in the line of the advancing and receding
hosts, in the very gulf-stream of the war," read its postwar resolution to Sarah, "but the mad passions engendered by the conflict
were ever calmed in the presence of your abode."[1]

Sarah finally joined James on August 14, 1891, three weeks before her eighty-eighth birthday. No one questioned that for the
twenty-five years of their marriage theirs had been a love eternal.
"A noble woman, a devoted wife, a true friend, a sincere Christian,"
reads the inscription on her tomb, as she rests beside the man she
held dear for another forty-two years.[2] In the interim, the West that
James K. Polk had done so much to secure had become an integral
part of the American nation.

The state of Tennessee did not take over Polk Place as the Polks
had planned. Instead, James and Sarah were moved to a tomb on
the grounds of the Tennessee state capitol in 1893. Those who visit
may notice something else. Below the east steps of the capitol, there
is a statue of Andrew Jackson astride a horse. Old Hickory is lift-
ing his hat and looking generally westward. But his gaze also takes
in the little grove of magnolia trees that shelters the tomb of James
and Sarah Polk. Old Hickory's boy had done him proud.

ACKNOWLEDGMENTS

I have long appreciated that my passion for history was awakened at an early age. By my third-grade year, my grandfather was tutoring me in the presidents of the United States, as well as the starting lineup of the Cleveland Indians. The presidential list was shorter then—when you got to Eisenhower, you were finished—but I had particular trouble with the eight names between Andrew Jackson and Abraham Lincoln. Martin Van Buren was easy enough, and I could remember William Henry Harrison. But who came next?

Patiently, Grandpa repeated the names and had me recite them in a particular cadence: Tyler, Polk, Taylor—pause—Fillmore, Pierce, Buchanan. It wasn't long before I could rattle them off with barely a pause, but for years, the men behind the names were to me what they have remained to many people: a blur. Interestingly enough, however, most of these men interacted with each other for decades during one of the most turbulent yet dynamic eras of American history.

I am particularly pleased to have found a home at Random House and greatly appreciate Will Murphy's enthusiasm and guidance on this project. As always, I have nothing but high praise and enormous respect for Alexander Hoyt, my agent. I also extend my best wishes to that consummate gentleman of the publishing world, Hugh Van Dusen.

Much of this book is based on the two major primary sources from James K. Polk's lifetime. The first is his own diary, kept while he was in the White House and now once again available in its unabridged edition thanks to the James K. Polk Memorial Association. The other is the multivolume *Correspondence of James K. Polk*, a gargantuan undertaking begun in 1969 under the guidance of Herbert Weaver and now nearing completion under the expert hand of Wayne Cutler. I have also relied on the James K. Polk Papers in the Library of Congress. In quoting from these and other sources, I have taken the liberty to edit spelling and capitalization.

I must thank my "home" library, the Penrose Library of the University of Denver; as well as the John C. Hodges Library of the University of Tennessee at Knoxville, particularly Bob Huguenin; the Norlin Library of the University of Colorado; and the Denver Public Library. Additionally, I appreciate the research assistance of Fadra Whyte at the University of Pennsylvania and the cartographic skills of David Lambert at National Geographic Maps.

Many people extended me kind hospitality during my Polk travels, but I especially enjoyed the time spent with John Holtz-apple and Thomas Price at the James K. Polk Home in Columbia, Tennessee. Their subsequent review of the manuscript and assistance with photographs and maps is greatly appreciated.

NOTES

A PROLOGUE IN TWO PARTS

1. John O'Sullivan, "Annexation," *United States Magazine and Democratic Review* XVII, No. LXXXV (July and August 1845), p. 5.

1—OLD HICKORY'S BOY

1. Robert V. Remini, *Andrew Jackson and the Course of American Empire, 1767–1821* (New York: Harper & Row, 1977), pp. 3–5, 38–39, 41, 84.
2. Charles Sellers, *James K. Polk, Jacksonian, 1795–1843* (Norwalk, Conn.: Easton Press, 1987), pp. 7–8, 23–25.
3. Sellers, *Jacksonian*, pp. 28–30, 37–38.
4. Numerous biographers have erroneously reported Polk's condition and subsequent surgery as related to gallstones, not urinary stones. The synopsis here is based on Robert W. Ikard, "Surgical Operation on James K. Polk by Ephraim McDowell, or the Search for Polk's Gallstone," *Tennessee Historical Quarterly* 43 (1984), pp. 121–131, and Polk's own account in J. George Harris, *Polk Campaign Biography* (Knoxville, Tenn.: Tennessee Presidents Trust, 1990), p. 6, specifically, "was seized by a paroxysm."
5. "much the most promising": and Dialectic Society debate topics and University of North Carolina information from Sellers, *Jacksonian*, pp. 41–44, 47, 49.
6. "your proficiency in extemporaneous" and graduation, pp. 50–51, 54–55.
7. Sellers, *Jacksonian*, pp. 56–61.
8. "incomplete, and not authenticated" and "to commence an action": Herbert Weaver and Paul H. Bergeron, eds., *Correspondence of James K. Polk* Vol. I, *1817–1832* (Nashville: Vanderbilt University Press, 1969), pp. 9–10 (Polk to Houston, September 27, 1820). Hereinafter *Correspondence* fol-

lowed by the appropriate volume number and page reference. Full cita-
tions for the various editors, publishers, and publication dates of the vol-
umes of the Polk correspondence appear in the bibliography. (Note:
Nineteenth-century quotations have been edited for spelling and capitalization to facilitate reading.) "A victim of the use": Marquis James, *The
Life of Andrew Jackson* (Indianapolis: Bobbs-Merrill, 1938), p. 624.

9. "Now so help me": William C. Davis, *Three Roads to the Alamo: The Lives and
Fortunes of David Crockett, James Bowie, and William Barret Travis* (New York:
HarperPerennial, 1999), p. 73.

10. Most sources for Sarah's early life are maddeningly suspect. Many stories
derive from Anson and Fanny Nelson's memorial published in 1892 and the
particularly dubious Jimmie Lou Sparkman Claxton's *Eighty-eight Years
with Sarah Polk* (New York: Vantage Press, 1972). John Reed Bumgarner,
who might have provided a more solid foundation in *Sarah Childress Polk: A
Biography of the Remarkable First Lady*, chose to use these earlier works rather
indiscriminately and also incorporated some errors of his own. This vi-
gnette is compiled from: Sellers, *Jacksonian*, pp. 74–76; John Reed Bumgarner, *Sarah Childress Polk: A Biography of the Remarkable First Lady* (Jefferson,
N.C.: McFarland, 1997), pp. 17–18, 23–25, 34; and Anson and Fanny Nelson, *Memorials of Sarah Childress Polk* (Newtown, Conn.: American Political
Biography Press, 1994), pp. 4–7, 16–17, 38. Polk's comment about the Earl
portrait, "See those lovely raven curls," is in Bumgarner, p. 34. The exchange between Polk and Jackson about Sarah was apparently first reported in Sarah Agnes Wallace, "Letters of Mrs. James K. Polk to Her
Husband," *Tennessee Historical Quarterly* XI, No. 2 (March 1952), p. 180.

11. James teasing Sarah story in Nelson, *Sarah Childress Polk*, p. 16; "I am a
candidate": *Correspondence* Vol. I, p. 16 (Polk to William Polk, September
24, 1822).

12. "twenty-three gallons" and election results in Sellers, *Jacksonian*, p. 77.

13. Sellers, *Jacksonian*, pp. 92–93.

14. Sellers, *Jacksonian*, pp. 77–78, 81–84, 87–92; "I have been preparing":
Harris, *Polk Campaign Biography*, p. 9. (Until 1913, federal senators were
elected by state legislatures and not by popular vote.)

15. "I am a senator": Robert V. Remini, *Andrew Jackson and the Course of American Freedom, 1822–1832* (New York: Harper & Row, 1981), pp. 52–53.

2 – CARRYING THE WATER

1. Stefan Lorant, *The Glorious Burden: The American Presidency* (New York:
Harper & Row, 1968), pp. 116, 908.

2. Jackson-Clay differences in Remini, *Andrew Jackson and the Course of American Freedom,* p. 58, and "denouncing the anonymous slanderer" and Adams-Clay conversation, ibid., pp. 88–90.

3. "The delegation I believe" and "If you do this": Robert V. Remini, *Henry Clay: Statesman for the Union* (New York: W. W. Norton, 1991), pp. 259–260.

4. Lorant, *Glorious Burden,* pp. 116, 908.

5. "So you see": Harold D. Moser, et al., eds., *The Papers of Andrew Jackson* Vol. VI, *1825–1828* (Knoxville: University of Tennessee Press, 2002), pp. 29–30 (Jackson to Lewis, February 14, 1825).

6. "We see the predictions": Vol. VI, p. 37 (Jackson to Lewis, February 20, 1825); Jackson's "nay" vote in Remini, *Andrew Jackson and the Course of American Freedom,* p. 103.

7. "live on their horses" and election results in Sellers, *Jacksonian,* p. 98.

8. "Colonel Polk, by whom": James F. Hopkins, ed., *The Papers of Henry Clay* Vol. 4, *Secretary of State, 1825* (Lexington: University of Kentucky Press, 1972), p. 716 (Carroll to Clay, October 4, 1825).

9. Sellers, *Jacksonian,* pp. 100–101.

10. "This important election": *Correspondence* Vol. I, p. 38 (Polk to Jackson, April 3, 1826).

11. "it would not be" and "Yes, sir": Eugene Irving McCormac, *James K. Polk: A Political Biography* (Berkeley: University of California Press, 1922), pp. 17–18.

12. "the dastardly individual" and "the general impression": *Correspondence* Vol. I, p. 39 (Polk to Jackson, April 3, 1826).

13. Clay-Randolph duel in Remini, *Clay,* pp. 292–295; "I ought not" and "I do not fire": James F. Hopkins and Mary W. M. Hargreaves, eds., *The Papers of Henry Clay* Vol. 5, *Secretary of State, 1826* (Lexington: University of Kentucky Press, 1973), p. 253 (Clay to Brooke, April 19, 1826).

14. Sellers, *Jacksonian,* p. 111.

15. "pleasure to hear": *Correspondence* Vol. I, p. 41 (Jackson to Polk, May 3, 1826); "expect an excitement": ibid., p. 177 (Polk to Jackson, April 13, 1828).

16. "First, I deem" and "all that has been" and "My friend Colonel Polk's": pp. 196–198 (Polk to Jackson, September 8, 1828).

17. "The Adams men here": *Correspondence* Vol. I, pp. 207–208 (Polk to Kincannon, November 15, 1828).

18. For a detailed discussion of this issue, see Bray Hammond, *Banks and Politics in America from the Revolution to the Civil War* (Princeton, N.J.: Princeton University Press, 1957), pp. 328–365.

19. See McCormac, *Polk,* pp. 18, 191 for examples of Polk's views on keeping

slavery out of public policy, and see William Dusinberre, *Slavemaster President: The Double Career of James Polk* (New York: Oxford University Press, 2003), for a complete account of Polk's record as a slaveholder.

20. "Did you ever know": *Correspondence* Vol. I, p. 537 (Polk to Coffee, November 27, 1832).

21. "to solicit the Speakership" and "received an answer" and "the President was not": McCormac, *Polk*, p. 48.

22. "If Mr. Polk": Sellers, *Jacksonian*, p. 237; Jackson's reaction ibid., p. 242.

23. "The New England states": *Correspondence* Vol. III, pp. 299–300 (Jackson to Polk, September 15, 1835).

24. Election results in Lorant, *Glorious Burden*, p. 910; "the only man" and "go to the wilds": Davis, *Three Roads to the Alamo*, pp. 397, 399.

25. "had been unable": James, *Life of Andrew Jackson*, p. 724.

3—TENNESSEE AND OLD TIPPECANOE

1. Tennessee congressional and speaker results in Sellers, *Jacksonian*, pp. 35, 326; House of Representatives totals from John A. Garraty, *The American Nation: A History of the United States* (New York: Harper & Row, 1966), appendix; an example of Polk's urging early attendance for special session vote is from *Correspondence* Vol. IV, p. 210 (Polk to Blair, August 16, 1837).

2. Supporting Catron for Supreme Court in *Correspondence* Vol. IV, p. 73 (Polk to Jackson, March 3, 1837); "Never have we": Sellers, *Jacksonian*, p. 351 (Catron to Jackson, January 4, 1838).

3. *Correspondence* Vol. IV, p. 340 (Walker to Polk, January 25, 1838); p. 362 (Walker to Polk, February 7, 1838).

4. "forty fat sheep" and "arising from exposure" and "he had been strongly": Nashville *Union*, September 3, 1838.

5. "the highest and most" and vote in *Congressional Globe*, 25 Cong., 3rd Sess. p. 238 (March 3, 1839); "While you were Speaker": *Correspondence* Vol. V, p. 356 (Blackwell to Polk, December 30, 1839).

6. Nelson, *Sarah Childress Polk*, pp. 54–55.

7. McCormac, *Polk*, p. 142; "very little more": Nashville *Republican Banner*, April 15, 1839, quoted in McCormac, *Polk*, p. 145; "The day was": *Correspondence* Vol. V, p. 113 (Polk to Sarah Polk, April 14, 1839); "thirty-seven of the state's": Sellers, *Jacksonian*, pp. 369–370; "I am anxious": *Correspondence* Vol. V, p. 154 (Sarah Polk to Polk, June 25, 1839).

8. Sellers, *Jacksonian*, pp. 372–373; vote percentage in Sam W. Haynes, *James K. Polk and the Expansionist Impulse* (New York: Pearson Longman, 1997), p. 45; vote totals in John Seigenthaler, *James K. Polk* (New York:

Times Books, 2004), p. 65; "the return of": *Correspondence* Vol. V, p. 186 (Jackson to Polk, August 13, 1839).

9. "I am duly sensible": *Correspondence* Vol. V, p. 213 (Polk to Haynes, August 27, 1839); "this triumphant regeneration": ibid., p. 197 (Pierce to Polk, August 20, 1839).

10. Johnson's Senate vote in Lorant, *Glorious Burden,* p. 149; Johnson's domestic life in Sellers, *Jacksonian,* pp. 400–401; "I am the most": James, *Life of Andrew Jackson,* p. 738.

11. "shed tears" and "convinced delegates": Remini, *Clay,* p. 552; "sit the remainder": Freeman Cleaves, *Old Tippecanoe: William Henry Harrison and His Time* (New York: Charles Scribner's Sons, 1939), pp. 320–321.

12. "ultimate wishes": *Correspondence* Vol. V, pp. 340–341 (Yell to Polk, December 12, 1839); see also pp. 281–282, 312–314 (J. L. Martin to Polk, November 2 and 26, 1839) for more discussion of Polk's presidential ambitions; "nominated for vice president" and "the plan that": Sellers, *Jacksonian,* p. 405.

13. "all that can": *Correspondence* Vol. V, p. 397 (Johnson to Polk, February 27, 1840); "To all I": ibid., p. 428 (Grundy to Polk, April 15, 1840).

14. "probably founded" and "Henceforth": Nashville *Republican Banner,* June 20, 1840. Critics routinely talk of political bias in twenty-first-century reporting, but it must be remembered that in the nineteenth century, many newspapers served as political mouthpieces closely allied to major parties. The Nashville *Republican Banner* was a Whig device and the Nashville *Union* a Democratic one.

15. "attempt to run": *Correspondence* Vol. V, p. 652 (Burton to Polk, March 9, 1841); "a perfect 'Tippecanoe run' ": Nashville *Republican Banner,* December 12, 1840.

16. "solemn, almost grotesque": Sellers, *Jacksonian,* p. 431; "a promising young man": Nashville *Union,* March 29, 1841; "my venerable competitor": McCormac, *Polk,* p. 182.

17. "maintained such an air": Sellers, *Jacksonian,* p. 431; "Why, boys": Nashville *Republican Banner,* March 30, 1841.

18. Sellers, *Jacksonian,* pp. 436–437.

19. "When I think": *Correspondence* Vol. V, p. 674 (Sarah Polk to Polk, April 8, 1841).

20. "Bring on your team": Nashville *Union,* April 8, 1841.

21. "wearied and worn" and "so hoarse that" and "boarded a stage": Sellers, *Jacksonian,* p. 442–444.

22. Vote totals in Seigenthaler, *James K. Polk,* pp. 67–68; "Governor Polk deserves": Martin Van Buren Papers, Manuscript Division, Library of Congress, Washington, D.C. (Jackson to Van Buren, August 16, 1841).

4—THE LAST DEFEAT

1. "We must keep" and "The sober second": Sellers, *Jacksonian,* p. 449.

2. "I believe your": *Correspondence* Vol. V, p. 722 (Turney to Polk, August 12, 1841); "wanted nothing that": Sellers, *Jacksonian,* p. 451; "Before the reverberation": Nashville *Republican Banner,* October 4, 1841; "If I shall ever": Sellers, *Jacksonian,* p. 452.

3. McCormac, *Polk,* p. 188.

4. Norma Lois Peterson, *The Presidencies of William Henry Harrison & John Tyler* (Lawrence: University Press of Kansas, 1989), pp. 19–20; Cleaves, *Old Tippecanoe,* p. 5.

5. "The impression which": Reginald C. McGrane, ed., *The Correspondence of Nicholas Biddle Dealing with National Affairs, 1807–1844* (Boston: Houghton Mifflin, 1919), pp. 337–338 (Biddle to Webster, December 13, 1840); "Mr. Clay, you forget": Lyon G. Tyler, *The Letters and Times of the Tylers* (Richmond, Va.: Whittet & Shepperson, 1885) Vol. II, p. 10.

6. "kept referring to Tyler": Remini, *Clay,* p. 580.

7. "President Tyler is": *National Intelligencer,* April 7, 1841.

8. "Go you now": Tyler, *Letters* Vol. II, pp. 33–34; "Clay is unhappy": Van Buren Papers (Wright to Van Buren, June 21, 1841).

9. "Tyler dares not": Tyler, *Letters* Vol. II, p. 41; "predominates over": Remini, *Clay,* p. 584, quoting New York *Herald,* July 30, 1841.

10. "a broader, deeper": Donald B. Cole, *Martin Van Buren and the American Political System* (Princeton, N.J.: Princeton University Press, 1984), p. 392.

11. Sellers, *Jacksonian,* pp. 466–467; "interesting often and some times": Robert Seager II, ed., *The Papers of Henry Clay* Vol. 9, *The Whig Leader, January 1, 1837–December 31, 1843* (Lexington: University Press of Kentucky, 1988), p. 704 (Clay to Sargent, May 31, 1842). See also Clay's similar comment that "not much on politics was discussed": ibid., p. 706 (Clay to Crittenden, June 3, 1842).

12. "The bargain is struck": Nashville *Republican Banner,* May 13, 1842.

13. "The contest that": Sellers, *Jacksonian,* p. 457, and see also "the ground was laid": pp. 472–473; "The labor of canvassing": *Correspondence* Vol. VI, p. 143 (Polk to Van Buren, December 8, 1842). The twenty-three-hundred-mile four-month Polk-Jones campaign on horseback crisscrossing Tennessee might not have had a rival for an individual statewide race—save perhaps the Lincoln-Douglas campaign of 1858 in Illinois—until Lyndon Johnson appeared determined to visit every Texas hamlet and farm by helicopter during his 1948 U.S. Senate campaign.

14. Polk clan descendants in William R. Polk, *Polk's Folly: An American Family*

History (New York: Doubleday, 2000), p. 157; Ickard, "Surgical Operation," pp. 130–131; "Present me respectfully": *Correspondence* Vol. III, p. 271 (Laughlin to Polk, August 21, 1835).

15. "I must confess": *Correspondence* Vol. VI, p. 259 (Sarah Polk to Polk, March 29, 1843).

16. "I never wanted": *Correspondence* Vol. VI, p. 276 (Sarah Polk to Polk, May 3, 1843); "You must cheer up": ibid., p. 316 (Polk to Sarah Polk, June 9, 1843); "You continue to write": ibid., p. 319 (Polk to Sarah Polk, June 18, 1843).

17. "was to be decided": Nashville *Union,* April 25, 1843; Sellers, *Jacksonian,* p. 475; "There is my banner": Nashville *Republican Banner,* March 29, 1843.

18. Presidential-choice debate in Nashville *Republican Banner,* July 3, 1843; debate and "Sir, I dare you to name": ibid., July 10, 1843.

19. "If you succeed": *Correspondence* Vol. VI, p. 317 (Armstrong to Polk, June 12, 1843).

20. "A Whig State": Nashville *Republican Banner,* August 11, 1843; Sellers, *Jacksonian,* pp. 487–488.

21. "It is no time": *Correspondence* Vol. VI, p. 331 (Polk to Armstrong, August 7, 1843); calendar of Polk papers, in *Correspondence* VI, pp. 662–663.

22. "now in a clear": *Correspondence* Vol. VI, p. 332 (Polk to Van Buren, August 18, 1843).

23. "The politics of Tennessee" and "The Tennessee Dynasty": Sellers, *Jacksonian,* p. 490; "it is as mortifying": *Correspondence* Vol. VI, p. 396 (Van Buren to Polk, December 27, 1843).

24. "the election in Tennessee": Seager, *Papers of Henry Clay,* Vol. 9, pp. 846–847 (Clay to Campbell, August 19, 1843).

5—HANDS OFF TEXAS

1. "They commence by introducing" and "proceed, upon the most": Frederick Merk, *Manifest Destiny and Mission in American History* (New York: Vintage Books, 1966), pp. 20–21.

2. Remini, *Andrew Jackson and the Course of American Empire,* pp. 389–390; "free-wheeling": Remini, *Andrew Jackson and the Course of American Freedom,* pp. 218–220; "authorized you to": Remini, *Andrew Jackson and the Course of American Democracy, 1833–1845* (New York: Harper & Row, 1984), pp. 352–356, 359.

3. Remini, *Andrew Jackson and the Course of American Democracy,* pp. 360–362; for two accounts of Houston's failed marriage see M. K. Wisehart, *Sam*

Houston, American Giant (Washington: Robert B. Luce, 1962), pp. 38–50, and Marquis James, *The Raven: A Biography of Sam Houston* (New York: Book-of-the-Month Club, 1990), pp. 72–85.

4. "We are looking": *Correspondence* Vol. III, pp. 567–568 (Hardeman to Polk, March 31, 1836).

5. "perhaps, the most important": Charles F. Adams, ed., *Memoirs of John Quincy Adams* Vol. IV (Philadelphia: J. B. Lippincott, 1875), p. 274; "a very large portion": *Congressional Globe*, 25 Cong., 1st Sess., pp. 24–26.

6. La Branche nomination in James D. Richardson, ed., *A Compilation of the Messages and Papers of the Presidents* (New York: Bureau of National Literature, 1897) Vol. IV, pp. 1500–1501; "to Sam Houston's republic": James, *Life of Andrew Jackson*, p. 719.

7. Julius W. Pratt, *A History of United States Foreign Policy* (Englewood Cliffs, N.J.: Prentice-Hall, 1955), pp. 226–227.

8. Peterson, *Presidencies of William Henry Harrison & John Tyler*, pp. 150–153, 180–183, 198–199; Pratt, *History of United States Foreign Policy*, pp. 227–228. Part of Upshur's confidence in a Senate ratification appears to have come from the fact that the Senate readily confirmed his own recess appointment when his views on annexation were well known.

9. "would deplore any": Richardson, *Messages and Papers* Vol. V, p. 2115 (Tyler's third annual message, December 1843).

10. Cole, *Martin Van Buren*, p. 390.

11. "the victory of next year": Seager, *Papers of Henry Clay* Vol. 9, p. 873 (Clay to Berrien, October 27, 1843).

12. "I think with you": *Correspondence* Vol. VII, p. 7 (Ramsey to Polk, January 4, 1844); "I fear some": ibid., p. 87 (Johnson to Polk, March 10, 1844).

13. Peterson, *Presidencies of William Henry Harrison & John Tyler*, pp. 201–203.

14. Peterson presents a good summary of these competing views and their documentation, pp. 203–206 and footnotes 5–8 on p. 300.

15. David M. Pletcher, *The Diplomacy of Annexation: Texas, Oregon, and the Mexican War* (Columbia: University of Missouri Press, 1973), p. 136.

16. "Should it meet" and "Texas voluntarily steps": Richardson, *Messages and Papers*, Vol. V, pp. 2160–2164 (Tyler to Senate, April 22, 1844).

17. "a peg to declare" and "marches through Louisiana": John Spencer Bassett, ed., *Correspondence of Andrew Jackson* (Washington: Carnegie Institution, 1933) Vol. VI, p. 202 (Jackson to Brown, February 9, 1843); "while Britain favored": Pletcher, *Diplomacy of Annexation*, p. 143; "the weakest and most" and "number, comfort, intelligence" and "in reality": Clyde N. Wilson, ed., *The Papers of John C. Calhoun* Vol. XVIII, *1844* (Columbia: University of South Carolina Press, 1988), pp. 273–278 (Calhoun to Pak-

enham, April 18, 1844); Charles M. Wiltse, *John C. Calhoun, Sectionalist, 1840–1850* (Indianapolis: Bobbs-Merrill, 1951), p. 170.

18. "his well-known lack": Remini, *Clay*, p. 635; "If St. Paul": Henry Thomas Shanks, ed., *The Papers of Willie Person Mangum* Vol. III, *1839–1843* (Raleigh, N.C.: State Department of Archives and History, 1953), p. 468 (Johnston to Mangum, September 14, 1843); "Are you for": Charleston *Mercury,* April 4, 1844; "I think I can": Mrs. Chapman Coleman, ed., *The Life of John J. Crittenden, with Selections from His Correspondence and Speeches* (Philadelphia: J. B. Lippincott, 1871), pp. 217–218 (Clay to Crittenden, March 24, 1844); "Raleigh letter" appeared in the Washington *National Intelligencer,* April 27, 1844, republished in Arthur M. Schlesinger Jr., ed., *History of American Presidential Elections, 1789–1968* Vol. I (New York: Chelsea House, 1971), pp. 814–817.

19. "acting too secretly": Cole, *Martin Van Buren*, p. 393; see also Van Buren to Hammett, April 20, 1844 in the Washington *Globe*, April 27, 1844, republished in Schlesinger, *History of American Presidential Elections* Vol. I, pp. 822–828.

20. "I have no doubt": James, *Life of Andrew Jackson*, p. 766; "a dead political duck": Bassett, *Correspondence of Andrew Jackson* Vol. VI, p. 283 (Jackson to Blair, May 7, 1844); "I have shed": ibid., p. 286 (Jackson to Blair, May 11, 1844); "to turn the current": Remini, *Andrew Jackson and the Course of American Democracy*, p. 498, and see also p. 597, note 38.

6 – A SUMMONS FROM OLD HICKORY

1. "It is important": *Correspondence* Vol. VII, pp. 131–132 (Donelson to Polk, May 10, 1844); "I send you" and "I cannot see" and "I told you": ibid., p. 131 (Armstrong to Polk, May 10, 1844).
2. "mortifying": *Correspondence* Vol. VI, p. 396 (Van Buren to Polk, December 27, 1843); "I think a serious": ibid., p. 65 (Johnson to Polk, May 20, 1842).
3. "a vast majority": *Correspondence* Vol. VII, p. 99 (Chase et al. to Polk, March 30, 1844); "Having at no time": ibid., pp. 105–106 (Polk to Chase et al., April 23, 1844). Polk's delay in answering Chase was due to his absence from Columbia on business at his Mississippi plantation and not from any procrastination. Polk received the Chase letter on April 21.
4. "I have only a moment": *Correspondence* Vol. VII, p. 116 (Johnson to Polk, May 3, 1844).
5. Jackson's letter urging annexation finally appeared in the Nashville *Union*

on May 16, 1844, and in the Washington *Globe* on May 23, 1844; "Texas must be ours!" and "extending our laws": Bassett, *Correspondence of Andrew Jackson* Vol. VI, p. 272 (Jackson to Blair, March 5, 1844); "a good deal": *Correspondence* Vol. VII, p. 97 (Johnson to Polk, March 29, 1844); "The scepter shall": Charles Sellers, *James K. Polk, Continentalist, 1843–1846* (Norwalk, Conn.: Easton Press, 1987), pp. 71–72.

6. All quotes from *Correspondence* Vol. VII, pp. 134–135 (Polk to Johnson, May 13, 1844). That Johnson was up to the task of promoting Polk's presidential ambitions is best evidenced by his comments during the *vice* presidential hunt. In January 1844, Johnson privately wrote to Sarah Polk with the latest in Washington gossip. He observed that her husband was "now encountering the very identical difficulties as to the *Vice* that he would have to do for the first office of the government and if he can overcome the one he could have done the other." Ibid., p. 45n (Johnson to Sarah Polk, January 14, 1844).

7. All quotes from *Correspondence* Vol. VII, pp. 136–137 (Polk to Johnson, May 14, 1844).

8. All quotes from *Correspondence* Vol. VII, pp. 125–126 (Johnson to Polk, May 8, 1844).

9. All quotes from *Correspondence* Vol. VII, pp. 139–140 (Polk to Johnson, May 15, 1844), except "never for a moment" and "someone has to take": ibid., pp. 137–138 (Polk to Johnson, May 14, 1844). For secondary accounts and other analyses of these three days, see Sellers, *Continentalist*, pp. 70–73; McCormac, *Polk*, pp. 231–234; and Remini, *Andrew Jackson and the Course of American Democracy*, pp. 499–502.

7—BALTIMORE, 1844

1. Timothy Jacobs, ed., *The History of the Baltimore & Ohio: America's First Railroad* (New York: Crescent Books, 1989), pp. 12–15, 28, 33; population figures are from 1840 census; by comparison, Washington, D.C., had twenty-three thousand residents and Nashville, Tennessee, seven thousand.

2. "will bring home": Remini, *Clay*, pp. 260–261; "it would have been wiser": Seager, *Papers of Henry Clay* Vol. 9, pp. 709–710 (speech at Lexington, Kentucky, June 9, 1842).

3. "Henry Clay of Kentucky" and "a sense of delicacy": Remini, *Clay*, pp. 644–646; Whig platform in Schlesinger, *History of American Presidential Elections*, Vol. I, p. 807; "I do not think": Thurlow Weed Barnes, *Memoir of*

Thurlow Weed (Boston: Houghton, Mifflin, 1884), p. 120 (Clay to Weed, May 6, 1844).

4. Sellers, *Continentalist*, p. 76; "You will find": *Correspondence* Vol. VII, p. 119 (Polk to Johnson, May 4, 1844); "he is one": ibid., p. 140 (Polk to Johnson, May 15, 1844).

5. "I can beat Clay": Sellers, *Continentalist*, p. 61. Calhoun's reference was to those New England Federalists who gathered at the Hartford convention in 1814 dissatisfied with the course of the War of 1812. A month later, Jackson's victory at New Orleans was announced and the Federalist party never recovered from the stigma of being perceived as defeatists.

6. Sellers, *Continentalist*, pp. 77–79, 84–89.

7. Proceedings of the Democratic National Convention, Baltimore, May 27–30, 1844, in Schlesinger, *History of American Presidential Elections*, Vol. I, pp. 829–839; "would play as bold": Sellers, *Continentalist*, pp. 89–91; "I will be heard": James C. N. Paul, *Rift in the Democracy* (Philadelphia: University of Pennsylvania Press, 1951), pp. 157–158.

8. "I said to them": *Correspondence* Vol. VII, pp. 158–159 (Pillow to Polk, May 28, 1844).

9. "It flashed in my mind": *Correspondence* Vol. VII, p. 318 (Bancroft to Polk, July 6, 1844).

10. "If a single vote" and "never before or since": Sellers, *Continentalist*, pp. 94–95; Cole, *Martin Van Buren*, p. 395.

11. "the name of Governor Polk": Van Buren Papers (Butler to Van Buren, May 31, 1844).

12. "You should have heard": *Correspondence* Vol. VII, p. 318 (Bancroft to Polk, July 6, 1844); Proceedings in Schlesinger, *History of American Presidential Elections*, Vol. I, pp. 839–841, specifically, "the bosom friend," p. 841; Sellers, *Continentalist*, pp. 95–97.

13. Proceedings in Schlesinger, *History of American Presidential Elections*, Vol. I, pp. 845–849; "he always knew": Sellers, *Continentalist*, pp. 97–98.

14. "Your nomination": *Correspondence* Vol. VII, pp. 161–162 (Johnson to Polk, May 29, 1844); "Never was there": ibid., p. 162 (Pillow to Polk, May 29, 1844).

15. Sellers, *Continentalist*, pp. 98–99.

16. "the domestic institutions" and "that our title": 1844 Democratic platform in Schlesinger, *History of American Presidential Elections*, Vol. I, pp. 799–801.

17. "We are more disposed": Sellers, *Continentalist*, p. 101; "Are our Democratic friends": Shanks, *Papers of Willie Person Mangum* Vol. IV, *1844–1846*, p. 134 (Clay to Mangum, June 7, 1844); "a ridiculous thing" and "the Whigs will have to": Sellers, *Continentalist*, p. 101; "The great mass":

McCormac, *Polk*, p. 258n; "a man of ability" and "Mr. Van Buren being": Sellers, *Continentalist*, p. 103; "I suppose miracles": James K. Polk Papers, Manuscript Division, Library of Congress, Washington, D.C. (Huntsman to Polk, June 11, 1844).

18. "The dark sky": Bassett, *Correspondence of Andrew Jackson* Vol. VI, p. 296 (Donelson to Jackson, May 29, 1844); "I hear it whispered": Washington *Madisonian*, May 30, 1844, reprinted in the Nashville *Republican Banner*, June 10, 1844.

19. The phrase "dark horse" may have originally appeared in an 1831 novel called *The Young Duke* by Benjamin Disraeli. That line reads: "A dark horse which had never been thought of, and which the careless St. James had never even observed in the list, rushed past the grandstand in sweeping triumph." (William Safire, *Safire's New Political Dictionary* [New York: Random House, 1993], p. 167.) Just when it was applied to Polk is debatable. Safire speculates that the term came into use after Polk and before Pierce—a rather narrow window. Polk biographer McCormac does not use the term, although Sellers does.

8—"WHO IS JAMES K. POLK?"

1. "Our friends here": *Correspondence* Vol. VII, p. 188 (Armstrong to Polk, June 3, 1844); "pleased beyond measure": ibid., p. 198 (Armstrong to Polk, June 5, 1844); "Daughter, I will": James, *Life of Andrew Jackson*, p. 773; "Who is James K. Polk?" Nashville *Republican Banner*, June 7, 1844; "refer the inquirer": Nashville *Union*, June 8, 1844.

2. "I write as I" and "In your acceptance": *Correspondence* Vol. VII, p. 166 (Brown to Polk, May 30, 1844).

3. "that under no circumstances": Richardson, *Messages and Papers* Vol. IV, p. 1864; "I think you should": *Correspondence* Vol. VII, p. 174 (Laughlin to Polk, May 31, 1844).

4. "turn a deaf ear": *Correspondence* Vol. VII, p. 161 (Hubbard et al. to Polk, May 29, 1844); "It has been well" and "I deem the present" and "the most effective means": ibid., pp. 241–242 (Polk to Hubbard et al., June 12, 1844); "I said nothing": ibid., p. 276 (Polk to Johnson, June 24, 1844). One is tempted to speculate on the impact of Polk's one-term pledge on future presidents. One of Polk's admirers was Theodore Roosevelt, who as a twenty-seven-year-old wrote in his 1886 biography of Thomas Hart Benton that "no foot of soil to which we had any title in the Northwest should have been given up." (Theodore Roosevelt, *Thomas Hart Benton* [Boston: Houghton Mifflin, 1895], p. 268.) On Inauguration Day 1905, a hale and

hearty Theodore Roosevelt—who had just won election to what would be his first full term—stunned supporters and adversaries alike by declaring in much the same vein as Polk had done in 1844 that he would not seek re-election. Four years later, very much desiring to remain in office, Roosevelt was a victim of his own reticence and yielded to his handpicked successor, William Howard Taft—only to run against Taft as a Bull Moose in 1912 and assure the election of their Democratic opponent, Woodrow Wilson.

5. Sellers, *Continentalist*, pp. 118–119; "The Texas question will" and "You must recollect": *Correspondence* Vol. VII, p. 168 (Walker to Polk, May 30, 1844); "In adjusting the details": ibid., p. 267 (Polk to Kane, June 19, 1844); "Nothing has surprised me": Remini, *Clay*, p. 649.

6. "order his majority" and "Clay is exceedingly proud": *Correspondence* Vol. VII, pp. 214–215 (Catron to Polk, June 8, 1844); Texas vote in Pratt, *History of United States Foreign Policy*, p. 229; "a bride adorned": Bassett, *Correspondence of Andrew Jackson* Vol. VI, p. 264 (Houston to Jackson, February 16, 1844).

7. "in the country" and "I believe General Jackson": *Correspondence* Vol. VII, pp. 384–385 (Polk to Donelson, July 23, 1844).

8. "cease his war": *Correspondence* Vol. VII, pp. 388–389 (Polk to Jackson, July 23, 1844); "to preserve his popularity": ibid., p. 410 (Donelson to Polk, July 29, 1844); "write a letter": ibid., p. 338 (Walker to Polk, July 10, 1844).

9. "I have but one": Bassett, *Correspondence of Andrew Jackson* Vol. VI, p. 305 (Jackson to Blair, July 26, 1844); "his great desire": Tyler, *Letters* Vol. III, pp. 143–144 (Jackson to Lewis, July 26, 1844); "a greater popularity": Bassett, *Correspondence of Andrew Jackson* Vol. VI, p. 306 (Jackson to Mason, August 1, 1844).

10. "Why my dear friend" and "scarcely able to wield": *Correspondence* Vol. VII, p. 401 (Jackson to Polk, July 26, 1844); "I concur fully": p. 430 (Polk to Jackson, August 3, 1844).

11. "handful of prostituted" Sellers, *Continentalist*, p. 137; "held the fate" Tyler, *Letters* Vol. II, p. 342; Bassett, *Correspondence of Andrew Jackson* Vol. VI, p. 315 (Tyler to Jackson, August 18, 1844).

12. "having been twice" and "Who is the opponent" and "a blighted burr": Sellers, *Continentalist*, pp. 139–141.

13. Polk dueling charges and "a drunkard, a duelist": McCormac, *Polk*, p. 273; "The standard of Henry Clay": Adams, *Memoirs of John Quincy Adams* Vol. XII, p. 45 (June 5, 1844).

14. "Forty of these": Ithaca (New York) *Chronicle*, August 21, 1844; "the grossest and basest": *Correspondence* Vol. VIII, p. 151 (Polk to Ingersoll,

October 4, 1844); "any last-minute smear": Safire, *Safire's New Political Dictionary*, p. 670.

15. All quotes from Remini, *Clay*, pp. 659–661.

16. "you will get": *Correspondence* Vol. VII, p. 300 (Jackson to Polk, June 29, 1844); "Ohio is a doubtful state" and "And now for the main": ibid., p. 362 (Harris to Polk, July 18, 1844).

17. "compelled to decide": *Correspondence* Vol. VII, p. 184 (Wright to Polk, June 2, 1844); Polk's response, ibid., pp. 244–246 (Polk to Wright, June 12, 1844); "neither I, nor": ibid., p. 431 (Polk to Jackson, August 3, 1844); "an outstanding hero": Oscar D. Lambert, *Presidential Politics in the United States, 1841–1844* (Durham, N.C.: Duke University Press, 1936), p. 196.

18. Sellers, *Continentalist*, pp. 151–157; McCormac, *Polk*, pp. 250–251, and see also pp. 281–282.

19. Election results from Schlesinger, *History of American Presidential Elections*, Vol. I, p. 861; *"the lords of the spindles"*: *Correspondence* Vol. VIII, p. 350 (Douglas to Polk, November 22, 1844). Polk fell only 210 votes short of the combined Clay-Birney total in Michigan (out of 55,728 total votes) and he beat the combined Clay-Birney total in Indiana by 208 votes (out of 140,154); Polk carried Louisiana 13,782 to 13,083. For the Plaquemines Parish vote fraud, see Edward Stanwood, *A History of Presidential Elections*, 3rd ed. (Boston: Houghton Mifflin, 1888), pp. 159–160; election results in Lorant, *Glorious Burden*, p. 911; "If the Whig abolitionists": ibid., p. 183. One additional what-if concerns the Whig selection of Theodore Frelinghuysen to be Clay's running mate. If the choice had been Millard Fillmore of New York instead—as it might well have been—might that possibly have translated into additional "hometown" votes for the Whig ticket from either Polk or Birney?

20. "Who is J. K. Polk": McCormac, *Polk*, p. 282.

9—MAKING GOOD ON TEXAS

1. "a mere *Tom Tit*": Sellers, *Continentalist*, p. 159; "of a ruffian": Adams, *Memoirs of John Quincy Adams* Vol. XII, p. 110 (November 25, 1844); "If the recent foreigners": Remini, *Clay*, p. 664; "will be a continuance": Tyler, *Letters*, Vol. III, p. 155 (Tyler to Waller, September 13, 1844).

2. "the triumph of every thing": Sellers, *Continentalist*, p. 157; "Mr. Polk begins": *Le journal des débats*, December 8, 1844, quoted in Pletcher, *Diplomacy of Annexation*, p. 170.

3. "Allow me to congratulate": *Correspondence* Vol. VIII, p. 321 (Bouck to

Polk, November 15, 1844); "take some thought": ibid., p. 315 (Brown to Polk, November 13, 1844); "I have been betting": ibid., p. 370 (Harry to Polk, November 28, 1844); "The glorious result": Bassett, *Correspondence of Andrew Jackson* Vol. VI, p. 334 (Jackson to Donelson, December 2, 1844).

4. "shabbily used": Pletcher, *Diplomacy of Annexation,* p. 164, and see also pp. 175–176; Wiltse, *John C. Calhoun, Sectionalist,* pp. 203–204; Tyler advises Jackson of Donelson appointment in Bassett, *Correspondence of Andrew Jackson* Vol. VI, pp. 319–320 (Tyler to Jackson, September 17, 1844); Donelson appointment and military assurance in Wilson, *Papers of John C. Calhoun* Vol. XIX, pp. 800–802 (Calhoun to Donelson, September 17, 1844).

5. "every day's delay": Wilson, *Papers of John C. Calhoun* Vol. XX, p. 350 (Donelson to Calhoun, November 23, 1844); Peterson, *Presidencies of William Henry Harrison & John Tyler,* pp. 249–250; "A controlling majority": Richardson, *Messages and Papers* Vol. V, pp. 2197–2198.

6. "Let us get annexation": Wilson, *Papers of John C. Calhoun* Vol. XX, p. 628 (Donelson to Calhoun, December 26, 1844); Peterson, *Presidencies of William Henry Harrison & John Tyler,* p. 252.

7. Peterson, *Presidencies of William Henry Harrison & John Tyler,* pp. 255–256; "a state, to be formed": *Congressional Globe,* 28th Cong. 2nd Sess., p. 244 (February 5, 1845).

8. Urged Old Hickory's early arrival in *Correspondence* Vol. I, pp. 211–213 (Polk to Jackson, December 1, 1828); "Texas will be brought": Barnes, *Memoir of Thurlow Weed* Vol. 2, p. 130 (Hunt to Weed, February 15, 1845); "The arrival of the President" and "is for Texas": Shanks, *Papers of Willie Person Mangum* Vol. IV, p. 268 (Mangum to Caldwell, February 20, 1845); Mangum in this letter also quoted Polk, strong believer in party discipline that he was, as saying that any "Democrat who shall falter"—that is to say, vote against him on Texas—"will have thrown upon him a fearful responsibility"; "literally crush": ibid., p. 128 (Mangum to Priestly Mangum, May 29, 1844).

9. Peterson, *Presidencies of William Henry Harrison & John Tyler,* pp. 256–259; McCormac, *Polk,* pp. 313–317; Walker amendment vote in *Congressional Globe,* 28th Cong., 2nd Sess., pp. 359–360 (February 27, 1845); on Polk assurances to Benton, see R. R. Stenberg, "President Polk and the Annexation of Texas," *Southwestern Social Science Review* XIV, pp. 333–356 (1934); "would not have": Sellers, *Continentalist,* pp. 206–208.

10. This version of Polk's inaugural address is from Richardson, *Messages and Papers* Vol. V, pp. 2223–2232, specifically, "two of these," p. 2225; "Every lover of his country" and "all distinctions of birth," p. 2226; "It is a source of deep regret," pp. 2226–2227; "We need no national banks" and "be speedily paid off," p. 2227; "Texas was once a part" and "congratulate my

country," p. 2229; "the question of annexation" and "Foreign governments" and "to enlarge its limits," p. 2230; "the right of the United States"
and "Our title," p. 2231; "in our country," p. 2232.

11. "If I should be": Nelson, *Sarah Childress Polk*, p. 80; "Hail to the Chief":
William Seale, *The President's House: A History* (Washington, D.C.: White
House Historical Association, 1986), Vol. I, p. 267; "supped with the true-
blue": Sellers, *Continentalist*, p. 211.

12. Pletcher, *The Diplomacy of Annexation*, pp. 184–185; McCormac, *Polk*, pp.
353–354; "an act of aggression": John Bassett Moore, ed., *The Works of
James Buchanan* (New York: Antiquarian Press, 1960) Vol. VI, p. 119n
(Almonte to Calhoun, March 6, 1845).

13. Sellers, *Continentalist*, pp. 221–223.

14. "lest such a communication" and "at this time": Richardson, *Messages and
Papers* Vol. V, pp. 2232–2233; "if any such pledges": Milo Milton Quaife,
ed., *The Diary of James K. Polk During His Presidency, 1845 to 1849* (Chicago:
Chicago Historical Society, 1910) Vol. IV, pp. 41–43 (July 31, 1848),
reprint by the James K. Polk Memorial Association, Columbia, Tennessee, 2005, hereinafter *"Diary"*; for the charge of misunderstanding or
duplicity, see Sellers, *Continentalist*, pp. 219–220.

15. "the power behind": *Correspondence* Vol. IX, pp. 346–347 (Yell to Polk,
May 5, 1845); "I congratulate you": James, *Life of Andrew Jackson*, p. 781;
"General Houston has redeemed": James, *The Raven*, p. 357; "I knew
British gold": Bassett, *Correspondence of Andrew Jackson*, Vol. VI, p. 412
(Jackson to Polk, May 26, 1845).

16. Texas votes in Pratt, *History of United States Foreign Policy*, p. 235; "Be assured my friend": Bassett, *Correspondence of Andrew Jackson* Vol. VI, pp.
413–414 (Jackson to Polk, June 6, 1845); "I have seen": and for Jackson's death, see Houston's account, ibid., p. 415n (Houston to Polk,
June 8, 1845).

10—STANDING FIRM ON OREGON

1. Sellers, *Continentalist*, p. 213.

2. "I intend to be": *Correspondence* Vol. VIII, p. 456 (Polk to Johnson, December 21, 1844); "I must be": *Correspondence* Vol. IX, p. 234 (Polk to
Jackson, March 26, 1845); "Our friend [Polk]": McCormac, *Polk*, pp.
321–322.

3. Polk's Cabinet letter draft in McCormac, *Polk*, pp. 325–326.

4. "I cannot proclaim": Moore, *Works of James Buchanan*, Vol. VI, pp.
110–112 (Buchanan to Polk, February 18, 1845).

5. 1827 negotiation in Pletcher, *Diplomacy of Annexation,* pp. 104–105; "whether it was wise" and Polk's 1829 opposition to forts are in McCormac, *Polk,* p. 557; the two cornerstone accounts of the settlement of the Northwest are in Oscar Osburn Winther, *The Great Northwest* (New York: Alfred A. Knopf, 1955), and David Lavender, *Land of Giants: The Drive to the Pacific Northwest, 1750–1950* (Garden City, N.Y.: Doubleday, 1956).

6. Winther, *Great Northwest,* pp. 115–117.

7. Oregon Trail overview from Merrill Mattes, *The Great Platte River Road* (Lincoln: University of Nebraska Press, 1987), pp. 11–14, 23; "the beginning of" and "the roughest road": Winther, *Great Northwest,* pp. 122–123; "I think our true policy": Seager, *Papers of Henry Clay* Vol. 9, p. 828 (Clay to Worthington, June 24, 1843); "would not yield": Pletcher, *Diplomacy of Annexation,* p. 136; "Whoo ha!" and 1849 census in Winther, *Great Northwest,* pp. 121, 124; "Go to the West": *Congressional Globe,* 29th Cong. 1st Sess., p. 180 (January 10, 1846).

8. "a fall so profound": Robert L. Schuyler, "Polk and the Oregon Compromise of 1846," *Political Science Quarterly* 26 (1911), pp. 457–458; 1844 Democratic platform in Schlesinger, *History of American Presidential Elections,* Vol. I, pp. 799–801; Polk's inaugural in Richardson, *Messages and Papers,* Vol. V, p. 2231.

9. Schuyler, "Polk and the Oregon Compromise," pp. 446–447.

10. McCormac, *Polk,* pp. 567–573; "found himself embarrassed": Moore, *Works of James Buchanan,* Vol. VI, p. 203 (Buchanan to Pakenham, July 12, 1845); "scarcely courteous": *Diary,* Vol. I, p. 2 (August 26, 1845); "more consistent with fairness": Moore, *Works of James Buchanan,* Vol. VI, p. 220 (Pakenham to Buchanan, July 29, 1845); see also ibid., pp. 186–194 (Buchanan to McLane, July 12, 1845) for a summary of the American position.

11. Summons to Buchanan in Moore, *Works of James Buchanan,* Vol. VI, pp. 223–224 (Polk to Buchanan, August 7, 1845); Polk-Buchanan debate in *Diary,* Vol. I, pp. 2–5 (August 26, 1845); "a large and splendid": Moore, *Works of James Buchanan,* Vol. VI, p. 252 (Buchanan to Pakenham, August 29, 1845); "wise statesmanship": *Diary,* Vol. I, pp. 11–12 (August 30, 1845).

12. Edwin A. Miles, "Fifty-four Forty or Fight—An American Political Legend," *Mississippi Valley Historical Review,* XLIV (1957–1958), pp. 291–309; "the fulfillment of our": O'Sullivan, "Annexation," *United States Magazine* XVII, No. LXXXV, p. 5; see also Julius W. Pratt, "John L. O'Sullivan and Manifest Destiny," *New York History,* XIV (1933), p. 213; "This national policy": New York *Morning News,* October 13, 1845.

13. Pakenham's unofficial visit: *Diary,* Vol. I, pp. 62–64 (October 21, 1845);

"seemed to be troubled" and other quotes: ibid., pp. 66–67 (October 23, 1845); "The truth is": ibid., pp. 107–108 (November 29, 1845).

14. Polk-Benton meeting: in *Diary*, Vol. I, pp. 68–72 (October 24, 1845).

15. First annual message in Richardson, *Messages and Papers*, pp. 2242–2249; "out-Monroes Monroe": Dexter Perkins, *A History of the Monroe Doctrine* (Boston: Little, Brown, 1963), p. 79.

16. "from my established rule" and "I remarked to him": *Diary*, Vol. I, pp. 154–155 (January 4, 1846).

11 — EYEING CALIFORNIA

1. Walter R. Borneman, *Alaska: Saga of a Bold Land* (New York: Harper Collins, 2003), pp. 81–83.

2. Gene A. Smith. "The War That Wasn't: Thomas ap Catesby Jones's Seizure of Monterey," *California History*, LXVI, No. 2 (1987), pp. 104–113.

3. McCormac, *Polk*, pp. 558–560; "Texas might not": Tyler, *Letters* Vol. II, p. 261; "I never dreamed": ibid., p. 448.

4. Thomas Larkin synopsis from Thomas Oliver Larkin, *First and Last Consul: Thomas Oliver Larkin and the Americanization of California*, ed. John A. Hawgood (Palo Alto, Calif.: Pacific Books, 1970); "I imagine that you": Smith, "The War That Wasn't," p. 113; "enough wild Yankees": Pratt, *History of United States Foreign Policy*, p. 241.

5. Sellers, *Continentalist*, pp. 231–232.

6. "For who can arrest": Washington *Union*, June 2, 1845; "A corps of properly organized": ibid., June 6, 1845.

7. "England must never": *Correspondence* Vol. X, p. 113 (Armstrong to Polk, August 4, 1845); "The expression of American": ibid., p. 128 (McCall to Polk, August 7, 1845); "The northern provinces": ibid., p. 183 (Douglas to Polk, August 25, 1845); "To make your administration": ibid., p. 220 (Yell to Polk, September 10, 1845).

8. *Correspondence* Vol. X, pp. 44–45 (Fitz to Polk, July 10, 1845).

9. "Let this railroad": *Correspondence* Vol. X, pp. 96–97 (Fletcher to Polk, July 24, 1845); "we shall see" and "An interesting essay": ibid., pp. 227–229 (Fletcher to Polk, September 13, 1845).

10. McCormac, *Polk*, pp. 386–387; "the last drop": Sellers, *Continentalist*, pp. 333–334.

11. Buchanan's instructions to Larkin in Moore, *Works of James Buchanan*, Vol. VI, pp. 275–278 (Buchanan to Larkin, October 17, 1845).

12. "do all in your power": Sellers, *Continentalist*, pp. 334–335; "ascertain with

certainty": 30th Cong., 1st Sess., House Ex. Doc. No. 60, p. 231 (Bancroft to Sloat, June 24, 1845).

13. "a confidential conversation" and "secret instructions": *Diary*, Vol. I, pp. 83–84 (October 30, 1845); see also John A. Hussey, "The Origin of the Gillespie Mission," *California Historical Society Quarterly*, XIX (March 1940), pp. 43–58.

14. Much has been written about John Charles Frémont over the years, most of it by partisans of one camp or the other. For a recent and balanced treatment, see Tom Chaffin, *Pathfinder: John Charles Frémont and the Course of American Empire* (New York: Hill and Wang, 2002), from which this summary has been compiled.

15. Chaffin, *Pathfinder*, pp. 242–243; "found me 'young' ": John Charles Frémont, *Memoirs of My Life* (Chicago: Belford, Clarke, 1887), pp. 418–419.

16. Chaffin, *Pathfinder*, pp. 252–253; "some conversation occurred": *Diary*, Vol. I, pp. 71–72 (October 24, 1845).

17. Chaffin, *Pathfinder*, pp. 276, 281–288, specifically "Flitting about," p. 295; "The pear is near": Larkin, *First and Last Consul*, p. 55 (Larkin to Leidesdorff, April 23, 1846).

18. Frémont, *Memoirs*, pp. 488–490.

12 — MISSION TO MEXICO

1. "maintain the Texas title": *Correspondence* Vol. IX, p. 450 (Polk to Donelson, June 15, 1845); "the Rio Grande" and "to approach as near": 30th Cong., 1st Sess., House Exec. Doc. No. 60, pp. 82–83 (Marcy to Taylor, July 30, 1845); "General Taylor at" and "little apprehension": *Correspondence* Vol. X, p. 105 (Polk to Armstrong, July 28, 1845); Taylor's orders in *Diary*, Vol. I, p. 9 (August 29, 1845).

2. "needlessly angry" and "unknown to the Mexicans": Sellers, *Continentalist*, pp. 230–231; "can never under any": Moore, *Works of James Buchanan*, Vol. VI, p. 133 (Buchanan to Parrott, March 28, 1845).

3. This summary of Mexican politics is taken from John S. D. Eisenhower, *So Far from God: The U.S. War with Mexico, 1846–1848* (New York: Random House, 1989), and Pletcher, *Diplomacy of Annexation*.

4. "possessing suitable qualifications" and Parrott negotiations in Pletcher, *Diplomacy of Annexation*, p. 275.

5. "it was expedient" and "One great object": *Diary*, Vol. I, pp. 33–35 (September 16, 1845).

6. *Correspondence* Vol. X, pp. 250–251 (Polk to Slidell, September 17, 1845); *Diary*, Vol. I, p. 36 (September 17, 1845).

7. Slidell's instructions in Moore, *Works of James Buchanan,* Vol. VI, pp. 294–306 (Buchanan to Slidell, November 10, 1845); "I will say however": *Correspondence* Vol. X, pp. 362–363 (Polk to Slidell, November 10, 1845).

8. "A few months more": *La voz del pueblo,* December 3, 1845, quoted in Pletcher, *Diplomacy of Annexation,* p. 354; "a war would": *Correspondence* Vol. X, pp. 449–450 (Slidell to Polk, December 29, 1845); "Be assured": Pratt, *History of United States Foreign Policy,* p. 246.

9. *Diary,* Vol. I, pp. 223–225 (February 13, 1846), p. 226 (February 14, 1846), and pp. 233–234 (February 17, 1846).

10. For various interpretations regarding Polk's commitment to the Slidell mission, see Sellers, *Continentalist,* pp. 337–338, 399–400; McCormac, *Polk,* pp. 393–394; Eisenhower, *So Far from God,* pp. 45–48; and Pletcher, *Diplomacy of Annexation,* pp. 352–357, 365.

11. "the proper remedies": *Correspondence* Vol. X, p. 363 (Polk to Slidell, November 10, 1845); the standard biography of Taylor is K. Jack Bauer, *Zachary Taylor: Soldier, Planter, Statesman of the Old Southwest* (Baton Rouge: Louisiana State University Press, 1985).

12. Pletcher, *Diplomacy of Annexation,* pp. 375–376.

13. Bauer, *Zachary Taylor,* p. 149.

13—"AMERICAN BLOOD UPON AMERICAN SOIL"

1. *Diary,* Vol. I, p. 363 (April 28, 1846).

2. *Diary,* Vol. I, pp. 375–376 (May 3, 1846).

3. *Diary,* Vol. I, pp. 379–380 (May 5 and 6, 1846).

4. *Diary,* Vol. I, p. 382 (May 8, 1846) and pp. 384–387 (May 9, 1846).

5. Polk's war message in Richardson, *Messages and Papers,* Vol. V, pp. 2287–2293 (May 11, 1846).

6. *Congressional Globe,* 29th Cong., 1st Sess., pp. 794–795 (May 11, 1846).

7. "no more men" and "abstained from engaging": *Diary,* Vol. I, pp. 390–392 (May 11, 1846); "the door was open" and "extremely averse": William Nisbet Chambers, *Old Bullion Benton, Senator from the New West: Thomas Hart Benton, 1782–1858* (Boston: Little, Brown, 1956), pp. 306–308; Sellers, *Continentalist,* p. 419.

8. "a more formal report" and "I did not consider" and "in going to war" and "stand and fight" and "there was no connection" and "one of the most": *Diary,* Vol. I, pp. 395–399 (May 13, 1846); "We go to war": Moore, *Works of James Buchanan,* Vol. VI, pp. 484–485 (Buchanan to United States Ministers, May 14, 1846).

9. "Go for the expedient": *Correspondence* Vol. IV, p. 233 (Catron to Polk, September 10, 1837).

10. Walter R. Borneman, *1812: The War That Forged a Nation* (New York: HarperCollins, 2004), pp. 47–51.

11. Edmund Morris, *The Rise of Theodore Roosevelt* (New York: Coward, McCann & Geoghegan, 1979), p. 610.

12. These descriptions of the battles of Palo Alto and Resaca de la Palma are based on Bauer, *Zachary Taylor,* pp. 149–165; Eisenhower, *So Far from God,* pp. 71–85; and David Lavender, *Climax at Buena Vista* (Philadelphia: J. B. Lippincott, 1966), pp. 66–79; specifically, "their main dependence": Bauer, *Zachary Taylor,* p. 152; "Gentlemen, you will prepare" and "long black hair": Eisenhower, *So Far from God,* pp. 81–83; "Take those guns": Bauer, *Zachary Taylor,* p. 161; also, "For myself, a young second-lieutenant": U. S. Grant, *Personal Memoirs of U. S. Grant,* Vol. 1 (New York: Charles L. Webster, 1885), p. 92; "I think you will find": John Y. Simon, *The Papers of Ulysses S. Grant,* Vol. 1: *1837–1861* (Carbondale: Southern Illinois University Press, 1967), p. 87 (Grant to Julia Dent, May 11, 1846). Grant's Mexican War letters to his future wife, Julia Dent, are very romantic and quite a contrast to the gruff image of him frequently portrayed.

13. "to renew negotiations": Richardson, *Messages and Papers,* Vol. V, p. 2293 (May 11, 1846); "would eagerly embrace": Pletcher, *Diplomacy of Annexation,* p. 396; "If Mexico makes peace": Lilian Handlin, *George Bancroft, the Intellectual as Democrat* (New York: Harper & Row, 1984), p. 219.

14—54°40′ OR COMPROMISE!

1. Miles, "Fifty-four Forty or Fight," p. 302; "our title to the whole" and "without violating" and "an overland mail": Richardson, *Messages and Papers,* Vol. V, pp. 2245–2247 (first annual message, December 2, 1845).

2. *Diary,* Vol. I, pp. 134–135 (December 23, 1845) and p. 149 (December 30, 1845); "ease off" and "some *fresh* negotiator" and "enable Great Britain": *Correspondence* Vol. X, p. 431 (Brown to Polk, December 17, 1845).

3. Polk-Allen conversation in *Diary,* Vol. I, p. 139 (December 24, 1845); House vote and text in *Congressional Globe,* 29th Cong. 1st Sess., pp. 349–350 (February 9, 1846); "probably ask the Senate": Miles, "Fifty-four Forty or Fight," pp. 302–305; "no one spoke *ex cathedra*" and "authorized no one": *Diary,* Vol. I, p. 262 (March 4, 1846), and see also pp. 270–271 (March 7, 1846).

4. All quotes from Miles, "Fifty-four Forty or Fight," pp. 305–306.

5. "If he don't settle": Coleman, *Life of John J. Crittenden*, p. 235 (Crittenden to Letcher, March 9, 1846).

6. "proper line of settlement" and "notice should be": *Diary*, Vol. I, pp. 324–325 (April 9, 1846); "Great Britain was never": Polk Papers, Manuscript Division, Library of Congress (Polk to Nicholson, April 2, 1846).

7. "a naked notice": *Diary*, Vol. I, p. 334 (April 17, 1846); "amicable settlement": *Congressional Globe*, 29th Cong., 1st Sess., p. 680 (April 16, 1846); "safest for the House": *Diary*, Vol. I, p. 335 (April 17, 1846); "The long delay" and "The truth is": ibid., pp. 344–345 (April 22, 1846).

8. Sellers, *Continentalist*, pp. 409–412; see also Julius Pratt, "James K. Polk and John Bull," *Canadian Historical Review* XXIV (1943), pp. 344–349, and Robert L. Schuyler, "Polk and the Oregon Compromise," pp. 460–461; navigation rights discussion and "The 54°40' men" and "I felt excited": *Diary*, Vol. I, pp. 452–453 (June 6, 1845), and see also pp. 454 and 456 on Buchanan's political motivations in initially opposing submission; "more intimately connected": Sellers, *Continentalist*, p. 412; "My opinions and my actions": Richardson, *Messages and Papers*, Vol. V, pp. 2299–2300 (June 10, 1846).

9. "Where now is" and "Phifty-Phour Phorty" and "a traitorous alliance": Miles, "Fifty-four Forty or Fight," p. 307.

10. "at what rate duties": Sellers, *Continentalist*, p. 327; "It was the poor man's": ibid., p. 455; "Now, we must pay": ibid., p. 456.

11. Sellers, *Continentalist*, pp. 446, 457–458, 467; "vastly the most important": *Diary*, Vol. II, p. 11 (July 3, 1846).

12. Richardson, *Messages and Papers*, Vol. V, p. 2258 (first annual message, December 2, 1845).

13. Sellers, *Continentalist*, pp. 468–470; McCormac, *Polk*, pp. 670–672.

14. "Congress should initiate" and "Let gentlemen say": Sellers, *Continentalist*, p. 453; "remain uncommitted": *Diary*, Vol. I, pp. 288–289 (March 13, 1846); "To call the mouth" and "Should this bill": Richardson, *Messages and Papers*, Vol. V, pp. 2310–2316 (veto message, August 3, 1846); see also Sellers, p. 473, for Senate vote, and Richardson, p. 2252, for national-debt figure.

15. "If Santa Anna endeavors": McCormac, *Polk*, pp. 439–440; Pletcher, *Diplomacy of Annexation*, pp. 445–447; Lavender, *Climax at Buena Vista*, p. 84; "to provide for any expenditure": Richardson, *Messages and Papers*, Vol. V, pp. 2309–2310.

16. "for the purpose of defraying": McCormac, *Polk*, pp. 441–443; "neither slavery nor": Sellers, *Continentalist*, pp. 479–483; "After an excited debate" and "Had there been time": *Diary*, Vol. II, pp. 75–77 (August 10, 1846);

Congressional Globe, 29th Cong., 1st Sess., pp. 1217–1218 (House vote, August 8, 1846), pp. 1220–1221 (Senate debate, August 10, 1846).

15 — TO SANTA FE AND BEYOND

1. Sellers, *Continentalist*, pp. 422–423; "should be to march": *Diary*, Vol. I, p. 400 (May 14, 1846); "to acquire for the U.S.": ibid., pp. 438–439 (May 30, 1846).
2. The principal and highly laudatory biography of Kearny is Dwight L. Clarke, *Stephen Watts Kearny, Soldier of the West* (Norman: University of Oklahoma Press, 1961).
3. "It has been decided" and other quotes, War Department orders of June 3, 1846, and Marcy to Kearny, all in Clarke, *Kearny*, pp. 394–397.
4. The best history of Bent's Fort is David Lavender's *Bent's Fort* (Garden City, N.Y.: Doubleday, 1954).
5. Clarke, *Kearny*, pp. 113–114; for two versions of the Bents' reaction to the use of their post, see ibid., p. 109, and Lavender, *Bent's Fort*, p. 273.
6. "The road from Santa Fe": W. H. Emory, *Notes on a Military Reconnaissance from Fort Leavenworth, in Missouri, to San Diego, in California, including part of the Arkansas, Del Norte, and Gila Rivers*, 30th Cong., 1st Sess., House Ex. Doc. 41, pp. 35–36.
7. "As a military man": Clarke, *Kearny*, p. 117; "The President desires": ibid., p. 398 (Marcy to Kearny, June 18, 1846).
8. Clarke, *Kearny*, pp. 126–127, 136; "we were too thirsty": ibid., pp. 143, 148.
9. "taken possession of Santa Fe" and "General Kearny has": *Diary*, Vol. II, pp. 169–170 (October 2, 1846); Congressional request for information in *Congressional Globe*, 29th Cong. 2nd Sess., p. 33 (December 17, 1846); "exceeded the power": *Diary*, Vol. II, p. 282 (December 19, 1846).
10. "conciliate them, attach them": *Diary*, Vol. I, p. 444 (June 2, 1846); "the right of emigration" and "I could not interfere": ibid., pp. 205–206 (January 31, 1846); Sellers, *Continentalist*, pp. 425–426; McCormac, *Polk*, p. 422.
11. "a leap in the dark": Clarke, *Kearny*, pp. 161, 165–166.
12. "General Taylor, I fear": *Diary*, Vol. II, p. 119 (September 5, 1846).
13. This description of the battle of Monterrey is based on Bauer, *Zachary Taylor*, pp. 170–185; Eisenhower, *So Far from God*, pp. 98–151; and Lavender, *Climax at Buena Vista*, pp. 94–121; specifically, "the town is ours": Eisenhower, *So Far from God*, p. 131; "it would be judicious": Bauer, *Zachary Taylor*, p. 184.

14. *Diary*, Vol. II, pp. 144–145 (September 19, 1846); McCormac, *Polk*, p. 445; "had the enemy in his power": *Diary*, Vol. II, p. 181 (October 11, 1846); "a great error": ibid., p. 183 (October 12, 1846).

15. "requisite notice": Lavender, *Climax at Buena Vista*, pp. 129–130.

16. "He is evidently": *Diary*, Vol. II, pp. 249–250 (November 21, 1846).

17. Lavender, *Climax at Buena Vista*, pp. 132–135, 146–150, 169–172, specifically, "all that we shall find," p. 132, and "discovered that rows," p. 150.

18. This description of the battle of Buena Vista is based on Bauer, *Zachary Taylor*, pp. 185–207; Eisenhower, *So Far from God*, pp. 166–191; and Lavender, *Climax at Buena Vista*, pp. 147–213; specifically, "General, we are whipped": Eisenhower, *So Far from God*, p. 188; "A little more grape": Lavender, *Climax at Buena Vista*, p. 210; "No result so decisive": Eisenhower, *So Far from God*, p. 191; casualties numbers are from Bauer, *Zachary Taylor*, pp. 205–206.

19. "The truth is": *Diary*, Vol. II, p. 462 (April 7, 1847).

16 — MR. POLK'S WAR

1. "They jest want": James Russell Lowell, *The Biglow Papers* (Chicago: Henneberry Company, no date), p. 24; "Mr. Polk's War": Boston *Daily Atlas*, May 16, 1847.

2. Richardson, *Messages and Papers*, Vol. V, pp. 2321–2356 (second annual message, December 8, 1846), specifically, "the injuries we had sustained," p. 2322; "It remains to be seen," p. 2342; and "The war has not been waged," p. 2344.

3. For an appreciative biography of Scott, see John S. D. Eisenhower, *Agent of Destiny: The Life and Times of General Winfield Scott* (New York: Free Press, 1997).

4. "the most perilous of all positions": Eisenhower, *Agent of Destiny*, pp. 225–226; "I have strong objections": *Diary*, Vol. II, p. 242 (November 17, 1846); "was so grateful": ibid., p. 245 (November 19, 1846).

5. *Diary*, Vol. II, pp. 221–223 (November 7, 1846); see also Chambers, *Old Bullion Benton*, pp. 308–309.

6. "not coming, my dear General": Bauer, *Zachary Taylor*, p. 190; Eisenhower, *So Far from God*, pp. 253–265, specifically, "the largest amphibious invasion," p. 255.

7. "This was joyful news": *Diary*, Vol. II, p. 465 (April 10, 1847); Eisenhower, *So Far from God*, pp. 269–283, specifically, "a desperate undertaking," p. 281, and "going down the hill," p. 282n; for a similar account of

Pillow's actions, see George B. McClellan, *The Mexican War Diary of George B. McClellan*, ed. William Starr Myers (Princeton, N.J.: Princeton University Press, 1917), pp. 81–87.

8. "Brigadier General Pillow": 30th Cong., 1st Sess., Senate Ex. Doc. No. 1, p. 257 (Scott to Marcy, April 19, 1847).

9. "Such is the jealousy" and "with no assurance": *Diary*, Vol. II, pp. 465–468 (April 10, 1847); for a biography of Nicholas Trist, see Robert W. Drexler, *Guilty of Making Peace: A Biography of Nicholas P. Trist* (Lanham, Md.: University Press of America, 1991).

10. "if he found" and "I was willing to make": *Diary*, Vol. II, pp. 471–475 (April 13, 1847).

11. "I did this": *Diary*, Vol. II, p. 480 and pp. 478–479 (April 16, 1847); Calhoun for Taylor: ibid., p. 470 (April 12, 1847).

12. "that the writer must" and "any of my Cabinet" and "he had not" and "a great outrage": *Diary*, Vol. II, pp. 482–486 (April 21–22, 1847); see also New York *Herald*, April 20, 1847.

13. "further active military operations": 30th Cong., 1st Sess., House Ex. Doc. No. 60, p. 941 (Marcy to Scott, April 14, 1847); "I see that the Secretary of War": ibid., p. 815 (Scott to Trist, May 7, 1847); "from him, who": ibid., p. 820 (Trist to Scott, May 9, 1847); "I fear Scott and Trist": Eisenhower, *So Far from God*, p. 301.

14. "Between them the orders": *Diary*, Vol. III, pp. 76–79 (July 9, 1847).

15. Eisenhower, *So Far from God*, pp. 295–298.

16. For North Carolina trip, see *Diary*, Vol. III, pp. 37–50 (May 28–June 5, 1847); for New England trip, see John Appleton, *North for Union: John Appleton's Journal of a Tour to New England Made by President Polk in June and July 1847*, ed. Wayne Cutler (Nashville, Tenn.: Vanderbilt University Press, 1986); "journey was undertaken": ibid., p. 3; "a section of my country" and "If Mr. Van Buren": *Diary*, Vol. III, pp. 73–74 (July 7, 1847); Wilmot Proviso votes in Pletcher, *Diplomacy of Annexation*, p. 475.

17 — OLD BULLION'S SON-IN-LAW

1. Chaffin, *Pathfinder*, pp. 315, 326–327, 331–335.

2. Eisenhower, *So Far from God*, pp. 215–216; Chaffin, *Pathfinder*, pp. 344–350; "more the effect of a parade": Frémont, *Memoirs*, p. 566.

3. Kearny orders in Clarke, *Kearny*, pp. 394–397 (Marcy to Kearny, June 3, 1846), and see also pp. 175–176; Chaffin, *Pathfinder*, p. 351; Eisenhower, *So Far from God*, pp. 217–221; "proper and prudent" and "punished, fined"

and "that trouble was coming": George P. Hammond, ed., *The Larkin Papers* (Berkeley: University of California Press, 1955), Vol. V, pp. 311–313 (Larkin to Rachel Larkin, December 14, 1846).

4. For these quotes and an exhaustive analysis of the battle of San Pasqual, although defensive of Kearny's role, see Clarke, *Kearny*, pp. 190–232.

5. For two accounts of the Kearny-Stockton-Frémont conflict, see Clarke, *Kearny*, pp. 235–287 and Chaffin, *Pathfinder*, pp. 367–378, as well as Senator Benton's vituperative account in Thomas Hart Benton, *Thirty Years' View* (New York: D. Appleton, 1856), Vol. II, pp. 715–719; "governor and commander-in-chief": Clarke, *Kearny*, p. 268.

6. "perfectly well and has": Clarke, *Kearny*, p. 257; "without passing through": Benton, *Thirty Years' View*, Vol. II, p. 716; Stockton and Kearny orders in Clarke, *Kearny*, pp. 276–278.

7. Benton's conditions and "I should have selected": *Diary*, Vol. II, pp. 411–413 (March 8, 1847); Eliza Benton's wedding, ibid., pp. 427–428 (March 18, 1847).

8. "An unfortunate collision": *Diary*, Vol. II, p. 493 (April 30, 1847); "fully satisfied": *Diary*, Vol. III, p. 11 (May 4, 1847).

9. "Mrs. Frémont seemed anxious": *Diary*, Vol. III, pp. 52–53 (June 7, 1847); Benton-Polk conversation in *Diary*, Vol. III, pp. 120–123 (August 17, 1847).

10. Kearny's first visit in *Diary*, Vol. III, p. 168 (September 11, 1847); "no conversation took place": ibid., p. 175 (September 16, 1847).

11. Jones and Benton pressure in *Diary*, Vol. III, pp. 176–177 (September 18, 1847); "see the manifest injustice": Pamela Herr and Mary Lee Spence, eds., *The Letters of Jessie Benton Frémont* (Urbana: University of Illinois Press, 1993), pp. 35–36 (JBF to Polk, September 21, 1847); "Colonel Frémont is under arrest": *Diary*, III, pp. 180–181 (September 25, 1847).

12. See Polk's diary for late September and early October 1847 for a chronicle of the first couple's illnesses; "Quite a number came in": *Diary*, Vol. III, pp. 194–195 (October 18, 1847).

13. Benton's threat in *Diary*, Vol. III, pp. 197–199 (October 22, 1847); "if I do not": *Diary*, Vol. II, p. 445 (March 29, 1847); John Randolph Benton's behavior and "I have always been" and "I will grant": *Diary*, Vol. III, pp. 202–204 (October 25, 1847).

14. "no reason why this case": *Diary*, Vol. III, p. 205 (October 26, 1847); "should you conquer": Clarke, *Kearny*, pp. 259–260; "whether the facts as proved": *Diary*, Vol. III, pp. 335–336 (February 12, 1848); Sunday Cabinet meeting, ibid., pp. 336–338 (February 13, 1848); "justice" and "in consideration of distinguished": Chaffin, *Pathfinder*, p. 381.

15. "The party was": *Diary*, Vol. III, pp. 340–342 (February 16, 1848); "I

meet Colonel Benton": ibid., p. 442 (May 2, 1848); "From the day I": *Diary*, Vol. IV, p. 227 (December 10, 1848).

18—A PRESIDENT ON THE SPOT

1. "I am fifty-two": *Diary*, Vol. III, p. 210 (November 2, 1847).
2. Third annual address in Richardson, *Messages and Papers*, Vol. V, pp. 2383–2384; "establish whether the particular spot": *Congressional Globe*, 30th Cong., 1st Sess., p. 64 (December 22, 1847); "for their indomitable valor" and "unnecessarily and unconstitutionally": ibid., p. 95 (January 3, 1848); "Let the President answer": ibid., Appendix, p. 94 (January 12, 1848).
3. "where kings have always stood" and "Allow the President": Abraham Lincoln, *Speeches and Writings, 1832–1858* (New York: Library of America, 1989), pp. 175–176 (Lincoln to Herndon, February 15, 1848).
4. "excite the jealousy": *Diary*, Vol. II, pp. 13–14 (July 6, 1846); "customary and usual" and "the call of the House": Richardson, *Messages and Papers*, Vol. V, pp. 2415–2417 (January 12, 1848); note that Polk also claimed executive privilege early in his administration in refusing to release an accounting for a State Department contingency fund—some of which was related to Texas. But his reasoning then was that it was John Tyler who had originally made the privilege claim, and it would set a dangerous precedent for one president to override the privilege claims of a predecessor; see Richardson, ibid., pp. 2281–2286 (April 20, 1846).
5. Eisenhower, *So Far from God*, pp. 304–305; Wallace Ohrt, *Defiant Peacemaker: Nicholas Trist in the Mexican War* (College Station: Texas A&M University Press, 1997), p. 117; "fidelity and devotion": 30th Cong., 1st Sess., House Ex. Doc. No. 60, p. 831 (Trist to Buchanan, July 23, 1847).
6. Eisenhower, *So Far from God*, pp. 303–327; Eisenhower, *Agent of Destiny*, pp. 270–284.
7. McCormac, *Polk*, pp. 483–486; "to an immediate decision" and "only to gain time": *Diary*, Vol. III, pp. 171–172 (September 15, 1847); Eisenhower, *So Far from God*, pp. 334–342.
8. Cave Johnson's comment regarding "General" Pillow in *Correspondence* Vol. VII, p. 164 (Pillow to Polk, May 30, 1844); "I have great confidence": *Diary*, Vol. III, pp. 112–113 (August 7, 1847); Nathaniel Cheairs Hughes Jr. and Roy P. Stonesifer Jr., *The Life and Wars of Gideon J. Pillow* (Chapel Hill: University of North Carolina Press, 1993), p. 41, "I can only say": p. 95 (Pillow to Mary Pillow, August 27, 1847), and "a gentleman, who has," p. 104 (Pillow to Mary Pillow, October 18, 1847).

9. Hughes and Stonesifer, *Gideon J. Pillow,* pp. 107–112; specifically, "Pillow was in command" and "General Scott gave," p. 107, and "to embezzle the public," p. 111; "assassin-like tactics" and "*praised* and *glorified* Scott": Polk Papers, Manuscript Division, Library of Congress (Pillow to Polk, November 24, 1847); Eisenhower, *Agent of Destiny,* pp. 310–313.

10. "unfortunate collisions": *Diary,* Vol. III, p. 266 (December 30, 1847); "A most embarrassing state": ibid., p. 271 (December 31, 1847); "The whole affair": Hughes and Stonesifer, *Gideon J. Pillow,* p. 113 (Pillow to Mary Pillow, November 25, 1847).

11. Details of Cabinet decision on Scott's removal in *Diary,* Vol. III, pp. 278–280 (January 3, 1848); Hughes and Stonesifer, *Gideon J. Pillow,* pp. 114–119, specifically, "That an idiot monkey" and "General Pillow will find," p. 115; "all statements of fact": Polk Papers, Manuscript Division, Library of Congress (Pillow to Polk, November 2, 1848).

12. "no further proceedings": Hughes and Stonesifer, *Gideon J. Pillow,* p. 119; "did not concur": *Diary,* Vol. IV, pp. 7–8 (July 6, 1848); "do [Pillow] full justice": *Diary,* Vol. III, p. 507 (July 1, 1848); "for their acceptable services": Winfield Scott, *Memoirs of Lieut.-General Scott* (New York: Sheldon, 1864), Vol. II, p. 583n.

13. "clear that [Pillow]": *Diary,* Vol. III, pp. 434–435 (April 25, 1848); "General Pillow is a gallant": *Diary,* Vol. IV, p. 17 (July 13, 1848); "amiable and possessed of": Scott, *Memoirs,* Vol. II, p. 416.

19—SECURING THE SPOILS

1. "of twenty of the principal" and "We have both learned": McCormac, *Polk,* pp. 511–512 (Scott to Trist, July 17, 1847). The memoirs of Colonel Ethan Allen Hitchcock, *Fifty Years in Camp and Field* (New York: G. P. Putnam's Sons, 1909), are the key source for Pillow's initial support of the scheme, but it should be remembered that Hitchcock was a strong Scott partisan who came to vilify Pillow; Pillow soon claimed to Polk that he had been duped into agreeing to it.

2. McCormac, *Polk,* pp. 491, 515–517; for Mexico's initial offer, see 30th Cong., 1st Sess., Senate Ex. Doc. No. 52, pp. 195–201 (Trist to Buchanan, September 4, 1847); see also Mexican commissioners' initial instructions, ibid., pp. 330–333.

3. "If Mexico continued obstinately": *Diary,* Vol. III, p. 161 (September 4, 1847); "the Mexican Government had" and "the Mexicans still refused" and "would embarrass the administration": ibid., pp. 163–165 (September 7, 1847); "sincerely hope that": ibid., p. 167 (September 9, 1847).

4. *Diary,* Vol. III, pp. 170–171 (September 14, 1847); "a mere mockery" and "we do not believe": Moore, *Works of James Buchanan,* Vol. VII, pp. 425–427 (Buchanan to Trist, October 6, 1847); resolves to recall Trist in *Diary,* Vol. III, p. 185 (October 4, 1847); "Mexico must now": ibid., p. 186 (October 5, 1847).

5. "I can never approve": *Diary,* Vol. III, pp. 196–197 (October 21, 1847); "Mr. Trist has managed": ibid., p. 199 (October 23, 1847); "As this fact" and "to reiterate your recall": Moore, *Works of James Buchanan,* Vol. VII, pp. 442–443 (Buchanan to Trist, October 25, 1847). The third notice is in Moore, ibid., p. 444 (Buchanan to Trist, October 27, 1847).

6. McCormac, *Polk,* pp. 520–526, specifically, "I have bid adieu," p. 523; "that a baser, villain," p. 524n; "If the present opportunity," p. 525; and "I will make a treaty," p. 524.

7. "the just and long-deferred" and "to make a permanent": Richardson, *Messages and Papers,* Vol. V, pp. 2386–2387, 2394; "taking the whole of Mexico": *Diary,* Vol. III, p. 229 (November 23, 1847).

8. "in the strongest terms": *Diary,* Vol. III, pp. 245–246 (December 11, 1848); Trist instructions to suspend in Moore, *Works of James Buchanan,* Vol. VII, p. 427 (Buchanan to Trist, October 6, 1847); "most surprising" and "He may, I fear": *Diary,* Vol. III, p. 283 (January 4, 1848); "His conduct astonishes": ibid., p. 286 (January 5, 1848); "the most extraordinary document" and "to order him off": ibid., pp. 300–301 (January 15, 1848).

9. McCormac, *Polk,* pp. 536–538; for the full text of the treaty, see *Treaties and Other International Agreements of the United States of America, 1776–1949,* Vol. 9 (Washington: U.S. Government Printing Office, 1972), pp. 791–806.

10. "Mr. Trist has acted": *Diary,* Vol. III, p. 345 (February 19, 1848); Sunday evening Cabinet meeting, ibid., pp. 346–347 (February 20, 1848); Buchanan discussion and Polk's reasons for submitting, ibid., pp. 347–350 (February 21, 1848), specifically, "A majority of one branch," p. 348, and "if [the treaty] was," p. 350.

11. Richardson, *Messages and Papers,* Vol. V, pp. 2423–2424 (February 22, 1848).

12. "The first proposal": Adams, *Memoirs of John Quincy Adams,* Vol. IV, p. 275; "not worth a dollar": Pratt, *History of United States Foreign Policy,* p. 261; "difficult, upon any": *Diary,* Vol. III, p. 366 (February 28, 1848); "apt to think that": ibid., p. 367 (February 29, 1848); "If the Democratic party": ibid., p. 371 (March 3, 1848); "If the treaty in": ibid., p. 366 (February 28, 1848).

13. McCormac, *Polk,* pp. 548–550; Pratt, *History of United States Foreign Policy,* pp. 261–262; "perfectly familiar with": *Diary,* Vol. III, p. 391 (March 18,

1848); Mexican vote and "not to ratify" and "It was a treaty": Richard Griswold del Castillo, *The Treaty of Guadalupe Hidalgo* (Norman: University of Oklahoma Press, 1990), p. 53.

14. "if a tolerable wagon road": Clarke, *Kearny*, p. 233; "continue as good to the Pacific": Emory, *Notes on a Military Reconnaissance*, pp. 45–126; Gadsden negotiations in Pratt, *History of United States Foreign Policy*, pp. 285–286, 614n.

15. *Diary*, Vol. IV, pp. 1–2 (July 4, 1848); "the war in which" and "The extensive and valuable": Richardson, *Messages and Papers*, Vol. V, p. 2437 (July 6, 1848).

20 – THE WHIGS FIND ANOTHER GENERAL

1. "the trouble he had given" and "the dissenting members": *Diary*, Vol. III, p. 282 (January 4, 1848).

2. McCormac, *Polk*, p. 713; "gratifying to me": *Diary*, Vol. III, p. 454 (May 19, 1848), and see also his diary entries of May 17 and 18, 1848; "My mind has been": *Diary*, Vol. I, p. 142 (December 24, 1845); "I will do my duty": *Diary*, Vol. II, p. 328 (January 14, 1847); "the president reiterated": *Diary*, Vol. III, p. 448 (May 13, 1848); John S. Jenkins, *The Life of James Knox Polk* (Auburn, N.Y.: James M. Alden, 1850), pp. 307–308.

3. "The public have no idea": *Diary*, Vol. IV, p. 261 (December 29, 1848).

4. "refused to lend": McCormac, *Polk*, pp. 714–715; "an honest and hearty": *Diary*, Vol. III, pp. 334–335 (February 10, 1848).

5. "in the manner of the Dutch" and "Hunker": Safire, *Safire's New Political Dictionary*, pp. 45, 318; McCormac, *Polk*, p. 715; Cole, *Martin Van Buren*, pp. 412–413.

6. "as old as his gait": Remini, *Clay*, p. 687; Bauer, *Zachary Taylor*, pp. 234–238, specifically "The Candidate was very," p. 238n; Johnson's other key postal accomplishment was to ratify a postal convention with Great Britain that put American vessels on equal footing with their British counterparts and that eliminated what had been a British monopoly on carrying mail on the high seas.

7. "By many, and often": Lincoln, *Speeches and Writings, 1832–1858*, p. 185 (Lincoln to Herndon, June 12, 1848); Free-Soil party in Cole, *Martin Van Buren*, pp. 413–415 and McCormac, *Polk*, pp. 715–716; "This is a most dangerous": *Diary*, Vol. III, p. 502 (June 24, 1848).

8. "the only means of allaying" and "the distracting subject of slavery": *Diary*, Vol. III, pp. 501–502 (June 24, 1848); McCormac, *Polk*, pp. 635–642; "Had [Oregon] embraced" and "embrace merely" and "geo-

graphical discriminations": Richardson, *Messages and Papers*, Vol. V, pp. 2457–2460 (August 14, 1848); *Diary*, Vol. IV, pp. 74–78 (August 14, 1848); *Congressional Globe*, 30th Cong., 1st Sess., pp. 1081–1082 (August 14, 1848).

9. "to meet in convention" and "extraordinary": *Diary*, Vol. IV, pp. 136–137 (September 30, 1848); "abrogate their": McCormac, *Polk*, pp. 644–645.

10. "I am decidedly in favor": *Diary*, Vol. III, p. 446 (May 10, 1848); "if Cuba was ever": ibid., pp. 476–477 (June 2, 1848); McCormac, *Polk*, pp. 700–704; Buchanan's instructions to Saunders in Moore, *Works of James Buchanan*, Vol. VIII, pp. 90–102 (Buchanan to Saunders, June 17, 1848); and see also *Diary*, Vol. III, pp. 485–488 (June 8, 1848).

11. Strother's Hotel visit in *Diary*, Vol. IV, pp. 99–102 (August 27–28, 1848).

12. *Diary*, Vol. IV, pp. 114–115 (September 1, 1848); "were old customers": ibid., p. 124 (September 18, 1848); "One of these": ibid., p. 127 (September 20, 1848); "I am a friend": ibid., pp. 134–135 (September 28, 1848).

13. "bestir yourself": Hughes and Stonesifer, *Gideon J. Pillow*, p. 121.

14. "Upon each recurrence": *Diary*, Vol. IV, p. 177 (November 2, 1848); "Information received" and "Without political information" and "elected by the Federal party": ibid., p. 184 (November 8, 1848); vote totals in Lorant, *Glorious Burden*, p. 912.

21 – HOMEWARD BOUND

1. "The Mississippi, so lately": Richardson, *Messages and Papers*, Vol. V, p. 2484; "the President represents": ibid., Vol VI, p. 2515; "The mere passage": ibid., p. 2517.

2. Gold display in *Diary*, Vol. IV, p. 224 (December 7, 1848); "The agitation of the slavery": ibid., p. 251 (December 22, 1848); "from the commencement" and "Congress adjourned" and "We have a country": ibid., pp. 231–233 (December 12, 1848); "I feared there were": ibid., p. 299 (January 20, 1849); and see also McCormac, *Polk*, pp. 651–655.

3. "its consolidating tendency" and "my signature of the bill": *Diary*, Vol. IV, pp. 371–372 (March 3, 1849).

4. "before he called": *Diary*, Vol. IV, pp. 350–351 (February 24, 1849); Taylor's visit, ibid., pp. 352–353 (February 26, 1849); "Mr. Buchanan is": ibid., p. 355 (February 27, 1849).

5. Taylor dinner in *Diary*, Vol. IV, pp. 358–359 (March 1, 1849).

6. Polk's will is most easily found in Mark E. Byrnes, *James K. Polk: A Biographical Companion* (Santa Barbara, Calif.: ABC-CLIO, 2001), pp. 257–259.

7. "I feel exceedingly relieved": *Diary*, Vol. IV, pp. 372–373.

8. Information from Senate Historical Office at www.senate.gov.

9. "were too distant" and "in a very low voice" and "I hope, sir" and "a well meaning old man": *Diary*, Vol. IV, pp. 374–376 (March 5, 1849).

10. Polk's journey home based on *Diary*, Vol. IV, pp. 376–416, specifically, "not only a warm," p. 384 (March 9, 1849); "We had a dusty," p. 387 (March 12, 1849); "suffering from [a] violent" and "greatly fatigued," p. 395 (March 16, 1849); "too far on my journey," p. 397 (March 18, 1849); "Perceiving that I could" and "a sumptuous breakfast," p. 401 (March 21, 1849); "took a cup of coffee," p. 402 (March 21, 1849); "against my own wishes," p. 403 (March 21, 1849); "a triumphal march" and "the cordial welcome," pp. 405–406 (March 22, 1849); "I hope, gentlemen," p. 409 (March 25, 1849); "well satisfied," p. 413 (March 28, 1849).

11. "I can perceive": *Diary*, Vol. IV, p. 418 (April 5, 1849); "two or three rooms" and "to take possession": ibid., p. 425 (April 24, 1849); ibid., pp. 426, 439; "to arranging my library," ibid., p. 440 (June 2, 1849).

12. "I love you, Sarah": Byrnes, *James K. Polk*, pp. 51–52.

13. Inscription on Polk tomb at Tennessee state capitol, Nashville.

22 – A PRESIDENTIAL ASSESSMENT

1. See Jenkins, *The Life of James Knox Polk;* "the gatherer of those fruits": James Schouler, *History of the United States of America Under the Constitution,* Vol. V. (New York: Dodd, Mead, 1891), p. 127; James Grant Wilson and John Fiske, eds., *Appleton's Cyclopaedia of American Biography* (New York: D. Appleton, 1888), Vol. V, pp. 54–55.

2. "not be controlled": Richardson, *Messages and Papers,* Vol. VI, p. 2731 (March 4, 1853); Pratt, *History of United States Foreign Policy,* pp. 284–286.

3. "I suppose there is": Hughes and Stonesifer, *Gideon J. Pillow,* p. 317.

4. Arthur M. Schlesinger Jr., "Rating the Presidents: Washington to Clinton," *Political Science Quarterly* 112 (1997), pp. 179–190; other presidential polls include James Taranto and Leonard Leo, eds., *Presidential Leadership: Rating the Best and the Worst in the White House* (New York: Free Press, 2004), in which Douglas Brinkley terms Polk "the most successful one-term president the United States has known [p. 63]." By comparison, the 1996 Schlesinger poll ranked John Tyler thirty-two out of thirty-nine and at the bottom of the "below average" category, just above "failure." Considering all that Tyler did to secure the annexation of Texas and defeat a

national bank—even at the cost of alienating his own party—one might argue that Tyler, too, accomplished his avowed goals and deserves better.

5. "the only President who": Arthur M. Schlesinger Jr., *The Imperial Presidency* (Boston: Houghton Mifflin, 1973), p. 384; "I have made myself": *Diary*, Vol. IV, p. 131 (September 23, 1848); for treasury oversight history, see Charles A. McCoy, *Polk and the Presidency* (Austin: University of Texas Press, 1960), pp. 74–81; "the President represents": Richardson, *Messages and Papers*, Vol. VI, p. 2515.

6. Garraty, *The American Nation*, p. 316.

EPILOGUE: SARAH

1. "What shall I say": Nelson, *Sarah Childress Polk*, pp. 171–172; "You were in the line": ibid., pp. 176–177.

2. Inscription on Polk tomb at Tennessee state capitol, Nashville.

BIBLIOGRAPHY

BOOKS

Appleton, John. *North for Union: John Appleton's Journal of a Tour to New England Made by President Polk in June and July 1847,* ed. Wayne Cutler (Nashville: Vanderbilt University Press, 1986).

Barnes, Thurlow Weed. *Memoir of Thurlow Weed* (Boston: Houghton Mifflin, 1884).

Bauer, K. Jack. *Zachary Taylor: Soldier, Planter, Statesman of the Old Southwest* (Baton Rouge: Louisiana State University Press, 1985).

Benton, Thomas Hart. *Thirty Years' View* (New York: D. Appleton, 1856).

Bergeron, Paul H. *Antebellum Politics in Tennessee* (Lexington: University Press of Kentucky, 1982).

———. *The Presidency of James K. Polk* (Lawrence: University Press of Kansas, 1987).

Borneman, Walter R. *Alaska: Saga of a Bold Land* (New York: HarperCollins, 2003).

———. *1812: The War That Forged a Nation* (New York: HarperCollins, 2004).

Bumgarner, John Reed. *Sarah Childress Polk: A Biography of the Remarkable First Lady* (Jefferson, N.C.: McFarland, 1997).

Byrnes, Mark E. *James K. Polk: A Biographical Companion* (Santa Barbara, Calif.: ABC-CLIO, 2001).

Chaffin, Tom. *Pathfinder: John Charles Frémont and the Course of American Empire* (New York: Hill and Wang, 2002).

Chambers, William Nisbet. *Old Bullion Benton, Senator from the New West: Thomas Hart Benton, 1782–1858* (Boston: Little, Brown, 1956).

Christman, Margaret C. S. *1846: Portrait of the Nation* (Washington, D.C.: Smithsonian Institution Press, 1996).

Clarke, Dwight L. *Stephen Watts Kearny, Soldier of the West* (Norman: University of Oklahoma Press, 1961).

Cleaves, Freeman. *Old Tippecanoe: William Henry Harrison and His Time* (New York: Charles Scribner's Sons, 1939).

Cole, Donald B. *Martin Van Buren and the American Political System* (Princeton, N.J.: Princeton University Press, 1984).

Coleman, Mrs. Chapman, ed. *The Life of John J. Crittenden, with Selections from His Correspondence and Speeches* (Philadelphia: J. B. Lippincott, 1871).

Dallek, Robert. *Hail to the Chief: The Making and Unmaking of American Presidents* (New York: Hyperion, 1996).

Davis, William C. *Three Roads to the Alamo: The Lives and Fortunes of David Crockett, James Bowie, and William Barret Travis* (New York: HarperPerennial, 1999).

De Voto, Bernard. *The Year of Decision: 1846* (Boston: Houghton Mifflin, 1942).

Drexler, Robert W. *Guilty of Making Peace: A Biography of Nicholas P. Trist* (Lanham, Md.: University Press of America, 1991).

Dusinberre, William. *Slavemaster President: The Double Career of James Polk* (New York: Oxford University Press, 2003).

Eisenhower, John S. D. *Agent of Destiny: The Life and Times of General Winfield Scott* (New York: Free Press, 1997).

———. *So Far from God: The U.S. War with Mexico, 1846–1848* (New York: Random House, 1989).

Garraty, John A. *The American Nation: A History of the United States* (New York: Harper & Row, 1966).

Grant, U. S. *Personal Memoirs of U.S. Grant* (New York: Charles L. Webster, 1885).

Griswold del Castillo, Richard. *The Treaty of Guadalupe Hidalgo* (Norman: University of Oklahoma Press, 1990).

Hammond, Bray. *Banks and Politics in America from the Revolution to the Civil War* (Princeton, N.J.: Princeton University Press, 1957).

Handlin, Lilian. *George Bancroft, the Intellectual as Democrat* (New York: Harper & Row, 1984).

Harnsberger, Caroline Thomas, ed. *Treasury of Presidential Quotations* (Chicago: Follett, 1964).

Harris, J. George. *Polk Campaign Biography* (Knoxville: Tennessee Presidents Trust, 1990). (Originally published in ten installments in the Nashville *Union* in 1844.)

Haynes, Sam W. *James K. Polk and the Expansionist Impulse* (New York: Pearson Longman, 1997).

Hitchcock, Ethan Allen. *Fifty Years in Camp and Field* (New York: G. P. Putnam's Sons, 1909).

Hughes, Nathaniel Cheairs, Jr., and Roy P. Stonesifer Jr. *The Life and Wars of Gideon J. Pillow* (Chapel Hill: University of North Carolina Press, 1993).

Jacobs, Timothy, ed. *The History of the Baltimore & Ohio: America's First Railroad* (New York: Crescent Books, 1989).

James K. Polk Memorial Association. *Provisions and Politics: Recipes Honoring First Lady Sarah Childress Polk* (Columbia, Tenn.: James K. Polk Memorial Association, 2003).

James, Marquis. *The Life of Andrew Jackson* (Indianapolis: Bobbs-Merrill, 1938). (Incorporating *The Border Captain* and *Portrait of a President*.)

———. *The Raven: A Biography of Sam Houston* (New York: Book-of-the-Month Club, 1990). (Originally published in 1929.)

Jenkins, John S. *The Life of James Knox Polk* (Auburn, N.Y.: James M. Alden, 1850).

Johannsen, Robert W. *To the Halls of the Montezumas: The Mexican War in the American Imagination* (New York: Oxford University Press, 1985).

———., et al. *Manifest Destiny and Empire: American Antebellum Expansionism*, ed. Sam W. Haynes and Christopher Morris (College Station: Texas A&M University Press, 1997).

Klein, Philip Shriver. *President James Buchanan, a Biography* (University Park: Pennsylvania State University Press, 1962).

Lambert, Oscar D. *Presidential Politics in the United States, 1841–1844* (Durham, N.C.: Duke University Press, 1936).

Larkin, Thomas Oliver. *First and Last Consul: Thomas Oliver Larkin and the Americanization of California*, ed. John A. Hawgood (Palo Alto, Calif.: Pacific Books, 1970).

Lavender, David. *Bent's Fort* (Garden City, N.Y.: Doubleday, 1954).

———. *California: Land of New Beginnings* (Lincoln: University of Nebraska Press, 1987).

———. *Climax at Buena Vista* (Philadelphia: J. B. Lippincott, 1966).

———. *Land of Giants: The Drive to the Pacific Northwest, 1750–1950* (Garden City, N.Y.: Doubleday, 1956).

———. *The Southwest* (New York: Harper & Row, 1980).

Leonard, Thomas M. *James K. Polk: A Clear and Unquestionable Destiny* (Wilmington, Del.: S.R. Books, 2001).

Lorant, Stefan. *The Glorious Burden: The American Presidency* (New York: Harper & Row, 1968).

Lord, Walter. *A Time to Stand* (New York: Harper, 1961).

Lowell, James Russell. *The Biglow Papers* (Chicago: Henneberry Company, no date).

Mattes, Merrill. *The Great Platte River Road* (Lincoln: University of Nebraska Press, 1987).

McClellan, George B. *The Mexican War Diary of George B. McClellan*, ed. William Starr Myers (Princeton, N.J.: Princeton University Press, 1917).

McCormac, Eugene Irving. *James K. Polk: A Political Biography* (Berkeley: University of California Press, 1922).

McCoy, Charles A. *Polk and the Presidency* (Austin: University of Texas Press, 1960).

Merk, Frederick. *Manifest Destiny and Mission in American History* (New York: Vintage Books, 1966).

Morris, Edmund. *The Rise of Theodore Roosevelt* (New York: Coward, McCann & Geoghegan, 1979).

———. *Theodore Rex* (New York: Random House, 2001).

Nelson, Anson and Fanny. *Memorials of Sarah Childress Polk* (Newtown, Conn.: American Political Biography Press, 1994). (Originally published 1892.)

Neustadt, Richard E. *Presidential Power, the Politics of Leadership* (New York: Wiley, 1960).

Ohrt, Wallace. *Defiant Peacemaker: Nicholas Trist in the Mexican War* (College Station: Texas A&M University Press, 1997).

Parton, James. *Life of Andrew Jackson* (New York: Mason Brothers, 1860).

Paul, James C. N. *Rift in the Democracy* (Philadelphia: University of Pennsylvania Press, 1951).

Perkins, Dexter. *A History of the Monroe Doctrine* (Boston: Little, Brown, 1963). (Originally published in 1941 as *Hands Off: A History of the Monroe Doctrine.*)

Peterson, Norma Lois. *The Presidencies of William Henry Harrison & John Tyler* (Lawrence: University Press of Kansas, 1989).

Pletcher, David M. *The Diplomacy of Annexation: Texas, Oregon, and the Mexican War* (Columbia: University of Missouri Press, 1973).

Polk, James K. *Polk: The Diary of a President, 1845–1849,* ed. Allan Nevins (London: Longmans, Green, 1929).

Polk, William R. *Polk's Folly: An American Family History* (New York: Doubleday, 2000).

Pratt, Julius W. *A History of United States Foreign Policy* (Englewood Cliffs, N.J.: Prentice-Hall, 1955).

Remini, Robert V. *Andrew Jackson and the Course of American Democracy, 1833–1845* (New York: Harper & Row, 1984).

———. *Andrew Jackson and the Course of American Empire, 1767–1821* (New York: Harper & Row, 1977).

———. *Andrew Jackson and the Course of American Freedom, 1822–1832* (New York: Harper & Row, 1981).

———. *Henry Clay: Statesman for the Union* (New York: W. W. Norton, 1991).

———. *Martin Van Buren and the Making of the Democratic Party* (New York: Columbia University Press, 1959).

Roosevelt, Theodore. *Thomas Hart Benton* (Boston: Houghton Mifflin, 1895).

Safire, William. *Safire's New Political Dictionary* (New York: Random House, 1993). (Previously published in 1968 as *The New Language of Politics.*)

Sandburg, Carl. *Abraham Lincoln: The Prairie Years*, Vol. Two (New York: Harcourt, Brace & World, 1926).

Schlesinger, Arthur M., Jr. *The Imperial Presidency* (Boston: Houghton Mifflin, 1973).

———. ed. *History of American Presidential Elections, 1789–1968* (New York: Chelsea House, 1971).

Schouler, James. *History of the United States of America Under the Constitution* (New York: Dodd, Mead, 1891).

Scott, Winfield. *Memoirs of Lieut.-General Scott* (New York: Sheldon and Company, 1864).

Seale, William. *The President's House: A History* (Washington, D.C.: White House Historical Association, 1986).

Sears, Louis Martin. *John Slidell* (Durham, N.C.: Duke University Press, 1925).

Seigenthaler, John. *James K. Polk* (New York: Times Books, 2004).

Sellers, Charles. *James K. Polk, Continentalist, 1843–1846* (Norwalk, Conn.: Easton Press, 1987). (Originally published by Princeton University Press, 1966.)

———. *James K. Polk, Jacksonian, 1795–1843* (Norwalk, Conn.: Easton Press, 1987). (Originally published by Princeton University Press, 1957.)

Skowronek, Stephen. *The Politics Presidents Make: Leadership from John Adams to George Bush* (Cambridge, Mass.: Belknap Press, 1993).

Sprague, Marshall. *The Great Gates: The Story of the Rocky Mountain Passes* (Boston: Little, Brown, 1964).

Stanwood, Edward. *A History of Presidential Elections*, 3rd ed. (Boston: Houghton Mifflin, 1888).

Taranto, James, and Leonard Leo, eds. *Presidential Leadership: Rating the Best and the Worst in the White House* (New York: Free Press, 2004).

Udall, Stewart. *The Forgotten Founders: Rethinking the History of the Old West* (Washington, D.C.: Island Press, 2002).

Wellman, Paul I. *Glory, God, and Gold* (Garden City, N.Y.: Doubleday, 1954).

Wilson, James Grant, and John Fiske, eds. *Appleton's Cyclopaedia of American Biography* (New York: D. Appleton, 1888).

Wiltse, Charles M. *John C. Calhoun, Sectionalist, 1840–1850* (Indianapolis: Bobbs-Merrill, 1951).

Winther, Oscar Osburn. *The Great Northwest* (New York: Alfred A. Knopf, 1955).

Wisehart, M. K. *Sam Houston, American Giant* (Washington, D.C.: Robert B. Luce, 1962).

ARTICLES

Grant, C. L. "Cave Johnson and the Presidential Campaign of 1844," *East Tennessee Historical Society's Publications* 25, pp. 54–73.

Goodpasture, Albert V. "The Boyhood of President Polk," *Tennessee Historical Magazine* VII (April 1921), pp. 36–50.

Haynes, George. "President of the United States for a Single Day," *American Historical Review* XXX, No. 2 (January 1925), pp. 308–310.

Horn, James J. "Trends in Historical Interpretation: James K. Polk," *North Carolina Historical Review* XLII, No. 4 (October 1965), pp. 454–464.

Hussey, John Adam. "The Origin of the Gillespie Mission," *California Historical Society Quarterly* XIX (March 1940), pp. 43–58.

Ikard, Robert W. "Surgical Operation on James K. Polk by Ephraim McDowell, or the Search for Polk's Gallstone," *Tennessee Historical Quarterly* 43 (1984), pp. 121–131.

Miles, Edwin A. "Fifty-four Forty or Fight—An American Political Legend," *Mississippi Valley Historical Review* XLIV (1957–1958), pp. 291–309.

Osborne, Ray Gregg. "Political Career of James Chamberlain Jones," *Tennessee Historical Quarterly* 7, pp. 195–228, 322–334.

O'Sullivan, John. "Annexation," *United States Magazine and Democratic Review* XVII, No. LXXXV (July and August 1845), p. 5.

Paullin, Charles O. "The Early Choice of the Forty-ninth Parallel as a Boundary Line," *Canadian Historical Review* IV (1923), pp. 127–131.

Pratt, Julius. "James K. Polk and John Bull," *Canadian Historical Review* XXIV (1943), pp. 341–349.

———. "John L. O'Sullivan and Manifest Destiny," *New York History* XIV (1933), pp. 213–234.

Schlesinger, Arthur M., Jr. "Rating the Presidents: Washington to Clinton." *Political Science Quarterly* 112 (1997), pp. 179–190.

Schuyler, Robert L. "Polk and the Oregon Compromise of 1846," *Political Science Quarterly* 26 (1911), pp. 443–461.

Smith, Gene A. "The War That Wasn't: Thomas ap Catesby Jones's Seizure of Monterey," *California History* LXVI, No. 2 (June 1987), pp. 104–113.

Stenberg, R. R. "President Polk and the Annexation of Texas," *Southwestern Social Science Review* XIV (1934), pp. 333–356.

Wallace, Sarah Agnes. "Letters of Mrs. James K. Polk to Her Husband," *Tennessee Historical Quarterly* XI, No. 2 (1952), pp. 180–192; continued in No. 3, pp. 282–288.

PAPERS and GOVERNMENT DOCUMENTS

Adams, Charles F., ed. *Memoirs of John Quincy Adams* Vol. IV (Philadelphia: J. B. Lippincott, 1875).

Adams, Henry, ed. *The Writings of Albert Gallatin* Vol. I (New York: Antiquarian Press, Ltd., 1960). (Originally published in Philadelphia by J. B. Lippincott, 1879.)

Bassett, John Spencer, ed. *Correspondence of Andrew Jackson* (Washington, D.C.: Carnegie Institution, 1933).

Cutler, Wayne, and James P. Cooper, Jr., eds. *Correspondence of James K. Polk* Vol. VII, *January–August 1844* (Nashville: Vanderbilt University Press, 1989).

Cutler, Wayne, and Robert G. Hall II, eds. *Correspondence of James K. Polk* Vol. IX, *January–June 1845* (Knoxville: University of Tennessee Press, 1996).

Cutler, Wayne, Robert G. Hall II, and Jayne C. Defiore, eds. *Correspondence of James K. Polk* Vol. VIII, *September–December 1844* (Knoxville: University of Tennessee Press, 1993).

Cutler, Wayne, and Carese M. Parker, eds. *Correspondence of James K. Polk* Vol. VI, *1842–1843* (Nashville: Vanderbilt University Press, 1983).

Cutler, Wayne, and James L. Rogers II, eds. *Correspondence of James K. Polk* Vol. X, *July–December 1845* (Knoxville: University of Tennessee Press, 2004).

Cutler, Wayne, Earl J. Smith, and Carese M. Parker, eds. *Correspondence of James K. Polk* Vol. V, *1839–1841* (Nashville: Vanderbilt University Press, 1979).

Emory, W. H. *Notes on a Military Reconnaissance from Fort Leavenworth, in Missouri, to San Diego, in California, including part of the Arkansas, Del Norte, and Gila Rivers,* 30th Cong., 1st Sess., House Ex. Doc. 41, pp. 35–36.

Frémont, John Charles. *Memoirs of My Life* (Chicago: Belford, Clarke, 1887).

Hammond, George P., ed. *The Larkin Papers: Personal, Business, and Official Correspondence of Thomas Oliver Larkin, Merchant and United States Consul in California* (Berkeley: University of California Press, 1955).

Herr, Pamela, and Mary Lee Spence, eds. *The Letters of Jessie Benton Frémont* (Urbana: University of Illinois Press, 1993).

Hopkins, James F., ed. *The Papers of Henry Clay* Vol. 4, *Secretary of State, 1825* (Lexington: University of Kentucky Press, 1972).

Hopkins, James F., and Mary W. M. Hargreaves, eds. *The Papers of Henry Clay* Vol. 5, *Secretary of State, 1826* (Lexington: University of Kentucky Press, 1973).

Hunt, Gaillard, ed. *The Writings of James Madison* Vol. VIII, *1808–1819* (New York: G. P. Putnam's Sons, 1908).

Lincoln, Abraham. *Speeches and Writings, 1832–1858* (New York: Library of America,1989).

McGrane, Reginald C., ed. *The Correspondence of Nicholas Biddle Dealing with National Affairs, 1807–1844* (Boston: Houghton Mifflin, 1919).

Meriwether, Robert L., ed. *The Papers of John C. Calhoun* Vol. I, *1801–1817* (Columbia: University of South Carolina Press, 1959).

Moore, John Bassett, ed. *The Works of James Buchanan* Vol. VI, *1844–1846* (New York: Antiquarian Press, 1960).

Moser, Harold D., et al., eds. *The Papers of Andrew Jackson* Vol. VI, *1825–1828* (Knoxville: University of Tennessee Press, 2002).

Polk, James K. James K. Polk Papers, Manuscript Division, Library of Congress, Washington, D.C.

Quaife, Milo Milton, ed. *The Diary of James K. Polk During His Presidency, 1845 to 1849* (Chicago: Chicago Historical Society, 1910). (Reprint by the James K. Polk Memorial Association, Columbia, Tenn., 2005.)

Richardson, James D., ed. *A Compilation of the Messages and Papers of the Presidents* (New York: Bureau of National Literature, Inc., 1897).

Seager, Robert, II, ed. *The Papers of Henry Clay* Vol. 9, *The Whig Leader, January 1, 1837–December 31, 1843* (Lexington: University Press of Kentucky, 1988).

Shanks, Henry Thomas, ed. *The Papers of Willie Person Mangum* (Raleigh, N.C.: State Department of Archives and History, 1950–1956).

Simon, John Y. *The Papers of Ulysses S. Grant* Vol. 1, *1837–1861* (Carbondale: Southern Illinois University Press, 1967).

30th Cong., 1st Sess., House Ex. Doc. No. 1.

30th Cong., 1st Sess., House Ex. Doc. No. 52.

30th Cong., 1st Sess., House Ex. Doc. No. 60.

Treaties and Other International Agreements of the United States of America, 1776–1949, Vol. 9 (Washington, D.C.: U.S. Government Printing Office, 1972).

Tyler, Lyon G. *The Letters and Times of the Tylers* (Richmond, Va: Whittet & Shepperson, 1885).

Van Buren, Martin. Martin Van Buren Papers, Manuscript Division, Library of Congress, Washington, D.C.

Weaver, Herbert, and Paul H. Bergeron, eds. *Correspondence of James K. Polk* Vol. I, *1817–1832* (Nashville: Vanderbilt University Press, 1969).

———., eds. *Correspondence of James K. Polk* Vol. II, *1833–1834* (Nashville: Vanderbilt University Press, 1972).

Weaver, Herbert, and Wayne Cutler, eds. *Correspondence of James K. Polk* Vol. IV, *1837–1838* (Nashville: Vanderbilt University Press, 1977).

Weaver, Herbert, and Kermit L. Hall, eds. *Correspondence of James K. Polk* Vol. III, *1835–1836* (Nashville: Vanderbilt University Press, 1975).

Williams, Amelia W., and Eugene C. Barker, eds. *The Writings of Sam Houston, 1813–1863* (Austin: University of Texas Press, 1938–1943).

Wilson, Clyde N., ed. *The Papers of John C. Calhoun* (Columbia: University of South Carolina Press, 1990).

Wiltse, Charles M., ed. *The Papers of Daniel Webster: Speeches and Formal Writings* Vol. 1, 1800–1833 (Hanover, N.H.: University Press of New England, 1986).

NEWSPAPERS

Boston *Daily Atlas*
Charleston *Mercury* (South Carolina)
Congressional Globe (Washington, D.C.)
Nashville *Republican Banner*
Nashville *Union*
National Intelligencer (Washington, D.C.)
New York *Herald*
New York *Morning News*
Washington *Globe*

INDEX

Maps are indicated by *italicized* page numbers.

ABOUT THE AUTHOR

WALTER R. BORNEMAN's recent books on American history include *Alaska: Saga of a Bold Land; 1812: The War That Forged a Nation; 14,000 Feet: A Celebration of Colorado's Highest Mountains* (with photographer Todd Caudle, and winner of the 2005 Colorado Humanities Program Book Award); and *The French and Indian War: Deciding the Fate of North America.*

He is best known in Colorado's mountains, where he lives, as the coauthor of *A Climbing Guide to Colorado's Fourteeners,* in print for twenty-five years. Borneman has a master's degree in American history from Western State College and a law degree from the University of Denver. He is the president of the Walter V. and Idun Y. Berry Foundation, which funds postdoctoral fellowships in children's health at Stanford.